Multimedia Literacy

THIRD EDITION

Multimedia Literacy

THIRD EDITION

Fred T. Hofstetter

University of Delaware

Boston   Burr Ridge, IL   Dubuque, IA   Madison, WI   New York   San Francisco   St. Louis
Bangkok   Bogotá   Caracas   Lisbon   London   Madrid
Mexico City   Milan   New Delhi   Seoul   Singapore   Sydney   Taipei   Toronto

McGraw-Hill Higher Education

A Division of The **McGraw-Hill** *Companies*

MULTIMEDIA LITERACY

Published by McGraw-Hill/Irwin, an imprint of The McGraw-Hill Companies, Inc. 1221 Avenue of the Americas, New York, NY, 10020. Copyright © 2001, 1997, 1995, by The McGraw-Hill Companies, Inc. All rights reserved. No part of this publication may be reproduced or distributed in any form or by any means, or stored in a data base or retrieval system, without the prior written consent of The McGraw-Hill Companies, Inc., including, but not limited to, in any network or other electronic storage or transmission, or broadcast for distance learning. Some ancillaries, including electronic and print components, may not be available to customers outside the United States.

This book is printed on acid-free paper.

domestic   1 2 3 4 5 6 7 8 9 0 QPD/QPD 0 9 8 7 6 5 4 3 2 1 0
international   1 2 3 4 5 6 7 8 9 0 QPD/QPD 0 9 8 7 6 5 4 3 2 1 0

ISBN 0-07-365998-3

Publisher: *David Kendric Brake*
Senior sponsoring editor: *Jodi McPherson*
Editorial coordinator: *Alexandra Arnold*
Senior marketing manager: *Jeff Parr*
Project manager: *Kelly L. Delso*
Production supervisor: *Michael R. McCormick*
Senior designer: *Matthew Baldwin*
Supplement coordinator: *Susan Lombardi*
Media technology producer: *David Barrick*
Cover and interior design: *Gary Palmatier, Ideas to Images*
Compositor: *Robaire Ream, Ideas to Images*
Typefaces: *10/12 Minion (text), Myriad (display)*
Printer: *Quebecor Printing Book Group/Dubuque*

Library of Congress Cataloging-in-Publication Data

Hofstetter, Fred T. (Fred Thomas), 1949–
    Multimedia literacy / by Fred T. Hofstetter.— 3rd ed.
        p. cm.
    Includes bibliographical references and index.
    ISBN 0-07-365998-3 (softcover: alk. paper)
    1. Multimedia systems. 2. Computer literacy. I. Title.

    QA76.575. H645 2001
    006.7—dc21
                                                        00-027779

INTERNATIONAL EDITION ISBN 0-07-116420-0

Copyright © 2001. Exclusive rights by The McGraw-Hill Companies, Inc., for manufacture and export.

This book cannot be re-exported from the country to which it is sold by McGraw-Hill.

The International Edition is not available in North America.

www.mhhe.com

Dedication

To JoAnn Balingit,
for your eyes.

Contents

PART FOUR — Looking Into the Future of Multimedia 135

Introduction

As onetime chairman of Chrysler Corporation, Lee Iacocca said, "Lead, follow, or get out of the way." So it is with multimedia. Never has an industry grown so quickly or had such an impact on the way we receive, process, and communicate ideas.

This book is designed to teach you about the world of multimedia—how multimedia is changing the world we live in, how to use it effectively, why it became a multibillion-dollar industry so quickly, and the impact it will have on your way of life. This book will also teach you how to tell when someone is using multimedia, how to see through the hype, and most important, how to do it yourself—how to create your own multimedia applications and make them sizzle with effectiveness.

This book defines and teaches the basic skills of multimedia. Skills that will enable you to create beautifully typeset text, full-color pictures, animation, audio commentary, motion video clips, and stereo sound tracks. Skills that let you surf the Internet, download multimedia objects, and create multimedia Web pages. Skills that let you put any word or picture anyplace on your computer screen and make any part of the screen into a trigger that you can link to any object on your computer. When a user selects one of the triggers, the object of the link will appear. This object can be text, a picture, a sound, a movie, an animation, a Web page, or an application on your computer or network.

Think about the power this provides: Once you can display an object on your computer screen and link it to any other object on your computer, you have gained control over all your computer's capabilities. You can have your computer provide you with instant access to every note you ever took, every talk you ever gave, and every slide you ever photographed. You can create an effective presentation that includes instant access to all of your company's information when your boss asks you for a report. You can author a multimedia title and publish it on a CD-ROM or mount it on the World Wide Web. You can broadcast multimedia creations to anyone with a multimedia PC connected to the Internet. Would you like to be able to do some of these things? Then this is the book for you.

Organization

This book has eight parts. The first four are conceptual, dealing with definitions, principles, applications, hardware, future trends, and social issues; the rest of the book is a tutorial, which teaches you how to create multimedia applications and publish them on the World Wide Web. The CD-ROM is full of *Show-Me* movies that will help you master the tutorial. The Web site links to hundreds of Web pages that bring what you read to life through color pictures, stereo sound, animation, demonstrations, and full-motion video clips.

Part One defines multimedia, tells you who uses it for what, describes how it is changing the world, tells you who needs to know about it, and provides a taxonomy of multimedia objects that you can use when creating your own applications.

Part Two deals with multimedia applications. Dozens of full-color screen prints and photos illustrate how multimedia is being used in classrooms, boardrooms, homes, retail stores, just-in-time training, cinema, video arcades, government, and industry. The Web site that accompanies this book links to demonstrations of these applications and the development packages that were used to create them.

Part Three focuses on multimedia hardware. Remember how the VHS and Beta videotape standards competed for market share when home VCRs were invented? There are even more competing multimedia standards today. Part Three tells you what the standards are, recommends a strategy to follow, and provides a checklist of features to look for when buying a multimedia computer.

Part Four looks into the future of multimedia and discusses how it will impact us all. Acknowledging the rapid rate at which the technology is advancing, Part Four describes how you can keep up with this fascinating field, continue to increase your multimedia skills, and help influence future uses of multimedia.

Parts Five through Seven provide you with a multimedia toolkit. Step-by-step tutorials guide you through the creation of text, graphics, sound, and video. You will learn how to manipulate text, import clip art, digitize photographs, draw new pictures, record sound, make CD audio clips, edit digital video, create buttons, and interact with the user. Then you will use these skills to create a multimedia application on the History of Flight.

Part Eight concludes the book with a tutorial on multimedia publishing, providing you with strategies and techniques for distributing your applications.

The book concludes with a glossary that defines the terms a multimedia-literate person should know. The author has coined a new term that combines the words *multimedia* and *literate* into the adjective *multiliterate,* which is what you will be when you finish this book:

> **mul·ti·lit·er·ate** \ ˌməl-tē-ˈli-tə-rət \ *adj* : understanding the principles of multimedia, its impact on the world, and how to use it for attaining business, professional, educational, and personal objectives.

Interactive CD-ROM Brings the Book to Life

The CD-ROM packaged with this book is known as the *Multilit* CD. The CD is tied to each chapter in the tutorial part of the book and includes:

- Clip art, clip music, and clip video to get you started creating multimedia applications

- Dozens of *Show-Me* movies teaching you how to use multimedia graphics, sound, and video software

- *Show-Me* movies also illustrates the step-by-step tutorial that shows you how to create multimedia applications using PowerPoint

- A keynote presentation created with PowerPoint as an example of the kind of application the tutorial will enable you to create

Web Site Links the Book to the Internet

The Web site that accompanies this book is known as the *Multilit* Web site. The Web address of the *Multilit* Web site is

http://www.mhhe.com/cit/hofstetter

There is a corresponding chapter at the Web site for each chapter in the book. The Web site contains:

- Demonstrations of many of the most popular commercial multimedia packages available today

- Links to online clip libraries full of photographs, sound effects, songs, animations, and videos

- Shareware versions of the graphics programs, video tools, and multimedia utilities used in the tutorials

- An electronic version of the chapter titles and goals, with bookmarks taking you to materials to help you reach your goals

- Hundreds of links to more information about stimulating topics raised in the book

- Links to buyer's guides that will help you shop for multimedia computers and accessories

The book, the CD, and the Web site are designed to serve either as a course of instruction that can be used in more formal settings, or for self-study by those learning more informally. The reading level and computer skills required are appropriate for any business professional, teacher, executive, college student, marketing rep, audiovisual professional, or high-school student.

- Chapter 1 illustrates how multimedia impacts everyone's way of life, with charts and graphs that show why it is to anyone's advantage to become multiliterate.

- Chapter 2 provides a taxonomy of multimedia, and the Web site brings the taxonomy to life with multimedia examples in full color with stereo sound, animation, and full-motion video clips.

- Chapters 3 through 8 survey multimedia applications in business, education, entertainment, government, health, and public information. The book provides a comprehensive overview of these applications while the Web site links to demonstrations that allow you to take products for a "test drive" and consider whether you would like to purchase a retail copy.

- Chapter 9 profiles several of the development packages that were used to create these applications. The book explains the purposes of the different packages and provides the Web site links to free trial versions and demonstrations of their features.

One of the most important issues in multimedia is deciding what hardware to buy.

- Chapter 10 reviews the competing multimedia standards and recommends a strategy for coping with the differences in brand-name platforms.

- Chapter 11 presents the components of a multimedia computer.

- Chapter 12 provides a checklist that will come in handy when you buy a multimedia computer.

- Chapter 13 shows you how to configure a multimedia computer so you can minimize its complexity and maximize its versatility.

- The Web site links to individual product Web sites and multimedia buyer's guides that can help you compare and purchase computers and peripherals.

The next four chapters look into the future of multimedia:

- Chapter 14 explores the multimedia frontiers of electronic publishing, fiber-optic superhighways, rural datafication, appliance-based computing, and virtual reality.

- Chapter 15 reviews emerging video, voice, and datacommunication technologies and shows how they are creating a new form of multimedia called telecomputing.

- Chapter 16 addresses the issues raised by the impact multimedia is having on our sensibilities and moralities, questions who is in control, describes the problems multimedia is causing, and suggests what you can do to solve them.

- Chapter 17 offers suggestions for staying abreast of new developments in this fast-paced field and how to contribute your own ideas to the continued evolution of multimedia.

Hands-On Tutorial and Projects

The rest of the book is a hands-on tutorial you complete on your multimedia computer.

- Chapters 18 through 25 cover introductory multimedia tools and techniques. The book provides step-by-step instructions for the tools and techniques that you will use to create multimedia projects.

- The CD includes *Show-Me* movies that you can watch whenever you would like to see a detailed video explanation of one of the step-by-step tutorials.

- Chapters 26 through 32 contain a project in which you will create a simple multimedia application on the History of Flight. You will use multimedia on the CD to make the aircraft come to life with full-color slides, audio clips, and full-motion video.

- For students with Internet access, Chapter 33 teaches World Wide Web search strategies and shows how to download multimedia objects from the Internet.

- Chapters 34 through 38 present more multimedia tools and techniques, including image manipulation, video editing, advanced drawing, chart making, and designing your own custom style templates.

- The projects culminate in Chapters 39 and 40, where you learn how to distribute applications on CD, on diskettes, or on the World Wide Web.

- As a grand finale, Chapters 41 and 42 teach you how to broadcast presentations live over the Internet and hold online meetings in which you can share your application live with other users on the Internet.

Instructor's Guide

An *Instructor's Guide* accompanies *Multimedia Literacy*. The guide includes suggested course outlines, a test bank, teaching tips, hints for helping students when they encounter difficulties, and strategies for using the text, CD, and Web site in class.

How to Access the *Show-Me* Movies on the CD-ROM

The CD that comes with this book is known as the *Multilit* CD. The CD is very easy to use on any computer that has a Web browser, such as Microsoft Internet Explorer or Netscape Navigator. Simply insert the CD into your CD or DVD drive. Use the Windows Explorer, My Computer, or Macintosh Finder to locate the file called *index.htm* in the root of the CD. Double-click the *index.htm* file to launch it. The index of movies on the CD will appear on-screen in your computer's Web browser window. Follow the links to watch the movie of your choice.

The movies on the *Multilit* CD will play on any Windows or Macintosh computer with a CD-ROM or DVD drive and either the Microsoft Internet Explorer or Netscape Navigator Web browser. If one or more movies do not play on your computer, install the latest version of the Web browser of your choice from either www.microsoft.com or www.netscape.com. If the movie still does not play, install the latest version of the QuickTime Player from www.apple.com. All of these downloads are free of charge.

Acknowledgments

Creating this book is one of the most exciting projects I have worked on. While researching it I made many new friends, and the brainstorming that ensued inspired new ideas and innovations.

I want to acknowledge and thank all of my students, who continue to teach me a lot.

Pat Fox, Trident Technical College's professor of computer graphics and CD-ROM designer par excellence, produced the *Multilit* CD. She recorded the *Show-Me* movies and created the index that allows users to access the movies from a Web browser. When you try the CD, you will surely agree that Pat is an expert in making hypermedia easy to use.

When Mary Tise enrolled in the Multimedia Literacy course offered at the University of Delaware, she created for her final project a PowerPoint version of the *History of Flight* application. It worked extremely well, demonstrating that PowerPoint had gained the hyperlinking capability needed to base the third edition's tutorial on PowerPoint. I will always be grateful to Mary for pointing the way to this important new direction.

When Becky Merino, Julie Bockrath, and Ann Lenzini took the Multimedia Literacy course, they created PowerPoint versions of the Information Superhighway application and granted permission for the author to include some of their screens on the *Multilit* CD. I'm grateful to Becky, Julie, and Ann for their creativity and resourcefulness.

University of Delaware research professor L. Leon Campbell provided valuable service as the author's "intelligent agent" on the Internet. Almost daily, Leon sent the author information about new media and the Web from his extensive surfing of the network. Leon is a valued friend and colleague.

Caravel Academy teacher Judith Conway and University of Delaware professors Frank Murray, Al Cavalier, and Lou Mosberg contributed to the section on cognitive psychology in Chapter 4. I am grateful for their insight and collegiality.

When Frank Ruggirello worked for McGraw-Hill, he managed the first edition of this book. Rhonda Sands of McGraw-Hill succeeded him and oversaw the production of the second edition. Jodi McPherson followed Rhonda and managed the third edition. I am grateful to Frank, Rhonda, and Jodi for many inspirations and contributions, especially for providing the resources needed to create the *Multilit* CD and the *Multilit* Web site.

Finally, the Spring 2000 multimedia class at Trident Technical College spent the semester under the expert tutelage of Pat Fox, working with an early draft of the manuscript to make sure the tutorials worked properly. We will always be grateful to: James All, Corrie Arend, James Ball, Stephanie Butski, David Crossley, Michael Doyle, Elisabeth Gann, Paul Reid Hanna, Robert Hennessee, Rachel Honour, John Klein, Amanda McNeely, Judith Perry, Stephen Place, Billie Rexroad, Crystal Smith, Greg Smith, Vincent Smith, and Laura Stevenson-Wood.

Information Technology at McGraw-Hill/Irwin

InformationTechnology

At McGraw-Hill Higher education, we publish instructional materials targeted at the higher education market. In an effort to expand the tools of higher learning, we publish texts, lab manuals, study guides, testing materials, software, and multimedia products.

At McGraw-Hill/Irwin (a division of McGraw-Hill Higher Education), we realize that technology has created and will continue to create new mediums for professors and students to use in managing resources and communicating information to one another. We strive to provide the most flexible and complete teaching and learning tools available as well as offer solutions to the changing world of teaching and learning.

McGraw-Hill/Irwin is dedicated to providing the tools for today's instructors and students to successfully navigate the world of Information Technology.

- **Seminar Series**—McGraw-Hill/Irwin's Technology Connection seminar series offered across the country every year demonstrates the latest technology products and encourages collaboration among teaching professionals.

- **McGraw-Hill/Osborne**—This division of The McGraw-Hill Companies is known for its best-selling Internet titles, *Harley Hahn's Internet & Web yellow pages,* and the *Internet Complete Reference for more information,* visit Osborne at **www.osborne.com.**

- **Digital Solutions**—McGraw-Hill/Irwin is committed to publishing digital solutions. Taking your course online doesn't have to be a solitary adventure, nor does it have to be a difficult one. We offer several solutions that will allow you to enjoy all the benefits of having your course material online. For more information, visit Osborne at **www.mhhe.com/solutions/index.mhtml.**

- **Packaging Options**—For more information about our discount options, contact your McGraw-Hill/Irwin sales representative at 1-800-338-3987 or visit our web site at **www.mhhe.com/it.**

Resources for Instructors

We understand that in today's teaching environment offering a textbook alone is not sufficient to meet the needs of the many instructors who use our books. To teach effectively, instructors must have a full complement of supplemental resources to assist them in every facet of teaching from preparing for class, to conducting a lecture, to assessing students' comprehension. *Multimedia Literacy* offers a complete, fully integrated supplements package and Web site, as described below.

Instructor's Resource Kit

The **Instructor's Resource Kit** is a CD-ROM, containing the Instructor's Manual in both MS Word and PDF format, Brownstone test generating software, and accompanying test item files for each chapter. The features of each component of the Instructor's Resource Kit are highlighted below.

- **Instructor's Manual:** The Instructor's manual contains a list of learning objectives, a chapter overview, and a lecture outline for each text chapter. Also included are solutions files for all end-of-chapter exercises and recommended course outlines. The guide incorporates teaching tips, hints for helping students when they encounter difficulties, and strategies for using the text, CD, and Web site in class.

- **Computerized Test Bank:** The *Multimedia Literacy* test bank contains over 500 multiple choice, true/false, fill-in the blank, short answer, and essay questions. Each question will be accompanied by the corresponding correct answer.

Digital Solutions to Help You Manage Your Course

PAGEOUT

PageOut is our Course Web Site Development Center that offers a syllabus page, URL, McGraw-Hill Online Learning Center content, online exercises and quizzes, gradebook, discussion board, and an area for student Web pages.

Available for free with any McGraw-Hill/Irwin product, **PageOut** requires no prior knowledge of HTML, no long hours of coding, and a way for course coordinators and professors to provide a full-course Web site. PageOut offers a series of templates—simply fill them with your course information and click on one of 16 designs. The process takes under an hour and leaves you with a professionally designed Web site. We'll even get you started with sample Web sites, or enter your syllabus for you! PageOut is so straightforward and intuitive, it's little wonder why over 12,000 college professors are using it.

For more information, visit the PageOut Web site at **www.pageout.net.**

ONLINE LEARNING CENTERS/WEB SITES

The Online Learning Center (OLC) Web site that accompanies *Multimedia Literacy* is accessible through our Information Technology Supersite at **www.mhhe.com/it** or at Hofstetter's book site **www.mhhe.com/cit/hofstetter.** This site provides additional learning and instructional tools to enhance comprehension of the concepts presented in the text. The OLC/Web site is divided into these three areas:

Information Center: Contains information about the text, supplements, and the author.

Instructor Center: Offers downloads and relevant links for professors.

Student Center: Contains chapter objectives, definitions, additional Web links, and statistics pertaining to each text chapter—over 25 links per chapter!

ONLINE COURSES AVAILABLE

Online Learning Centers (OLCs) are your perfect solutions for Internet-based content. Simply put, these Centers are "digital cartridges" that contain a book's pedagogy and supplements. As students read the book, they can go online and take self-grading quizzes or work through interactive exercises. These also provide students appropriate access to lecture materials and other key supplements.

Online Learning Centers can be delivered through any of these platforms:

- McGraw-Hill Learning Architecture (TopClass)
- Blackboard.com
- Ecollege.com (formally Real Education)
- WebCT (a product of Universal Learning Technology)

McGraw-Hill has partnerships with WebCT and Blackboard to make it even easier to take your course online. Now you can have McGraw-Hill content delivered through the leading Internet-based learning tool for higher education.

At McGraw-Hill., we have the following service agreements with WebCT and Blackboard:

Instructor Advantage   Instructor Advantage is a special level of service McGraw-Hill offers in conjuction with WebCT designed to help you get up and running with your new course. A **team of specialists** will be immediately available to ensure everything **runs smoothly** through the **life** of your adoption.

Instructor Advantage Plus   Qualified McGraw-Hill adopters will be eligible for an even higher level of service. A certified WebCT or Blackboard specialist will provide a full day of on-site training for you and your staff. You will then have unlimited e-mail and phone support through the life of your adoption. Please contact your local McGraw-Hill representative for more details.

Technology Connection Seminar Series

McGraw-Hill/Irwin's Technology Connection seminar series offered across the country every year demonstrates the latest technology products and encourages collaboration among teaching professionals.

MS Office 2000 Applications Texts and CDs

McGraw-Hill offers three applications series: The *O'Leary Series*, The *Advantage Series*, or The *Interactive Computing Series*. Each series features its own unique approach to teaching MS Office in order to meet the needs of a variety of students and course goals.

- The *O'Leary Series* features a project-based, step-by-step walk through of applications.
- The *Advantage Series* features a case-based, what, why and how approach to learning applications to enhance critical thinking skills.
- The *Interactive Computing Series* features a visual, two-page spread to provide a more skills-based approach to learning applications.

Each series offers Microsoft® OfficeUser Specialist (MOUS) approved courseware to signify that it has been independently reviewed and approved in complying with the standards of content coverage related to the Microsoft® Exams and Certification Program. For more information on Microsoft's MOUS certification program, please visit Microsoft's Web site at **www.microsoft.com/office/traincert/**.

Also available for applications are the *Interactive Computing Series* Computer-Based Training CD-ROM tutorials. These CD-ROMs offer a visual, interactive way to develop and apply software skills. The CD-ROM features a unique "skills-concepts-steps" approach, and includes interactive exercises and performance-based assessment. These CD-ROMs are simulated, so there is no need for the actual software package on the computer.

Skills Assessment

McGraw-Hill/Irwin offers two innovative systems to meet your skills assessment needs. These two products are available for use with any of our applications manual series.

ATLAS (Active Technology Learning Assessment System) is one option to consider for an application skills assessment tool from McGraw-Hill. ATLAS allows students to perform tasks while working live within the Microsoft applications environment. ATLAS provides flexibility for you in your course by offering:

- Pre-testing options
- Post-testing options
- Course placement testing
- Diagnostic capabilities to reinforce skills
- Proficiency testing to measure skills
- ATLAS is Web-enabled, customizable, and is available for Microsoft® Office 2000

SimNet (Simulated Network Assessment Product)—SimNet is another option for a skills assessment tool that permits you to test students' software skills in a simulated environment. SimNet is available for Microsoft® Office 97 (deliverable via a network) and Microsoft® Office 2000 (deliverable via a network and the Web). SimNet provides flexibility for you in your course by offering:

- Pre-testing options
- Post-testing options
- Course placement testing
- Diagnostic capabilities to reinforce skills
- Proficiency testing to measure skills

For more information on either skills assessment software, please contact your local sales representative, or visit us at **www.mhhe.com/it**.

Interactive Companion CD-ROM

This free student CD-ROM, designed for use in class, in the lab, or at home by students and professors alike, includes a collection of interactive tutorial labs that illustrate some of the most popular and difficult concepts in information technology. By combining video, interactive exercises, animation, additional content, and actual "lab" tutorials, we expand the reach and scope of the textbook. The lab titles are listed below:

Available Now:

- Computer Anatomy
- Binary Numbers
- Storage
- E-Mail
- Learning to Program I
- Learning to Program II
- Network Communications

- Intro to Multimedia
- Databases
- Workplace Issues (ergonomics/privacy/security)

Coming Soon:

- User Interfaces
- Photo Editing
- Word Processing
- Spreadsheets
- Directories, Folders, Files
- Using Files
- CPU Simulator
- Troubleshooting
- Web Pages and Html
- SQL Queries

PowerWeb

PowerWeb is an exciting new online product available from McGraw-Hill. A nominally priced token grants students access through our Web site to a wealth of resources—all corresponding to computer literacy. Features include an interactive glossary; current events with quizzing, assessment, and measurement options; Web survey; links to related text content; and WWW searching capability via Northern Light, an academic search engine. Visit the PowerWeb site at **www.dushkin.com/powerweb**.

Part One

People retain only 20% of what they see and 30% of what they hear. But they remember 50% of what they see and hear, and as much as 80% of what they see, hear, and do simultaneously.

—Computer Technology Research Corporation

Multimedia is the buzzword of the decade. Like most buzzwords, it has been used in many contexts. You find it on the covers of books, magazines, CD-ROMs, video games, and movies. It is used in advertising shoes, hairstyles, drugs, cars, computers, soft drinks, beer, kitchen floors, vacations, airplanes, televisions, telephones, houses, museums, newspapers, arcades, theme parks, Olympic Games, and shopping malls. Sometimes the term is used to add hype to products that have nothing to do with multimedia. The many uses and abuses of the word *multimedia* have led to confusion over just what multimedia is. For this reason, a book on multimedia literacy must begin by defining it.

1

Definitions

After completing this chapter, you will be able to:

▓ Define multimedia, describe why it is effective, and explain how it will be important to life in the twenty-first century

▓ Demonstrate how multimedia is changing the world through telecommuting, home shopping, electronic publishing, and computer-based education

▓ Show how fast multimedia is growing in business, industry, homes, online services, and education

▓ Identify and define the components of a multimedia PC

▓ Define the Internet and the World Wide Web and understand how they provide access to multimedia resources on a worldwide basis

● To define multimedia properly, one must go beyond stating what it is and put the term in context. In this chapter you will not only get a standard "textbook" definition of multimedia, but also learn why it is important, how fast it is growing, how it is changing the world, and who needs to know about it. The term **multimedia PC** will be defined, along with the nomenclature needed to understand the specifications of a multimedia computer. Then you will learn how the Internet and the World Wide Web are being used to distribute multimedia applications on a worldwide basis.

What Is Multimedia?

Multimedia is the use of a computer to present and combine text, graphics, audio, and video with links and tools that let the user navigate, interact, create, and communicate. As depicted in Figure 1-1, this definition contains four components essential to multimedia. First, there must be a computer to coordinate what you see and hear, and interact with you. Second, there must be links that connect the information. Third, there must be navigational tools that let you traverse the web of connected information. Finally, because multimedia is not a spectator sport, there must be ways for you to gather, process, and communicate your own information and ideas.

If one of these components is missing, you do not have multimedia. For example, if you have no computer to provide interactivity, you have mixed media, not multimedia. If there are no links to provide a sense of structure and dimension, you have a bookshelf, not multimedia. If there are no navigational tools to let you decide the course of action, you have a movie, not multimedia. If you cannot create and contribute your own ideas, you have a television, not multimedia.

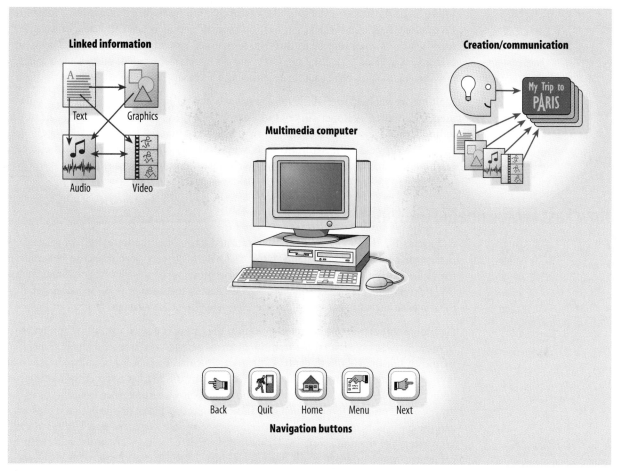

Figure 1-1 Multimedia is the use of a computer to present and combine text, graphics, audio, and video with links and tools that let the user navigate, interact, create, and communicate.

Why Is Multimedia Important?

Multimedia is fast emerging as a basic skill that will be as important to life in the twenty-first century as reading is now. In fact, multimedia is changing the nature of reading itself. Instead of limiting you to the linear presentation of text as printed in books, multimedia makes reading dynamic by giving words an important new dimension. In addition to conveying meaning, words in multimedia serve as triggers that readers can use to expand the text in order to learn more about a topic. This is accomplished not only by providing more text but by bringing it to life with sound, pictures, music, and video.

The more you learn about multimedia, the more books pale by comparison. For example, suppose you read a lengthy document and want to refer back to the page on which a certain idea was mentioned. You check the index, but the topic you want is not listed. Try as you might while paging through the book, you just cannot find what you read earlier. A multimedia document solves this problem by letting you search the full text for key words to find any topic or combination of topics. In fact, a multimedia document can refer not only to information within itself, but also to all the other documents to which it has been linked, and to all the documents to which they have been linked. Multimedia uses links to let you navigate the universe of connected information at the speed of light. Comparing this global network of multimedia to our highway system that lets motorists travel almost anywhere, the U.S. government has named the network the **Information Superhighway**.

Multimedia is highly effective. As research and publishing company Computer Technology Research (CTR) Corporation reports, people retain only 20% of what they see and 30% of what they hear. But they remember 50% of what they see *and* hear, and as much as 80% of what they see, hear, and do *simultaneously*. That is why multimedia provides such a powerful tool for teaching and learning.

Multimedia will help spread the Information Age to millions of people who have not yet used a computer. A Roper survey sponsored by IBM found that more than half of the respondents did not want a computer that required a manual to use it (*Washington Post* 12/27/93, Business: 13). Multimedia provides the computer industry with the key to reaching this untouched market, which will cause computer use to skyrocket.

How Fast Is Multimedia Growing?

As Figures 1-2 through 1-6 illustrate, multimedia is one of the fastest-growing markets in the world today. As the installed base of CD-ROM drives approaches the 200-million mark, DVD (digital video disc) drives have become one of the hottest consumer items. DVD drives can play CDs and also provide access to thousands of broadcast-quality movies with surround sound and up to 26 times more data storage.

Figure 1-2 shows that online subscriptions to the Internet passed the 50-million mark in significantly less time than more traditional forms of mass media reached their audiences. By the end of the twentieth century, nearly two-thirds of U.S. households already had home computers. Although the growth occurs in all market segments, the analyst agency Dataquest reports that first-time buyers are now coming from households in the lower socioeconomic levels, which may indicate that the digital divide between the haves and the have-nots may gradually be narrowing (*San Jose Mercury News* 2/8/99, *Multilit* Web site). By the time you read this, nearly half of American households will be connected to the Internet, as illustrated in Figure 1-3.

Looking at worldwide growth, the online business research firm eMarketer forecasts that the total Internet population will increase to 350 million users by 2003. As Figure 1-4 illustrates, this is a 267% increase from the 95 million people using the Internet at the end of 1998.

Fueling this growth are advances in technology (see Figure 1-6 on page 11) and price wars that have dramatically lowered the cost of multimedia computers. The growing number of consumers has created a larger market for multimedia titles, and new tools

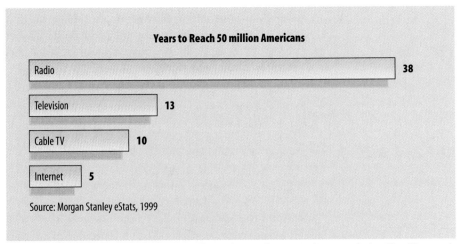

Figure 1-2 How many years it took for different forms of mass media to reach the 50-million mark.
Source: Morgan Stanley *eStats* 12/2/99, *Multilit* Web site.

U.S. Net User Household Growth trends		
Year	**Millions of Households**	**% of Total U.S. Households**
1996	6.5	6.6%
1997	14.5	14.5%
1998	24.4	24.2%
1999	28.0	27.6%
2000	32.0	31.4%
2001	35.3	34.4%
2002	44.0	42.7%

Source: Morgan Stanley eStats, 1999

Figure 1-3 The growth of American households with home computers connected to the Internet. *Source:* Morgan Stanley *eStats* 12/2/99, *Multilit* Web site.

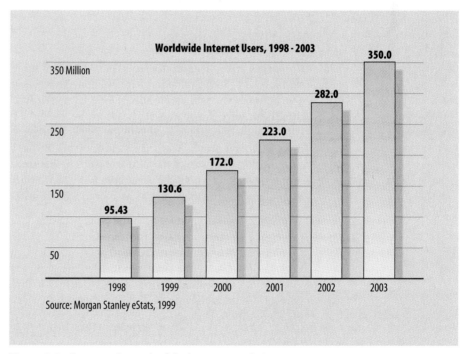

Figure 1-4 Forecasted growth of the Internet population. *Source:* Reuters, *CNET News.com* 7/7/99, *Multilit* Web site.

are enabling more people to become developers. The second half of this book, for example, is a hands-on tutorial that will enable you to begin creating multimedia applications.

Online multimedia services are booming. By the end of the twentieth century, Cisco Systems estimated that the online infrastructure was generating $115 billion in revenue annually and accounted for 372,462 high-tech jobs (*The Industry Standard* 6/20/99, *Multilit* Web site). Because only 27.6% of computer owners currently belong to an Internet service, there is plenty of room for growth. And grow it will! AT&T Broadband & Internet Services already provides cable television entertainment and information programming services to more than 10 million customers across the country and is actively developing competitive local cable telephone services (AT&T news release 9/2/99, *Multilit* Web site).

Educational use of multimedia is also skyrocketing. According to the Software and Information Industry Associaton (SIIA), U.S. K-12 schools spent $4.8 billion on instructional technology in 1998, with PC budgets increasing at a rate of about 20% per year (SIAA 1999, *Multilit* Web site).

For more statistics on the information technology industry, follow the *Multilit* Web site links to Dataquest Interactive. Once you subscribe to Dataquest, you can request up-to-the-minute statistics about trends in multimedia, networking, videoconferencing, and a wide range of personal computer products and services. Dataquest charges a small fee for each chart or graph you download.

How Is Multimedia Changing the World?

Multimedia is redefining the communication system that forms a significant part of the infrastructure of our society. An unprecedented number of mergers among companies jockeying for position in this fast-paced field are combining the telephone, television, and personal computer into a mass market multimedia utility.

Mergers and Alliances

Broadview investment service reports that 374 digital-media deals were made in the first six months of 1999, valued at $36.5 billion. That was up from 112 mergers valued at $4.6 billion in the first six months of 1998 (Broadview 7/28/99, *Multilit* Web site). All of these deals were overshadowed, however, by the $36.75 billion merger of Viacom and CBS, proposed in September 1999, which was the largest media deal to date. As Reuters news service reported, "Viacom's acquisition of CBS has created an Internet powerhouse with interests that span entertainment, sports, finance, and all manner of e-commerce properties" (Reuters, *CNET News.com* 9/7/99, *Multilit* Web site). Follow the *Multilit* Web site link to the Viacom/CBS merger to see an overview of their combined holdings.

When Microsoft teamed up with the NBC network to create MSNBC.COM, the brand power of a TV network eased the transition of TV viewers to become online users, and the online service became a regular part of the way these people use television (*Broadcasting & Cable* 5/6/96: 43). In a similar move, America Online invested $1.5 billion in Hughes Electronics Corporation, owner of the DirecTV satellite service, so AOL could market DirectTV enhanced with AOL's Internet-on-TV services (*San Jose Mercury News* 6/22/99, *Multilit* Web site). AOL then began the new millennium by announcing the largest media deal to date, namely, the $182 billion acquisition of Time Warner. The new company, which is called AOL Time Warner, marries the world's biggest online service provider with the largest media conglomerate.

Telecommuting

Multimedia is changing our place of work. According to a Deloitte & Touche report, **telecommuting** (working from home using computers, modems, and fax machines) accounted for 45% of all new jobs from 1987 to 1992 (*Atlanta Constitution* 1/2/94: E2). By the middle of 1998, 15.7 million workers in the United States were telecommuting at least one day per month (Cyber Dialogue, 10/28/98, *Multilit* Web site).

A survey by Work/Family Directions research group found that 20 to 40% of employees would like to telecommute (*Wall Street Journal* 12/14/93: B1). More than half of U.S. businesses permitted telecommuting in 1996, with 1.5 million companies having telecommuting policies then in place (*USA Today* 6/18/96: E7). The California earthquakes made many new converts to telecommuting, given the significant long-term damage to traffic routes around Los Angeles (*Investor's Business Daily* 1/27/94: 4). In addition to reducing traffic congestion, an Arthur D. Little study points out how telecommuting can cut gas consumption and air pollution. For example, a 10 to 20% reduction in the number of trips in the United States would save 3.5 billion gallons of gas per year (*Atlanta Constitution* 12/2/93: A19). Telecommuting has also had an impact on the clothing industry, causing suit sales to plummet as more people work from home (*St. Petersburg Times* 1/3/94: 19).

Microsoft provides the world with excellent telecommuting software for free. Called *NetMeeting*, it enables real-time voice and data communications over the Internet. Two or more people can thereby share applications, transfer files, view and illustrate a shared whiteboard, and chat with each other. Chapter 42 contains a step-by-step tutorial on using *NetMeeting* to share a PowerPoint application with other users. To download the *NetMeeting* software, follow the *Multilit* Web site link to *NetMeeting*.

Home Shopping

Multimedia is changing how the world shops. Instead of wearing yourself out trekking from store to store, trying to find the size and style you like and then waiting in line to pay for it, teleshopping services let you shop from home. According to a CommerceNet/ Nielsen survey, by 1999 the number of online shoppers had increased to 55 million people. Of these, 28 million made purchases online, 9 million bought something online at least once a month, and a million made weekly purchases online (*CommerceNet* 6/17/99, *Multilit* Web site). By 1999, electronic shopping sales had surged to more than $98 billion annually and are forecast to rise to $1.2 trillion by 2003 (*eMarketer, CNET News.com* 7/7/99, *Multilit* Web site). Figure 1-5 shows how the percentage of online shoppers is expected to grow.

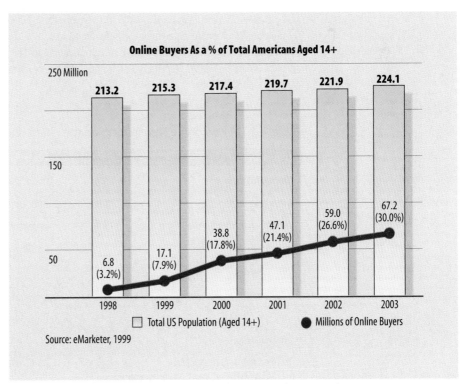

Figure 1-5 Projected growth in the percent of Americans shopping online.
Source: eMarketer, CNET News.com 7/7/99, Multilit Web site.

Business and Advertising

Multimedia is changing the face of business. Online shopping and banking are creating a cashless society by eliminating the need for printed money. American Express, for example, is enabling its cardholders to make deposits, invest in money market funds, purchase certificates of deposit, and pay bills through an online service called American Express Membership B@nking (*Wall Street Journal* 7/23/99.) The Gartner Group predicts that bill-paying over the Internet will become business as usual by 2002, when all banks will offer online bill payment (*USA Today* 8/4/99).

The online brokerage market is poised to lead the growth of the financial services sector with assets projected to grow from $415 billion in 1998 to $3 trillion by 2003 (NUA Internet Surveys 9/6/99, *Multilit* Web site). Online brokerages provide a way for the average citizen to purchase stocks online, instead of having to buy them through a traditional stockbroker. Forrester research predicts that buying stocks online will be particularly popular in Europe, with online brokerage accounts predicted to rise from 1.3 million in 2000 to 14 million in 2004. Giga Information Group predicts that worldwide, corporations will save as much as $1.25 trillion by doing business over the Internet (*Washington Post* 8/4/99).

Advertising is paying for the costs of operating Web services, much like advertising covers the cost of television broadcasts so you can watch TV for free. For example, commercial ads pay for the popular search engine Yahoo at http://www.yahoo.com. In 1998, advertisers spent $1.9 billion advertising on the Internet, exceeding the estimated $1.6 billion spent on outdoor advertising that same year (*Internet Index* 5/31/99, *Multilit* Web site).

Electronic Publishing

Multimedia is changing how we read newspapers by eliminating the need for the paper and offering all the features of multimedia, including full-text search, graphics, audio, and video. According to the Kelsey Group, more than 2700 newspapers are experimenting with electronic ventures, compared to only 42 in 1989; contributing to the need for these experiments is the fact that half of young people aged 18 to 24 do not read newspapers at all (*US News & World Report* 5/16/94: 60). Table 1-1 lists a few of the newspapers you can read on the Web.

Table 1-1   A Few of the Newspapers on the World Wide Web

Newspaper	Web Address
Chicago Tribune	http://www.chicago.tribune.com
Los Angeles Times	http://www.latimes.com
New York Times	http://www.nytimes.com
San Jose [CA] Mercury News	http://www.sjmercury.com
USA Today	http://www.usatoday.com
Virginian-Pilot	http://www.pilotonline.com
Wall Street Journal	http://interactive.wsj.com
Washington Post	http://www.washingtonpost.com
4,000 other links to newspapers, magazines, broadcasters, and news services	http://www.newslink.org

Teaching and Learning

Electronic publishing also impacts the education industry. Schools are beginning to invest former textbook budgets in multimedia technology, for example, by equipping students with laptop computers to access course materials online (*Electronic-school.com* 6/99, *Multilit* Web site). After studying hundreds of controlled experiments in which computers were used in college and high-school courses, elementary education, and adult high-school equivalency programs, Kulik (1985, 1986, 1991, and 1994) reports overall learning gains averaging more than a letter grade higher (effect size = .32), and significant reductions in the time required for students to learn (averaging 34% in college and 24% in adult education). Chapter 4 surveys some of these applications and analyzes how computers are changing the nature of education.

Mass Media

The Internet is competing with television for people's free time. A survey conducted by the Emerging Technologies Research Group shows Internet users spending an average of 6.6 hours a week on the Net, time previously spent watching TV, listening to the radio, or making long-distance phone calls. The average session was 68 minutes (*Tampa Tribune* 1/12/96: B&F1). A Nielsen study reported similar results, concluding that Internet users spend more time online than TV viewers spend with their VCRs (*Dow Jones News* 10/30/95). The percentage of women using the Internet has increased steadily, from 33% of users in 1996 to 46% in 1999 (*CommerceNet/Nielsen Survey* 6/17/99, *Multilit* Web site).

Who Needs to Know About Multimedia?

Ask yourself a few historical questions:

- Who needed to know how to read books after the printing press was invented?
- Who needed to know how to drive cars after highways got built?
- Who needed to know how to call someone when telephones were invented?

Now ask:

- Who needs to know how to use a multimedia computer to access the Internet?

Anyone who plans to learn, teach, work, play, govern, serve, buy, or sell in the information society needs to know about multimedia. Just imagine the consequences of not knowing about it. For example, suppose you are a journalist who cannot create a hypermedia document and transmit it across a network; how long do you think you will be employable? What about paramedics who cannot upload a picture of a wound and get expert advice on how to treat it? Or architects and designers who cannot use computers to simulate and troubleshoot products before they are built? Or merchandisers who do not know how to advertise products on the network? Or teachers who cannot use multimedia to bring their classrooms to life? Or businesspeople who cannot access corporate data when it is needed to make the right decision? Or governments without the technology needed to detect and deter aggression?

To state the case succinctly: Everyone who plans to function productively in twenty-first-century society needs to know about multimedia.

What Is a Multimedia PC?

A **multimedia PC** is a computer that has a CD-ROM or DVD drive and supports 8-bit and 16-bit waveform audio recording and playback, MIDI sound synthesis, and MPEG movie watching, with a central processor fast enough and a RAM large enough to enable you to play and interact with these media in real time, and with a hard disk large enough to store multimedia works that the user can create. In order for you to understand this definition of a multimedia PC, a few terms need to be defined.

RAM and MB

RAM stands for random access memory; it is the main memory at the heart of a computer in which multimedia programs execute. RAM is measured in megabytes (**MB**). *Mega* means million, and *byte* is the unit of measure for computer memory. A byte can hold a single character, and a megabyte can hold a million characters. Although some programs can run in smaller amounts of RAM, anyone serious about multimedia should have a computer equipped with at least 48 MB of RAM.

Processor and MHz

The **processor** is the brain in your computer where calculations and decisions get made. Processor speed is measured in **MHz**, which stands for megahertz. *Mega* means million, and *hertz* is one cycle per second.

Intel is the biggest manufacturer of the processors found in multimedia computers. Figure 1-6 shows how the relative power of the various Intel processors is a function of their model number and processor speed. The more powerful the processor, the faster the multimedia computer will respond. For the latest information on Intel processor speed comparisons, follow the *Multilit* Web site link to the Intel iCOMP index.

Hard Drive

A **hard drive** is a magnetic storage device on which computer programs and data are stored. Like RAM, hard drives are measured in megabytes, also called megs, or in gigabytes, also called gigs. A gigabyte is a thousand megabytes. The larger the hard drive, the more programs and data the computer can store. A multimedia PC should have at least 640 megabytes. The hard drive will hold, for example, the multimedia applications that you will create in the tutorial part of this book. If you plan to record digital video onto your hard drive, it needs to be as large as you can afford to make it.

CD-ROM

CD-ROM stands for compact disc—read-only memory. A CD-ROM can store about 680 MB (megabytes) of data. That is enough to hold the text of 200 Bibles. Because compact discs are inexpensive to produce yet provide so much storage, CD-ROM became the medium of choice for publishing multimedia applications in the twentieth century.

The speed of a CD-ROM drive is measured in how many thousands of characters (bytes) it can read per second. In computer spec sheets, the character *K*, which stands for *kilo* (the Greek word for thousand), is used to represent 1000 characters, or 1 kilobyte (KB). The first CD-ROM drives could transfer data at a rate of 150 KB per second. Double-speed CD-ROM drives can transfer data at twice that speed, or 300 KB per second.

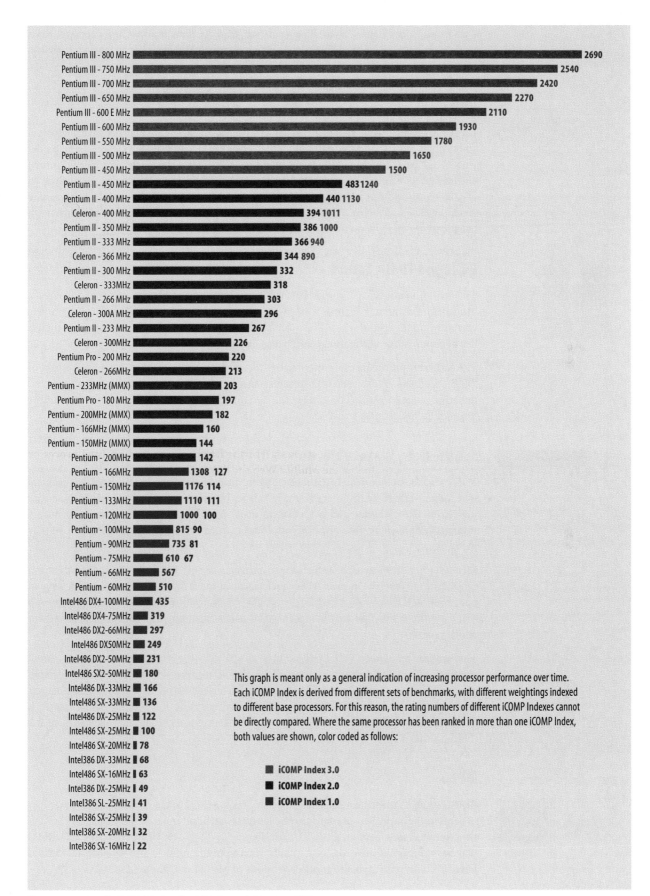

Processor	Value	Value 2
Pentium III - 800 MHz	2690	
Pentium III - 750 MHz	2540	
Pentium III - 700 MHz	2420	
Pentium III - 650 MHz	2270	
Pentium III - 600 E MHz	2110	
Pentium III - 600 MHz	1930	
Pentium III - 550 MHz	1780	
Pentium III - 500 MHz	1650	
Pentium III - 450 MHz	1500	
Pentium II - 450 MHz	483	1240
Pentium II - 400 MHz	440	1130
Celeron - 400 MHz	394	1011
Pentium II - 350 MHz	386	1000
Pentium II - 333 MHz	366	940
Celeron - 366 MHz	344	890
Pentium II - 300 MHz	332	
Celeron - 333MHz	318	
Pentium II - 266 MHz	303	
Celeron - 300A MHz	296	
Pentium II - 233 MHz	267	
Celeron - 300MHz	226	
Pentium Pro - 200 MHz	220	
Celeron - 266MHz	213	
Pentium - 233MHz (MMX)	203	
Pentium Pro - 180 MHz	197	
Pentium - 200MHz (MMX)	182	
Pentium - 166MHz (MMX)	160	
Pentium - 150MHz (MMX)	144	
Pentium - 200MHz	142	
Pentium - 166MHz	1308	127
Pentium - 150MHz	1176	114
Pentium - 133MHz	1110	111
Pentium - 120MHz	1000	100
Pentium - 100MHz	815	90
Pentium - 90MHz	735	81
Pentium - 75MHz	610	67
Pentium - 66MHz	567	
Pentium - 60MHz	510	
Intel486 DX4-100MHz	435	
Intel486 DX4-75MHz	319	
Intel486 DX2-66MHz	297	
Intel486 DX50MHz	249	
Intel486 DX2-50MHz	231	
Intel486 SX2-50MHz	180	
Intel486 DX-33MHz	166	
Intel486 SX-33MHz	136	
Intel486 DX-25MHz	122	
Intel486 SX-25MHz	100	
Intel486 SX-20MHz	78	
Intel386 DX-33MHz	68	
Intel486 SX-16MHz	63	
Intel386 DX-25MHz	49	
Intel386 SL-25MHz	41	
Intel386 SX-25MHz	39	
Intel386 SX-20MHz	32	
Intel386 SX-16MHz	22	

This graph is meant only as a general indication of increasing processor performance over time. Each iCOMP Index is derived from different sets of benchmarks, with different weightings indexed to different base processors. For this reason, the rating numbers of different iCOMP Indexes cannot be directly compared. Where the same processor has been ranked in more than one iCOMP Index, both values are shown, color coded as follows:

- ■ iCOMP Index 3.0
- ■ iCOMP Index 2.0
- ■ iCOMP Index 1.0

Figure 1-6   Intel's iCOMP index for i386 through Pentium III Processors.

Quadruple-speed drives, also called 4x drives, transfer data at 600 KB per second. Even faster drives are available, with speeds ranging from 17x (2550 KB per second) to 40x (6000 KB per second).

DVD

DVD stands for digital versatile disc. It can hold 4.7 GB (gigabytes) per layer, which is seven times more than a CD can hold. Dual-layer DVDs can hold 8.5 GB on a single side, with 17 GB on a double-sided, dual-layer disc. A DVD has the same diameter (120mm) and thickness (1.2mm) as a compact disc. DVD drives can play back CDs as well as DVDs, so you do not need a CD-ROM drive if your computer has a DVD drive. The most popular feature of a DVD is that it can play back full-length feature films with broadcast-quality video and surround sound.

8-Bit and 16-Bit Sound

The term **bit** stands for binary digit. A bit can have one of two values: 0 or 1. When a multimedia computer records a sound, a stream of bits gets recorded to represent the vibrations in the sound wave. The more bits that are used to sample the wave, the higher the dynamic range of the music you hear.

The earliest multimedia computers had 8-bit sound, which produces a dynamic range of 50dB (decibels). More recent computers also have 16-bit sound, which increases the dynamic range to 98dB. The greater the dynamic range, the more faithfully the volume levels in the music play back.

Synthesizer, Wavetable, and MIDI Playback

MIDI stands for Musical Instrument Digital Interface. MIDI is the most economical way for multimedia computers to make music, because instead of recording the entire waveform like a digital audio recording does, MIDI encodes only the performance information (such as note on, note off, louder, softer) needed for a synthesizer to play the music.

MIDI setups often involve external equipment, such as music keyboards and sound modules that play the music. This external equipment is costly, however. To let you play back MIDI without needing external devices, multimedia computers contain a MIDI synthesizer driver that can play MIDI songs through your computer's waveform audio board.

The synthesizer driver will rarely sound as good as the external equipment would, however. Enter the wavetable, which is a list of numbers that describe the desired waveshape of a sound. Every sound has a characteristic waveshape that determines the timbre or kind of sound you hear. You will learn more about waveshapes in Chapter 2. The wavetable helps MIDI do a better job of creating waveshapes that produce the desired sounds.

MPEG

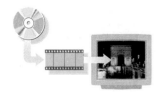

MPEG stands for Motion Picture Experts Group. MPEG is the format that is emerging as the new digital video standard for the United States and most of the world. MPEG-1 is the noninterlaced version of MPEG designed for playback from ordinary CD-ROM players. MPEG-2 is the broadcast quality version used on DVD and satellite TV such as DirecTV. You will learn about other versions of MPEG in Chapter 15.

What Is the Internet?

The **Internet** is a worldwide connection of more than 72 million computers that use the Internet Protocol (IP) to communicate. The Internet Protocol was invented for the U.S. Department of Defense Advanced Research Projects Agency (ARPA). The goal was to create a network that would continue to function if a bomb destroyed one or more of the network's nodes; information would get rerouted automatically so it could still reach its address. As a result of this bomb-proof design, any user on the Internet can communicate with any other user, regardless of their location.

Figure 1-7 illustrates the web that is formed by the interconnections of computers on the Internet in the United States. More than 190 countries and territories around the world are similarly connected to the Internet, forming a worldwide tele-communications network.

Every computer on the Internet has a unique IP address. An IP address consists of four numbers separated by periods. The numbers range from 0 to 255, so that the smallest possible address is 0.0.0.0 and the largest is 255.255.255.255. The number of IP addresses this scheme allows is 256^4, which is 4,294,967,296. This provides room for adding more computers as the network grows.

IP addresses can be hard to remember. For example, the Web server at the Library of Congress has the IP address 140.147.248.7. The White House is at 198.137.241.30. The Smithsonian is 160.111.7.240. If you had to remember numbers like these, the Internet would not be very user-friendly.

To make IP addresses easier for human beings to remember, a domain name system (DNS) was invented to permit the use of alphabetic characters instead of numbers. For example, instead of having to remember that the Library of Congress is at 140.147.248.7

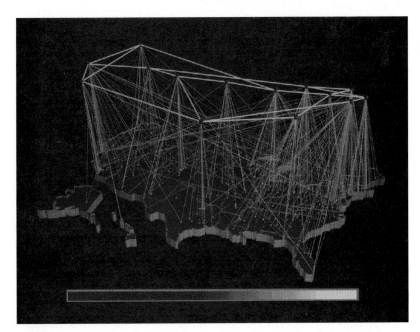

Figure 1-7   This image is a visualization study of inbound traffic measured in billions of bytes on the NSFNET T1 backbone for September 1991. The traffic volume range is depicted from purple (0 bytes) to white (100 billion bytes). The NSFNET is one of the most important parts of the Internet in the United States.

Source: Rendered by Donna Cox and Robert Patterson, National Center for Supercomputing Applications/University of Illinois. The data was collected by Merit Network, Inc.

you can use its domain name www.loc.gov. The White House is www.whitehouse.gov, and the Smithsonian is www.si.edu. Domain names have the format:

hostname.subdomain.top-level-domain

In the United States, top-level domains normally consist of one of the following:

.edu	educational
.com	commercial
.gov	government
.mil	military
.net	network support centers
.org	other organizations

In the rest of the world, top-level domains are usually country codes, such as *fr* for France. The subdomain refers to the network to which a computer is connected, and the host name refers to the computer itself. For example, in the domain name www.louvre.fr, which is the World Wide Web server at the famous Louvre museum in Paris, the top-level domain *fr* indicates that the server is located in France, the subdomain *louvre* tells you that the server is on the Louvre's network, and the host name *www* identifies this computer as the Louvre's World Wide Web server.

The International Ad Hoc Committee (IAHC) has proposed adding seven new top-level domain names. The new names are .firm, .store, .web, .arts, .rec, .info, and .nom. For more information about the new names and the status of this proposal, follow the *Multilit* Web site links to the *Generic Top Level Domain Memorandum of Understanding*.

What Is the World Wide Web?

The **World Wide Web (WWW)** is a networked hypertext system that allows documents to be shared over the Internet. Developed at the European Particle Physics Center (CERN) in Geneva, Switzerland, the Web's original purpose was to let researchers all over the world collaborate on the same documents without traveling.

Hypertext is a word coined by Ted Nelson (1965). It refers to text that has been linked. When you view a hypertext and click a word that has been linked, your computer launches the object of that link. The links give the text an added dimension, which is why it is called *hyper*.

When the Web started, it was purely text-based. In 1993, the National Center for Supercomputer Applications (NCSA) released Mosaic, a graphical user interface that made the Web extremely easy to use. In addition to text, Mosaic allowed Web pages to contain pictures, with links to audio and video as well. This led to the Web becoming the most popular service on the Internet.

In 1994, Netscape Communications Corporation was started by some of Mosaic's developers, and over the next few years, a program called Netscape Navigator became a very popular Web browser. Microsoft also created a Web browser called the Microsoft Internet Explorer, which rivals Netscape Navigator. The popularity of Microsoft Internet Explorer and Netscape Navigator diminished the need for continued work on Mosaic, and in 1997, the NCSA quietly discontinued work on it, opting instead to work on other advanced Internet technologies.

In the July 1996 issue of *Technology Review* is a fascinating interview with Tim Berners-Lee, the person credited with inventing the World Wide Web. You can find the interview online by following the *Multilit* Web site links to "The Web Maestro: An Interview with Tim Berners-Lee."

exercises

1. Give examples of how multimedia has affected (a) the nation as a whole, (b) your local community, and (c) your personal life.

2. In your chosen career or profession, would telecommuting be appropriate? How would it help or hinder your work?

3. This chapter described how multimedia is changing the world through mergers and alliances, telecommuting, home shopping, electronic publishing, and computer-based learning. How else do you see multimedia changing the world?

4. Compare the advantages and disadvantages of online shopping as you see them. What impact does online shopping have on traditional stores and shopping malls?

5. Think of an example showing how a computer helped you learn something. What was the subject matter? What role did the computer play? Did you learn better because of the computer? Why or why not?

6. Of all the different kinds of occupations you can think of, which ones need multimedia the most? The least? What is your chosen occupation? Why will you need to know about multimedia to do well in this line of work?

7. Find out the domain name of the computer network at your school or place of work. If you have an e-mail address on that network, the domain name will be the part of your e-mail address after the @ sign. For example, if your e-mail address is santa.claus@toymakers.northpole.com, the domain name is toymakers.northpole.com.

2 Taxonomy of Multimedia Objects

After completing this chapter, you will be able to:

▧ **Define and recognize linked objects in a multimedia application**

▧ **Understand the present-day limits of creating those objects**

▧ **Think about what new kinds of objects there may be in the future as multimedia technology progresses**

▧ **Consider whether the digitization of media is making communication better or worse, and understand the appropriate role of technology**

● The definition of multimedia in the previous chapter emphasizes the important role that links play in giving users a way to interact and navigate. This chapter defines the objects of those links by providing a taxonomy of multimedia. There are six kinds of objects: text, graphics, sound, video, animation, and software. The roles each kind plays in a multimedia system are described here.

Text

Although it is possible to have multimedia without text, most multimedia systems use text because it is such an effective way to communicate ideas and provide instructions to users. There are four kinds of text: printed, scanned, electronic, and hypertext.

Printed Text

Printed text, like the words in this paragraph, appears on paper. Suppose you want to use printed text as the basis for a multimedia document. In order for a multimedia computer to read printed text, you need to transform the text into machine-readable form. The most obvious way to do this is to type the text into a word processor or text editor, but that is tedious and time-consuming. A faster way would be to scan the text.

Scanned Text

Low-cost scanners that can read printed text and convert it into machine-readable form to produce **scanned text** are widely available. There are three basic kinds of scanners: flatbed, handheld, and sheet-fed. Flatbed scanners are more expensive because of the motors and pulleys that move the scanner over the paper. Handheld scanners cost less because you move the scanner over the paper manually, thereby avoiding the cost of the flatbed enclosure and mechanism. Sheet-fed scanners have a slot into which you insert the page you want scanned. Regardless of the kind of scanner you have, advances in the optical character recognition (OCR) software that comes with scanners have increased scanning accuracy.

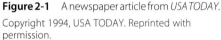

Figure 2-1 A newspaper article from *USA TODAY*. Copyright 1994, USA TODAY. Reprinted with permission.

Figure 2-2 The newspaper article being scanned with a handheld scanner.

For example, consider the newspaper article in Figure 2-1. Figure 2-2 shows it being scanned by a handheld scanner. You can see the results of the scan in Figure 2-3. Notice how a couple of characters have a caret (^) in front of them. The scanning software marks characters with a caret when it is not sure whether it has accurately recognized them. If you compare Figure 2-3 to the original text in Figure 2-1, however, you will see that every character is correct.

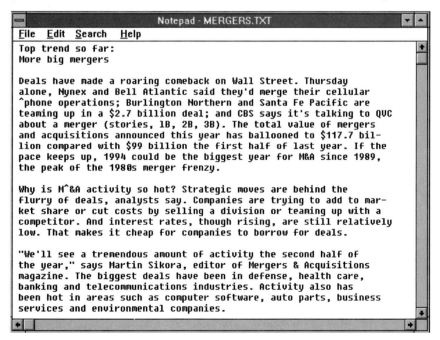

Figure 2-3 The results of the scan. The caret (^) marks characters about which the scanner was unsure.

The author used a handheld scanner extensively while writing this book. Instead of typing quotes from books and magazines, the author simply swiped the scanner over the quotes and flowed the scanned text into this document. As this book goes to press, the most portable scanner is the IRISPen, which is a pen-sized scanner that allows you to scan text into any Windows or Macintosh application. It scans editable text into the current cursor position. For more information, follow the *Multilit* Web site links to handheld scanners.

Electronic Text

A tremendous number of texts are available in machine-readable form, because almost everyone who writes books or publishes manuscripts today does so with word processing and electronic publishing equipment. Because they can be read by a computer and transmitted electronically over networks, such texts are referred to as **electronic texts**. For example, this book was written with Microsoft Word 2000.

Electronic text was used extensively in writing this book. Internet news feeds and other networked resources provided a rich store of information that would otherwise have taken years to research. You will learn how to access these news feeds in the online resources section of Chapter 17.

Hypertext

The prefix *hyper* may be the most important word in this book, because it refers to the process of linking, which makes multimedia interactive. The word *hypertext* was coined by Ted Nelson (1965). **Hypertext** refers to text that has been linked. When you view a hypertext and click a word that has been linked, your computer launches the object of that link. Any one of the objects listed in this taxonomy of multimedia can be the object of such a link. The links give the text an added dimension, which is why it is called hyper.

Graphics

It has often been said that a picture is worth a thousand words. However, that is true only when you can show the picture you want when you need it. Multimedia lets you do this when graphics are the object of a link. Graphics often appear as backdrops behind text to create a pictorial framework for the text. Pictures can also serve as icons, intermixed with text, representing options that can be selected; or pictures can appear full-screen in place of text, with parts of the picture serving as triggers which, when selected, launch other multimedia objects or events.

Bitmaps

A **bitmap** is a picture stored as a set of pixels that correspond to the grid of dots on a computer screen. To display the picture, the computer sets each dot on the screen to the color specified for it in the bitmap. You can create bitmaps with any graphics editor, such as the Paint program that comes with Windows, or commercial drawing programs such as Adobe Photoshop or CorelDRAW. In Chapter 34, you will learn how to use Paint Shop Pro (Windows) or GraphicConverter (Macintosh) to capture into a bitmap any graphic displayed on your computer screen from any software program, including frames from live video feeds.

Over the years many different graphics formats have been invented for storing images on computers. Table 2-1 lists the most common formats and identifies their intended purpose.

Table 2-1   The Most Common Computer Graphics Formats

Filename Extension	Intended Purpose
.bmp	Windows bitmap; the BMP file is the most efficient format to use with Windows
.dib	Windows device-independent bitmap; used to transfer bitmaps from one device or process to another
.gif	Graphics Interchange Format (GIF); invented by CompuServe for use on computer networks, GIF is the prevalent graphics format for images on the World Wide Web
.mac	Macintosh MacPaint format
.jpg	JPEG image, named for the standards committee that formed it: the Joint Photographic Experts Group; intended to become a platform-independent graphics format
.pcd	Kodak's Photo CD graphics file format; contains five different sizes of each picture, from "wallet" size to "poster" size
.pcx	Zsoft Paintbrush graphics format; popular in the DOS world
.pic	PC Paint graphics format
.pict	The Macintosh standard image format
.png	Portable Network Graphics format. Pronounced ping, *.png* is the patent and license-free format approved by the W3C (World Wide Web Consortium) to replace the patented GIF format
.tga	Truevision Targa format; *tga* stands for Targa, which is a video capture board
.tif	Tagged Image File Format (TIFF); known as "the variable standard" because there are so many kinds of TIFF subformats
.wpg	WordPerfect graphics format

Vector Images

Vector images are stored as a set of mathematical equations called algorithms that define the curves, lines, and shapes in a picture. For images that do not contain a lot of continuous color changes, vectors are a more-efficient way to store the image than bitmaps. Consider a diagonal line, for example. A bitmap stores each point along the diagonal as an RGB color value. A vector image, on the other hand, simply stores the line's starting point, direction, length, and color.

Vector images have two advantages over bitmaps. First, vector images are scalable, meaning that you can use graphics programs to enlarge or reduce the size of the image without any loss of quality. Second, because vector images normally have smaller file sizes than bitmapped graphics, vectors download more quickly over the Internet.

AutoDesk is the leading manufacturer of vector-based software. Their AutoCAD software uses vector-based graphics to create working models of architectural and mechanical drawings. AutoDesk has created plug-ins that enable Web browsers to display vector drawings and let users interact with AutoCAD models. To download the plug-ins and manipulate some sample AutoCAD drawings, follow the *Multilit* Web site links to the AutoDesk plug-ins. For more information about vector technology and standards, follow the links to the Vector Zone.

Clip Art

Creating graphics by hand is time-consuming. To save time there are extensive libraries of clip art that you can use in multimedia productions. By following the *Multilit* Web site links to clip art, you will discover dozens of online clip libraries. Many have broad,

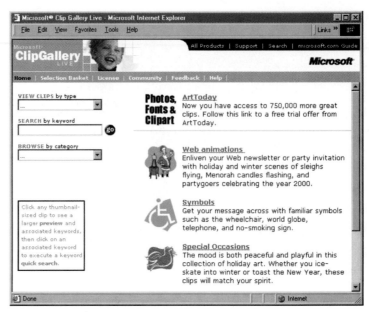

Figure 2-4   Microsoft's online clip library provides you with hundreds of thousands of royalty-free images.

general categories including photographs, icons, animations, background tiles, buttons, and bullets, while other libraries focus on a visual theme such as nature or scientific images. You can usually use clip-art images royalty free, but make sure you read the license carefully because restrictions may apply. You may be required to include a courtesy hyperlink to the clip library's Web site, for example.

In Chapter 21, you will learn how to use Microsoft's online clip library. Figure 2-4 shows how it lets you search for clip art by type, key word, or category.

Digitized Pictures

Video capture boards let you connect a video camera, VCR, videodisc player, or live video feed to your computer and grab frames instantly into bitmaps that can be used in multimedia applications. Think of the pictorial breadth this technology provides: Since video digitizers accept a video signal as input, they can digitize anything a video camera can see. Any photograph, slide, or picture from any book or magazine can be digitized in full color and linked into your multimedia application. Because copyright law prohibits unlawful copying and distribution, however, make sure you study the copyright and fair use guidelines presented in Chapter 16.

Snappy Video Snapshot is an image capture module that connects to the printer port on the back of a desktop or laptop PC. Snappy can capture images up to 1500 × 1125 pixels with up to 16 million colors. Since you do not have to put anything inside your computer, Snappy is much easier to install than a video capture card. You should be aware, however, that Snappy does not capture full-motion movies like video capture boards do; Snappy just does what its name implies, which is to "snap" still pictures from the output of a video camera or other video source. For more information, follow the *Multilit* Web site links to Snappy.

Figure 2-5 The e-photo Web site for Eckerd Drugs.

Courtesy of Eckerd Corporation; Kodak is a registered trademark of Eastman Kodak Company, and PhotoNet is a registered trademark of PictureVision Inc. Copyright 1996–2000.

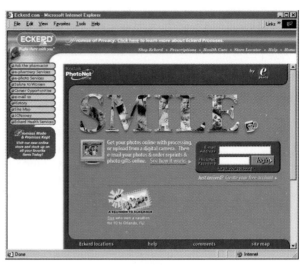

Figure 2-6 Kodak PhotoNet online.

Courtesy of Eckerd Corporation; Kodak is a registered trademark of Eastman Kodak Company, and PhotoNet is a registered trademark of PictureVision Inc. Copyright 1996–2000.

If you do not have a capture board or a Snappy, you can shoot a roll of film and take it to a mass market retail store, such as Eckerd Drugs, where it only costs about $4 extra to get a diskette with up to 15 pictures, $5 for up to 28 images, and $6 for 29 or more exposures. The diskette has software that lets you view the pictures on your PC and export the images in different graphics formats.

Figure 2-5 shows Eckerd's e-photo Web site. Clicking the link to online photo services takes you to Kodak PhotoNet online, as illustrated in Figure 2-6. How this works is fascinating. You take your film to any participating Eckerd drugstore and request Kodak PhotoNet online by simply checking the appropriate box and providing your e-mail address. You will receive an e-mail message notifying you when your negatives and prints are ready to be picked up and how you can access your scanned photos online. Digital camera users have the option of creating a free online account and purchasing a "roll of space" into which you can upload photos and place an order for high-quality prints.

For more information about digital photo processing and to preview the Kodak PhotoNet online gallery, follow the *Multilit* Web site link to the Eckerd drugstore e-photo digital image center. For the latest information about digital cameras, click the *Multilit* Web site's digital camera link.

Hyperpictures

Just as words can serve as triggers in a hypertext, so also can parts of pictures. When parts of pictures are used to trigger multimedia events, they are called **hyperpictures**. In Chapter 23, you will learn how to make any part of any image be a trigger that you can link to any text, graphic, sound, or video on your computer, or to any Web page or other multimedia resource on the Internet. The triggers can be any size or shape, and you can make them invisible. There is no limit to the number of triggers you can put on a hyperpicture. When the user mouses over a trigger, the cursor changes shape to tell the user that spot is a hyperlink. If the user clicks there, your link will trigger.

Sound

There are four types of sound objects that can be used in multimedia productions: waveform audio, MIDI sound tracks, compact disc (CD) audio, and MP3 files.

Waveform Audio

Just as video digitizers can be used to grab any picture a camera can see, **waveform audio** digitizers can record any sound you can hear. Every sound has a waveform that describes its frequency, amplitude, and harmonic content. Waveform audio digitizers capture sound by sampling this waveform thousands of times per second; the samples are stored on a computer's hard disk in a file that usually has a *.wav* filename extension, which stands for waveform. Figure 2-7 shows a waveform in the process of being sampled, and Figure 2-8 shows the samples from the corresponding *.wav* file.

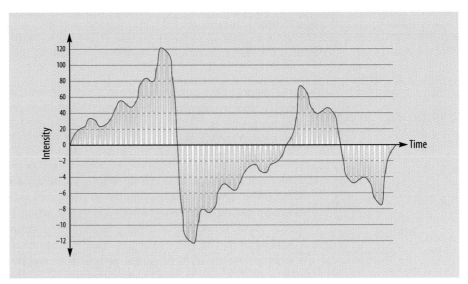

Figure 2-7   Waveform in the process of being sampled; the vertical lines show the points at which samples are taken.

0	33	80	−122	−56	−21	40	−43
15	47	96	−96	−47	−15	43	−40
21	56	122	−80	−33	0	47	−46
24	52	117	−84	−26	10	42	−66
34	48	85	−78	−24	35	18	−74
32	55	0	−55	−32	74	−18	−35
24	78	−85	−48	−34	66	−42	−10
26	84	−117	−52	−24	46	−47	0

Figure 2-8   Samples taken from the waveform in Figure 2-7.

The *Multilit* Web site provides links to Web sites offering free, downloadable waveform audio in a wide range of genres including contemporary and classical music, movie soundtracks, television programs, and sound effects. Read the license carefully because restrictions may apply, especially if you are planning to charge a fee for the application in which you use the clip.

MIDI

MIDI stands for Musical Instrument Digital Interface. It provides a very efficient way of recording music. Instead of recording the waveform of the sound, which requires a lot of storage, MIDI records the performance information required for your computer's sound chip to play the music. For example, there are MIDI codes for turning notes on and off, making them loud or soft, changing their timbre or tone quality, and bending them or adding other special effects. MIDI files have a *.mid* filename extension. They can be randomly accessed down to an accuracy of 1/128 second.

The MIDI folder on the *Multilit* CD contains several MIDI songs that were provided courtesy of Midisoft Corporation. In addition, the *Multilit* Web site provides links to MIDI archives where you can download thousands of MIDI songs from the Internet. As always, read the license carefully and observe the copyright and fair use guidelines presented in Chapter 16.

Audio CD

Audio CDs can hold up to 75 minutes of high-fidelity recorded sound. The sampling rate is 44,100 samples per second, which is fast enough to record any sound audible to humans. The samples are 16 bits, producing a dynamic range of 98dB, which is discrete enough to record faithfully a quiet whisper or a loud scream. The addressing used in CD-ROM drives permits multimedia computers to randomly access a song on the CD with split-second accuracy down to 1/75 of a second.

In Chapter 24, you will learn how to make any track or sound clip play from an audio CD during a multimedia presentation. At the *Multilit* Web site, you will find links to CD audio stores where you can find just about any song in the world, from your favorite recording artist to that hard-to-locate classical recording. There is even a link to a custom disc company that will burn a one-of-a-kind CD containing just the songs you want.

CD Plus, CD Extra, and Enhanced CD

CD Plus, also known as **CD Extra** or **Enhanced CD**, is a music CD that can also function as a CD-ROM, with computer data included on the music disc. If you put the CD Plus into a conventional audio CD player, you hear the music as usual. Insert the CD Plus into a multimedia PC, and the computer programming provides you with dazzling computer graphics, navigation, and interactivity.

To find out whether an audio CD has these features, put it in your computer's CD or DVD drive, and wait to see if an enhanced window pops up offering you a menu of extra features on the CD.

MP3

MP3 stands for MPEG Audio Layer 3. It is an audio file format that uses an MPEG audio codec to encode (compress) and decode (decompress) recorded music. MP3 can compress a CD audio track into a substantially smaller sized file requiring significantly less bandwidth to transmit over the Internet without degrading the original sound track's quality.

To download a free MP3 player, find MP3 Web sites, and create MP3 files from your favorite audio CD, follow the *Multilit* Web site links to MP3. If you do not personally own the CD, and/or if the MP3 files are not for your own personal use, please observe the copyright and fair use guidelines presented in Chapter 16. Because the MP3 technology makes it so easy to violate copyright, the kind of software used to create an MP3 file from an audio CD is called a **ripper**.

Hyperaudio

Sound tracks are played over time. Many multimedia creation tools allow you to time the occurrence of objects to sync points in the music. When audio is used to trigger multimedia objects, it is referred to as **hyperaudio**.

Video

Video provides a rich and lively resource for multimedia applications. There are four types of video that you can use as the objects of links in multimedia applications: live video feeds, videotape, videodisc, and digital video.

Live Video Feeds

Live video feeds provide interesting real-time objects of multimedia links. Any television channel or live camera feed can be the object of a link. Suppose you are teaching civics and you want to illustrate how a bill works its way through Congress. C-SPAN, the Cable-Satellite Public Affairs Network, operates one channel that covers proceedings on the floor of the House of Representatives, and another channel devoted to the Senate; it also broadcasts interviews and call-in shows, congressional hearings, speeches, and press conferences.

If you teach a subject in which current events are important, your multimedia software can put you just a mouse click away from CNN, the 24-hour news channel that summarizes the news every 30 minutes. Or suppose you are a plant supervisor needing to inspect what is happening on one of your assembly lines; a mouse click can instantly display a live video feed on your multimedia computer screen.

Webcams let you watch live video feeds from all over the world. From freeway traffic to surfing beaches, day care centers to college dorm rooms, Webcams can be found just about anywhere. For a look at some of the more popular Webcams, follow the *Multilit* Web site links, where you will find articles about Webcam use and a search engine that indexes more than 11,000 cameras.

Videotape

The most widespread video medium is videotape. Almost everyone owns a VCR, and nearly every shopping center has a video store that rents movies on videotape. Corporations use videotape to provide just-in-time training, and public libraries have collections of instructional videotapes.

Videotapes can be the object of multimedia links. This medium is limited by two factors, however. First, videotapes are linear. The information is stored on tape in a serial fashion, and in order to access it you may have to wait a long time for the tape to fast-forward or rewind to the spot you want; this can take as long as three minutes. Second, most videotape players are not computer controllable. This means that you must manually press the *play, stop, fast-forward,* and *rewind* buttons yourself to use videotape in a multimedia presentation. Happily, Sony Hi8 videotape players are computer controllable, through a protocol called the Video System Control Architecture (VISCA), which can control up to seven devices. A wide range of Sony video products are VISCA controllable, including camcorders, VCRs, and monitors. For more information, follow the *Multilit* Web site links to Sony and VISCA.

Videodisc

There are two industrywide formats for videodiscs: CAV and CLV. CAV discs can store up to 54,000 still frames or 30 minutes of motion video with a stereo sound track. The frames are addressed by specifying numbers from 1 to 54,000. The CAV format lets you display still frames as well as play motion sequences.

CLV discs can store up to an hour of video on each disc side, which is twice as much video as CAV discs hold. But unless you have an expensive high-end player such as the Pioneer LD-V8000, you cannot show still frames from CLV discs.

Because of its fast random access and minimal consumption of the multimedia computer's resources, videodisc became one of the most popular twentieth-century means of providing video to multimedia applications in education, government, and industrial training. The popularity of videodisc has waned, however, due to the emergence of digital video and DVD, which are discussed next.

Digital Video

Digital video is the most promising and exciting video storage medium. Like waveform audio, digital video is stored in files on a hard disk, CD-ROM, or DVD. Because the video is digital, it can be served over computer networks, alleviating the need for videotapes and videodisc players. Digital video can be randomly accessed by frame, letting you play specific clips.

High-speed Pentium processors can play full-screen video without needing any special hardware installed. Slower computers need to have digital video boards installed to play movies full-screen. Otherwise, the video plays back in a window about one-quarter the size of the screen. Chapter 24 will teach you how to insert, size, and position movies. In Chapter 35, you will learn how to edit digital video and create movie clips.

DVD

DVD stands for digital versatile disc, but when a DVD's purpose is to play back a movie, it can more properly stand for digital video disc. DVD uses MPEG-2 to compress a full-length feature film onto a 4.7-inch disc. The movie plays back beautifully, with surround sound and 540 horizontal lines of full-color video. It is common for a DVD to offer the viewer a choice of languages, with or without subtitles, and sometimes the user can choose to view alternate endings to a movie. All this combined with backward-compatibility that lets you play audio CDs has led to the DVD player becoming a hot consumer item. Just as CD audio provided multimedia developers with split-second access to practically all recorded music, so also does DVD promise to create a digitally accessible store of all feature movies. Follow the *Multilit* Web site links to DVD news, reviews, and buying guides.

Hypervideo

Like sound tracks, video clips are played over time. Many multimedia creation tools allow you to time the occurrence of objects to sync points in the video. When video is used to trigger other multimedia events, it is referred to as **hypervideo**.

Animation

In multimedia, **animation** is the use of a computer to create movement on the screen. There are four kinds of animation: frame, vector, computational, and morph.

Frame Animation

Frame animation makes objects move by displaying a series of predrawn pictures, called frames, in which the objects appear in different locations on the screen. If you think about how a traditional movie plays in a theater, you can understand how frame animation works. In a movie, a series of frames moves through the film projector at about 24 frames per second. You see movement on the screen because each frame contains a picture of what the screen should look like at the moment that frame appears. Why 24 frames per second? Because that is the threshold beneath which you would notice flicker or jerkiness on the screen.

Vector Animation

A vector is a line that has a beginning, a direction, and a length. **Vector animation** makes objects move by varying these three parameters for the line segments that define the object. Macromedia is the industry leader in vector-based animation software. Macromedia's Flash software uses vector graphics to create animations and interactive graphics for use on the Web. Macromedia has published the Flash file format (*.swf*) as an open standard. For more information, follow the *Multilit* Web site links to Macromedia Flash, where you can visit a gallery of Web pages containing Flash animations and download Flash for a free 30-day trial period.

Computational Animation

Suppose you want to move a word across the screen. There are two ways to do that. You could create a series of frames that show the word inching its way across the screen, with each frame representing one moment in time as the word moves. But this would be inefficient, because the frames consume precious memory, and it takes a lot longer for an artist to draw the frames. In **computational animation**, you move objects across the screen simply by varying their x and y coordinates. The x coordinate specifies the horizontal position of the object, that is, how far across the screen. The y coordinate specifies the vertical position, that is, how far down the screen.

Morphing

Morphing means to transition one shape into another by displaying a series of frames that creates a smooth movement as the first shape transforms itself into the other shape. For example, Figure 2-9 shows the *David* morphing into the *Mona Lisa*. You can run this example on the *Multilit* CD. To run it, use the Windows Explorer or the Macintosh Finder to display the contents of the *Movies* folder, then double-click the movie named

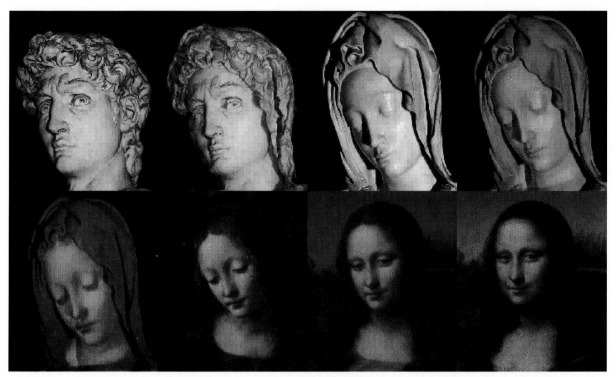

Figure 2-9　*David* morphs into the *Pieta*, then into *The Virgin of the Rocks*, and finally into the *Mona Lisa*.

morph. It would take a lot of time and patience to create a morph like this by hand. Morphing software creates the transitional frames automatically. Morphing is discussed in more depth in Chapter 5 in the section on cinematic special effects.

Software and Data

One of the most powerful concepts in multimedia is the seamless integration you can achieve by creating links to documents and datasets. When a user triggers a link to a word-processed document, such as a Microsoft Word *.doc* file for example, your computer automatically launches the software application (MS Word in this example) and uses it to display the document. Similarly, a link to an Excel spreadsheet's *.xls* file makes your computer launch Excel to display the spreadsheet. In Chapter 23 you will learn how to make these kinds of links to software and data objects.

Finding Multimedia Resources on the World Wide Web

The World Wide Web is a rich resource for finding multimedia objects of all types. In Chapter 33 you will learn strategies for locating objects via key word or subject-oriented searching. Web searches provide quick and easy access to millions of text documents, statistical datasets, pictures, sound tracks, musical scores, movies, animations, multimedia utilities, Web page creation tools, and software applications of all types. You will learn how to download these objects to your computer for use in your multimedia applications. You will also learn the proper bibliographic form for citing online resources in term papers and scholarly publications.

e x e r c i s e s

1. Scan a newspaper article into your word processor. Compare the scanned text to the original. How accurate was the scan? What hardware did you use to do the scan? What software? What problems do you see in scanner technology? *Note:* If you do not have a scanner, visit your local computer lab to complete this assignment.

2. Get a friend to take your picture with a 35mm camera. Have your friend zoom in close, taking the picture portrait style. Take the film to Eckerd drugstore and get it developed with the option to have a diskette returned along with your slides or prints. Run the software on the disk you get back from Eckerd, and see if your photo looks OK. What impresses you, and what disappoints you about your appearance on-screen? In Chapter 34 you will learn imaging techniques that can improve the look of your photo.

3. Printed books do not have hypertext ability. Do you believe that hypertext makes documents so powerful as to render printed books obsolete? If so, what kinds? All books, or just certain kinds? For example, is hypertext more important in an encyclopedia than in a novel?

4. Digital audio and video make it possible to digitize anything you can see or hear and edit it seamlessly, without leaving a trace. For example, a *New York Newsday* cover photograph showed ice skaters Nancy Kerrigan and Tonya Harding practicing together when in fact they were not (*New York Times* 2/17/94: A12). Will this capability make it increasingly difficult for judges in courtroom trials to admit audio recordings and videotapes into evidence?

5. Insert some audio CDs into your computer's CD or DVD drive. List the CDs you try. Do any of the CDs pop up a window that lets you access enhanced features on the CD? If so, name the CD that is enhanced, and tell what the enhanced features let you do that a plain audio CD does not. *Note:* Do not confuse the enhanced window with your computer's audio CD player. If an audio CD is not enhanced, your computer will probably pop up the CD audio player. What you are looking for in this exercise is an enhanced window that lets you do more than just play the music on the CD.

6. As multimedia technology progresses, the list of objects in the taxonomy this chapter presents will increase. Can you think of any new kinds of objects that have already been invented? How about the future? Dream up and describe a new multimedia object that future technology could support.

Part Two

Survey of Multimedia Applications

Tell me and I will forget; show me and I may remember; involve me and I will understand.

— Chinese proverb

Imagine if our kids' test scores were as high as their Nintendo scores.

— Computer Curriculum Corporation advertisement

The purpose of this multimedia application survey is to make you aware of the tremendous growth and development of multimedia throughout business, education, government, industry, and entertainment. The applications are illustrated with full-color pictures to give you an idea of what they are like. Demonstrations of many of these applications have been linked to the *Multilit* Web site.

Perusing these application summaries may give you ideas for multimedia titles you would like to develop. If you have an idea for an application that you do not find mentioned here, chances are it has not yet been developed, and there may be an opportunity for you to be the first to market it. On the other hand, if you find titles described here that are similar to your idea, you will know that the market is already developing, and examining these applications will help you gauge how your idea measures up against the competition. To find out if a title has already been developed, follow the *Multilit* Web site links to online catalogs of multimedia titles.

3

Business and Industry

After completing this chapter, you will be able to:

■ Understand how multimedia is transforming business and industry into a global economy

■ Consider the appropriate uses of point-of-sale kiosks, videoconferencing, and just-in-time training systems

■ Examine how these technologies are being used in your local community

■ Predict whether digital video will replace the VCR as the primary means of distributing video recordings

■ Experience what it is like to shop for merchandise on the World Wide Web

■ Define the term *day trading* and know why to be careful if you try it

● Multimedia provides businesses with powerful new ways to reach and service customers. Interactive multimedia merchandising is replacing storefronts with point-of-sale kiosks and home-shopping networks that have increased sales dramatically. Videoconferencing permits face-to-face meetings without traveling. Multimedia teaching systems provide just-in-time training whenever and wherever needed, significantly reducing corporate training costs. Global networking makes these services available anytime, anywhere.

Interactive Multimedia Merchandising

Anyone who shops has been frustrated by the time and effort required to locate a product you want in the style, color, and size you need. How often have you been told that what you want is out of stock? This section discusses how multimedia computers are being used in specific businesses to solve this problem. These businesses provide interactive merchandising systems that can help you find the product you want in the size you need, and that permit you to comparison-shop without having to spend all day visiting different stores.

Merchandising Kiosks

If you are tall like the author, and have big feet, Florsheim's merchandising kiosk is a godsend. It lets you shop for shoes by style, size, and color by touching the screen and following voice instructions. The kiosk includes a keyboard that lets you enter your name, address, and credit card number, and the system then arranges for drop-shipping the shoes via UPS overnight.

According to Computer Technology Research (CTR), "The Florsheim stores with kiosks report a 20% overall increase in shoe sales, not only through the automated system but also by freeing store salesmen [and women] to handle more customers faster and more expeditiously." In addition to locating kiosks in more than 300 company-operated stores, Florsheim has placed kiosks in 320 Sears department stores and is experimenting with kiosk placements at selected JC Penney stores. You can also shop Florsheim Online at http://www.florsheim.com.

Video Merchandising

Olmstead (1993) describes how kiosks are boosting retail sales by providing customers with in-store video search capabilities. FastTake Video kiosks, for example, let consumers preview movie trailers, search titles, and order movies for next-day delivery. Retailers get monthly updates to the database, advertising opportunities, point-of-purchase promotions, demographic targeting, and studio/retailer cross promotion. Installation and field service are provided by IBM Corporation. Figure 3-1 shows the FastTake kiosk. Customers are drawn to the futuristic design of the kiosk and the movement of the trailers playing on the menu. Under Editor's Pics you can find more details about featured videos whose trailers run in a continuous loop on the home screen. Through Just for Kids you find children's videos on the kiosk. Under New Releases you can quickly view this month's new features. In Coming Soon you search for new releases that will be available in the months ahead.

Blockbuster Video, meanwhile, is marketing videos on the Web at http://www.blockbuster.com. In addition to searching movie categories and titles, Blockbuster has a feature called Blockbuster Recommends that helps you find movies that suit your tastes. You rate movies you have seen, and Blockbuster Recommends diagnoses your tastes and suggests new movies based on your personal preferences. The more movies you rate, the more the wizard learns about your personal tastes. You can register online for free to use the service, which remembers your preferences from session to session so you can come back anytime for another personal movie recommendation. Follow the *Multilit* Web site links to learn more about video merchandising.

Virtual Shopping

The Information Superhighway provides consumers with convenient shopping in any store connected to an online service. This benefits not only the shopper, but also the manufacturer. Online shopping bypasses the traditional distributor to put an information-rich virtual storefront right where a preferred customer is waiting. By enabling the manufacturer to compile and analyze customer habits and buying trends, the network boosts sales, letting vendors market specific products directly to the consumers most likely to buy them.

Consider the Galleria 21 virtual shopping mall at London's Heathrow Airport. A touch-screen kiosk provides online access to dozens of stores, including Royal Doulton, Bally, Waterford Crystal, Burberry's, and The Scotch House.

Figure 3-1   The FastTake Video Merchandising Kiosk.

Galleria 21 guarantees speedy delivery of purchases almost anywhere in the world. Galleria 21 is multilingual, accepts a wide variety of credit cards, and recognizes worldwide monetary standards.

MontegoNet Solutions designs, manufactures, and markets Internet kiosks for use in bank lobbies, cyber cafés, concert halls, convention centers, hotel lobbies, retail stores, museums, and exhibit halls. Internet kiosks expand the virtual shopping experience by integrating it with personal services such as banking, faxing, and e-mail. NCR and CyberFlyer Technologies are marketing Internet kiosks to banks as replacements for automated teller machines (ATM). In addition to withdrawing and depositing money, consumers can browse through their checking accounts and inspect their 401(k) retirement records. Kinko's has added Internet access to its entire chain of more than 800 copy shops, connecting customers for $12 an hour through ISDN lines provided by GTE. Follow the *Multilit* Web site links to learn more about Internet kiosks.

Virtually any store planning to stay in business in the twenty-first century has established a Web site. Table 3-1 lists the Web addresses of some Internet shopping sites and describes what they do. Anyone with a Web browser can visit these stores online. Secured payment services such as CyberCash have made it safe for consumers to shop online and charge purchases to their credit cards. For more information, follow the *Multilit* Web site link to CyberCash.

Table 3-1 World Wide Web Online Shopping Locations

World Wide Web Address	What You'll Find There
http://malls.com	A mall of malls, featuring hundreds of online theme malls, city malls, and global malls
http://www.amazon.com	One of the most innovative online shopping sites, originally for books and CDs, now for anything you want to buy or sell
http://www.1800flowers.com	The online store for 1-800-flowers, where you can order flowers, gourmet food, and gifts appropriate for any season
http://ipw.internet.com	A wide range of information technology products, including network connections, Internet providers, World Wide Web products, digital cameras, video products, and more
http://www.isn.com	The Internet Shopping Network (ISN), the first online retailer in the world when it was launched in April 1994; here you'll find an online auction where you can buy or sell a wide range of products including furniture, electronics, jewelry, sporting goods, and toys
http://www.wal-mart.com	Online access to the world's largest retail store chain
http://www.landsend.com	Lands' End, a direct merchant of traditionally styled, casual clothing for men, women, and children, as well as soft luggage and products for the home
For an extensive list of Internet shopping sites on the Web, go to www.yahoo.com and search for the key words "online malls" and "online shopping."	

Comparison Shopping

Back in the good old days, when you bought products at a shopping mall and wanted to make sure you were getting a good price, you could walk to three or four different stores and compare prices. In the online shopping world, on the other hand, with tens of thousands of stores online, how can you ever compare all the prices? The answer is easy: You can use online comparison-shopping services.

At the Yahoo shopping service, for example, you can type the name of a product, and within a few seconds, Yahoo will search its directory of thousands of stores and millions of products. Then you click the option to sort the hits by price, and Yahoo does your comparison shopping for you. The Lycos search engine also offers a comparison shopping service. If you do not know the specific product name you are looking for, Lycos steps you through the process of determining your needs and helps you decide what product to buy. The AltaVista search engine offers Smart Shopping, which lets you search the Web for products to buy, see how other users rate products and merchants, and compare products side by side.

To learn more about comparison shopping, follow the *Multilit* Web site links to the Yahoo shopping service, Lycos Comparison Shopping, and AltaVista Smart Shopping. For a list of other shopping agents, go to www.yahoo.com and search for shopping agents.

Videoconferencing

Due to the high cost of transportation and the large amount of employee time spent traveling to meetings, videoconferencing is on the rise. More than 50 countries have videoconferencing equipment, and in North America alone there are more than 10,000 videoconferencing rooms. One of the largest public networks is in Kinko's stores. To find out whether your local Kinko's store has videoconferencing, follow the *Multilit* Web site links to Kinko's. Figure 3-2 shows a videoconference in progress.

Figure 3-2 A videoconference in progress.

Not everyone can afford expensive videoconferencing equipment and high-speed dedicated communications lines. A lower-cost alternative on the Internet is CU-SeeMe (pronounced *see you see me*), which is one of the more creative product names created in the twentieth century. *CU* stands for Carnegie-Mellon University, where the CU-SeeMe videoconferencing technology was invented in 1993. Anyone who has a multimedia PC with an installed video camera can get on the Internet and establish a real-time videoconference via the CU-SeeMe software. In 1998, White Pine Software acquired complete ownership of the trademark, source code, and all intellectual property rights to CU-SeeMe, which lets up to 50 people participate in a videoconference with chat and an electronic whiteboard. For larger meetings, White Pine offers a more expensive alternative called MeetingPoint. For more information, follow the *Multilit* Web site links to CU-SeeMe, MeetingPoint, and White Pine Software.

One of the fastest-growing videoconferencing networks is based on Microsoft's NetMeeting software. Microsoft lets you download the NetMeeting software for free. In Chapter 42, you will learn how to get online with NetMeeting and use it to share multimedia applications over the Internet. If you have a videoconferencing camera, people in the meeting will also be able to see you. Follow the *Multilit* Web site links to NetMeeting and Microsoft's recommendations for cameras to use with it.

Logitech sells a complete line of videoconferencing cameras that can turn any multimedia PC into a videoconferencing terminal. Prices for the Logitech cameras range from $49.95 to $149.95. They plug in to your computer's USB or parallel port, thereby alleviating the need to open your computer and install a digital video board. Eventually, video lenses the size of pens will be integrated into laptop computers that can be used as portable videoconferencing terminals.

For case studies of different approaches to videoconferencing, follow the *Multilit* Web site link to the *ComputerWorld* focus article in which Burden (1999) describes how different industries are using NetMeeting and CU-SeeMe as well as Intel's ProShare, Lucent's MMCX, Corel's CorelVideo, White Pine's MeetingPoint, and PictureTel's Concorde and LiveShare products.

Multimedia Travel Systems

Travel is a natural subject for multimedia because the more you can show customers about where they will travel, what their accommodations will be like, and what they will be able to do at their destination, the more likely the person will enjoy the trip and want to use your service again. That is the goal of Web-based travel services that include fare finders, travel news, featured vacation packages, and online booking for lodging and transportation by land, rail, air, or sea. At travelocity.com, for example, you can find the lowest fare or best schedule on more than 400 airlines.

Fodor's Travel Online offers a comprehensive service that allows you to create a custom mini-guide for more than 110 global destinations. The user can request information about transportation, accommodations, entertainment, and restaurants. In addition to showing lush, graphic images of your dream vacation, Fodor's offers the *Living Language* Web page, which helps you learn more than 500 fundamental travel phrases in French, German, Italian, and Spanish.

To test-drive some online travel services, follow the *Multilit* Web site links to multimedia travel systems.

Financial Services

Anyone who invests in the stock market knows what a dramatic effect current events have on the day-to-day value of volatile stocks. This is why the financial services industry is using multimedia to provide on-screen windows that display broadcast videos and news feeds from the Cable News Network (CNN), Reuters, Dow Jones News, Knight-Ridder, and CNN's Financial Network (CNNfn). Brokers can buy or sell quickly when news breaks. Follow the *Multilit* Web site links to tour these Web-based news feeds.

EntryPoint is a customizable Internet toolbar that puts a stock market ticker on your computer screen, as illustrated in Figure 3-3. You can customize the ticker to show the precise stocks you want to monitor, and EntryPoint provides you with news stories telling how the companies are doing. Lots of other EntryPoint services are available, including local and national news, weather, sports, online shopping, and e-commerce services. You can download the toolbar for free by following the *Multilit* Web site links to EntryPoint.

The Securities and Exchange Commission (SEC) has a Web site providing access to corporate filings made with federal agencies one day after they are filed with the agency. Located at http://www.sec.gov, the SEC site also contains policy initiatives, speeches, and enforcement actions.

Figure 3-3   The EntryPoint toolbar displays a customizable stock ticker.

Real Estate

Another natural for multimedia is the real estate industry. Visiting properties for sale consumes a tremendous amount of time for brokers and buyers alike. Multimedia computers enable buyers to visit hundreds of properties virtually, view on-screen photos of homes, inspect floor plans, see street maps, and study neighborhood demographics to minimize the number of actual visits required. *Computer Technology Research* (page 53) tells how multimedia cut in half the number of houses customers would see before deciding which one to buy, resulting in a 50% increase in sales.

At realtor.com, for example, you can search more than 1.3 million homes, locate the area you want, find a realtor, identify lenders in the area, and plan how to finance your new home. Checklists help prevent you from forgetting something important. Virtual tours let you pan around 360-degree views of selected properties. At ColdwellBanker.com, you can find out information about any neighborhood in the United States, attend virtual open houses, and apply for a mortgage. At HomeQuest Network, you can view videos of selected homes and take a virtual tour online. Follow the *Multilit* Web site links to tour your dream home virtually.

Corporate Training

Corporate America spends a fortune on training. The American Society for Training and Development (ASTD) estimates that as much as $210 billion is spent on employee training each year; 78% of this amount is the cost of participant time and expenses incurred while attending training sessions. Analyzing these costs, Dennis (1994) notes that "Even a small reduction in participant time could make a large impact; for instance, a 5% reduction in training time could save employee time worth $8 billion a year." International Data Corporation, an Internet market research firm, forecasts an explosive growth of Internet-based training (IBT), from $197 million in 1997 to more than $5.5 billion in 2002, which represents a compounded annual growth rate of nearly 95% (ASTD 1998, *Multilit* Web site).

Many corporations have used multimedia to reduce training costs and improve employee productivity. For example, Figure 3-4 shows how Omaha-based transportation giant

Figure 3-4   The Harriman Dispatching Center controls 2,500 trains on 34,000 miles of track.
Photo provided by Union Pacific Railroad.

Union Pacific's Harriman Dispatching Center controls the operation of more than 2,500 trains daily across 34,000 miles of track. Cantwell (1993) notes that Union Pacific used multimedia to reduce training costs by 35% while increasing the speed at which trainees learn by 30% and boosting retention by 40%. The Union Pacific courseware was developed with Allen Communication's Quest authoring system.

Arnold (1993) describes how trainers at AT&T use multimedia to prepare employees to handle blackouts. For obvious reasons, the field managers will not let technicians train on live equipment. So AT&T uses multimedia to simulate a live situation. Figures 3-5 through 3-7 show how AT&T designed their screen displays. On the right of the screen is a text window in which printed instructions appear. On the left is a presentation window in which graphics, animation, and video appear. Beneath that is a smaller window that displays the active part of the tool. Technicians train on dozens of tasks and subtasks until they master the learning objectives. This learning strategy saved AT&T considerable costs by eliminating the need to fly 2,000 technicians to corporate headquarters for training.

Large libraries of multimedia training materials are available. For example, the ITC Learning Corporation publishes the Enterprise Learning System consisting of more than 700 titles used by more than 5,000 companies. Lesson libraries include instrumentation, information technology, operator performance, call center training, PC skills, regulatory compliance, technical/vocational skills, and basic skills. The Instrument Society of America (ISA) publishes a series of online courses covering analyzers, control valves, digital instrumentation, electronic maintenance, industrial measurement, process control calibration, control safety, pneumatic maintenance, and troubleshooting. Interactive Media Communications (IMC) publishes a series of CD-ROMs and videotapes dealing with laboratory and operator safety. Follow the *Multilit* Web site links to learn more about the ITC, ISA, and IMC courseware libraries.

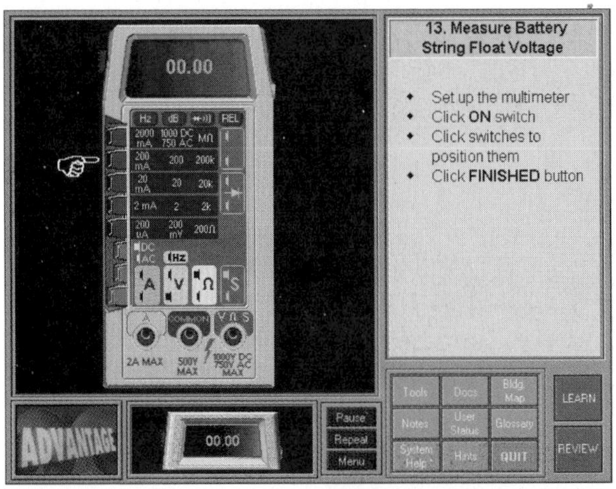

Mass Market Applications

Multimedia is wide open for entrepreneurs who can make a lot of money dreaming up ways to use it in mass market applications. For example, nearly everyone is concerned about their appearance, and choosing hairstyles has mass

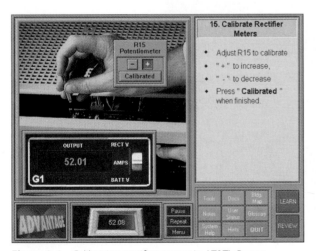

Figure 3-5 Measuring battery string float voltage in AT&T's Regen Hut application.

Figure 3-6 Calibrating rectifier meters in AT&T's Regen Hut application.

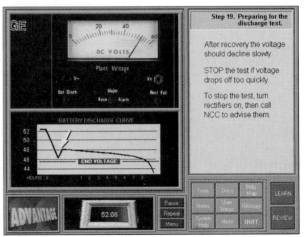

Figure 3-7 Preparing for the discharge test in AT&T's Regen Hut application.

Figure 3-8   A Styles-On-Video system in action in a hair salon.

Figure 3-9   The Styles-On-Video system consists of a multimedia computer with video camera, digital video capture card, VCR, pen, and digitizing tablet.

market appeal. Figure 3-8 shows how New Image Industries has made clever use of multimedia to help you decide what hairstyle suits you best. The Styles-On-Video system uses a multimedia computer with a video capture board and a camera to digitize your head onto the computer screen. Then the operator uses the digitizing tablet and stylus pen shown in Figure 3-9 to remove your hair. The system proceeds to put other hairstyles on your head to show what you would look like in different fashions and hair colors, as shown in Figure 3-10. Then the system creates a videotape that you can study privately or show friends to get their opinion on which style you should choose. Follow the *Multilit* Web site links to find out where the nearest Styles-On-Video imaging salon is in your area.

Figure 3-10   Styles-On-Video lets you explore your hairstyle fantasies.

Day Trading

Day trading is the use of the Internet to track the value of individual stocks and buy or sell them rapidly depending on how the market goes. You buy a stock whose value is rising, for example, and you hope that its value will continue climbing for the seconds or minutes that you own the stock. Be careful how you react to the glitzy television ads enticing you to become a day trader. While it is possible to make a lot of money day trading, you can also lose a lot. Testifying before the U.S. Senate about this new form of trading, SEC Chairman Levitt warned that "Most individual investors do not have the wealth, the time, or the temperament to make money and to sustain the devastating losses that day trading can bring" (SEC Congressional Testimony 9/16/99, *Multilit* Web site). With this caveat, follow the *Multilit* Web site links if you want to learn more about day trading.

exercises

1. Have you ever used a point-of-sale kiosk? Where? Did it have multimedia? Compare the way it functioned to traditional shopping; did the kiosk complement, replace, or make traditional shopping unnecessary?

2. Find a point-of-sale kiosk in your community. Describe its look and feel. Observe people using it and describe any problems or advantages you observe.

3. What are the obstacles to digital video replacing the VCR as the primary means of distributing video recordings? If your home has access to a digital video service, how has the service impacted the use of your VCR? Do you rent more or fewer videotapes from your local video store? Why?

4. Visit your local Kinko's and ask to see their videoconferencing facilities. Do you think videoconferencing has become a viable business at Kinko's? For whom and for what purpose? Would you use it in your planned line of work, or for personal matters? Why?

5. Visit a local realty office and find out whether its realtors use multimedia to sell homes. If so, ask what is the benefit; if not, find out why they do not use multimedia.

6. Visit a local business and find out whether it has ever used multimedia computers for training. How is computer-based training used in your chosen profession?

Education

After completing this chapter, you will be able to:

▪ **Describe how multimedia computers provide a powerful environment for achieving the goals of the cognitive movement in education**

▪ **Understand how multimedia computers are being used across the curriculum in a wide range of subjects**

▪ **Sample demonstrations of state-of-the-art applications linked to the *Multilit* Web site**

▪ **Assess how up-to-date your local schools are in adopting multimedia technologies for teaching and learning**

▪ **Question whether technology will make any major difference in the structure of schooling**

● As articulated by Brown, Collins, and Duguid (1989), skills and knowledge are too often taught out of context, as ends in and of themselves. To overcome this, teachers are using multimedia to bring into the classroom real-life examples of situations that provide the contextual framework so important for learning. Brown calls this use of multimedia **situated learning**. Multimedia gives teachers instant access to thousands of slides, videos, sound tracks, and lesson plans. These materials can be called up instantly, either for classroom use or as a networked resource for student exploration, discovery, reflection, and cooperative learning. Among educational researchers, the capability to demonstrate vividly and convincingly the real-world applicability of knowledge has become known as **anchored instruction** (The Cognition and Technology Group at Vanderbilt, 1990).

The benefits of multimedia are well documented by Professor James Kulik (1985, 1986, 1991, and 1994) and his associates at the University of Michigan. During the past 20 years, Kulik has analyzed hundreds of controlled experiments on the effectiveness of computer-based learning. Although the term *multimedia* did not exist then, many of the studies used graphics, sound, and video in a manner now referred to as multimedia. Overall, the findings indicate that average learning time has been reduced significantly (sometimes by as much as 80%), and achievement levels are more than a standard deviation higher (a full letter grade in school) than when multimedia is not used.

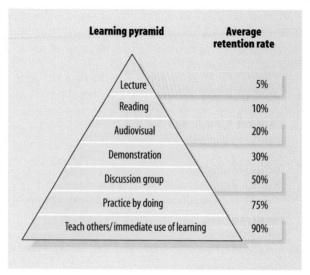

Figure 4-1 The learning pyramid.

Source: National Training Laboratories (NTL) Institute, Bethel, Maine.

The Kulik studies are classified according to grade levels. The Information Superhighway is linking universities, colleges, schools, and homes into a continuum that is helping to break down the distinctions between these grade levels. The Internet is enabling students of all ages to collaborate on worldwide projects, share discoveries, and develop strategies for acquiring knowledge in a social context. As the Learning Pyramid in Figure 4-1 shows, the more actively involved students are in the teaching and learning process, the more knowledge gets retained.

Cognitive Versus Behavioral Psychology

Much of what happens in the traditional classroom was influenced heavily by the behaviorist movement, which dominated American psychology from about 1920 to 1970. Chief among the behaviorists was Skinner (1938, 1953), who saw that human behavior is powerfully shaped by its consequences. Moreover, Skinner felt that psychology was essentially about behavior and that behavior was largely determined by its outcomes. Although Skinnerian methods have been effective in learning how to train animals and helping human beings modify their behavior, the behaviorists fell short of what is most important in education for most educators. To educate, you must do more than modify behavior. To educate, you must help the student learn how to develop strategies for learning. Such is the goal of the cognitive movement in education as defined by Bruning (1995: 1):

> *Cognitive psychology* is a theoretical perspective that focuses on the realms of human perception, thought, and memory. It portrays learners as active processors of information—a metaphor borrowed from the computer world—and assigns critical roles to the knowledge and perspective students bring to their learning. What learners do to enrich information, in the view of cognitive psychology, determines the level of understanding they ultimately achieve.

It is appropriate that Bruning borrows from the computer world in his definition of cognitive psychology. As you will see in the educational applications surveyed in this chapter, multimedia computers provide a powerful environment for helping achieve the goals of the cognitive movement in education. As articulated by Piaget (1969), students learn better when they can invent knowledge through inquiry and experimentation instead of acquiring facts presented by a teacher in class. It is difficult for a teacher to provide this kind of environment for each student in a traditional classroom. Since there is only one teacher for many students, it is physically impossible for the teacher to support each student's individual needs. Multimedia computers help by providing students with a world of interconnected knowledge to explore. The screen-capture and downloading tools you will learn in the tutorial section of this book enable students to collect what they discover and construct a framework for organizing and understanding. Thus, the student becomes an active processor of the information, and knowledge is the by-product.

Since the learner is portrayed as an active processor who explores, discovers, reflects, and constructs knowledge, the trend to teach from this perspective is known as the *constructivist movement* in education. As Bruning (1995: 216) explains, "The aim of teaching, from a constructivist perspective, is not so much to transmit information, but rather to encourage *knowledge formation* and development of metacognitive processes for judging, organizing, and acquiring new information." Several theorists have embellished this theme. Rumelhart (1981), following Piaget, introduced the notion of *schemata,* which are mental frameworks for comprehension that function as *scaffolding* for organizing experience. At first, the teacher provides instructional scaffolding that helps the student construct knowledge. Gradually, the teacher provides less scaffolding until the student is able to construct knowledge independently. For example, in the History of Flight tutorial in Part Six of this book, a lot of scaffolding is provided at first as an aid to learning how to develop a multimedia application; gradually, the scaffolding is removed until the student is able to create new multimedia works independently. Skinner and the behaviorists used related techniques known as *prompting* and *fading.* A hierarchy of sequential prompts firms up and reinforces a student's skill, and fading removes the prompts gradually until the student can perform a task independently.

Vygotsky (1978) emphasized the role of social interactions in knowledge construction. Social constructivism turns attention to children's interactions with parents, peers, and teachers in homes, neighborhoods, and schools. Vygotsky introduced the concept of the *zone of proximal development,* which is the difference between the difficulty level of a problem a student can cope with independently and the level that can be accomplished with help from others. In the zone of proximal development, a student and an expert work together on problems that the student alone could not solve successfully.

A challenge for software designers is to create programs that can function as the expert in the zone where learning and development take place. Software that succeeds can help transform the traditional teacher-centered classroom into a more learner-centered environment. Table 4-1 compares the teacher-dominated and cognitive perspectives. As you review the software surveyed in this chapter, keep this comparison in mind and reflect on the role multimedia computers can and should play in the contemporary classroom.

Table 4-1   Comparison of the Teacher-Dominated and Cognitive Perspectives on Education

Teacher-Dominated Perspective	Cognitive Perspective
Teacher centered	Learner centered
Teachers present knowledge	Students discover and construct knowledge
Students learn meaning	Students create meaning
Learner as memorizer	Learner as processor
Learn facts	Develop learning strategies
Rote memory	Active memory
Teacher structures learning	Social interaction provides instructional scaffolding
Repetitive	Constructive
Knowledge is acquired	Knowledge is created
Teacher provides resources	Students find resources
Individual study	Cooperative learning and peer interaction
Sequential instruction	Adaptive learning
Teacher manages student learning	Students learn to manage their own learning
Students learn others' thinking	Students develop and reflect on their own thinking
Isolationist	Contextualist
Extrinsic motivation	Intrinsic motivation
Reactive teachers	Proactive teachers
Knowledge transmission	Knowledge formation
Teacher dominates	Teacher observes, coaches, and facilitates
Mechanistic	Organismic
Behavioralist	Constructivist

Art

The ability to display more than 16 million colors lets computers exhibit artwork in true colors that rival those on the printed page. But unlike books, in which the pictures are static and unconnected, multimedia computers offer art educators all the advantages of hypermedia. For example, consider Softkey's *Leonardo*. Figure 4-2 shows how the user has instant access to every painting, invention, and writing of this Renaissance master. The biography chronicles the events that shaped da Vinci's life and contains hyperlinks that transport you to articles, paintings, videos, and models of his inventions. Figure 4-3 shows how the timeline correlates events in Leonardo's life to world history. Follow the *Multilit* Web site link for more information about *Leonardo*.

Now that graphics are available worldwide on the Internet, museums all over the world are making artwork accessible on the Information Superhighway. The Spring 1994 newsletter of The Getty Center for Education in the Arts discusses the role of the Internet in discipline-based art education:

Figure 4-2 The database in Softkey's *Leonardo 2.0.*

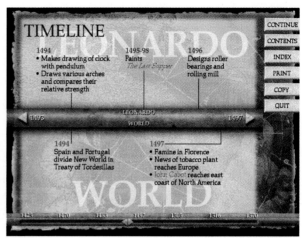

Figure 4-3 The timeline in Softkey's *Leonardo 2.0.* The highlighted words are hyperlinks.

Imagine a national network devoted to discipline-based art education (DBAE) in its myriad, evolving applications. This network would open communications between teachers, administrators, school board members, scholars, policy makers, students, artists, community arts groups, art associations, and parents. It would provide access to new ideas, products and research; innovative programs; opportunities for collaboration; current literature; discussions of ideas; and training techniques. Through print or electronic media it would offer forums for sharing, exchanging, informing, testing, discussing, learning, surveying, or advocating among an expanding community of practitioners, scholars, and advocates.

Getty has been working diligently to make this dream come true. To experience the wealth of resources available for art educators, follow the *Multilit* Web site links to Getty's art education site. Also linked to the *Multilit* Web site are:

- Archives of American Art—The Smithsonian Institute's easy-to-navigate digital art library

- ArtFul Minds—An art education Web site where teachers will find theoretical information and practical applications about brain research, arts education, technology use, and integration

- ArtMuseum.net—An Intel partnership with some of the world's leading art museums using Macromedia Flash and Shockwave, RealPlayer, and Live Picture Zoom to provide you with a virtual experience touring art exhibits online

- ArtsEdge—The Kennedy Center's online showcase including such titles as the African Odyssey Interactive, the Duke Ellington Centennial Celebration Site, and Look in the Mythic Mirror, an integrated mythology curriculum Web site

- National Gallery of Art—Virtual tours that use a free version of the Live Picture Zoom Viewer, which lets you move from room to room and zoom in to your favorite masterpieces

Biology

Biology teachers are taking advantage of multimedia's ability to bring classrooms to life with animations, full-motion video clips, and stereo sound. Multimedia curriculum resources include animals, dissection, genetics, heredity, and cell biology.

Animals

How We Classify Animals teaches taxonomy. Distributed by the Society for Visual Education (SVE), this multimedia CD begins by explaining the two broad groups of animals (vertebrates and invertebrates). Students examine the different types and categories of animal life such as sponges, animals with stinging cells, worms, jointed animals, soft-bodied animals, spiny-skinned animals, fish, amphibians, birds, and mammals. A HyperStax interface allows for fully interactive browsing and testing options with a scorekeeper. The teacher's guide features activities that make connections among a wide range of content areas, including language arts, health and nutrition, social studies, art, and critical thinking. For more information, follow the *Multilit* Web site links to SVE & Churchill Media.

Mammals: A Multimedia Encyclopedia is a multimedia CD from the National Geographic Society that covers more than 200 mammals, from aardvark to zorilla. There are 45 full-motion video clips, 150 authentic animal vocalizations, 700 captioned full-screen photographs, fact boxes, and range maps you access with your mouse. Essays about the animals provide the equivalent of 600 pages of text.

Oceans Below is a simulated CD-ROM scuba diving adventure by Amazing Media. After checking your gear on the deck of the ship, reading a small guidebook that turns into a slide show on topics like altered depth perception and ocean conservation, and selecting one of 17 dives (see Figure 4-4), you can view a fish chart like the plastic sheets real divers use (see Figure 4-5). Then, as you dive, the world beneath the waves emerges. You explore the depths with your mouse as many colorful images of sea creatures appear. For example, clicking on a picture of a lionfish lets you watch a video of it—within the frame of a face mask (see Figure 4-6)—and listen to a description.

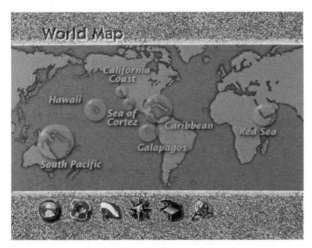

Figure 4-4 The world map takes you to any one of 17 exciting dives in Amazing Media's *Oceans Below*.

Figure 4-5 Narrated sea life charts identify the fish you encounter in *Oceans Below*.

Figure 4-6 Full-motion videos play inside the frame of a face mask in *Oceans Below.*

Dissection

The Curry School of Education has a frog dissection tutorial on the World Wide Web. The tutorial contains highly interactive activities in which the student clicks on a picture of a frog to mark the beginning and end of an incision. If the student is wrong, feedback is provided. When the student gets the answer right, the incision is made, and another picture shows the results. You can try this out by following the *Multilit* Web site links to the Interactive Frog Dissection Tutorial.

Genetics and Heredity

Exploring Genetics and Heredity is a multimedia CD from Clearvue that uses narrated diagrams and microphotographs to explain DNA structure, meiosis, mitosis, the nature and regulation of genetic material, and the basic patterns of heredity, including an extensive presentation of Mendel's law. Clearvue also publishes three separate CDs entitled *Genetics, Heredity,* and *Evolution,* treating these topics in more detail. For more information, follow the *Multilit* Web site links to Clearvue.

Virtual FlyLab (VFL) is an interactive Web site for genetics instruction. Developed by Dr. Robert Desharnais at California State University at Los Angeles, VFL enables students to conduct genetic experiments by "breeding" fruit flies over the Web and observing the patterns of inheritance in the offspring. Students can also formulate hypotheses and conduct statistical tests. You can find Virtual FlyLab online by following the *Multilit* Web site link to Virtual Courseware for Science Education.

Cell Biology

Clearvue's *Cell Biology* consists of two multimedia CDs that cover biological concepts and cellular processes. *Part I: Cell Structure & Function, Cell Cycle, Mitosis & Cell Division, Meiosis* compares prokaryotic and eucaryotic cells and presents the structure and function of organelles in plant cells. After outlining the phases of the cell cycle, stages of mitosis, and cell division, the CD introduces the basic mechanism of meiosis and examines the sequence of events, sources of genetic variability, cytology of meiotic cell division, and the differences and similarities between mitosis and meiosis. *Part II: Membranes, Cell Motility* describes how lipid and protein molecules assemble to form cellular membranes and introduces the fluid mosaic model and supporting evidence, as well as major pathways for the transport of molecules through membranes. Cell motility is examined with respect to microtubules and microfilaments.

You can find out more about how multimedia computers are being used in biology teaching by following the *Multilit* Web site links to the National Association of Biology Teachers (NABT) and the Human Genome Project.

Chemistry

Illman (1994) reviews the work of several chemistry teachers who are using multimedia tools to make presentations in classrooms, publish electronic journals, illustrate the periodic table, develop animations of ions and molecules, and make multimedia chemistry instruction available on the Internet. Illman predicts that personal computers will become widespread in teaching chemistry due to the wide range of problems multimedia can solve.

For example, one of the most perplexing problems in teaching chemistry is that students do not get enough time in the laboratory to conduct experiments. Many schools cannot provide the quantity or quality of lab experience needed for a good education in chemistry. Students are no longer permitted to handle some important chemicals that have been found to cause cancer. Other experiments are too dangerous, expensive, or time-consuming. Enter the multimedia CD-ROM *Exploring Chemistry*. Published by Falcon Software, *Exploring Chemistry* is a comprehensive introductory chemistry course covering both inorganic and organic topics. Its 150 lessons provide 180 hours of instruction. The interactive lab design by Professors Stanley G. Smith and Loretta L. Jones (1993) uses full-motion video to let students conduct lab experiments repeatedly until the students master the material. Students can try experiments on the CD that would be too risky to perform in person, such as the grain dust explosion illustrated in Figure 4-7. The step-frame option lets the students view the explosion as it develops; each frame represents a thirtieth of a second.

Figures 4-8 and 4-9 show the equilibrium experiment, which lets you mix a variety of chemicals, observe the reactions, and learn from the results. The two chemicals used in the experiment, potassium chromate and potassium dichromate, have been widely used in chemistry education. Recently, they have been found to be carcinogens, so the only safe way to teach about them is through simulations like this. The simulations are so realistic that when you click a chemical with your mouse and see a hand pour the chemical into the beaker, it is as if your own hand poured it in. For more information about *Exploring Chemistry*, follow the *Multilit* Web site link to Falcon Software.

Figure 4-7   The grain dust explosion lasts only a quarter of a second; students view it in stages by stepping through each frame of video.

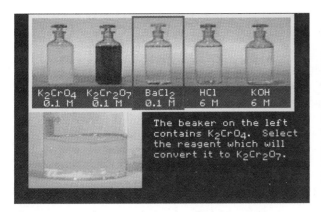

Figure 4-8 Students mix chemicals to find the one that changes potassium chromate into potassium dichromate.

Figure 4-9 The result of entering a wrong answer in the equilibrium experiment.

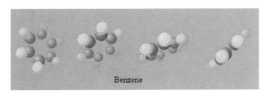

Figure 4-10 Java rotations of a model of a benzene molecule. Rotating the chemical model leads the user to discover that the centers of the six carbon atoms and six hydrogen atoms in benzene are coplanar.

Active technologies on the World Wide Web are helping solve another problem in teaching chemistry: visualizing the structure of chemical models. In a textbook, students are limited to a static photo that shows only one position. On the Web using active technologies such as Sun's Java, Macromedia's Shockwave, or Microsoft's ActiveX, students can rotate chemical models by clicking and dragging with a mouse. For example, Figure 4-10 shows different stages in the rotation of a model of a benzene molecule on a Java Web page. To try this and other chemical models on the Web, point your Java-enabled browser at http://www.udel.edu/fth/java/MoleculeViewer.

Speaking of textbooks, there is now a multimedia alternative to the best-selling introductory chemistry text *Chemistry and Chemical Reactivity*. Professor John Kotz, primary author of the text, has created a multimedia CD-ROM entitled *Saunders Interactive General Chemistry CD-ROM with Activchemistry*, which is distributed by Saunders College Publishing. The CD includes more than 600 screens with thousands of full-color photos and illustrations, video clips with narration and sound effects, animations, and 3-D molecular model rotations generated with CAChe Scientific software, which enables students to manipulate the models in real time. The multimedia materials contain content-sensitive hyperlinks to the complete textbook. Virtual Minilabs let students perform experiments on-screen, manipulate variables, and observe results. The CD-ROM comes packaged with a printed workbook in which students record their observations. For more information, follow the *Multilit* Web site links to Interactive General Chemistry.

Civics

Instead of teaching civics with textbooks that only describe it, multimedia lets teachers bring civics to life with multimedia CD-ROMs, live video feeds from Congress, and online access to government agencies and offices. The *Multilit* Web site has links, for example, to the White House, the U.S. House of Representatives, and the Senate. To find another agency, follow the link to the Louisiana State University Libraries' comprehensive *U.S. Federal Government Agencies Directory*.

To provide more of a historical perspective, Compton's NewMedia publishes *U.S. Civics*, a guide to U.S. history from the 1700s to the present. Biographies, government structure, reference manuals, and sample tests round out this educational database.

Economics

A big problem in teaching economics is the static nature of the charts and graphs printed in economics textbooks. Students need to be able to manipulate the data and view changes interactively to gain an understanding of complex economics concepts.

McGraw-Hill is addressing this problem with two multimedia CD-ROMs for the best-selling McConnell *Economics* textbook. The first CD is entitled *Microeconomics*. It covers supply and demand, elasticities, cost, pure competition, monopoly, and tax incidence. The second CD is called *Macroeconomics*. Topics include national accounts, the aggregate expenditure model, aggregate demand and supply, the Federal Reserve and monetary policy, inflation/unemployment, money, banking, and money creation.

If you compare Figures 4-11 and 4-12, you can see how the *Economics* CD-ROM brings economics to life. Figure 4-11 is one of the graphs in the textbook. The student sees only one view and cannot change anything. Figure 4-12 is the same graph on the *Microeconomics* CD. Buttons enable the student to shift the production possibilities and view the results in a table of data that updates automatically when the student changes the graph.

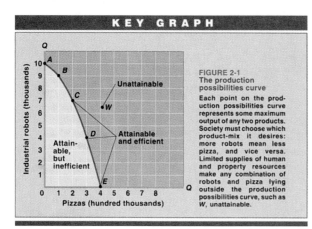

Figure 4-11   How the Production Possibilities curve appears in the *Economics* textbook. The student cannot interact with it.

Economics, 13E by C. McDonnell and Stanley Brue. Copyright © 1996 McGraw-Hill Companies. Reprinted by permission.

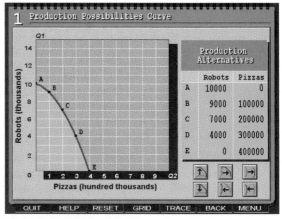

Figure 4-12   The multimedia version of the Production Possibilities curve lets the student manipulate the graph and study changes in the data.

Economics, 13E by C. McDonnell and Stanley Brue. Copyright © 1996 McGraw-Hill Companies. Reprinted by permission.

Foreign Languages

When abroad, try conversing in a foreign language you supposedly learned in school and you will quickly grasp the importance of multimedia in foreign-language instruction. Although books can teach grammar and vocabulary, they cannot interact with you the way people converse. Enter multimedia.

Multimedia computers are a natural for teaching language. Digital audio provides pronunciation capabilities, and full-motion video can put students in real-life situations. Exploiting these features, Syracuse Language Systems has teamed with Random House to publish the award-winning *Living Language Multimedia* series on CD-ROM. The series includes four products:

- *All-in-One Language Fun* contains instruction in Spanish, French, German, Japanese, and English—all on one CD. Designed for ages three to 12, the CD teaches hundreds of words and phrases through multimedia versions of familiar games, including bingo, jigsaw puzzles, Concentration, Simon says, and more. Digital audio of native speakers' voices helps users learn how to pronounce the words.

- *TriplePlay Plus* takes an important leap forward. It uses speech recognition software licensed from Dragon Systems to listen, analyze, and help improve your pronunciation. *TriplePlay Plus* is available in English, French, German, Hebrew, Italian, Japanese, and Spanish versions. Figure 4-13 shows how interactive comic strips depict everyday situations to build comprehension and conversation skills at a slow or natural rate of speech.

- *Let's Talk* uses Dragon speech recognition to teach on one CD more than 2200 words in each of four languages: French, German, Italian, and Spanish. Native speakers provide the model, and a "recognition meter" shows how well your pronunciation matched it.

Figure 4-13 An interactive comic strip in *TriplePlay Plus* from Syracuse Language Systems.

Figure 4-14   A conversational situation presented by *Your Way* from Syracuse Language Systems.

- *Your Way* is a language course based on branching conversations in six everyday settings: social engagements, dining out, hotels and accommodations, around town, travel, and medical needs. For example, Figure 4-14 shows a situation in a restaurant. Challenging games, extensive reference sections, and a multimedia glossary add to the richness of *Your Way*.

The Syracuse CDs have won many awards, including the Milia d'Or 1998 Reference and Education Award, the Family PC 1998 Family Tested Award, as well as a series of Consumer Electronics Show, Technology & Learning, and NewMedia INVISION awards. Highly praised is the use of speech recognition to teach pronunciation. According to Syracuse president Martin Rothenberg, "Using the automatic speech recognition games in *TriplePlay Plus*, language learners can develop a natural-sounding accent and confidence in their speaking skills. Learners will immediately know if they are saying words and phrases correctly, and will be able to practice and improve as they play. The games are also designed so that a native-speaker's voice is always available as a pronunciation model." Except for the specially designed dynamic microphone packaged with the software, no additional hardware is required. For more information about these and other products, follow the *Multilit* Web site link to Syracuse Language Systems.

Another award-winning CD called *Kidspeak* from XOOM aims to make learning a second language easy for grade-school children. Designed to take advantage of intuitive language learning abilities, *KidSpeak* combines animation with interactive games, puzzles, and songs. It has no drills, tests, or anything unpleasant. Instead, children believe they are playing with their animated friends as they acquire second language skills. To learn more, follow the *Multilit* Web site links to *KidSpeak*.

Geography

The highly visual nature of geography makes it a natural for multimedia. The National Geographic Society has pulled out all the stops with Xpeditions, a Web site developed in partnership with MCI WorldCom. If you follow the *Multilit* Web site link to the National Geographic Xpeditions, you'll find an interactive atlas that lets you see and print more than 1800 maps, take virtual tours delivered via Apple's QuickTime 3D technology, and browse an archive of the U.S. National Geography standards. Xpeditions won the 1999 Coadie award for best new education online product. It is part of MCI WorldCom's MarcoPolo project, which is bringing standards-based content online in subjects across the curriculum. To learn more about this exciting project, follow the *Multilit* Web site links to MarcoPolo. For more information about other multimedia products from the National Geographic Society, follow the *Multilit* Web site links, where you'll find the *Complete National Geographic,* a set of CD-ROMs containing every page of the magazine including the original photography.

A cleverly designed CD-ROM is Brøderbund Software's *Where in the World Is Carmen Sandiego?* Carmen and her gang of villains are stealing the treasures of the world. Sixty countries are involved, with hundreds of animations and thousands of audio clues, including 500 digitized in foreign languages. The student uses Funk & Wagnall's *World Almanac* to help solve the crime, doing research to find out where to go next to find the criminal and the loot. Figure 4-15 shows the high-tech on-screen tools. Clues include languages spoken, landmarks, and cultural sites. As you can see in Figure 4-16, places are illustrated with pictures from *National Geographic* and accompanied by songs from the Smithsonian. Thus, *Carmen* teaches geography in the context of world culture. The latest release offers an immersive environment in which the student can take a 360-degree walking tour, creating the illusion that the student actually is in the place being explored.

Although *Carmen* is so popular that hundreds of middle schools have held Carmen Sandiego Geography Days, some teachers have trouble figuring out how to integrate programs like *Carmen* into teaching, because it shifts the focus from teacher-centered to

Figure 4-15　On-screen tools in *Where in the World Is Carmen Sandiego?* include the videophone (left), Dataminder (bottom center), and Note Pad (bottom right).

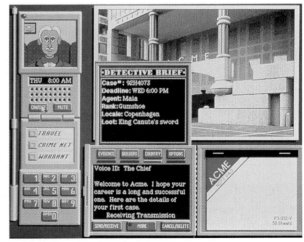

Figure 4-16　Dramatic photographs place players in 45 countries around the world.

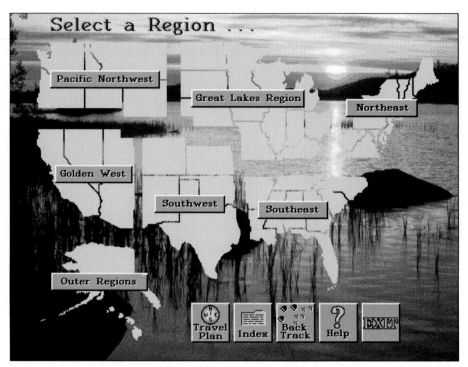

Figure 4-17   This map appears when you start the *National Parks of America* CD-ROM. Clicking the buttons lets you navigate down through Regional and State menus to individual parks.

student-centered instruction. As Neuwirth (1994) explains, "This game cannot be used in a classroom setting. It is not a very didactic tool as the teacher is not given any time for talking to the student during the game." Follow the *Multilit* Web site links to learn more about *Carmen* and other award-winning Brøderbund products distributed by The Learning Company.

National Parks of America by Multicom is more utilitarian. Figures 4-17 through 4-19 show how this multimedia CD uses the metaphor of a map to let you navigate to any park in the country and virtually tour it before deciding whether to plan an actual trip there. There are more than 900 photographs by renowned nature photographer David Muench. The CD lets you locate and select any one of 230 parks by name or geographic location or by specific criteria such as camping or hiking. You can research park background information or just tour through dramatic videos and the magnificent beauty of Muench's photographs, as shown in Figure 4-19.

Environmental Systems Research Institute's *ArcView* is a geographic information system (GIS) that lets you create and query geographically oriented databases. Using the combined power of the computer, geography, data, and their imaginations, students can develop hypotheses and test scenarios to develop an understanding of the world. For example, Figure 4-20 shows how you can query what countries produced more energy than they consumed in a certain year. Figure 4-21 shows a satellite plot of irrigated fields in part of Kansas. *ArcView* ships with six CD-ROM databases covering different aspects of the United States and the world. In addition, you can create your own databases and import data from dBase or plain text data files. For more information, follow the *Multilit* Web site link to *ArcView*.

Figure 4-18 At the state level, *National Parks of America* lets you view a map that locates each park in the state.

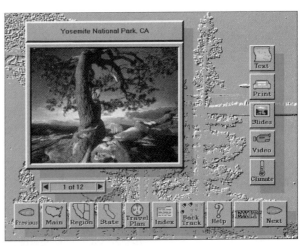

Figure 4-19 At the park level, *National Parks of America* lets you access detailed information about each park and view spectacular photos.

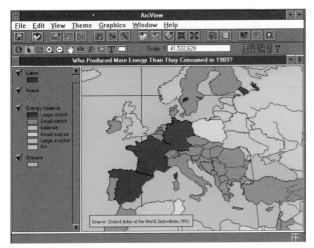

Figure 4-20 An *ArcView* plot answers the question of who produced more energy than they consumed in 1989.

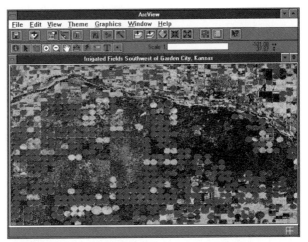

Figure 4-21 *ArcView* plots the irrigated fields southwest of Garden City, Kansas.

History

There are many ways multimedia brings history to life. CD-ROM versions of traditional history textbooks have audio and video with full-text search; multimedia has inspired the creation of new history resources on CD-ROM for which no prior book exists; and the Internet provides online access to source documents, newsletters, and discussion groups.

History Textbooks on CD-ROM

D.C. Heath and the Voyager Company have developed multimedia CD-ROM versions of established history textbooks. D.C. Heath has published the American history text *The Enduring Vision, Interactive Edition*. In addition to the text and photographs of the printed version, the CD-ROM includes 3000 pages of historic documents, U.S. Census data from 1790 to 1990, and audio and video recordings that include footage of President Franklin D. Roosevelt's war message to Congress.

Who Built America? is a CD-ROM by Voyager. Developed by history professor Roy Rosenzweig at George Mason University, it covers the period from the centennial celebration of 1876 to the Great War of 1914. In addition to the text of the printed version, the CD contains historic documents, audio recordings, videos including *The Great Train Robbery,* and more than a thousand pictures.

Dorling Kindersley has created a multimedia CD version of its *Eyewitness Encyclopedia of World History.* The CD covers 10 historical eras from the earliest records of human habitation to Nelson Mandela's election as president of South Africa. Equal treatment is given to Europe, Asia, Africa, the Americas, and Oceania. Online references include Everyday Life, Culture, Inventions, and a Who's Who that provides biographies of historically important personalities.

Multimedia History Titles

Several history titles have been developed on CD-ROM without first appearing as a book. The National Geographic Society has published on CD-ROM *The Presidents: A Picture History of Our Nation,* which describes the personal and political lives of U.S. leaders. This encyclopedic reference tool for home, library, and classroom features historic moments on video, famous speeches, a historical perspective and commentary on each president, more than a thousand captioned photographs, election maps and essays, a political party index, a multimedia timeline that provides a social and historical context for each president, and photo essays on the presidency. The CD also has a narrated tutorial, a pop-up glossary, a game, and the ability to print captions, essays, and speeches.

Figure 4-22 shows The Ultimate Titanic Collection, which includes three CD-ROMs from CyberFlix that use multimedia to bring history to life. In *Titanic: An Interactive Journey,* you relive the story of the world's most famous luxury ocean liner and its catastrophic loss. In a game-like format, you discover thousands of amazing facts about the vessel, travel on its maiden voyage, witness the world-shattering events that led to the loss of more than 1,500 lives, and find out what happened in the aftermath. In the adventure game, *Titanic: Adventure Out of Time,* you play the role of a British secret agent who can change the course of history, depending on how you gather clues and solve puzzles as you navigate a 3-D reconstruction of the Titanic. A bonus CD contains seven more guided tours of the Titanic.

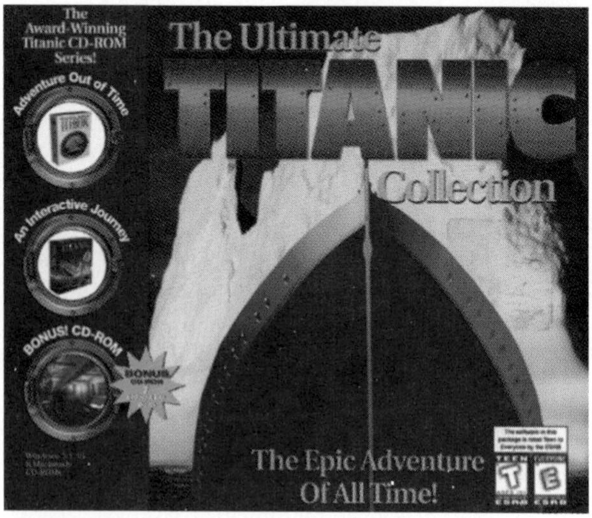

Figure 4-22 The Ultimate Titanic Collection contains three CD-ROMs from CyberFlix.

Wars

Quanta Press and Compton's NewMedia publish a series of war CD-ROMs. Titles include the *Civil War, World War II, Korea,* and *Vietnam.* In April 1991, Time Warner Interactive released *Desert Storm: The War in the Persian Gulf,* advertising it as "the first electronic magazine with over 6000 screens of selectable documentation covering the Gulf War." Users follow the evolution of a Gulf War story from its origins to the actual article as it eventually appeared in *Time* magazine. The CD includes *Time* correspondents' files, exclusive audio reports, 300 full-color photographs, and every story report in its original, unedited form, organized chronologically and indexed by subject. There is a glossary of high-tech weapons and a photo gallery, as well as exclusive audio reports, including "as-it's happening" correspondent analyses and interviews. An active timeline of the war lets the user see and hear a synopsis of each week's key events.

Compton's NewMedia offers a competing product, *Desert Storm with Coalition Command,* which comes with a game that lets you deploy ground forces from a sophisticated command post, set policies for providing information to the media, and get vital feedback through direct hotlines to the White House and Pentagon.

FlagTower's *World War II* is a multimedia CD-ROM that presents the Second World War from the British perspective. The CD provides a broad perspective on the war from Germany in the 1920s through postwar reorganization efforts, with explorations of the war's six theaters, in-depth examinations of the impact of the Treaty of Versailles, and a powerful collection of first-person accounts of the Holocaust.

The Assassination of J.F.K.

A CD-ROM that fosters debate is the award-winning *The JFK Assassination: A Visual Investigation.* Published by Medio, it includes more than 20 minutes of narrated overview, video clips from five films documenting the assassination, and computer animations showing conflicting bullet angles. Also included is the complete text of the *Warren Commission Report,* Jim Marrs's best-selling book *Crossfire,* and *The J.F.K. Assassination: A Complete Book of Facts.* Figures 4-23 through 4-26 show how you review the evidence and decide whether there was a conspiracy and who was involved in it.

Figure 4-23   The main menu in *The JFK Assassination* introduces you to the background leading up to the assassination, lets you visit the scene in Dealey Plaza, and presents Text, Analysis, and Films & Photos buttons to help you determine whether there was a conspiracy.

Figure 4-24   The Films & Photos screen from *The JFK Assassination* lets you view the Nix, Hughes, Zapruder, and Muchmore films.

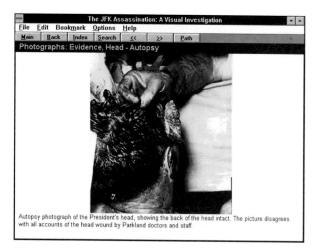

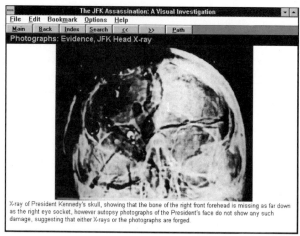

Figure 4-25 Autopsy photo from *The JFK Assassination* refuting the *Warren Commission Report.*

Figure 4-26 Evidence of forgery on *The JFK Assassination* CD-ROM.

Internet Resources for Historians

DeLoughry (1994) tells how the H-Net (history network) project at the University of Illinois at Chicago has set up 20 Internet mailing lists that have attracted more than 4500 subscribers in 47 countries. HNSOURCE at the University of Kansas provides historians easy access to historical texts and data located all over the network. The Historical Text Archives at Mississippi State University provide Internet users with such historical documents as the *Instruments of Surrender* signed by Japanese leaders at the end of World War II and *Up From Slavery,* the autobiography of Booker T. Washington. Cromohs, the *Cyber Review of Modern Historiography,* is an electronic journal that provides Web access to research on the principles and methodologies of historical research. The History Channel's speech archives provide full text and use RealAudio to let you listen to famous speeches ranging from the Reverend Martin Luther King's "I have a dream" speech to astronaut Neil Armstrong's commentary as he walked on the moon.

To learn more about these online history resources, follow the *Multilit* Web site links to H-Net, Cromohs, the University of Kansas History Group, the *Historical Text Archives,* and the History Channel.

Mathematics

Mathematics is one of the most highly developed multimedia application areas. Due to the computational nature of mathematics, computers can model the content, monitor student progress, and help students master educational objectives. The National Council of Teachers of Mathematics (NCTM) has issued a set of guidelines that rely heavily on computers as an agent for change in the way mathematics is taught. The NCTM guidelines encourage the teaching of math in real-world contexts in which students investigate problems that have meaning.

For example, Scott Foresman teamed with ABC to produce *Wide World of Mathematics,* in which video footage from ABC News and ABC Sports broadcasts is used to demonstrate how mathematics is used every day, in virtually every field of endeavor. Well-known runner Marty Liqouri takes students step-by-step over the New York City marathon course, using mathematics to compute the length of the course, the runners' rate of travel at different checkpoints, and the combined weight of the runners as they cross the Verazzano-Narrows Bridge. The Hubble space telescope provides a real-world setting for a treatment of very large and very small numbers. The construction of the Chunnel that connects France and England beneath the English Channel introduces dimensions and units. Hurricane Andrew situates prediction techniques with footage from forecasters at the National Hurricane Center. An NFL football game uses a playing field as a number line on which students learn addition and subtraction. To get a copy of a preview of the *Wide World of Mathematics,* call (800) 554-4411 and ask for the videotape demo (code number 37520-X) or the CD-ROM demo (code number 37521-8).

Multimedia is also being used to give a fresh look to classic math software such *Math Blaster* from Davidson. *Math Blaster: Episode 1—In Search of Spot* uses dazzling graphics, digitized speech, sound effects, and music to present more than 50,000 problems in addition, subtraction, multiplication, division, fractions, decimals, percents, number patterns, and estimation. *Math Blaster: Episode 2—Secret of the Lost City* builds on the skills learned in episode 1 by presenting problems that contain two and three operands, up to three-digit numbers, whole and negative numbers, decimals, fractions, and percentages. *Math Blaster Mystery—The Great Brain Robbery* builds prealgebra and word-problem skills as students explore a mysterious mansion. *Math Blaster Algebra* teaches algebra for grades 7 through adult.

Academic Systems markets a series of mathematics CD-ROMs that link students to the instructor's PC, so the teacher can monitor each student's progress and step in for individual assistance when needed. California State University (CSU) at Northridge reports a higher percentage (70%) of students are passing math than before (only 50% pass without the programs). "Before this I've always felt I never met a technology that didn't ultimately just cost me more money," says CSU Northridge's vice president for academic affairs (*Wall Street Journal* 4/3/96: B6). Follow the *Multilit* Web site link to Academic Systems for case studies on the use of *Interactive Mathematics.*

For more information on the NCTM standards, follow the *Multilit* Web site link to the Eisenhower National Clearinghouse. IBM publishes a booklet that keys math software to the standards. The title is *A Directory of Educational Objectives and IBM Elementary Mathematics Courseware.* To peruse this and other IBM K-12 support services, follow the *Multilit* Web site link to IBM K-12 Education. While you are visiting the *Multilit* Web site, be sure to check out TERC's expanding list of hands-on math and science learning materials.

Music

The music industry has been so totally transformed by multimedia technology that accreditation guidelines require that every music student learn about computer music applications, including music recording, editing, arranging, and printing. Midisoft's *Studio* is an example of the kind of software musicians are expected to know how to use. *Studio* is very easy to use because of its graphical tape-recorder controls. Anyone who knows how to work a tape recorder can use this program to record and play MIDI sequences. It even notates automatically anything you play on a MIDI keyboard. *Studio* is great for teaching class piano; music teachers can record each one of their students on a different track, complete with orchestral accompaniment, which is highly motivating for students when they rehearse. The latest version of *Studio* lets you record and edit waveform audio, including vocals played in sync with the MIDI tracks. For more information and to download free demos of *Studio* and other music products, follow the *Multilit* Web site link to Midisoft.

Figure 4-27   The guitar model in *Play Blues Guitar.*

Copyright © 1995 Play Music, Inc.

In *Play Blues Guitar,* published by Play Music, Inc., the student enters a virtual music studio in which blues guitarist Keith Wyatt teaches how to play several blues styles. There are music videos of each piece performed on stage. Hypertext study guides provide historical backgrounds and stylistic explanations. Then Wyatt brings you into his studio and gives lessons on how to play the style. Figure 4-27 shows the guitar model on which the notes to play appear as dots on the fretboard, providing the student with a powerful tool for learning the comps and riffs. The student can speed up or slow the tempo and watch as indicators light up on the fretboard, showing what notes to play in time with the music. Play Music also publishes a basic guitar course called *Play Guitar* and intermediate guitar lessons called *Play Rock Guitar.* For more information about these breakthrough products, follow the *Multilit* Web site link to Play Music.

Discovering Music by Voyetra Turtle Beach is a highly produced suite of music software for learning music history, recording music, printing scores, and improvising with an automatic accompaniment program. Figure 4-28 shows the main menu. You can

Figure 4-28   *Discovering Music* CD-ROM.

Copyright © 1995 Voyetra.

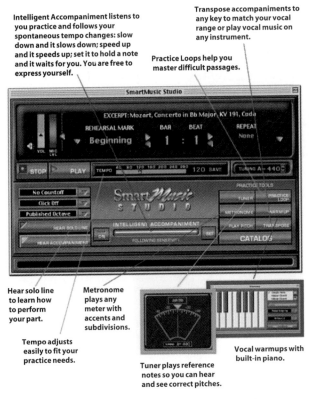

Intelligent Accompaniment listens to you practice and follows your spontaneous tempo changes: slow down and it slows down; speed up and it speeds up; set it to hold a note and it waits for you. You are free to express yourself.

Transpose accompaniments to any key to match your vocal range or play vocal music on any instrument.

Practice Loops help you master difficult passages.

Hear solo line to learn how to perform your part.

Metronome plays any meter with accents and subdivisions.

Tempo adjusts easily to fit your practice needs.

Tuner plays reference notes so you can hear and see correct pitches.

Vocal warmups with built-in piano.

Figure 4-29 SmartMusic®Studio screen display and feature highlights.

SmartMusic®Studio is a registered trademark of Coda Music Technology.

download Jammin' Keys, Music Writer, and Recording Station at very reasonable prices, or pay a little more for CD-ROM versions. For details and downloads, follow the *Multilit* Web site links to Voyetra Turtle Beach.

Coda Music Technology achieved a breakthrough with its *SmartMusic®Studio* intelligent accompaniment software. *SmartMusic®Studio* listens to and follows a soloist's tempo changes, providing a way for students to practice playing with an ensemble when human performers are not available. Music schools around the world are using *SmartMusic®Studio* to provide a more realistic practice experience for soloists. An extensive library of more than 5000 instrumental and vocal music accompaniments is available. Figure 4-29 illustrates the *SmartMusic®Studio* features. For more information and to get a free demo, follow the *Multilit* Web site link to Coda Music Technology.

Music Resources on the World Wide Web

The music library at Indiana University has assumed the task of indexing all the music resources on the Web. By pointing your Web browser at this excellent index, you can navigate through a wealth of musical treasures. For example, BMG's Classics World lets you browse the latest releases of classical music on CD-ROM. At the Classical Music MIDI Archives, you can download and play MIDI files for thousands of classical music compositions. Indiana's artist-specific index lists hundreds of performing musicians who have established Web sites. To learn more about these exciting online music resources, follow the *Multilit* Web site links to Classic World, the Classic MIDI Archives, and Indiana University's music library.

Physics

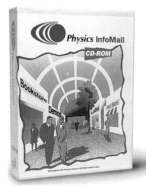

Figure 4-30 The *Physics InfoMall* CD-ROM.

Courtesy of www.learningteam.org.

Physics teachers are using multimedia to help achieve the goals of the National Science Education Standards, which call for providing students with opportunities to get involved in the active process of learning science. Escalada, Grabhorn, and Zollman (1996) used multimedia computers to develop visualization techniques that allow students to collect, analyze, and model motion data. Students use a video capture board to record experiments. Video Analyzer software makes it possible to collect two-dimensional spatial and temporal data, and a Visual Space-Time program combines parts of successive video images into a space-time diagram. These techniques enable students to make connections between concrete, everyday experiences and the abstract principles of physics.

Pictured in Figure 4-30, *Physics InfoMall* is a CD-ROM that contains the text and graphics from 19 physics textbooks and 3900 articles from *Physics Today, The Physics Teacher,* and *The American Journal of Physics.* The brainchild of University of Nebraska physicist Robert Fuller, *Physics InfoMall* provides a rich resource for physics teachers and students to research and explore. As Fuller explains, most students and physicists use books only to find examples of problems they are working on. The *Physics InfoMall* fulfills Fuller's dream of providing students with a compact, searchable CD-ROM resource from which physics examples can be cut and pasted and manipulated at will. Distributed by The Learning Team, *Physics InfoMall* includes a Problems Place containing

Figure 4-31   *The Video Encyclopedia of Physics Demonstrations.*

3000 problems and solutions, and a Demo and Lab Shop containing more than 1000 demos and laboratory exercises. For more information, follow the *Multilit* Web site link to the *Physics InfoMall.*

The Video Encyclopedia of Physics Demonstrations shown in Figure 4-31 is published by The Education Group. It consists of 25 videodiscs that present 600 demonstrations of basic physical principles. Most segments have narration (written scripts are included), and many segments feature slow-motion photography or computer animations. Topics include mechanics, waves, sound, fluid dynamics, heat, thermodynamics, electricity, magnetism, optics, and modern physics. An extensive 1500-page companion explains how to use the videos. In his very positive review of this package, Beichner (1993) describes how the series can be used to assign homework in which students use data from the videos: "For example, a series of balls of varying diameters and masses are dropped from nearly 4 meters. By stepping through the video a frame at a time, position measurements can be made as the balls fall. Time is included on each frame." The series is also available in middle school and primary school versions.

By the time you read this, a DVD version will be available. There is a video clip on the *Multilit* CD that shows examples from *The Video Encyclopedia of Physics Demonstrations.* To view it, use the Windows Explorer or the Macintosh Finder to locate the movie called *physics* in the *movies* folder, then double-click the movie to play it.

Science

Science teachers are using the Internet to provide students with collaborative learning experiences, access to scientific databases, and virtual visits to science laboratories. Reporting on the New Jersey Networking Infrastructure in Education project, Friedman, Baron, and Addison (1996) cite several compelling examples of science study via the Internet. Students gather samples from local pond water, measure chemical characteristics, examine organisms, and share observations with peers over the Internet. An ocean weather database that tracks ships at sea enables students to calculate the speed and direction of oceangoing vessels and predict arrival times.

Students visit the Plasma Physics Laboratory at Princeton University to access data from fusion experiments as quickly as Princeton scientists. Follow the *Multilit* Web site links to visit these projects online.

Multimedia CDs complement these online materials. *Science 2000+* is a comprehensive science curriculum for grades 5 to 8 published by Decision Development Corporation. Consistent with the most advanced science frameworks and employing the latest in educational technology, *Science 2000+* takes an activity-based, thematic approach to teaching science. Within its flexible and open-ended structure, students actively investigate and explore science. They gain a better understanding of a world increasingly shaped by science and technology, plus an insight into the importance of science in solving some of today's critical environmental and health issues. Organized into nine-week units, the curriculum in *Science 2000+* is connected by central themes and is oriented toward solving problems. Multiple disciplines, such as life, health, social, earth, physical and environmental sciences, math, anthropology, and language arts, are brought into play as students research real-life situations. To see how the activities in *Science 2000+* relate to the national science standards, follow the *Multilit* Web site link to Decision Development Corporation, click *Science 2000+*, and then click Curriculum.

Videodiscovery publishes a series of innovative videodiscs and multimedia CDs for teaching science. The *Science Forums* challenge students in sixth through ninth grades to grapple with real-world problems. Using a town meeting format, the forums present role-playing scenarios that focus on science, technology, and societal problems. For example, Figure 4-32 is from a forum on fossil fuel and the greenhouse effect. Students consider whether fossil fuel users should be taxed according to the amount of carbon dioxide that the fuels release into the atmosphere, with the tax revenue used to pay for the greenhouse effects of global warming.

Also from Videodiscovery is a series of *Science Sleuths* videodiscs and CDs, in which students solve wacky dilemmas using the research methods and tools of actual scientists. There are 24 open-ended mysteries, ranging from exploding grain silos to crashing computers. Through careful observation and research, students must develop a rational explanation and report their findings. For example, Figure 4-33 is from *The Case of*

Figure 4-32 Carbon dioxide turns the earth into a giant greenhouse by absorbing heat and trapping it inside the atmosphere. From *Science Forums*, volume I, "Fossil Fuel and the Greenhouse Effect."

Figure 4-33   A palentologist shows the fault line in which a dinosaur bone was found. From *The Case of the Misplaced Fossil* in *Science Sleuths*.

the Misplaced Fossil. An amateur paleontologist found a dinosaur bone from the Cretaceous Age (65 to 140 million years ago) in a Tertiary Stratum dating back to only 10 million years ago, and the student must explain the mystery of how it got there. Beautifully produced student manuals and instructor guides accompany the Videodiscovery discs and CDs. For a complete list of products, follow the *Multilit* Web site link to Videodiscovery.

Falcon Software's *Environmental Science: Field Laboratory CD-ROM* contains seven modules: stream pollution, minerals for society, energy from coal, radiation, legal control of the environment, streams and floods, and geology of homesite selection. Students learn how to define a problem, sample data, model phenomena, and draw conclusions. For more information, follow the *Multilit* Web site link to Falcon Software.

Elementary Education

Children's Software Revue (CSR) is a magazine and a Web site devoted to empowering children to foster their growth and development through quality software. As depicted in Figure 4-34, *CSR* reviews the software and informs teachers and parents about its relative merits. The Children's Software Finder lets you search for more than 4200 products by platform, subject, grade level, rating, or title.

One such title is the CD-ROM version of the best-selling *Macmillan Dictionary for Children* pictured in Figure 4-35. With 12,000 word entries, 1000 illustrations, and 400 sound effects, it has a spelling bee and hangman games, and a tour guide named Zak who helps kids learn how to pronounce words. Zak, who is a real ham, is likely to give you his personal reaction as you look up a word. Figure 4-36 shows a sample screen in which the student has looked up the word *apple*. The four icons along the right of the screen let the student look up other words, compile a word list, play games, and get help. The *Dictionary* also has word etymologies and language notes.

Figure 4-34   The Children's Software Revue (CSR) Web site.

Figure 4-35 The title screen from the best-selling *Macmillan Dictionary for Children*.

Figure 4-36 The result of looking up the word *apple* in the *Macmillan Dictionary for Children*.

The National Geographic Kids Online network (Kids Net) combines online computer activity with real-life interactions and experimentation. Electronic mail engages children in cooperative learning across the Internet. For example, consider the Acid Rain Project for which students designed acid rain collectors and inspected tombstones for acid rain damage. After compiling and analyzing the data, students shared results through e-mail. The result provided a comparison of acid rain damage throughout the United States and Canada. To find out about other Kids Net activities, follow the *Multilit* Web site link to Kids Net. While there, see the Kids Archive, which is full of stories about Kids Net accomplishments.

Another online collaborative network is organized by the KIDLINK Society. Since 1990, KIDLINK has united 175,000 children from 132 countries. Their primary means of communication is e-mail, although the children also use Internet chat rooms and videoconferencing. Kids can connect at any time to join conversations on a wide range of subjects. To join in, click KIDLINK at the *Multilit* Web site.

Reading and Writing

Multimedia computers enhance the teaching and learning of reading and writing by providing an environment that motivates students to read and makes it easy for students to begin writing at an early age. The software discussed here demonstrates how the computer addresses a variety of learning styles, puts students in control, encourages exploration and peer tutoring, and fosters the development of modern communication skills.

CD-ROMs that present stories for children in a hypermedia format are becoming very popular. The CDs display full-color illustrations and let the child click items on the screen to have words spoken, defined, or used in sentences, to trigger sound effects and animations, and to link to related materials. The only technical drawback is that although the CDs are highly interactive, the child cannot slow down the pace of the audio. In a controlled study of the impact of CD-ROM storybooks on children's reading comprehension, Matthew (1998) found that children who use CD-ROMs read equally as well but become significantly better storytellers than students who learn to read only from books.

Just Grandma and Me was the first title to appear in the *Living Books* series by Brøderbund. Based on the best-selling book by Mercer Mayer, the CD contains 12 pages of lively animations, music, sound effects, narration, and talking characters who teach early reading and storytelling skills. Its purpose is to enable children ages three to eight to explore the printed words, as well as the pictures, and to learn words, phrases, and complete sentences. Full Spanish and Japanese translations are included.

Arthur's Teacher Trouble, the second in Brøderbund's *Living Books* series, is based on the best-selling book by Marc Brown. This interactive, animated storybook features lively animations, original music, realistic sounds, and hundreds of words written, spoken, and even spelled out loud. By putting the child in control of exploring the printed words and the pictures, the CD engages kids in this "whole language" approach to learning. A full Spanish translation is included. Figure 4-37 illustrates the first page of the book. Active items include objects on the bulletin board, the window shades, the door, each student, and different parts of the professor's body.

One criticism of the *Living Books* has been that the animations take students on tangents that do not contribute to the story. More recent *Living Books* titles such as *The Tortoise and the Hare* and *New Kid on the Block* are linking the animations closer to the story, so the animations lead to better comprehension. *Dr. Seuss's ABC* was so popular that *Living Books* followed it with another Dr. Seuss classic, *Green Eggs and Ham*. The *Living Books* have won dozens of awards, including Best Overall Educational Program from the Software Publishers Association, Parent's Choice from the Parent's Choice Foundation,

Figure 4-37   The first page of *Arthur's Teacher Trouble*.

Figure 4-38 Reader Rabbit's *Complete Learn to Read System.*

and Best Early Childhood Software from the High/Scope Educational Research Foundation. For more information about the *Living Books,* follow the *Multilit* Web site link to The Learning Company.

Also from The Learning Company is a highly rated series of Reader Rabbit products. The series targets learners ranging in age from baby through toddler, preschool, kindergarten, and grade school. Figure 4-38 shows how Reader Rabbit's *Complete Learn to Read System* integrates multimedia CDs with flashcards, workbooks, and storybooks. First the students learn letters and sounds, then they read words and sentences. *Children's Software Revue (CSR)* has reviewed dozens of Reader Rabbit products. To read these reviews, follow the *Multilit* Web site link to *CSR* and use the Children's Software Finder to locate titles that begin with the words Reader Rabbit.

An Internet resource for young writers is the Alphabet Superhighway, which was created under the Department of Education's READ*WRITE*NOW! initiative. On the Alphabet Superhighway, students learn to create, locate, and communicate information through mentoring, guided discovery, competitions, and other online activities. The goal is to raise reading and writing achievement levels in the United States. Information is organized around Knowledge Neighborhoods, where general topics such as space, earth, peoples and cultures, and technology can be browsed. At the heart of the Alphabet Superhighway are places for students to display their work (such as the Cyberzine and Exhibit Center), and facilities for finding information (the Library and the Smart Searcher) and for learning and reinforcing skills and topics (the Traveling Tutor and the Challenge Chaser). The Traveling Tutor teaches a variety of topics including how to write better reports and how to draw graphs and diagrams. The Challenge Chaser presents challenges for students to write essays, search for information, spell words, and solve word puzzles. Smart Searcher helps find information, either within the Alphabet Superhighway or out on the Web. Assisting teachers and parents are a Teachers' Lounge and a Parents' Place. To visit, follow the *Multilit* Web site link to the Alphabet Superhighway.

1. What percentage of your teachers used multimedia in the classroom when you were in elementary school? What percentage of teachers do you believe will be using multimedia computers as a classroom teaching aid by the year 2010?

2. How do you believe multimedia technology will affect the future of schooling? If the Information Superhighway could serve all the nation's educational software to children at home, for example, would there be no further need for schools as we know them? Are there any aspects of schooling that technology cannot replace?

3. The *Macmillan Dictionary for Children* was shown in Figures 4-35 and 4-36. Follow the *Multilit* Web site link to the *Children's Software Review (CSR),* and find out whether *CSR* recommends the CD-ROM version of this dictionary. What rating does *CSR* give the *Macmillan Dictionary for Children?* Does *CSR* recommend any other multimedia dictionaries?

4. If you would like to learn more about cognitive psychology and the constructivist movement in education, see Bruning's textbook *Cognitive Psychology and Instruction* (Englewood Cliffs, N.J.: Merrill/Prentice-Hall, 1998, ISBN 0-13-716606-0). The introduction provides an excellent overview, history, and comparison of the behavioral and constructivist movements in education. Another excellent text is Mark and Cindy Grabe's *Integrating Technology for Meaningful Learning* (Boston: Houghton Mifflin, 1998, ISBN 0-395-87136-4). Chapter 2 is devoted to cognitive learning and technology tools.

5

Entertainment

After completing this chapter, you will be able to:

▦ **Understand how multimedia is transforming the entertainment industry by moving from passive to interactive art forms**

▦ **Recognize how multimedia techniques are being used to create cinematic special effects**

▦ **Question the ethics of digital cinema**

▦ **Understand how realistic and violent video arcade games have become**

▦ **Recognize how virtual reality is making interactive environments more immersing and persuasive**

● Much of the innovation in multimedia sound and graphics originates in the entertainment industry. There is intense competition among cinematographers and video game producers to deliver the most dazzling and engaging special effects. Interactive movies appearing on CD and DVD encourage the user to influence the story or play a role in it. Research and development in virtual reality are providing new visualization, mobility, and tracking devices that immerse the user so completely that the simulated experience seems real.

Cinema

Moviemakers are investing heavily in the development of multimedia software to make movies more engaging. Producers use multimedia computers to create realistic special effects through digital imaging, rendering, animation, morphing, superimposition, replacement, and surround sound. Remember, however, that although multimedia computers may have been used to produce a movie, watching the movie is not a multimedia experience unless you can interact with it and play a role in what happens.

Morphing

One of the more interesting multimedia effects is called **morphing**, a computer graphics technique in which one image is transformed into another in a seamless, uninterrupted segment. Duncan (1991) describes how morphing was used in the Arnold Schwarzenegger hit movie *Terminator II* to create the model 1000 terminator, a liquid metal machine that could imitate any form with which it came into contact. *Terminator II* went on to win Academy Awards for best visual effects, makeup, sound, and sound effects.

Morphing was used to convey a theme of racial harmony in Michael Jackson's music video *Black and White.* Duncan (1992) tells how 13 young people of varied racial and ethnic backgrounds were transformed into one another in a segment lasting only a minute.

Pictured in Figure 5-1, Avid's Elastic Reality software has rendered morphs for hundreds of television and feature film productions. It combines photographic realism with the freedom of artist-controlled elasticity; hence the name, Elastic Reality. Figure 5-2 shows how the artist can adjust distortion, color, rotation and layering priority over time. In Figure 5-3, the artist sets parameters on key frames for animating character expressions. To learn more, follow the *Multilit* Web site link to Avid's Elastic Reality.

The *Multilit* Web site links to several online examples of morphs that you can view for free. If you want to create morphs of your own, follow the link to SuperGoo, which lets you stretch, warp, and smear images in real time as though the images were liquid. SuperGoo saves the images in a series of key frames that work like a digital flip book you can render into a QuickTime movie. To create characters that not only morph but also speak and display emotions, follow the *Multilit* Web site link to Haptek's Virtual Friends.

Figure 5-1   Avid's Elastic Reality enables you to morph and warp still graphics to create high-quality animations.

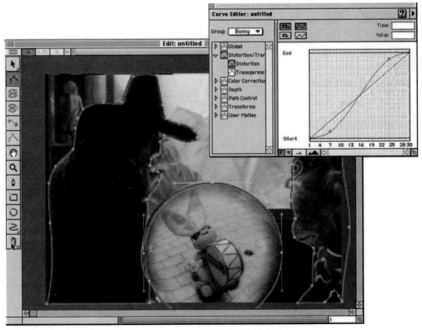

Figure 5-2   The curve editor in Avid's Elastic Reality adjusts distortion, color, rotation, and layering priority over time.

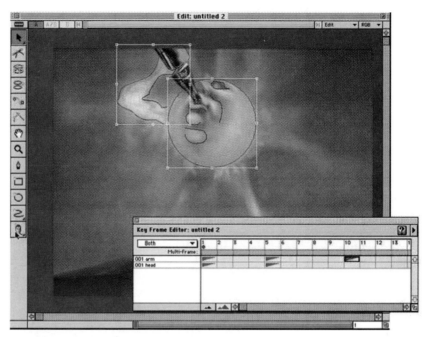

Figure 5-3   Avid's Elastic Reality has powerful key frame capabilities for animating character expressions.

Superimposition

When Gabe (played by Sylvester Stallone) failed in his attempt to rescue Sarah (Michelle Joyner) in the movie *Cliffhanger,* she fell thousands of feet to her death. Or so it seemed. In reality, Sarah fell only 35 feet into a stunt bag. Kaufman (1993) tells how an IBM Power Visualization System (PVS) superimposed her fall into the stunt bag over dramatic photographs of the Dolomites. Developed originally for high-end scientific visualization, the PVS is a rendering, compositing, editing, and viewing tool powerful enough to display composited shots at 30 frames per second (fps).

Animation

The dinosaurs in the Spielberg film *Jurassic Park* took animation to a new level. To tap the talent of stop-motion animators and translate it into the digital domain, a clever interface called the Dinosaur Input Device (DID) was created. As skilled animators moved mechanical dinosaurs to create realistic body movements, the DID created a wireframe model which was converted to a SoftImage file that could be refined through computer animation. Duncan (1993) describes how the mechanical models ensured that the dinosaur's spine, neck, tail, legs, and arms moved correctly, while the computer animated the fingers, toes, and mouth. Once the DID and SoftImage animations were complete, computer animators at Industrial Light & Magic (ILM) did the final rendering, adding breathing effects and the organic wobble of the dinosaur skin. ILM even made computer-generated rain stream off the back of the tyrannosaurus rex to establish realism in one rainy scene.

Toy Story is a Disney film produced by Pixar, which is probably the most innovative 3-D animation company in the world. If you have not seen *Toy Story,* treat yourself by viewing it. While you watch the film, remember that every single frame was computer-generated. At the end of the movie, view the credits. You will be impressed by the number of technicians involved and the new job positions created. Table 5-1 contains some interesting statistics about the production of *Toy Story*. Disney also publishes the CD-ROM *Toy Story Animated Story Book*. Designed for children ages three to nine, the CD follows the movie's story line and features educational games on basic skills taught in the context of the story.

Table 5-1 *Toy Story* Statistics

Object Type	Number
Number of bytes required to store the film information	1 trillion (1 terabyte)
Minutes of completed animation produced each week	3.5
Months it took to write the shader for Andy's hair (it took the longest)	9
"Built-in" lights on Buzz	10
Least number of minutes required to render a frame of film	45
Most number of hours required to render a frame of film	20
Number of characters	76
Minutes of computer animation	77
Number of Sun Workstations in Pixar's Renderfarm operating on a 24-hour basis	110
Texture maps for Buzz (plus an additional 450 to show scuffs and dirt)	189
Gigabytes required to store final frames	500
Number of avars (variables which an animator can control) for Buzz	700
Number of avars for Woody	712
Number of avars for Woody's face	212
Number of avars for Woody's mouth	58
Number of avars for Sid's backpack	128
Number of leaves on the trees in Andy's neighborhood	1.2 million
Number of shaders written for the production	1300
Final number of shots in the film	1561
Number of frames of computer animation in the film	110,064
Number of texture maps created for the film (most are painted digitally, but some are photographed and scanned; the carpet in Sid's house was taken from *The Shining*)	2000
Number of storyboards drawn	25,000
Number of lines in model program required to describe Buzz	34,864
Number of lines in model program required to describe Woody	52,865
Number of machine hours required to render frames	800,000
Number of lines of code needed to create the film's models	4.5 million

Building on the success of its predecessor, *Toy Story 2* provided another opportunity for Buzz and Woody to star in what was to become the top-grossing animated film to date. For more information about the movie and related products, follow the *Multilit* Web site links to *Toy Story 2*. To learn about the Renderman family of animation products used to create the *Toy Story* characters, follow the links to Pixar.

Digital Recasting

A series of Diet Coke commercials feature the classic black-and-white film stars Humphrey Bogart, Louis Armstrong, and James Cagney playing in full color alongside contemporary stars such as Elton John and Paula Abdul. How can Bogart, Armstrong, and Cagney star in a modern commercial? Were look-alikes found to play the parts of the classic actors? Or were the original films colorized and modern actors somehow superimposed onto them?

Hubbard (1992) explains how digital video techniques were used to create the Diet Coke commercials. First, the classic films were digitized. Then traditional and electronic rotoscoping techniques were used to extract the classic actors from their original environments. Next, the commercials were composited in layers, with a background layer of people seated and dancing, middle layers in which the archival characters interact with the modern actors, and a foreground layer in which people cross in front of the rotoscoped classic actors to impart a sense of reality. Finally, the original actors were colorized, and finishing touches were added, like putting Louis Armstrong's reflection alongside Elton John's on the top of the piano. Digital video editing permitted all of this to be done without any loss of quality. Traditional editing would have required many generations of videotape, with each video transfer progressively degrading the picture quality.

Video Games

Video games have come a long way since Pong and PacMan. Advances in computer graphics have replaced stick figures and cartoonlike drawings with actual photographs of scenes and characters digitized on multimedia computers. Digital audio has made video games more realistic by providing instant access to recordings of the actual sounds made by characters and objects in the game. New input devices use lasers and 3-D mice to let the user interact more intimately with objects on the screen.

The best place to see the new technology is in video arcades. As the technology progresses, the innovations that emerge first in the arcades become available in portable versions you can play at home. Unfortunately, some of the most violent and offensive games become mass market hits. As this book goes to press, the best-selling video game, *Mortal Kombat*, contains such graphic violence that it provoked a public outcry in favor of government intervention and rating systems for video games. Although *Mortal Kombat* has controls parents can set to limit the level of violence in the game, most kids are more computer literate than their parents and have already figured out how to make the games more violent. To find out about the latest release, follow the *Multilit* Web site link to *Mortal Kombat*. While there, look for links to *Quake*, which is *Mortal Kombat*'s primary competitor. In Chapter 16 you will be asked to consider whether graphically violent and sexually exploitative games increase the likelihood that young people will engage in similar behaviors in real life.

Interactive Movies

Interactive movies played on multimedia computers let the viewer influence how the story unfolds. In Cyan's *Myst*, for example, you are mysteriously transported to the ancient island shown in Figure 5-4. Soon you learn that your presence there is not an accident. You must travel through several 3-D photorealistic worlds to untangle a web of treachery and deceit. Live actors appear superimposed on stunningly rendered 3-D scenes, such as the graphic shown in Figure 5-5.

Figure 5-4　Cyan's *Myst* has surpassed 7 million copies sold.

Myst®Cyan, Inc.

Figure 5-5　Screen from the Channelwood Age in *Myst*.

Myst has a fully developed story line. The island was created by Artrus, who discovered the secret of writing books that create worlds and transport you from one world to another. But a plot against Artrus has apparently left his island and his worlds deserted. Your challenge is to uncover the story of *Myst* and find Artrus and his family. Filled with clever puzzles and unexpected twists and turns, *Myst* is a thinking game that requires 40 to 60 hours to complete. The user points and clicks with a mouse to solve the puzzle. The only directions explain merely how to move around. You can find out more by following the *Multilit* Web site link to *Myst*.

Also linked to the *Multilit* Web site is an interactive movie named *Dust: A Tale of the Wired West*. The year is 1882. You're a stranger in Diamondback, New Mexico. Mayhem follows rumors of lost Spanish silver. To discover the keys to your survival, you must unravel the mystery of the lost silver as you interact with more than 35 characters who remember your actions and behave accordingly. A strong story line pulls you into the drama as you experience interactive storytelling at its best.

Virtual Reality

Virtual reality (VR) refers to the use of a computer to immerse the user into a simulated experience so authentic it seems real. VR systems often use special hardware to enhance the experience, including visual displays (monitors, head-mounted viewing goggles, periscope booms, and direct eye scanning), tracking devices (data gloves, joysticks, body

Figure 5-6 The Cybertron gyroscopic virtual reality system.

Figure 5-7 3-D graphic produced with PhotoVR technology.

suits, or infrared tracking), and mobility devices (motion platforms, treadmills, stationary bicycles, trackballs, and flying mice that let you move in a 3-D space).

One of the most participatory VR systems is the Cybertron by Straylight. Figure 5-6 shows how the user maneuvers by bodily pivoting and tilting the gyro mechanism. Straylight uses quadraphonic CD audio and 3-D imaging to enhance the experience. For example, Figure 5-7 shows a scene from Straylight's PhotoVR, a photorealistic VR engine that lets users explore highly realistic 3-D virtual environments. PhotoVR imports 3-D designs created with CAD (computer-aided design) programs and lets the user move around the 3-D environment in real time. To learn more about these and other exciting VR products, follow the *Multilit* Web site link to Straylight.

Figure 5-8 shows CrystalEyes VR hardware from StereoGraphics that lets you interact with stereoscopic images as depicted in Figure 5-9. As you move your head from side to

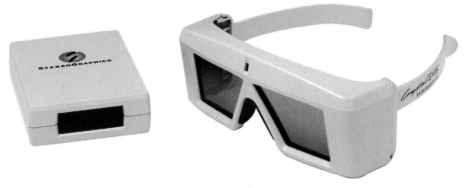

Figure 5-8 The CrystalEyes VR hardware consists of a lightweight, wireless set of 3-D liquid crystal shutter eyewear and an infrared emitter.

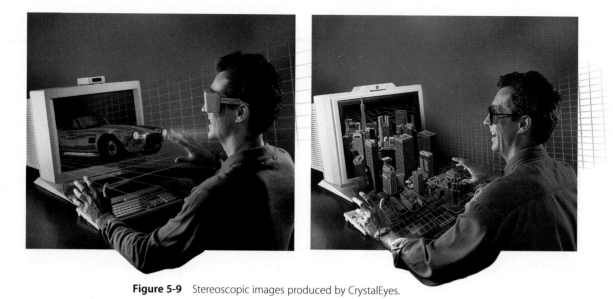

Figure 5-9   Stereoscopic images produced by CrystalEyes.

side, closer to or farther away from the monitor, the image on the display changes its perspective, creating the convincing illusion that the image is a real object. The tracking mechanism uses an infrared emitter. Thus, the user's hands are free to interact with other peripherals, such as the computer keyboard or mouse. For the latest information on CrystalEyes, follow the *Multilit* Web site link to StereoGraphics.

The entertainment industry is using VR to create virtual actors. Known as VActors, virtual actors appear on-screen as animated characters whose actions are controlled by humans wearing VR sensors. Special input devices track the actor's face, body, and hand movements. SimGraphics Engineering has created VActors for Nintendo to use in trade shows, live TV interviews, videodiscs, and mall tours. SimGraphics has also created VActors for Interplay Productions (*Mario Teaches Typing* CD-ROM), Fugi Television (touring exhibition), Hewlett-Packard (corporate video), and NHK (a high-definition television commercial). A VActor named Ratz the Cat is performed by comedian Paul Brophy on the British television shows *Live and Kicking* and *Children's BBC*. For more information on VActor technology, follow the *Multilit* Web site link to Cooper and Benjamin's treatise on *Dramatic Interaction in Virtual Worlds.*

Virtual reality has also brought Mark Twain to life in the form of *Twain-VR,* a 3-D character created by Color Concepts & Images. The brainchild of Lake Tahoe-based multimedia producer Gary Jesch in collaboration with Twain impressionist McAvoy Layne and co-producer Susan Margolis, virtual Mark Twain is spookily similar to the man himself in appearance, in his words and experiences, and in the way he sounds. For more information about Mark Twain and other virtual characters, follow the *Multilit* Web site link to CHOPS & Associates.

Tracking body movements is a tricky problem addressed by Ascension Technology Corporation's Flock of Birds tracking devices, which provide real-time, simultaneous tracking of up to 30 receivers over medium and long ranges. The Flock is typically used for head, hand, and body motion tracking in applications ranging from flight simulation and virtual reality to medical instrument localization and motion capture for character animation. The Flock can transmit up to 144 position and orientation measurements per second. For more information about the Flock, follow the *Multilit* Web site link to Ascension Technology.

Atlantis Cyberspace has a virtual reality entertainment Web site where you can find out about all of the commercially available VR systems and learn where the nearest VR theme park is in your locale. Follow the *Multilit* Web site link to Atlantis Cyberspace.

exercises

1. Attend the latest box office hit movie, or view the latest soft drink commercials. Watch for multimedia techniques. Try to find examples of digital imaging, rendering, animation, morphing, superimposition, replacement, and surround sound. How could the movie or commercial have been improved through more use of multimedia?

2. Get an interactive movie by either purchasing it from your local software store, borrowing it from a library, or buying it online at amazon.com. After playing the movie, answer these questions. What is the title of the movie you played? Who published it, and what is its copyright date? How interactive was the movie? How immersing was it? Did you really feel like you were an essential part of the movie? What role did you play? Were you able to influence the movie's outcome? Do you prefer this kind of involvement to just watching a traditional movie? Why or why not?

3. Digital editing techniques permit actors to play in scenes they have never visited physically. Singers are having their voices digitized so they can continue to record new songs after their singing voice wanes. Comment on the ethics of this. Will digitized actors and voices create problems for younger artists who cannot find work if older actors can continue to play long after they would have been forced into retirement without multimedia?

4. When the VCR was invented, it did not sell very well until videotapes of movies too sexually explicit and violent for TV became available. Will the success of multimedia similarly depend on the sale of violent and sexually explicit interactive titles, or could the industry survive if titles that provoke violent and sexually exploitative behavior were taken off the market?

5. Browse to vr-atlantis.com and choose "Where to experience VR" to find out where the nearest VR theme park is in your locale. Visit the theme park and try some VR. Describe the experience. Did you feel like you were actually "in" the situation in which the VR tried to immerse you? How real did the simulated experience feel?

6

Government and Politics

After completing this chapter, you will be able to:

▨ **Realize how multimedia can be used to improve access to state and local government**

▨ **Assess how your state is using multimedia, and determine whether the way it is using multimedia is good or bad for its citizens**

▨ **Understand how the city of Atlanta used multimedia to win its bid to host the Olympic Games**

▨ **Question whether multimedia makes too much information available too quickly to the public during wartime**

▨ **Realize how politicians are using the World Wide Web for virtual campaigning**

▨ **Find out how to check up on your congressional representatives to see how well they are representing your views on important votes**

▨ **Learn how the Internet is shifting the political power base from special interests groups to the citizenry**

● Government officials have turned increasingly to multimedia for solutions to problems inherent in governance. Multimedia kiosks make services more widely available and enable municipalities to respond more quickly to emergencies and disasters. Videoconferencing and the Internet provide ways for politicians to reach, canvass, and broaden their constituencies. Countries that want to be competitive in the new global economy are quickening the pace of the development of their national Information Superhighways. Governments are using the Internet to find out more about what is happening around the world and to document it for the United Nations. Since human nature unfortunately dictates that peacekeeping will inevitably break down, the military uses multimedia to wage war effectively.

Public Service Kiosks

CITY-INFO kiosks have been installed throughout Vienna, Austria, to offer citizens and travelers the ability to find information on addresses, points of interest, shops, restaurants, public transportation, hours of operation, guided tours, and the cost and location of tickets, buses, museums, and events. Set up in public areas like train stations, monuments, and other frequently visited places, the kiosks were designed to be easily recognizable yet blend in with their surroundings. The kiosks are connected to a network that updates them simultaneously. In their careful analysis of user reaction to the CITY-INFO kiosks, Professors Hitz and Werthner (1993) from the University of Vienna reported these results:

> It can be stated that the system is judged extremely positive (93%). . . . Typical users are young (43% under the age of 25), male (70%), tourists (55%) and well educated (32% high school, 34% university). They strongly recommend the usage of such a system (62% very much). . . . It is interesting that more than half would like to access such information via their [own] equipment and also 52% are willing to pay for such a service.

North Communications has deployed hundreds of kiosks across four continents, including municipal kiosks in the cities of Sacramento, Phoenix, New York, and Brisbane, Australia; and state government kiosks in California, Nebraska, Kansas, Hawaii, Arizona, New Mexico, and Texas. North has also set up federal government kiosks for Medicare, Social Security, veterans' benefits, and the U.S. Postal Service. As illustrated in Figure 6-1, North's product line covers motor vehicle services, employment services, public information products, legislative access, court automation, and TouchTeller financial services for banks and credit unions that want to take online banking to the streets.

For example, North developed a Quick Court kiosk for the Supreme Court of the State of Arizona. Now deployed throughout the state in court lobbies and libraries, the Quick Court kiosks provide information to litigants, produce legal documents for use in court cases, and increase public access to the courts. The kiosks use text, graphics, and an on-screen narrator to help litigants handle divorces, child support, name changes, affidavits, small claims, and landlord/tenant disputes.

Figure 6-1 Info/Media products available from North Communications. For the latest information, visit http://www.infonorth.com.

Figure 6-2   The TouchTeller kiosk from North Communications.

North has installed dozens of kiosks across the five boroughs of New York City. One of the more frequent uses is to pay parking fines, which netted the city a significant savings in transaction fees. Oxford Bank combined North's kiosks with the NetGain secure browser to create a new concept in branch banking. Customers now can access the bank's online Web services through touch-screen "TouchTeller" kiosks. Figure 6-2 shows the TouchTeller kiosk. To learn more about touch-screen kiosk applications, follow the *Multilit* Web site link to North Communications.

The State of Oregon's Employment Division uses multimedia kiosks in shopping malls, grocery stores, libraries, and community colleges to provide up-to-the-minute information about job openings that can be accessed simply by touching the screen. When the kiosk is not in use, it attracts users by playing video scenes of Oregon accompanied by lively stereo music. Referring to the kiosks in a press conference, then governor of Oregon Barbara Roberts stated, "We are going to change state government. We must be more efficient, and we must be smarter in how we deliver our services to the people in the state."

Figures 6-3 through 6-5 show screens from the Oregon kiosk. The purple buttons are active all the time and jump straight to the submenu of the button selected. All screens and videos are also available in Spanish by touching the ESPAÑOL button. For a list of Oregon kiosk locations, follow the *Multilit* Web site link to Oregon Kiosks.

Figure 6-3   A regional map showing Oregon Employment Division kiosk locations.

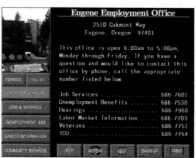

Figure 6-4   The result of pressing one of the red dots in Figure 6-3.

Figure 6-5   Oregon kiosk users can select the cities in which they are interested in finding jobs.

Electronic Town Meetings

CNN talk show host Larry King and CNN's *TalkBack Live* host Bobbie Battista are champions of the electronic town meeting, in which telephones are used to provide interactivity during television broadcasts. Since the number of people who can call in is limited by the length of the broadcast, interactive discussion groups on the Internet are being used to provide more people an opportunity to discuss their views. The Internet makes the meetings virtual, since they are no longer bounded by time or place. To participate, follow the *Multilit* Web site link to *TalkBack Live*.

The Internet is also becoming popular as a polling device on commercial television networks. Polls were formerly taken by asking viewers to call different phone numbers to register their response to a given question. Pollsters now advertise Internet addresses, which enable viewers to respond over the Information Superhighway. Many television shows are followed up by discussion sessions on computer networks, where the issues can be debated in more depth.

Internet and the National Information Superhighways

Realizing how any country that does not go online will be disenfranchised and unable to compete in the global economy, governments are spending billions of dollars to hasten the construction of their national Information Superhighways. The global connection of these highways into a worldwide network is referred to as the Internet. As this book goes to press, more than 170 countries are already connected, with more than 45,000 networks online on the Internet.

Experts disagree on whether the new technology will narrow or broaden the digital divide that separates the haves from the have-nots. As Mack (1999) reports, 88% of the world's Internet users are from wealthy nations. The average worker in Bangladesh, for example, would need to save for eight years just to buy a computer. There is only one telephone for every 100 people in Cambodia. Arpanet creator Paul LeBlanc counters that developing nations can leapfrog by taking advantage of newer technologies, for example, by constructing wireless cell phone towers instead of stringing wire to provide connectivity. For more arguments on both sides of this issue, follow the *Multilit* Web Site link to the Digital Divide.

For the reasons mentioned earlier, any country that does not go online and become proficient in using the Internet will become disenfranchised and seriously impede its ability to compete in the global economy.

Safeguarding National Interests

When serving as president of the United States, George Bush criticized the Central Intelligence Agency (CIA) for being so slow to issue reports, the White House learned more about world developments by watching commercial TV. The government now uses multimedia computers to provide officials with live TV feeds from news channels such as CNN, which appear in windows on the screen alongside other applications.

The government is also using the Internet to solve crimes. For example, the Federal Bureau of Investigation (FBI) posted a message on the Internet's NASA Network Information Center, asking for help in solving the Unabomber case, which involved a series of bombings targeting the computer industry, universities, and the aircraft and airline industries (*Wall Street Journal* 12/31/93: 10).

Warfare

The Gulf War and the war in Bosnia demonstrated how effectively multimedia can wage war. Imagine yourself in control of a smart bomb. You are seated at a multimedia computer, aiming a laser that steers the bomb. In a window, you view a live video feed from a camera in the smart bomb, showing precisely where it is headed. Your multimedia computer provides such fine control that you can fly the bomb into an air duct to penetrate an otherwise highly fortified building.

Although the accuracy of aerial multimedia weaponry lessens the need for ground forces, army combat is still a reality. When casualties occur, multimedia medicine steps in. For example, consider a group of army doctors at an EVAC hospital, facing a tough decision. Shrapnel has mutilated an artery and a vein in a soldier's leg. Conventional field medicine recommends amputation. Instead, doctors photograph the wound with a Kodak digital camera that has a small computer system interface (SCSI, pronounced *skuzzy*) port for plug-and-play capability. The images and patient history are uploaded via satellite to the Walter Reed Army Medical Center in Bethesda, Maryland, where specialists guide the field doctors through delicate reconstructive surgery that saves the leg. Detailed information on digital cameras is linked to the *Multilit* Web site.

Not all warfare uses conventional weapons. A more subtle form of **information warfare** is emerging. According to former CIA director John Deutch, the trend toward increased corporate reliance on telecommunications and networks is making the United States more vulnerable to information warfare tactics. "The electron, in my judgment, is the ultimate precision-guided munition. Virtually any single 'bad actor' can acquire the hardware and software needed to attack some of our critical information-based infrastructures. . . . We have evidence that a number of countries around the world are developing the doctrine, strategies and tools to conduct information attacks" (*Wall Street Journal* 6/26/96: B6). When serving as deputy U.S. attorney general, Jamie Gorelick warned that "an electronic Pearl Harbor" is a very real danger. About 250,000 intrusions into defense department computer systems are attempted each year, with about a 65% success rate (*BNA Daily Report for Executives* 7/17/96: A22). For more information about the use of information technologies in advanced defense applications, follow the *Multilit* Web site link to the Defense Advanced Research Projects Agency (DARPA) Information Technology Office, the Federal Bureau of Investigation, and the National Infrastructure Protection Agency.

Olympic Bidding

A big problem faced by the city of Atlanta at the outset of its bidding in 1988 for the 1996 Summer Olympics was lack of recognition as an international city. At that time only about 15 of the 90 voting members of the International Olympics Committee had ever been to Atlanta, which was known more for *Gone With the Wind* and similar visions of the Old South. Based on recommendations by Dr. Pat Crecine, then president of Georgia Tech, Atlanta used a multimedia campaign to promote a modern image of the city and project through realistic computer graphics what the planned stadium and other proposed facilities would be like. For example, Figure 6-6 shows the proposed Olympic dormitory complex, and Figure 6-7 shows the computer-generated "Golden

Figure 6-6   A computer graphics rendering of the proposed Olympic dormitory.

Figure 6-7   The computer-generated "Golden Athlete" carries the Olympic torch.

Athlete" who carries the Olympic torch into the proposed Olympic stadium. As Gamble-Risley (1992) describes the experience:

> Just sit down and prepare yourself to take a magnificent journey as you rush from space toward the Earth, plunge past fluffy clouds and down over snowcapped mountains, rivers and forest until you soar over Georgia and come to the city of Atlanta. After you've flown into the city, you'll come to a futuristic-looking stadium where you'll glide down corridors into an office, and exit out a window where you'll view the future site of the Olympic village. . . . From there, the tour is literally placed in the hands of the user who uses a trackball to take control over the adventure and can essentially go sight-seeing around the city.

After winning the bid, Atlanta's multimedia presentation evolved into a system called Atlanta Vision. Figure 6-8 shows how the system allows the observer to tour all of Georgia via a GIS (Geographical Information System) database system showcasing economic development opportunities and other highlights of the state.

Frederick Dyer and Mike Sinclair, who were codirectors of the Georgia Tech Multimedia Lab during Atlanta's quest for the Olympics, created 360-degree panoramic views by taking pictures from a helicopter with a motordrive 35mm camera. After digitizing the frames, the lab developed techniques for computer-correcting the resulting images for various distortions and then electronically composited them, resulting in images like the one shown in Figure 6-9. The multimedia presentation system continues to be enhanced and supported by the Georgia Power Company as a statewide, economic development tool for Georgia. A number of new multimedia ventures for Sports Technology, Coca Cola, dance technology groups, and others have been developed from the original technology. Today, more than a decade after its formation, the Lab is busier than ever with a wide variety of projects. Currently, key new activities include participation in the Video Development Initiative (ViDe) for the Internet2 project of the University Corporation for Advanced Internet Development (UCAID) and several distance education initiatives in Georgia.

For more information, contact codirectors Andy Quay and Ed Price at the Georgia Tech Interactive Media Technology Center. Their e-mail addresses are Andy.Quay@oip.gatech.edu and Ed.Price@oip.gatech.edu. Fred Dyer's e-mail address is fred@peachnet.edu. To learn more about how multimedia is being used to promote Olympic venues, follow the *Multilit* Web site links to various Olympic Games and Committees.

Figure 6-8 The Atlanta Vision kiosk uses a multiscreen panoramic presentation system.

Figure 6-9 Frederick Dyer and the 360-degree panoramic view upon which the Olympic rings float.

Politics

The Web has become a strategically important place to find out what is happening in politics and make your voice heard. If you follow the *Multilit* Web site links to VoteNet and VOTE.com, you will immediately see how the Web provides the most comprehensive vehicle for polling that the world has ever known. VOTE.com inventor Dick Morris hopes that voting on the Web will make individuals become so powerful that special interests no longer will be able to control the Congress because so many citizens will express their individual opinions.

You can find out how your congressional representatives are voting by following the *Multilit* Web site link to Thomas, where you will find the congressional record online. By following the link to C-Span, you can follow live video Web coverage of the House and Senate, browse the C-Span programming guide, and get a free membership to *C-SPAN in the Classroom*. You can also follow the *Multilit* Web site link to take a free peek into the *National Journal*'s Cloakroom, which is a members-only site that provides opportunities to make your voice heard, talk with others about issues that concern you, and reach out and communicate directly with decision makers in politics and government.

Virtual Campaigning

According to Buchanan (1994), the Internet played a significant role in Landon Curt Noll's election to the Sunnyvale (California) City Council. Noll recruited a third of his volunteer campaign organization directly from the Internet, on which voters asked why he was running for office and what he hoped to accomplish. Overall, Noll estimates he reached 50,000 voters through the Internet.

Wasserman (1999) reports that even though there are fewer campaign donations via the Internet, online contributors give more on average than offline contributors; moreover, online supporters are repeat contributors. John Aristotle Phillips, cofounder of Aristotle, a leading provider of campaign management software, predicts that by 2004, 80% of the money raised from individuals for political candidates will come from Internet sources. For the complete story, follow the *Multilit* Web site link to Finding Money on the Web.

The Internet has become so important to public officials getting elected that almost every political candidate has a Web site. To find out where the political candidate Web sites are, follow the *Multilit* Web site link to Yahoo's index of political candidate Web sites.

FinanceNet

FinanceNet is an independent public Internet network that was established by then Vice President Al Gore's National Performance Review in Washington, D.C. Operated by the National Science Foundation, FinanceNet is the information clearinghouse of the Joint Financial Management Improvement Program. FinanceNet reaches across geopolitical boundaries to link financial management staff worldwide to catalyze continuous improvements in employee productivity and taxpayer resources. To access it, follow the *Multilit* Web site link to FinanceNet.

Small-Business Assistance

The U.S. Business Advisor offers small businesses online access to guides and government forms needed to comply with regulations or apply for government-backed loans or other federal assistance. The goal is to provide small businesses with one-stop access to federal agencies that regulate and assist business (*Wall Street Journal* 2/14/96: B2). The U.S. Small Business Administration (SBA) offers a full range of services including information about start-up capital, how to secure financing, developing a business plan, attending SBA Training and Conferences, using the online Small Business Classroom, and conducting business online. To visit the U.S. Business Advisor and SBA Web sites, follow the *Multilit* Web site links.

Patent Searches

The U.S. government has a Web site where you can do patent searches online. Follow the *Multilit* Web site link to the U.S. Patent Office, then select Search U.S. Patent Bibliographic Data. This service is maintained by the Center for Networked Information Discovery and Retrieval (CNIDR), in cooperation with the U.S. Patent and Trademark Office (USPTO).

Internal Revenue Service

The Internal Revenue Service (IRS) has a Web site where you can find out about the tax code, download tax forms, and file your income tax return over the Internet. Follow the *Multilit* Web site link to visit the IRS online.

e x e r c i s e s

1. How is multimedia used by your state government? Do multimedia kiosks, for example, help tourists find their way around your largest cities? Is there an employment kiosk to help the unemployed find jobs? Is multimedia used to make disaster relief available to those who need it? Does your state use multimedia to deliver driver's license tests?

2. Think of three more ways multimedia could be used to improve government services to your community. Describe how you would want them implemented.

3. The city of Atlanta used multimedia to help win its bid to host the Olympic Games. How could your local government use multimedia to promote your cities and strengthen their economy?

4. President George Bush used to complain that he learned more from watching CNN on TV than he did from the CIA. So could terrorists. To what extent should news coverage of nationally sensitive information and events be curtailed? For example, during their amphibious landing on the beach in Somalia, soldiers complained that television lights betrayed their positions. Should wars be televised?

5. Browse to http://thomas.loc.gov and check the record to find out whether your congressional representatives are voting the way you want them to. Use the House and Senate directory to find out their e-mail addresses, and send them e-mail to express your views. What are the names and e-mail addresses of your state's U.S. senators? What is the name and e-mail address of your voting district's U.S. representative?

7

Medicine and Nursing

After completing this chapter, you will be able to:

▨ **Recognize the breadth of multimedia applications in health care for medical training, emergency preparedness, and virtual surgery**

▨ **Understand how health care professionals in your community should be using multimedia computers to prepare for emergency situations**

▨ **Find out whether your local health care professionals are taking advantage of online resources, videoconferencing, and interactive diagnostic programs**

● When life depends on something, people get serious about it. So it is with multimedia and health care. This chapter surveys applications that promise to provide you with better diagnosis when you get sick, more-efficient treatment, life skills to keep you healthy, and, in an emergency, health care professionals who either know what to do about the situation or who can use a multimedia computer to find out what to do before it is too late.

Medical Training

From the $39.95 *The Doctors Book of Home Remedies* by Compton's NewMedia to the $22,000 *American Heart Association Advanced Cardiac Life Support* training system by Actronics, multimedia computers are providing patients, doctors, and nurses with interactive health care training and medical references. Graphic Education's *Interactive Healthcare Directories* lists nearly 2,000 software titles developed for health-related education and reference. These programs cover both professional and consumer subject matter, including medicine, nursing, allied health, staff development, patient education, and health promotion. With the directory, you can quickly locate software covering anatomy, medical terminology, infection control, diabetes, and surgical procedures. Figure 7-1 shows the search screen. To locate titles on a given topic, you type in a key word or phrase. Clicking Quick Search brings up the titles that have your word or phrase in the title or subject fields. For a longer list of titles, you click Full Search to bring up titles that also contain your key word or phrase in the description of the software program. For more information, follow the *Multilit* Web site link to the *Interactive Healthcare Directories.*

The Interactive Patient is a Web site at Marshall University School of Medicine that simulates an actual patient encounter. This teaching tool for physicians, residents, and

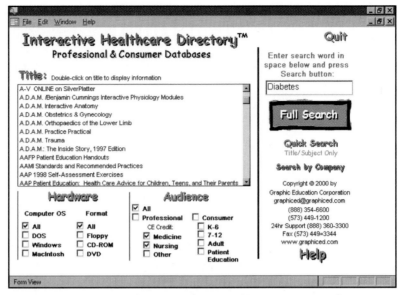

Figure 7-1 Search screen from the *Interactive Healthcare Directories* CD from Graphic Education Healthcare Multimedia.

medical students offers a case with a chief complaint to the user, who must then interact with the patient by requesting additional history, performing a physical exam, and reviewing laboratory data and X rays. After conducting the examination, the user is encouraged to submit a diagnosis and treatment plan. The system promises to evaluate and provide feedback on all submitted answers. To try the case yourself, follow the *Multilit* Web site link to The Interactive Patient.

For more information about nursing online, follow the *Multilit* Web Site links to the Nursing Center, the Sigma Theta Tau International Honor Society of Nursing, and Nurse Practitioner Central.

Anatomy and Physiology

Anatomy and Physiology is a double-sided videodisc from Videodiscovery that comes with a two-volume, 600-page, bar-coded directory. Students can observe the human structure in remarkable detail in the 1,500 3-D animations. Its 3,000 photographs and motion sequences are fully correlated to the nation's best-selling anatomy text. Nine mini-documentaries introduce medical career options and debate various topics. The videodisc also includes the acclaimed Bassett collection of human body dissections. For more information, follow the *Multilit* Web site link to Videodiscovery.

A fascinating place to visit on the Web is the National Library of Medicine's (NLM's) Visible Human Project. The NLM is using body-slicing techniques to create complete, anatomically detailed, 3-D representations of the male and female human body. Transverse CT, MRI, and cryosection images of male and female cadavers have been collected at 1-millimeter intervals. The long-term goal is to produce a system of knowledge structures that will transparently link visual knowledge forms to symbolic knowledge formats such as the names of body parts. To view a sampler of images, follow the *Multilit* Web site link to the Visible Human Project.

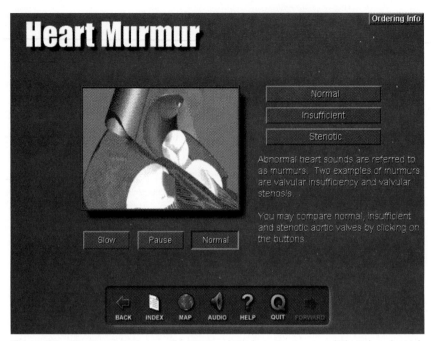

Figure 7-2   The Dynamic Human: The 3D Visual Guide to Anatomy and Physiology by Unk.

The Dynamic Human is a CD-ROM from Wm. C. Brown Publishers containing 3-D anatomical illustrations you can move around, light-up identification for the structures in all 11 body systems, and hundreds of animations showing how your body works. For example, Figure 7-2 shows how you can hear and see the difference between a normal heart and one with a heart murmur. The CD is full of dynamic models like this one, which you can pause at any time or play in slow motion. For a beautifully illustrated overview of the CD's contents and a detailed look at how the CD correlates with anatomy and physiology textbooks, follow the *Multilit* Web site link to *The Dynamic Human.*

Virtual Surgery

Imagine a surgeon using a head-mounted display to rehearse the removal of a brain tumor by moving surgical instruments through a 3-D view of the tumor. Imagine a physician using hand gestures to control tiny robots that swim through your blood vessels and fire lasers to vaporize cholesterol plaques that can cause heart attacks. Imagine being able to take a virtual walk through your body to see how a particular medication acts to prevent an asthmatic attack. According to Merril (1993), all of these scenarios are possible outcomes of current virtual reality research in medical applications. Figures 7-3 and 7-4 show how Merril uses texture mapping to wrap images of actual tissues onto the surface of surgical models.

HT Medical Systems has won many awards for its TELEOS software. TELEOS is the virtual reality authoring system that HT created for producing surgical training

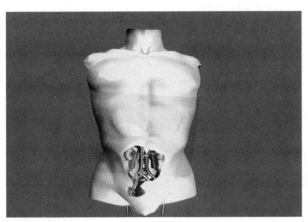

Figure 7-3 Physicians use virtual reality simulations to learn laparoscopic ("belly button") surgery.

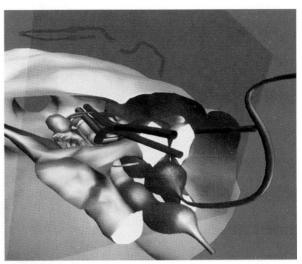

Figure 7-4 Texture mapping wraps images of actual tissues on the surface of surgical models.

simulations. The simulation products include CathSim, a computer-based system for intravenous therapy; PreOp Endoscopy Simulator, a realistic, computer-based system for teaching the motor skills and cognitive knowledge necessary to perform Endoscopy procedures; and the PreOp Endovascular Simulator, which trains clinicians in procedures such as balloon angioplasty, stent placement, and pacemaker leads placement. To get more information and find out what is new, follow the *Multilit* Web site link to HT Medical Systems, and click Products.

Also linked to the *Multilit* Web site is Laparoscopy.com, which uses a multimedia gallery full of sound, graphics, and video to demonstrate numerous types of laparoscopic surgery. You can even watch surgeries live through CUSeeMe videoconferencing.

Videoconferencing Network

Klinck (1993) describes how the Voluntary Hospitals of America (VHA), the nation's largest alliance of hospitals, is building a videoconferencing network to connect its 900 nonprofit hospitals. Based on VTEL Corporation's PC-based videoconferencing technology, the system will enable health care professionals at different hospitals to use videoconferencing for patient diagnosis and treatment. The equipment can capture videotape transmissions of medical images and clinical procedures, which is ideal for providing continuing medical education to physicians and other health care professionals. Doctors can annotate test results, allowing a more personal and immediate diagnosis. The system also permits the use of stethoscopes, EKG units, X rays, teleradiology systems, sonograms, and other medical devices. In time-sensitive cases, VTEL's system can allow for quick decisions vital to saving a patient's life. Figure 7-5 shows how the VTEL videoconferencing for health care model is designed to roll quickly from room to room as needed in a hospital.

For more information about the VHA project and many other health care videoconferencing applications, follow the *Multilit* Web site link to VTEL Online and click the option to see industries and customer profiles.

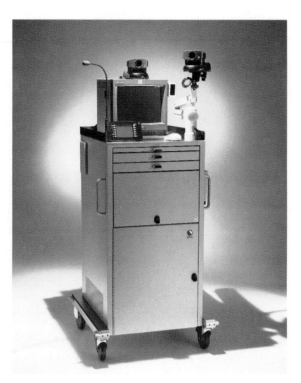

Figure 7-5 VTEL's HS2000 rollabout videoconferencing system allows for movement between surgical units, and to conference rooms or classrooms.

Online Resources

To allow physicians speedy access to the latest clinical research, the American Association for the Advancement of Science publishes the electronic *Online Journal of Current Clinical Trials.* The National Library of Medicine has endorsed this new online journal by including it in its MEDLINE database and its *Index Medicus.*

MEDLINE is the primary tool for searching medical information relating to health care administration, biomedical research, medicine, surgery, dentistry, and nursing, dating back to 1966. MEDLINE is online at the National Library of Medicine (NLM). Follow the Multimedia Literacy Web site link to the NLM Web site, where you can take MEDLINE for a free test drive, but after that you must pay a subscription fee for continued access.

In 1996, Jim Clark, founder of Silicon Graphics, Inc. (SGI) and Netscape Communications, created a new Internet business called Healtheon, with the goal of using the World Wide Web to help companies link together all of the institutions of care, including hospitals, health insurance companies, doctors' offices, medical labs, and patients' homes. Clark said: "We are providing a standard health care community interface, using the Internet as a medium, and providing services to health care providers" (*New York Times* 6/18/96: C4). Blue Cross & Blue Shield of Massachusetts became the first health care provider to sign on with Healtheon (*Wall Street Journal* 6/26/96: B6).

Just three years later in 1999, Healtheon merged with WebMD. With backing from more than 70 strategic partners, including DuPont, UnitedHealth Care, Merck-Medco, HealthSouth, Microsoft, Intel, CNN and Reader's Digest, Healtheon/WebMD launched its Web site, which is called WebMD.com. Its goal is to lead the evolution of health care and empower its participants by delivering revolutionary improvements to the way

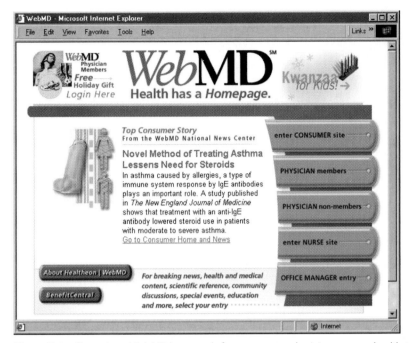

Figure 7-6   Shows how WebMD has portals for consumers, physicians, nurses, health teachers, and administrators.

physicians, consumers, and healthcare institutions communicate, share information, and conduct transactions. Figure 7-6 shows how WebMD has logons for consumers, physicians, nurses, health teachers, and administrators. To visit the site that aims to become the leading Internet-based healthcare network, follow the *Multilit* Web site link to WebMD.

The *Multilit* Web site also links to several other online medical resources, including the National Institutes of Health, the C. Everett Koop Institute, the Harvard Medical Web, HealthWeb, Healthfinder, Yahoo's Health Care Index, and the Medical Matrix, which is an extensive guide to Internet clinical medicine resources.

exercises

1. Your life or that of a loved one could depend on the extent to which your local health care provider uses multimedia in preparing its staff to handle medical situations correctly. Find out whether your local health care facility knows about the *Interactive Healthcare Directories*; ask how many of the interactive video training programs are in place and how many staff members have completed the training.

2. Is your doctor connected to the Internet? Ask about this during your next appointment. Find out how your doctor uses the network to stay current and learn about new procedures, such as by reading the *Online Journal of Clinical Trials*. Ask if your doctor subscribes to WebMD and logs on regularly. If not WebMD, what other online service does your doctor use to keep current with treatments that could one day save your life?

3. List three ways multimedia computers can help you maintain your personal health today. What other ways do you foresee technology being used to help improve your health in the future?

8

Encyclopedic Resources

After completing this chapter, you will be able to:

▧ **Take advantage of the encyclopedic resources on CD, DVD, and the Internet**

▧ **Appreciate the power of online searching as a research tool**

▧ **Understand how the Smithsonian, the Library of Congress, the Louvre, and museums and libraries all over the world have gone online**

▧ **Realize when and why the *Encyclopaedia Britannica* went online**

● A wealth of encyclopedic resources are available on multimedia CD and DVD and online via networks on the Information Superhighway. CD and DVD provide the convenience of owning the resource and being able to use it on any multimedia PC. Networks provide access to much more information, which is usually more up-to-date than the CD or DVD. By linking articles on disc to related Web sites, CD and DVD encyclopedias provide you with a way to get updated information online, thereby combining the best of both worlds.

Encyclopedias on CD and DVD

Anyone who has used a printed encyclopedia will appreciate the convenience of multimedia CD and DVD. Not only does it seem to take forever to find the information you want in a printed encyclopedia, but you also have to check all of the annual updates, which are printed in separate volumes. CD and DVD not only solve this problem by providing rapid full-text searching, but they also cost less. Thanks to the computer price wars, the entire multimedia PC costs less than the printed *Encyclopaedia Britannica.*

In 1985, Grolier became the first company to publish its printed encyclopedia in a multimedia CD version. Now the *Grolier Multimedia Encyclopedia* is available in a deluxe double-CD version containing 37,000 articles, 15,000 images, 1,200 maps, 177 videos, a 250,000-word dictionary, 150 Panorama photos, and more than 16 hours of sound. Another 22,000 articles are online on the Web. Research Starters provide students with multimedia lists that guide the beginner. The Online Knowledge Explorer provides access to 26,000 Grolier-selected Web sites and more than 500 free article updates every month. The DVD version, pictured in Figure 8-1, has 50% more video than the CD-ROM version. For more information, follow the *Multilit* Web site link to Grolier Online.

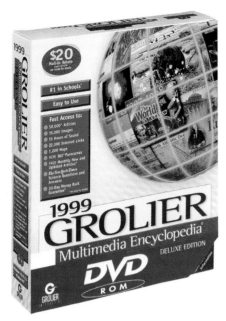

Figure 8-1 The DVD version of the *Grolier Multimedia Encyclopedia* has 50% more video than the double CD-ROM version.

Figure 8-2 Compton's interactive encyclopedia contains the full text and graphics of the 26-volume *Compton's Encyclopedia* plus multimedia enhanced sound and movies.

Compton's also publishes a multimedia version of its printed encyclopedia. Shown in Figure 8-2, *Compton's Encyclopedia Deluxe* contains the full text and graphics of the 26 printed volumes; thousands of pictures, drawings, and photos; easy-to-use research paths to retrieve information; an interactive world atlas with links to 121,000 related pictures and articles; enhanced sound and full-motion video for Windows; and the complete *Merriam-Webster OnLine Dictionary and Thesaurus.*

Compton's researched what tools would make the encyclopedia most useful and provides a rich set of options for browsing and searching. Search and Discover lets you search the encyclopedia for any topic. The timeline tool lets you access information on important people and events in U.S. and world history. An Outline view displays a general outline of history, and a Detail view offers detailed accounts of specific events. The Report Starter facilitates note-taking, outline-generating, and scholarly writing with proper bibliographic style. The Presentation Maker lets you bookmark articles, and multimedia resources then assemble them into a slide show with narration. Ask a Librarian lets you pose research questions at Compton's Web site, where you are promised a response within two working days. A planetarium lets you enter your longitude, latitude, date, and time to find out what celestial bodies will be visible then and there. For the latest information, follow the *Multilit* Web site link to Compton's.

Encarta is a multimedia encyclopedia by Microsoft. Pictured in Figure 8-3, *Encarta* includes more than 42,000 articles in 93 categories, a gallery with more than 7,000 photographic images, 170 videos and animations, 2,500 sound clips, and more than 19,000 Web links. Users access this information in several ways. The contents page lets you view all available resources at a glance, then jump to sidebars containing famous

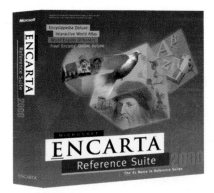

Figure 8-3 Microsoft *Encarta* has Natural Language Search, which brings up content related to questions you type in ordinary English.

Encarta Box shot reprinted with permission from Microsoft Corporation.

speeches, historical documents, and literary excerpts. There is an alphabetical index, a category browser that lets you narrow down topics by category and subcategory, a dynamic timeline that puts events in chronological order and lets you compare historical events around the world, and an atlas that lets you select places by zooming in on a map. You can use the Pinpointer search engine to search for specific words or phrases within any article, or you can use Natural Language Search, which lets you type questions in ordinary English that *Encarta* parses and links to relevant content. *Encarta* also lets you set bookmarks, take notes, and copy both textual and multimedia material into personalized files.

The DVD version of *Encarta* contains more than twice as many videos and four times as many 360-degree views than the CD-ROM version. For more information, follow the *Multilit* Web site link to *Encarta*.

It was not until 1995 that the *World Book Encyclopedia* and the *Encyclopaedia Britannica* began to retail on CD-ROM. These flagship encyclopedias delayed moving into an electronic form until market pressures required them to do so. Pictured in Figure 8-4, the *World Book* CD comes in three versions: standard, deluxe, and premier. The deluxe version adds more video and comes with wizards for creating quizzes, Web pages, reports, charts, and time lines. The premier version is speech enabled and includes *Rand McNally New Millennium World Atlas Deluxe, Merriam Webster's Reference Library,* and three *Information Please Almanacs.* The reference library contains a homework tool kit and research wizards. For more information, follow the *Multilit* Web Site link to World Book.

The *Encyclopaedia Britannica* comes on both CD and DVD. Both versions contain all 44 million words of the *Encyclopaedia Britannica* plus *Merriam-Webster's Collegiate Dictionary* and *Nations of the World,* and a comprehensive alphabetical index. There are more than 73,000 articles, 8,000 photographs, 1,200 maps, 33,000 Web links, and 1.4 million cross-referenced links. Topic Tours illustrate a variety of topics drawn from the database, such as moon exploration, African wildlife, and cathedrals of the world. The Analyst lets you compare data between nations and create

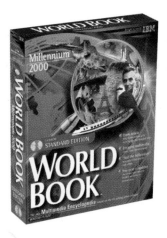
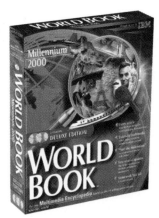
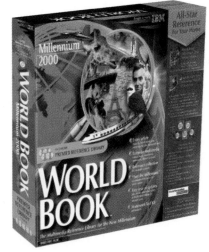

Figure 8-4 Published by World Book and IBM, the *World Book Encyclopedia* comes in three versions: standard, deluxe, and premier.

World Book graphics courtesy of World Book, Inc. World Book is a trademark of World Book, Inc. www.worldbook.com.

instant graphs and tables for use in research reports. The *Britannica* search engine lets you type questions in ordinary English, and it rank-orders the responses according to relevance. The *Britannica* can also be searched online, as described in the next section of this chapter. Comparing the electronic version to the printed encyclopedia, a librarian once told the author that schools like to have the printed encyclopedia because each student can research topics in a different volume, while only one student can use the CD at a time. The author replied: "That's fine as long as you are willing to restrict Johnny's knowledge to topics beginning with the letter *C*." For more information about the *Britannica* CD and the *Britannica* DVD, follow the *Multilit* Web site link to *Britannica*.

Online Encyclopedias

Someday the Information Superhighway may eliminate the need for CD and DVD by making available all of the necessary databases and programs in the form of a worldwide network, which will function as a public utility that will be as widespread as telephones and televisions are now. So popular is the Internet that any encyclopedia planning to stay in business is establishing an online service.

Consider the *Encyclopaedia Britannica*, for example. The obvious advantage of the online version is that you have access to all the latest information at once, as opposed to conducting separate searches through the printed volumes of the *Micropaedia*, the *Macropaedia*, and the annual *Book of the Year*.

Internet Resources

All over the world, museums have seized the opportunity to establish a presence on the World Wide Web and provide online access to their collections. This is especially advantageous for persons unable to travel to museums in person. Hundreds of museums are online, so many that you may not know where to start exploring them. Listed below are profiles of some of the more popular museum resources you will find online. The tutorial in Chapter 33 will provide you with search strategies for finding specific information on the Web. For a list of more than a thousand online museum references, use your Web browser to go to the Yahoo search engine at www.yahoo.com and type in the key word *museum*.

Library of Congress

The Library of Congress operates a Web site that lets you browse historical collections in the National Digital Library, visit Library Reading Rooms, search THOMAS (legislative information), access services of the Law Library of Congress (including the Global Legal Information Network), or locate government information. You can also search the Library of Congress online catalog. Online exhibits include Soviet government documents such as the directive from Lenin ordering the death of anti-Communist farmers; fifteenth-century manuscripts from the Vatican library; sections of the Dead Sea Scrolls along with maps and other images related to the scrolls; and an image bank that chronicles Christopher Columbus's 1492 trip to the Americas. Online access to the Library of Congress is free at www.loc.gov. Be sure to visit the online gallery of exhibitions and *American Memory: America's Story in Words, Sounds & Pictures.*

Smithsonian Institution

The Smithsonian Institution sponsors many Internet services that provide access to materials from its various museums and research arms. For example, the National Air and Space Museum, the National Museum of American Art, and the National Museum of Natural History are all online. You can search the Smithsonian databases, join discussion groups, and explore information on the Smithsonian's many museums, galleries, research centers, and offices. You can access all of these resources by following the *Multilit* Web site link to the Smithsonian. Especially relevant for readers of this book is the Virtual Smithsonian, a broadband service that uses multimedia to bring traveling exhibits such as *America's Smithsonian* to the Web.

Musée du Louvre

The world famous Musée du Louvre, the largest museum in western Europe, is online. By following the *Multilit* Web site link to the Louvre, you will find an electronic version of the *Louvre* magazine, a schedule of cultural activities, a guide to the collections, the history of the buildings, and thousands of images including the famous *Mona Lisa*. The Louvre uses QuickTime VR to provide 360-degree panoramic tours of more than 50 rooms in the museum.

exercises

1. Find out whether you can get access to CD or DVD encyclopedias at home, work, or school. What are the titles of the CD or DVD encyclopedias available to you? Where are they located?

2. Select a topic, such as the role Amelia Earhart played in aviation history. Then time how long it takes you to find information about her and construct an appropriate bibliography from a printed encyclopedia. Now try one of the CD or DVD encyclopedias mentioned in this chapter. How much time did the CD or DVD search save?

3. New technology has benefited researchers considerably. For example, the photocopy machine was invented while the author was a student. No longer did students have to write out by hand the materials we wanted to excerpt from books and magazines in the library; for 10 cents per page, we could make photocopies, thereby saving many hours of time handwriting. Today multimedia CD, DVD, and the Information Superhighway provide much more powerful tools. How do you see multimedia computers helping you conduct research?

4. There is a beautiful bitmap of the *Mona Lisa* online at the Louvre's Web site. Point your Web browser at www.louvre.fr and see if you can navigate to the *Mona Lisa:* Choose Les collections, then Peintures, then click on the *Mona Lisa* icon to see her full screen.

5. Visit the online encyclopedias listed in Figure 8-5. What services do they offer? What services are free, and which ones make you pay? Do they all offer full text online? How do the online services complement the CD or DVD version of the encyclopedias? Could any of these online services replace the disc, making the CD or DVD unnecessary?

Figure 8-5   Logos of online encyclopedias to click at the *Multilit* Web site.

Encarta logo reprinted with permission from Microsoft Corporation. Compton's Encyclopedia courtesy of The Learning Company. World Book graphics courtesy of World Book, Inc. World Book is a trademark of World Book, Inc. www.worldbook.com.

9 Application Development Packages

After completing this chapter, you will be able to:

- **Define the categories of application development packages and recognize the names of the major packages in each category**

- **Know when to use a presentation package, a hypermedia program, an animation package, or a full-fledged authoring tool**

- **Experience what the different packages are like by downloading product demonstrations and running them**

- **Define the term *Instructional Management System (IMS)* and know how to locate and compare the commercially available IMS products**

● There are six kinds of development software for creating multimedia applications: presentation packages, hypermedia programs, animators, authoring systems, Web page creation tools, and Instructional Management Systems. This chapter defines each kind, identifies the leading products, and provides links to demonstrations at the *Multilit* Web site.

As with most categorizations, there is an overlap among the classifications defined here. For example, some presentation packages provide a limited hypermedia capability; you can use hypermedia programs to create presentations; and full-fledged authoring systems can do just about anything. However, just as you would not normally use a sledgehammer to pound a finishing nail, so also do multimedia tools have their appropriate uses, according to which you will find them classified in this chapter.

Presentation Packages

The goal of **presentation packages** is to make it easy for you to produce convincing multimedia shows consisting of slides, audio clips, animations, and full-motion sequences. Industry leader PowerPoint is so-named because of how the package is intended to influence an audience.

Several graphics packages also have presentation capabilities. One of PowerPoint's competitors, for example, is Harvard Graphics, which is a high-powered graphics package with presentation capabilities.

PowerPoint

Microsoft PowerPoint is the leading presentation package with tens of millions of users worldwide. PowerPoint addresses the needs of business professionals and educators to create compelling graphics and present them effectively. Based on the slide-show metaphor shown in Figure 9-1, PowerPoint has a Slide Sorter that lets you drag slides and position them in the order you want to present them. You can drag and drop slides from one presentation to another and import charts and spreadsheet data from Microsoft Excel. An AutoContent Wizard helps you figure out what to say, and an Outliner helps organize and reorder thoughts by letting you selectively collapse and expand outline headings.

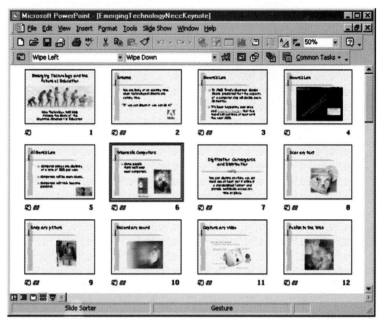

Figure 9-1 The Slide Sorter in PowerPoint shows you all your slides and lets you set up special presentation effects.

PowerPoint has an online clip library containing thousands of images, sounds, and animations to enhance your message. Styles and themes help you keep a consistent design throughout a presentation. Hyperlinking lets you interconnect words and images on your slides or link them to Web sites. PowerPoint also has a graphing feature that enables you to create your own charts, and an equation editor to create and display scientific and mathematical equations. A rehearsal feature helps you practice and learn how long a presentation will take, showing how much time you spent on each slide. You can print speaker's notes, audience handouts, and outline pages. More importantly, you can use PowerPoint to publish applications to the Web, giving your presentations a worldwide audience.

The tutorial part of this book in Chapters 18 to 42 is a step-by-step tutorial in how to design, create, and publish multimedia applications with PowerPoint.

Figure 9-2   Easy Presentations is a streamlined version
of Harvard Graphics intended for use by small businesses.

Harvard Graphics

Published by Software Publishing Corporation (SPC), Harvard Graphics competes
with PowerPoint for market share. To lower the price so more people can afford it,
SPC has created a streamlined version called Harvard Graphics Easy Presentations,
pictured in Figure 9-2. Features include the Advisor, which gives you step-by-step
guidance on design and content; Quick Tips, to save you time by suggesting handy
shortcuts; Design Tips, to keep you on track as you create a presentation; Design
Checker, to diagnose and repair stylistic or design problems; and Quick Looks, to
take the guesswork out of choosing a layout. For more information, follow the *Multilit*
Web site link to Harvard Graphics.

Hypermedia Programs

Hypermedia programs go beyond the linear slide-show metaphor used in presentation
packages to provide an infinite capability to link objects and enable users to navigate
among them. The most well-known hypermedia programs are HyperCard and
HyperStudio.

HyperCard

HyperCard uses the metaphor of a stack of cards. Each screen is regarded as a card you
can place anywhere in a stack and link to any other card. You can make simple stacks
without learning any programming. You need to learn HyperTalk (HyperCard's
programming language) to create more complex applications.

Thousands of HyperCard stacks are available, many of which are either free or available
for a small shareware fee. For more information about HyperCard, follow the *Multilit*
Web site link to HyperCard Heaven, which is the Web site for people who love HyperCard.

HyperStudio

Originally developed for the Mac, HyperStudio now runs on both Windows and Macintosh computers. It is one of the easiest and most powerful programs for use in schools. Teachers have had a lot of success with students using HyperStudio to create multimedia projects. HyperStudio makes it easy for students to snap pictures, edit QuickTime movies, and create projects combining text, sound, graphics, and video. To download a demo and get a free evaluation CD, follow the *Multilit* Web site link to HyperStudio.

Animation and Multimedia Sequencing

Animation is the use of a computer to create movement of objects on the screen. There are different levels of animation complexity. The simplest form of animation is called **frame animation**, in which the computer displays a stack of predrawn graphics that create a movie when shown in rapid succession. You can create frame animations by dropping predrawn images into the QuickTime Pro movie editor, which you will learn how to use in Chapter 35.

More sophisticated are applications that let you define graphic objects and make them move by manipulating real-time parameters that control the object. Morphing, which you studied in Chapter 5, is one such technique. The ultimate in animation is the kind of computer modeling and object rendering used to create the animated characters in the movie *Toy Story* and its sequel, *Toy Story 2*.

Multimedia sequencers are programs that let you show a series of audiovisual events, either one after the other or in synchronization with each other. These events often include animations. Discussed here are three programs that enable you to create animations and present them as part of a multimedia sequence, namely, Adobe Premiere, Autodesk 3D Studio, and Macromedia Director.

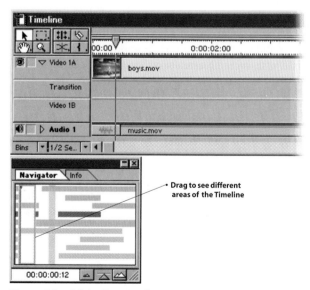

Figure 9-3 Adobe Premiere lets you create movies up to three hours long for broadcast, CD, or the Web.

Premiere

Adobe's Premiere is a video-editing tool with interactive motion path creation. Premiere has full-featured video capture and editing of 99 video and audio tracks with virtual clips to extend mixing capabilities. You can cut, copy, and paste with as many as 35 clips open simultaneously in the source monitor window. There are 75 transitions and 58 filters, plus tools for creating custom transitions and filters. Premiere displays clips "filmstrip style" and lets you zoom in for single-frame editing. Figure 9-3 shows how you can drag to see different areas of the movie's timeline. Motion control allows any still or moving image to fly along a path with twisting, zooming, rotation, and distortion effects. Premiere comes on a CD-ROM with clip media and video tutorials. To download a trial version, follow the *Multilit* Web site link to Adobe Premiere.

Figure 9-4   The Skating Baby created with with 3D Studio MAX and Character Studio by Kinetix.

3D Studio

Animation industry leader Autodesk has an animation division called Kinetix, which has the mission to bring professional animation software to your desktop. Imagine being able to create the animated skating baby shown in Figure 9-4. You can do this and more with 3D Studio VIZ from Kinetix. 3D Studio VIZ is a suite of products that is interoperable with the new generation of Autodesk design tools. A hybrid 3D character animation system called Biped combines with an interactive skinning system called Physique to provide a high-quality and cost-effective way to populate your 3D Studio worlds with characters that move with incredible realism. For full-motion demos of dancing babies and other animated characters, follow the *Multilit* Web site links to Autodesk and Kinetix. If you are a student or an educator, be sure to check out the educational discounts for Kinetix products.

Director

Macromedia's Director is the industry leader in multimedia sequencing. Witness groundbreaking applications like Brøderbund's *Living Books* and the Sting CD *All This Time,* which were created with Director. Figure 9-5 shows how Director is based on a movie production metaphor, complete with a cast (1), stage (2), and score (3). You import media into the cast window, then drag and drop cast members onto the stage. The Score controls the sequencing and can have up to 1,000 media channels.

Following the theatrical metaphor, actors can be cast and scripted to take on a life of their own as objects in an application. The Lingo object-oriented scripting language enables developers to create custom in-house code that plugs in to extend Director's built-in capabilities. Director files can play over the Internet using Shockwave, which comes as part of Macromedia's Director Shockwave Internet Studio. Director is the tool

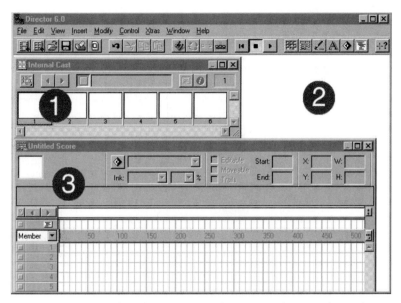

Figure 9-5 Director is based on a movie production metaphor, complete with a cast (1), stage (2), and score (3).

used to create Shockwave content, which appears on thousands of Web sites and has become one of the Internet standards for multimedia. You can also use Director to create enhanced CDs, which are audio CDs plus multimedia content that appears if you insert the CD into a computer. For the latest information on Director and Shockwave, follow the *Multilit* Web site link to Macromedia, where you can take the Internet Studio Tour and download a free trial version.

Authoring Systems

Full-fledged application development tools that let you present material, ask questions about it, evaluate user input, and branch accordingly are called **authoring systems**. In the past, before graphical user interfaces became popular, authoring was a tedious and time-consuming process, often requiring hundreds of hours of work to create one hour of completed material. Windowed environments led to the creation of graphically based authoring systems that have reduced considerably the time needed to create a sophisticated application. Two of the leaders are discussed here, namely, Authorware and ToolBook.

Authorware

Macromedia's Authorware is the leading multimedia authoring tool for interactive learning. Authorware is rooted in some pretty powerful technology. Its sophisticated judging, sequencing, and instructional management facility builds upon two decades of work by Authorware founder Mike Allen on a computer-assisted instruction (CAI) system called PLATO.

When Authorware merged with Macromind to create Macromedia in 1992, Macromind's Director (discussed earlier) became Authorware's multimedia engine, creating a blockbuster authoring system. Macromedia won publishing contracts with Paramount Publishing, Jostens Learning, HyperMedia Communications, and McGraw-Hill, and they formed strategic alliances with Apple Computer, 3DO, Bell Labs, Bell Atlantic, Brøderbund, Kaleida, and others.

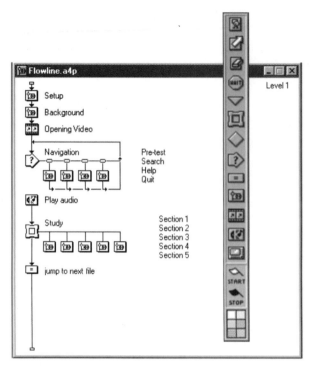

Figure 9-6 The flowline metaphor in Macromedia's Authorware.

Figure 9-6 shows how Authorware Professional uses a flowline metaphor to create logic structures from 13 design icons. The developer creates an application by selecting icons and dragging them onto the flowline. Double-clicking an icon opens it, allowing the developer to add content. As icons accumulate on the screen, the developer can click the Map icon to group related icons together. Thus, the developer can view the application from a top-down approach, maintaining perspective on how the various program modules interrelate.

Applications created with Authorware can be played over the Web via the Authorware Web Player, as illustrated in Figure 9-7. The application shown below was created by TraCorp, Inc., a multimedia training company in Phoenix, Arizona. To see examples of Authorware in action, and to download a free trial version, follow the *Multilit* Web site links to Macromedia Authorware.

Toolbook

ToolBook is published by click2learn. True to its name, ToolBook is based on a book metaphor. You develop applications by creating books full of pages, which can contain text, graphics, and buttons that enable user interaction. Toolbook has a scripting language called OpenScript in which you program interactive and navigational commands that define what the buttons do. You can also attach scripts to hot words in text fields. Particularly useful is a script recorder that will automatically create a script for actions you perform on the screen, such as navigating to a page in a book or creating an animation by moving an object around the screen. ToolBook comes with hundreds of prescripted multimedia objects that you can copy and paste into your application.

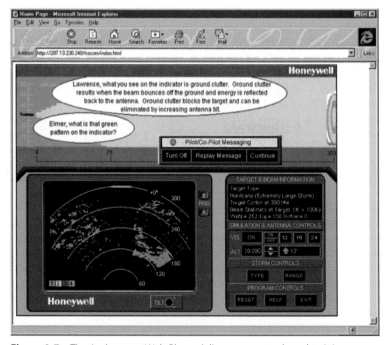

Figure 9-7 The Authorware Web Player delivers computer-based training over the Web with the Airborn Radar Management developed by TraCorp, Inc.

The ToolBook II Assistant makes it possible to deliver interactive learning programs over the Web. The ToolBook II Assistant uses a drag-and-drop interface to create course content consisting of text, graphics, audio, and video; then you publish the lesson using a wizard. ToolBook II Assistant applications use Dynamic HTML to synchronize the appearance of text and graphics over the Web.

To sample the kind of application you can create with ToolBook, follow the *Multilit* Web site link to click2learn, where you can survey the online learning showcase and request a trial version of ToolBook on CD. While there, check out click2learn.publisher, which lets you create and publish courses that click2learn sells, paying you 30% of the income in royalties.

Web Page Creation Tools

The Web is fast becoming the preferred medium for publishing multimedia applications. The leading packages for creating Web pages are Netscape Composer and Microsoft FrontPage.

Netscape Composer

Netscape Composer is the name of the WYSIWYG Web page editor that comes as part of the suite of tools in Netscape Communicator. When you create a Web page with Netscape Composer, you work on a screen that makes what you create appear just as it will when viewed in the Netscape Web browser. Hence the term *What-You-See-Is-What-You-Get (WYSIWYG)*. You can download Netscape Communicator free of charge by following the *Multilit* Web site link to Netscape. The textbook *Internet Literacy* contains a detailed tutorial on creating Web pages with Netscape Composer. Follow the *Multilit* Web site link to *Internet Literacy* for a detailed look at the contents of this Web page creation tutorial.

Microsoft FrontPage and FrontPage Express

Microsoft FrontPage is a fully featured Web site creation and management tool that is part of Microsoft Office, and Microsoft FrontPage Express is a scaled-down yet still highly useful version that comes for free with Microsoft Internet Explorer. You can download the latest version of Microsoft Internet Explorer for free by following the *Multilit* Web site link. One of the nice features you get in the Microsoft Office version of FrontPage is an HTML editor that lets you tweak the HTML codes by hand, just in case you want to use a feature that is not yet handled by the WYSIWYG tool. To learn more, follow the *Multilit* Web site link to Microsoft FrontPage. The textbook *Internet Literacy* contains a detailed tutorial on creating Web pages with Microsoft FrontPage Express. Follow the *Multilit* Web site link to *Internet Literacy* for a detailed look at the contents of this Web page creation tutorial.

Microsoft Word

Microsoft Word, which is the word-processing component of Microsoft Office, has a powerful Web page creation feature built in. To create a Web page version of a term paper, for example, you just open the term paper, then pull down the File menu and choose the option to Save as Web Page. If your term paper uses heading styles, the Web page maker creates a frame containing an outline of topics that the user can click to go to different places in your paper. You get all this capability without needing to know any HTML. For more information, follow the *Multilit* Web site link to Microsoft Word.

Microsoft PowerPoint

As you learned previously in this chapter, Microsoft's presentation software is called PowerPoint. PowerPoint has a powerful Web page creation feature built in. In Chapter 40, you will complete a step-by-step tutorial that will teach you how to create Web pages with PowerPoint. As in Web pages created with Microsoft Word, you get a frame containing an outline of your presentation on which the user can click a topic to bring up the corresponding slide.

Bringing Web Pages to Life

In today's media-centric world, you may not be content with a static Web page. Discussed here are four ways to bring Web pages to life: Animated GIFs, JavaScript, ActiveX, and Dynamic HTML.

ANIMATED GIFS

The simplest way to put motion on a Web page is to create an animated GIF, which is a special kind of GIF file containing multiple images that are shown in a sequence at specific times and locations on the screen. A looping option causes the Web browser to keep showing the frames continually, so the user sees an animation.

A shareware application that you can use to create animated GIFs is called the GIF Construction Set. To download it, click the GIF Construction Set icon at the *Multilit* Web site. For a tutorial on creating animated GIFs, follow the *Multilit* Web site links to the GIF Construction Set. You can also create animated GIFs with Microsoft GIF Animator, which you can download for free by following the links at the *Multilit* Web site.

JAVASCRIPT

True to its name, JavaScript is a scripting language that lets little programs called scripts be included on a Web page. Both Netscape and Microsoft support JavaScript. There are variations in how JavaScript runs on different platforms, however, so you need to test any scripts you create with any browsers that will be used to execute them. For more information about the origins and applications of JavaScript, follow the *Multilit* Web site to JavaScript Developer Central. There you will find sample code for creating rollovers, graphs, menus, dialog boxes, calendar popups, and layering effects. Figure 9-8 shows one of the rollover effects you can create with JavaScript. For even more JavaScript resources, go to www.cnet.com and search for JavaScript.

Figure 9-8   A rollover effect created with JavaScript at the AOL@School Web site. Notice how the photo changes as the user mouses over the menu choices.

Copyright © 2000 America Online, Inc. Used with permission.

ACTIVEX

ActiveX was begun by Microsoft as a way to create and distribute information over the Internet using existing software applications and data. ActiveX involves three concepts: controls, scripts, and documents. ActiveX controls enable a wide variety of applications and content to be embedded in HTML documents. Utilizing Microsoft's object linking and embedding technology, ActiveX controls enable you to incorporate any supported data type directly into the window of an ActiveX enabled Web browser such as the Microsoft Internet Explorer. More than a thousand ActiveX controls are available, from multimedia sound and video players to spreadsheets, charts, graphs, calculators, and paint programs. The Microsoft Internet Explorer itself is an ActiveX control that can be embedded inside other applications. For more information, follow the *Multilit* Web site link to ActiveX. To see dozens of controls that you can download and use, follow the link to the CNET ActiveX Control Library.

DYNAMIC HTML

Dynamic HTML makes Web pages dynamic by exposing all page elements as objects. These objects can be manipulated by changing their attributes or applying methods to them at any time. These manipulations can also be triggered by keyboard and mouse events on all page elements. The definition of the objects and how they can be manipulated is called the Document Object Model (DOM). The DOM defines, for example, how text or graphics can be added, deleted, or modified on the fly. Text can change color or size when a user mouses over it. Positioning coordinates can be updated at any time to create animated effects, without reloading the page. To learn more about Dynamic HTML, follow the *Multilit* Web site links to Dynamic HTML Central and the Dynamic HTML Web Workshop.

Instructional Management Systems

One of the hottest new kinds of Web-based software is the Instructional Management System (IMS). An IMS is an educational environment that can present instructional content, make assignments to students, administer tests, help instructors grade assignments, record student progress, provide feedback to students, and export grades and other kinds of records. In short, an IMS provides the educational infrastructure for organizing and delivering applications created by the other kinds of multimedia software discussed in this chapter.

There are two repositories of information about Instructional Management Systems. At Vanderbilt University, the Web of Asynchronous Learning Networks (ALN) has a product catalog in which all IMS vendors have been invited to list their products. To see this catalog, follow the *Multilit* Web site link to ALN, then choose Product Catalog— Product Listings. In Ontario, Canada, a consortium of universities has created a Web site called the NODE, which has a database called technologies for learning (tfl). To search this database, follow the *Multilit* Web site link to the NODE, then choose tfl database. Also linked to the *Multilit* Web site is Landonline, a Web site designed to help educators evaluate and select online delivery software. At Landonline, you can make side-by-side comparisons of IMS systems based on an analysis conducted by Professor Bruce Landon, Professor of Psychology at Douglas College.

One of the IMSs you will find talked about in these catalogs is Serf®, which was developed by the author of this book. As you might expect, there is a Serf-based multimedia literacy course that uses this book as the textbook, and there is also a Serf-based Internet literacy course that uses the author's *Internet Literacy* textbook. For more information about taking and developing courses with Serf, follow the *Multilit* Web site link to Serf.

exercises

1. What presentation packages does your school or business own? What were the primary reasons for selecting them over competing brands? Do you think this was a good decision? Why or why not?

2. Does your school or business own an authoring system? If so, which one? Why was it selected? Do you think this was a good decision? Why or why not?

3. What software would you personally use to create a presentation? Why do you prefer it over other brands? What improvements would you like to see the vendor make?

4. Given the features of the presentation packages, hypermedia programs, animators, and authoring systems presented in this chapter, what is your overall impression of the state of the art of multimedia application development? What additional capabilities would you like these tools to have?

5. What are the implications of the World Wide Web for multimedia publishing? How will active products like JavaScript, ActiveX, and Dynamic HTML influence the creation and distribution of multimedia titles? Will the online distribution of multimedia content over the Web diminish the popularity of CD and DVD as the preferred publishing medium? What are the potential drawbacks and pitfalls of Web-based multimedia publishing?

6. Follow the *Multilit* Web site link to Landonline. Fill out the form to compare two of the leading IMS packages you find listed there. What two packages did you choose, and how do they compare? Do you agree with the comparison? Based on this analysis, which one would you recommend, and why?

Part Three
Selecting Multimedia Hardware

Buying a multimedia computer may be the most complicated shopping you ever do. Four factors make it difficult. First, because there is no industrywide standard for multimedia, each vendor creates its own brand and produces multimedia applications that work with only its brand. Potential buyers hesitate because they know that getting Brand X will prevent them from running applications made for Brand Y. Second, there are so many options you can add on to a multimedia computer that even once you decide which brand to buy, you might still find it confusing when choosing multimedia peripherals. Third, it is hard to get a list of all the options that are available because vendors are interested in showing only those they sell. Finally, once you buy your computer and select the options you want, installing and getting them to work can be complicated and time-consuming.

The next four chapters in this book will help you overcome these dilemmas. The good news is that once you finally do get your multimedia computer up and running, you should not have many (hopefully, not any) problems. In other words, most of the difficulty will happen right at the beginning, and if you can persevere through the startup problems, your time and effort will be repaid by the many benefits you will reap from your multimedia computing.

CHAPTER 10

Competing Multimedia Standards

After completing this chapter, you will be able to:

▨ **Understand the competing standards of multimedia and comprehend what is meant by the phrase *multi multimedia***

▨ **Realize how lack of standardization retards the progress of multimedia development**

▨ **Consider the level at which standardization would be appropriate**

▨ **Know which multimedia formats will have the most longevity**

▨ **Understand the basic architecture of the Microsoft MCI (Media Control Interface)**

▨ **Gauge the market penetration of Apple's QuickTime**

▨ **Know how Jini extends the concept of Sun's Java to everyday appliances**

▨ **Consider the expanding role of Sony's PlayStation as a platform for educational multimedia**

● The multimedia computer industry is beset by an unfortunate lack of standardization. Instead of uniting the nation's best minds toward creating a compatible cross-platform system for multimedia, the computer industry is hard at work creating multiple standards and competing products. If this were happening accidentally, one might be more willing to tolerate the situation. Instead, vendors deliberately create disparity to differentiate their products from the competition and to make past purchases obsolete so customers will buy more hardware. In the area of graphics alone, there are more than 30 so-called standards for storing pictures in computer files. When an industry provides 30 different ways of doing something, there is no standard.

Computer industry leaders fail to recognize how self-defeating this lack of standardization is. They should learn a lesson from the musicians. During the early 1980s, the National Association of Music Merchants and the Audio Engineering Society began to discuss how a lack of standards was retarding the market for music synthesizers. Consumers were afraid to buy a keyboard because there was no guarantee that it would be compatible with later models in the same product line, much less with synthesizers made by other vendors. In 1983, the Musical Instrument Digital Interface (MIDI) standard was released, and all of the music merchants endorsed it. Consumers were no longer afraid of obsolescence, and music synthesizer sales mushroomed. Vendors made more money not so much because their market share increased, but because the entire market grew exponentially as a result of standardization.

Multi Multimedia

Instead of having one multimedia standard, consumers are faced with a complicated array of competing software and hardware platforms that the author (Hofstetter 1993) describes as "multi multimedia." When you create an application, you must be careful to store your objects in formats that will have the most longevity and compatibility. Otherwise the time and effort you spend will have to be reinvested when the so-called standards change.

Microsoft's MCI

Microsoft's MCI provides Windows users with a strategic approach to coping with this lack of standardization. *MCI* stands for Media Control Interface. The purpose of the MCI is to provide a device-independent means of developing multimedia software. The idea is that vendors who make multimedia hardware supply an MCI translation table for each device. Instead of hard-coding applications to specific devices, developers use MCI commands that get converted automatically by the translation table into the specific instructions needed to control the device. The MCI commands consist of generic multimedia instructions such as PLAY, RECORD, PAUSE, SEEK, SAVE, and STOP.

If you have a Windows PC, you can find out what MCI devices you have by clicking your Windows Start button, going to Settings—Control Panel, selecting Multimedia, and double-clicking Media Control Devices, as illustrated in Figure 10-1. To find out more about Microsoft's multimedia directions, follow the *Multilit* Web site links to Microsoft Windows Media.

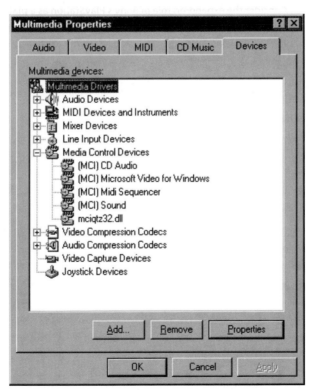

Figure 10-1 Microsoft MCI Drivers provide standardized control of CD Audio, Video for Windows, MIDI, and waveform sound devices.

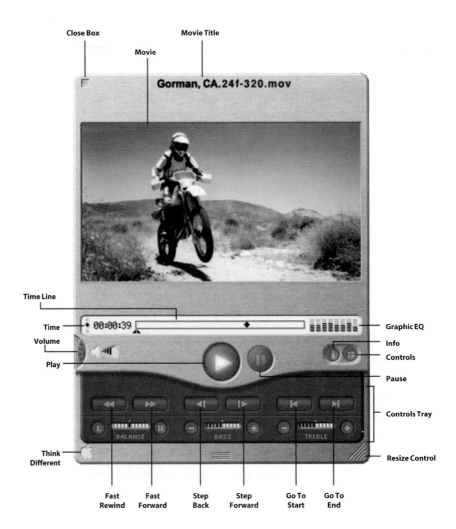

Figure 10-2   The Apple QuickTime Player.

Apple's QuickTime

Apple's QuickTime is to the Macintosh what the MCI is to Windows. Like the MCI, QuickTime supports digital audio, MIDI, compact disc, and digital video. QuickTime is emerging as a popular cross-platform standard for multimedia. Figure 10-2 shows the QuickTime Player, which runs on both Windows and Macintosh computers. In Chapter 35, you will learn how to edit movies with QuickTime Pro, which also runs on both Windows and Macintosh computers. When this book went to press, Apple claimed that 57% of Web sites that use video use QuickTime. For the latest information and to download the QuickTime Player for free, follow the *Multilit* Web site link to QuickTime.

Sun's Java and Jini

The goal of Sun's Java is to solve the problem of multi multimedia by creating a machine-independent technology for using the same application from any kind of machine—a Windows PC, a Macintosh computer, a network computer, a TV set-top box, a handheld computer, or an Internet phone. Through a connection technology called Jini, Sun is extending the Java concept to household appliances. Imagine a stove

Figure 10-3 Some of the devices that Sun plans to connect with its Jini technology.

that can send you an e-mail message warning you that someone forgot to turn it off when you left for vacation. Figure 10-3 shows some of the other devices that Sun plans to connect with its Jini technology.

Both of the major browsers—Netscape Navigator and Microsoft Internet Explorer—come with Java interpreters built in. Due to arguments and competition between Sun and Microsoft, however, you must double-check to make sure that Java applets you create for one platform will run on the other. For more information about Java, follow the *Multilit* Web site link to the Java technology home page. To learn more about Jini, follow the link to Jini Connection Technology.

Sony's PlayStation

Normally you wouldn't think of a game machine like the Sony PlayStation® game console in Figure 10-4 as a platform for more general-purpose kinds of multimedia. Lightspan, Inc. Software changed that with a product called Lightspan Achieve Now, which was created in conjunction with Sony. Lightspan Achieve Now is a comprehensive interactive software curriculum that conforms to state and national education standards. Developed by and for educators for use in elementary and middle schools. Lightspan Achieve Now is cleverly designed to run on a Windows PC or to go home on a Sony PlayStation® game console. Students take the PlayStation CDs home like any workbook or textbook. After a lesson in counting, for example, teachers hand out a CD that reinforces how to count by twos. Children solve math problems in an imaginary land known as Googol®, and they learn to read with Mars Moose®, pictured in Figure 10-5. Hollywood artists used Autodesk's 3D Studio animation software to create the characters and bring them to life. To get more information and try out demos of LightSpan, Inc. adventures, follow the *Multilit* Web site link to Lightspan Achieve Now.

Figure 10-4 The Sony PlayStation® game console, for which Lightspan, Inc. developed a series of curriculum-based, educational CDs called Lightspan Achieve Now.

Figure 10-5 Mars Moose® is a 3-D animated character with whom children learn to read in an emergent literacy program from Lightspan, Inc.

Coping with Multi Multimedia

Due to the competitive nature of our capitalistic society, in which vendors feel the need to differentiate products so the consumer will see the difference and buy their brands, we need to accept the fact that we are going to have to live with multi multimedia for the foreseeable future. The best strategy for coping with multi multimedia is to keep abreast of emerging multimedia standards and purchase the products that follow those standards. To locate the standards, follow the *Multilit* Web site links to the World Wide Web Consortium (W3C), the Internet Engineering Task Force (IETF), the Internet Society (ISOC), and the International Organization for Standardization (ISO), which has a special Information Technology Task Force (ITTF). All of these organizations are devoted to the creation of the standards that are needed to evolve and globalize the Internet and its underlying multimedia technologies and applications.

exercises

1. Visit your local computer store and find out what multimedia brands it carries. Does it sell Microsoft MCI-based multimedia PCs? Does it carry Apple QuickTime-based Macintoshes? Sony PlayStations? What other brands does it have? Ask which brand sells best in your community and why.

2. To standardize everything about multimedia today would be a mistake. The field is still too young for that, and there must be room for experimentation. On the other hand, certain objects could be standardized now. For example, there are more than 30 "standard" ways of storing bitmaps. The time and effort spent converting images from one format to another could be saved by an industrywide standard for storing bitmaps. Are there other multimedia objects that should be standardized now? List them and state why.

3. Explain how Microsoft's MCI helps developers cope with the multi multimedia dilemma.

4. SMIL is an emerging standard for delivering multimedia sequences of synchronized text, images, sound, and video over the Web. Go to the World Wide Web Consortium site at w3c.org and follow the links to SMIL. What does SMIL stand for? What is the current status of the SMIL standard? Have any major vendors come out with products based on SMIL? Name the product that you consider to be the most significant to support SMIL.

11

Multimedia Computer Components

After completing this chapter, you will be able to:

▓ **Recognize the components of a multimedia computer**

▓ **Understand the shopping terminology needed to make intelligent choices when purchasing a multimedia computer**

▓ **Know the difference between a mouse and a trackball, 8-bit and 16-bit audio, analog and digital video, CD-ROM and DVD, modems and network cards, flatbed and handheld scanners, and inkjet and laser printers**

▓ **Understand the data communication terminology needed to procure equipment for connecting your multimedia computer to the Internet**

● There are five categories of components in a multimedia computer: the system unit, multimedia accessories, read/write storage, auxiliary input devices, and communication options. Understanding these components will enable you to follow the multimedia computer checklists provided in Chapter 12.

System Unit

At the heart of every computer is the central processor, which is the "brain" in which computations are performed. The system unit includes the central processor and the electronics required to support it. System units normally ship with a color monitor and a pointing device.

Central Processor

The **central processor** has a numerical name that indicates the basic type and speed of the processor. Processors from Intel, which is the largest manufacturer, have the numbers 286, 386, 486, or Pentium, which would have been called 586 had the patent office not ruled that the number could not be trademarked. Instead of calling the next generation of processors the P6 as originally planned, Intel decided to call it the Pentium Pro, because of the mass market popularity of the name *Pentium*. For the same reason, Intel named the next generation Pentium III. Figure 1-5 in Chapter 1 compares the speed of the most popular Intel central processors. For comparison ratings of the most recent Intel processors, follow the *Multilit* Web site link to the Intel iCOMP benchmark. For comparison ratings of Macintosh processors, follow the link to Macintosh benchmarks.

RAM

RAM stands for random access memory; it is the main memory at the heart of a computer in which multimedia programs execute. RAM is measured in megabytes (MB). *Mega* means million, and *byte* is the unit of measure for computer memory. A byte can hold a single character, and a megabyte can hold a million characters. **Meg** is another abbreviation for megabyte.

Because multimedia objects are big, you need a large amount of RAM to make a multimedia computer work well: 32 MB is the minimum required, but many applications need 48 MB to run well. Large programs like Windows NT require 64 MB to run well. In general, the more RAM you have, the better your multimedia applications will perform.

Color Display

Color displays are also referred to as color monitors. Measured along the diagonal, they come in screen sizes ranging from 8 to 50 inches or more. The most typical sizes range from 12 to 19 inches. Larger monitors are very expensive and normally are purchased for classrooms or boardrooms, where many people need to be able to see the display.

Independent of the number of inches is the number of **pixels** the computer can display on the monitor. The minimum number for multimedia is 640 pixels across by 480 pixels down the screen. On computer spec sheets, this is expressed as 640 × 480 (the number across is always printed first, followed by the number down). Other common pixel grids are 800 × 600, 1024 × 768, 1280 × 1024, and 1600 × 1200. Many Webmasters are beginning to design their pages for 800 × 600 screens instead of the former 640 × 480 minimum. Any computer you purchase today, therefore, should be able to display at least 800 × 600 pixels.

Equally important is the number of colors the system unit can display. Older computers with VGA (video graphics array) had 4-bit color arrays that could display only 16 colors. Computers with SVGA (super VGA) had 8-bit arrays that could display 256 colors. Any computer you purchase today should be able to display at least 16-bit color, which can display 65,536 colors. Most computers being sold today have 24-bit color, which can display more than 16 million colors.

Pointing Device

The **mouse** is the most common pointing device on multimedia computers today. In the Windows world, mice have two or three buttons; for most applications, a two-button mouse works fine. On the Macintosh, the mouse has one button. Alternatives to mice include mouse pens, which let you write with a stylus instead of dragging a mouse; trackballs, which let you spin a ball instead; and the innovative TrackPoint, which is a tiny joystick mounted in the center of the keyboard on an IBM ThinkPad notebook computer. As shown in Figures 11-1 and 11-2, you work the TrackPoint with the tip of your index finger, eliminating the need for a surface on which to run a mouse.

Expansion Ports and Slots

When you purchase a multimedia computer, you should make sure it has expandability so you can add multimedia accessories later on. Four technologies are used for adding accessories on to a computer: USB, SCSI, FireWire, and expansion slots.

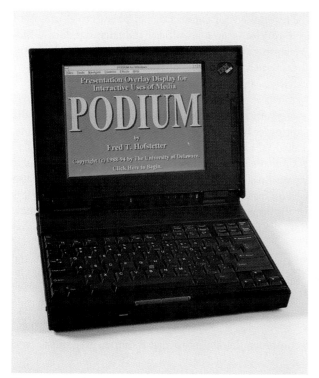

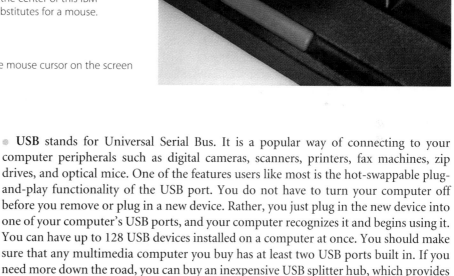

Figure 11-1   The tiny joystick in the center of this IBM ThinkPad's computer keyboard substitutes for a mouse.

Figure 11-2   A user positions the mouse cursor on the screen with the IBM TrackPoint device.

- **USB** stands for Universal Serial Bus. It is a popular way of connecting to your computer peripherals such as digital cameras, scanners, printers, fax machines, zip drives, and optical mice. One of the features users like most is the hot-swappable plug-and-play functionality of the USB port. You do not have to turn your computer off before you remove or plug in a new device. Rather, you just plug in the new device into one of your computer's USB ports, and your computer recognizes it and begins using it. You can have up to 128 USB devices installed on a computer at once. You should make sure that any multimedia computer you buy has at least two USB ports built in. If you need more down the road, you can buy an inexpensive USB splitter hub, which provides additional USB ports.

- **SCSI** stands for Small Computer System Interface. It lets you daisychain up to eight mass storage devices. Although many CD-ROM drives use SCSI, most computers do not come with an external SCSI connector to which you can attach additional SCSI devices. If your computer does not come with a SCSI connector and you need to connect a SCSI device, you will want to devote an expansion slot to installing a SCSI board. A wide range of SCSI devices are available, including internal and external hard drives, CD-ROM drives, and read/write optical drives. One of the most popular SCSI devices is the Iomega Jaz disk drive discussed in the section on multimedia read/write storage.

PCI Slots   ISA Slots

Figure 11-3   On this multi-media PC motherboard, ISA slots are outlined in blue, and PCI slots are bordered by red.

● **FireWire** is a high-speed serial technology for connecting peripherals to a computer. Originally developed by Apple, FireWire is now an official industry standard (IEEE 1394). If you are purchasing a Macintosh, make sure it has FireWire ports to which you can connect multimedia peripherals such as DV (digital video) camcorders and other high-speed devices like hard disk drives and printers.

● **Expansion slots** hold circuit cards you can plug in to add functionality to a multimedia PC. To be fully expandable, a computer needs to have at least one or two empty slots. Portable computers have slots called PC card slots. Desktop computers have slots called PCI, which stands for *Peripheral Component Interconnect.* Make sure your new computer has at least one or two empty expansion slots of each type. Desktop computers may also contain an older type of slot based on the Industry Standard Architecture (ISA), but ISA slots are slowly being replaced by the faster PCI slots, so do not be concerned if your new computer does not have ISA slots. Figure 11-3 shows a computer's motherboard that has both PCI and ISA slots.

Multimedia Accessories

Multimedia accessories give a computer the ability to make sound, play music, and record movies.

CD-ROM

By definition, multimedia computers have either a CD-ROM drive or a DVD drive that can play CD-ROMs as well as DVDs. Both are evolving technologies that keep improving. The original CD-ROM drives read computer data at a speed of 150 KB per second. Second-generation drives were twice as fast, reading data at 300 KB per second. Called double-speed or 2× speed drives, they could also read multisession CDs, which are discs that have had additional data written onto them in subsequent recording sessions. Quadruple-speed drives, also called 4× drives, transfer data at 600 KB per second. Even faster drives are available, with speeds ranging from 17× (2550 KB per second) to 40× (6000 KB per second). If you buy a computer with a CD-ROM drive, make sure it has at least a quadruple-speed drive.

DVD

A new CD-ROM format called DVD (digital versatile disc) is fast replacing CD-ROM in popularity. The DVD can hold seven times more than a conventional CD—4.7 GB (gigabytes) per layer, as compared to 680 MB for CD. Dual-layer DVDs can hold 8.5 GB on a single side, with 17 GB on a double-sided, dual-layer disc. DVD has the same diameter (120mm) and thickness (1.2mm) as a compact disc. Backward compatibility enables DVD drives to play CD-ROMs and audio CDs. For more information, including beautiful diagrams that show how DVDs are produced, follow the *Multilit* Web site link to the Sony DVD site.

Digital Audio

By definition, multimedia computers have the ability to record and play back waveform digital audio files. If your system does not have waveform audio, it is not a multimedia computer.

Figure 11-4   DeskTop Theatre 5.1 DTT 2500 Digital from Cambridge SoundWorks.

The original multimedia PC standard called for 8-bit sound, which produces a dynamic range of 50dB (decibels). Multimedia computers now also have 16-bit sound, which increases the dynamic range to 98dB. The greater the dynamic range, the more faithful the sound reproduction. For more information about the latest audio features, follow the *Multilit* Web site link to Creative Labs, the industry leader in multimedia sound.

Audio Speakers

You will need a pair of audio speakers to listen to the sound produced by your multimedia PC. If you get powered speakers with amplifiers built in, you will not need a separate amplifier. Otherwise, you will need an amplifier as well.

Sound has become so essential to multimedia that most computers come with speakers. Surround sound is an option on higher-end multimedia computers. You'll appreciate surround sound especially if you have a DVD drive, because many movies on DVD have Dolby Digital 5.1 surround sound. As illustrated in Figure 11-4, the nomenclature 5.1 refers to five surround speakers (left-front, center-front, right-front, left-rear, and right-rear) plus one subwoofer that produces low bass sounds. For more information about computer speakers, follow the *Multilit* Web site links to Boston Acoustics and Cambridge SoundWorks.

Graphics Accelerator

A **graphics accelerator** is a computer chip that helps your PC process the specialized calculations that 3D imaging requires. Graphics accelerators have memory called video RAM, which is measured in megabytes. In general, the more video RAM the graphics accelerator has, the faster it will work, and the more it will cost. If you plan to play the latest interactive games or use applications that do 3-D rendering, you will need a graphics accelerator. Some computers have the graphics accelerator built in on the motherboard, and others use graphics accelerator cards. If you are buying a Windows-based PC and you plan to add a graphics accelerator, make sure your computer has an Accelerated Graphics Port (AGP) slot. Newer motherboards have an AGP slot as well as the normal PCI peripheral slots.

Video Overlay

Video overlay allows a computer to display common video sources including video cameras, VCRs, and videodiscs while simultaneously displaying computer graphics. The overlay circuitry makes one of the colors in the computer graphics transparent; when that color appears on the screen with the video overlay driver activated, the video source shows through.

Some computers come with video overlay built in. To add it to a computer that does not already have it, you need to purchase a video overlay card. You must exercise caution when purchasing such a card. There are a lot of competing brands, and they do not all provide the features you may need. You should consider the following two features when making a purchase.

- **TV Tuner.** Some cards have a TV tuner on board. If you know in advance that you want a TV tuner in your computer, get it on your video overlay card to save the slot you will need when you add the tuner later.

- **Full Motion Video Capture.** Overlay cards do not necessarily enable you to record full-motion video; if you want to make video recordings, you need an overlay card that can capture moving video.

Figure 11-5 shows how the All-In-Wonder board from ATI Technologies can do all these things. For more information, follow the *Multilit* Web site link to ATI All-In-Wonder. Also linked to the *Multilit* site is the Hauppage WinTV overlay board.

Figure 11-5   The All-In-Wonder card surrounded by an artist's depiction of the things it can do.

TV Tuner

TV tuner cards give a multimedia computer the ability to tune in to both broadcast and cable television channels. Some have video overlay capability on board, whereas others require that you have a video overlay card to which you can connect the video output of your tuner card. If you know in advance that you will want a TV tuner, purchase an overlay card that has a TV tuner built in.

MIDI

MIDI stands for Musical Instrument Digital Interface. Because MIDI is a required part of the multimedia PC specification, you do not have a multimedia computer if you do not have MIDI. Make sure that any new computer you buy has wavetable synthesis built in to its MIDI circuitry. Wavetable synthesis enables MIDI to play digitally sampled instrument sounds that are stored in the wavetable. This makes the instrumental sounds much more realistic than those produced by older multimedia PCs that did not have the wavetable.

MPEG

MPEG is emerging as the new digital video standard for the United States and most of the world. MPEG stands for *Motion Picture Experts Group,* the name of the ISO standards committee that created it. By definition, a multimedia computer must be able to play MPEG, or it is not a multimedia PC. Four versions of MPEG have been worked on:

- **MPEG-1** is the noninterlaced version designed for playback from CD-ROMs.

- **MPEG-2** is the interlaced version intended for the all-digital transmission of broadcast quality TV. Adopted by the United States Grand Alliance HDTV specification, the European Digital Video Broadcasting Group, and the Digital Versatile Disc (DVD-ROM) consortium, MPEG-2 does surround sound. RCA's DirecTV service uses MPEG-2.

- **MPEG-3** was to be the HDTV version of MPEG, but then it was discovered that the MPEG-2 syntax could fulfill that need by simply scaling the bit rate, obviating the third phase.

- **MPEG-4** is a low-bandwidth version of MPEG that is being invented for transmitting movies over mobile and wireless communications networks and over the Internet.

For more information, follow the links to MPEG at the *Multilit* Web site.

Multimedia Read/Write Storage

Multimedia requires a lot of storage if you are into digital audio and video. The storage alternatives are discussed here.

Hard Disk Drive

When you purchase a multimedia computer, you should get as much hard disk built into it as you can afford. No matter how much capacity you get, you will eventually run out as your library of multimedia software grows. Hard disk size is measured either in megabytes or gigabytes. A *megabyte* is a million bytes, and a *gigabyte* is a billion bytes. Anyone serious about multimedia should have at least 4 gigs of hard disk space.

Iomega Zip Disk and Jaz Disk

Iomega's Zip and Jaz disk drives are attractive storage mediums for multimedia developers because the disks are removable. The Zip disk drive comes in a USB version that makes it very easy to move from one computer to another. Zip disks come in two densities: 100 MB (which holds the equivalent of 70 diskettes) and 250 MB (equivalent to 175 diskettes). Iomega also manufactures a Jaz drive that is faster and holds a lot more data. Jaz disks come in 1GB (1,070 MB) and 2 GB (2,140 MB) formatted capacity. The Jaz drive is a SCSI device. For the latest information, follow the *Multilit* Web site link to Iomega.

Recordable CD-ROM

Recordable CD-ROM is called **CD-R**; the *R* stands for recordable, indicating that you can record on the CD. Each CD-R disc can store about 650 MB. CD-R drives have fallen in price and are a very cost-effective way of backing up your data. In quantities of 50 or more, blank CD-R discs cost less than a dollar each.

Recordable DVD

Recordable DVD is called **DVD-R**. The DVD-R recorders and discs cost more than CD-R, but they also hold more data. DVD-R is an emerging technology. The first DVD-R discs can hold up to 3.95 gigabytes (3.95 billion bytes) of information on each side. Since the DVD format supports two-sided media, a total of 7.9 GB can be stored on a two-sided DVD-R disc. That is 12 times as much data as fits on a CD-R disc. Eventually, perhaps by the time you read this, DVD-R will be able to hold even more. To find out, follow the *Multilit* Web site link to DVD-R.

Communication Options

The datacommunication protocol used on the Internet is called **TCP/IP**, which stands for Transmission Control Protocol/Internet Protocol. Both the Windows and the Macintosh operating systems have support for TCP/IP built in. To connect your computer to the Internet via TCI/IP, you need either a modem or a network card. Most computers come with either a modem or a network card built in. When you purchase a new computer, you should think about whether you are going to connect it to the Internet via modem or network card, and make sure your new computer has what you need to get connected.

Telephone Modems

The most common means of connecting to the Internet from home is via plain old telephone service, also known as POTS. In order to communicate with the Internet over an ordinary telephone line, your computer must have a modem. Modems are so popular that most computers being sold today come with modems built in. Older models require the addition of external modems that connect to your computer's serial port, or modem cards that plug into one of your computer's expansion slots. Figure 11-6 illustrates how modems work by modulating and demodulating the computer's transmission; hence the term, *modem*.

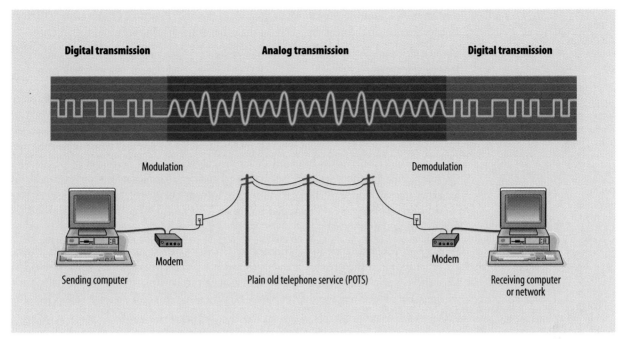

Figure 11-6   How modems work.

Modems have gotten steadily faster as computer technology has advanced. Modem speed is important because it determines how long you have to wait for information to arrive. Modem speed is often expressed in units known as bps, which stands for bits per second, or Kbps, which stands for a thousand bits per second. Common speeds are 14,400 bps (14.4 Kbps), 28,800 bps (28.8 Kbps), 33,600 bps (33.6 Kbps), and 56,000 bps (56 Kbps). Information traveling at 14,400 bps, for example, takes twice as long to arrive as it would at 28,800 bps.

ISDN

ISDN stands for Integrated Services Digital Network. It is the digital telephone system that is being installed by regional Bell companies in most of the United States. The basic rate service ranges in cost from $20 to $80 per month and offers a transmission speed of 144 Kbps, made up of two 64 Kbps data channels and one 16 Kbps control channel. In order to use ISDN to connect to the Internet, you will need to contact both your local telephone company and your Internet Service Provider, to find out whether ISDN is available in your area, and to make sure your ISP supports it.

DSL Modems

As datacommunications technology continues to advance, modems will continue to increase in speed. Someday, the so-called "high speeds" discussed in this book will seem slow. Digital subscriber line (DSL) modems, for example, can send data at speeds up to 2 million bits per second. If you are tempted to purchase such a modem, however, first make sure that your ISP can support it. To find out whether DSL is available in your community, follow the *Multilit* Web site link to the DSL Resource Center, where there is an excellent tutorial comparing DSL to the other ways of connecting to the Internet.

Network Cards

Network cards provide faster ways to access the Internet. If your school or workplace has high-speed Internet cabling, you should consider getting a network card so you can connect to the Internet at high speed. The most popular kind of network card is called **Ethernet** (pronounced *ee-thur-net*). Many multimedia computers come with Ethernet built in. Ethernet networks transmit data at high speed, up to 10 megabits per second (Mbps—mega means a million, so 10 Mbps means 10 million bits per second). At Ethernet speeds, a file that takes 10 minutes to transmit over a 14.4 Kbps modem arrives in just one second. Actual downloading times may vary depending on the number of users sharing the Ethernet.

When Bob Metcalfe invented Ethernet in 1973 as part of his Harvard Ph.D. thesis, Ethernet required the use of coaxial cable, which is the kind of wire used in cable TV. Now there is a so-called 10BaseT Ethernet that can use ordinary twisted-pair telephone wiring. There is also a newer 10/100BaseT Ethernet that can move data at rates up to 100 megabits per second.

Cable Modems

Cable modems offer high-speed Internet access over TV cables. Average costs range from $40 to $60 per month. Cable modems can theoretically offer speeds from 3 to 30 Mbps, but in the real world, where you are competing with other users in your neighborhood for available bandwidth, actual speeds range from 400 to 1440 Kbps. That is still a lot faster than an analog telephone modem. Many neighborhoods, however, do not yet have two-way cable modem service. When this book went to press, only about 30% of the TV cables in the United States had been converted to the hybrid fiber/coax (HFC) lines needed to deliver two-way cable modem service. To find out whether cable modem service is available in your neighborhood, contact your local cable TV company.

Auxiliary Input

The auxiliary input devices described here provide convenient ways to digitize preexisting texts and pictures for use with a multimedia computer. The program that converts scanned text into machine-readable characters is known as optical character recognition (OCR) software. OCR software does not necessarily ship with scanners, so if you plan to scan printed text into machine-readable form, make sure you have the necessary OCR software. The best OCR software is industry leader Caere Corporation's OmniPage. For the latest information, follow the *Multilit* Web site link to Caere, where you will find a comprehensive guide to scanners.

Handheld Scanners

Handheld scanners have fallen in cost while increasing in reliability. The author used a handheld scanner extensively to scan the quotations that appear in this book. If you are an educator, be sure to ask the vendor if there is an educational discount; most scanner manufacturers have special discounts for educators. As this book goes to press, the most portable scanner is the IRISPen, which is a pen-sized scanner that allows you to scan text into any Windows or Macintosh application. Pictured in action in Figure 11-7, the

Figure 11-7   The IRISPen scans editable text into the current cursor position.

IRISPen scans editable text into the current cursor position. For more information, follow the *Multilit* Web site links to handheld scanners.

Flatbed Scanners

Flatbed scanners do a nice job of scanning both text and graphics, and the price of color flatbed scanners has fallen steadily. If your budget permits, a flatbed scanner is a good addition for producing multimedia text and image objects. To find out more about flatbed scanners, follow the *Multilit* Web site link to industry leader Hewlett-Packard's family of ScanJet scanners.

Page-Fed Scanners

Page-fed scanners cost less and work as well as flatbed scanners, with the obvious constraint that you can feed only single pages into a page-fed scanner. On flatbed scanners, you can lay an open book down and scan the page without having to make a copy of it first to feed into a page-fed scanner. For this reason, a flatbed scanner is more versatile.

Slide Scanners

Slide scanners have a slot into which you insert a 35mm slide; their purpose is to scan the slide and produce a bitmap image of it. If you have a lot of 35mm slides to digitize, follow the *Multilit* Web site link to Polaroid, which sells a highly rated slide scanner. If you have only a few 35mm slides to digitize, however, it will be more cost-effective for you to send them to Kodak for digitizing onto a Photo CD. For more information, follow the *Multilit* Web site link to Kodak Photo CD.

Digital Cameras

As digital cameras fall in price and increase in resolution, they will eventually obviate the need for slides by making film unnecessary. High-end digital cameras already have color sharpness and resolution that rival the quality of a 35mm slide, which has an effective resolution of about 4000 × 4000 pixels. When this book went to press, for example, Kodak already was marketing professional digital cameras with resolutions exceeding 3000 × 2000 pixels. If you only need to snap pictures for display on a Web page, however, you won't need such an expensive camera. To compare the features and prices of digital cameras, follow the *Multilit* Web site link to CNET or the Computer Shopper and search for Camera. When you buy a camera, make sure it is capable of snapping a picture with the color depth and pixel resolution you need.

Snappy

Snappy Video Snapshot is an image capture module that connects to the parallel port on the back of a desktop or laptop PC. Snappy can capture still images from any video source, such as a camcorder, at resolutions up to 1500 × 1125 pixels with 16 million colors. There is a Snappy demo on the *Multilit* CD. To run the demo, go to the Demonstrations section, select Software, and click the Snappy button. For information about the latest version, follow the *Multilit* Web site link to Snappy.

Videoconferencing Cameras and WebCams

Videoconferencing cameras, also known as WebCams, have dropped in price so rapidly that they are becoming a mass-market consumer item. To compare prices and features among the cameras that are available, follow the *Multilit* Web site link to CNET or the Computer Shopper and search for WebCam. Chapter 35, which is a step-by-step tutorial on digital video recording and editing, features the Logitech QuickCam family of WebCams. The QuickCam comes in a USB version that can connect to any Windows PC or Macintosh with a USB port. When you purchase a WebCam, make sure your computer has the kind of port needed for connecting the camera.

Computer Projectors

Computer projectors connect to the monitor output of a multimedia computer to project the computer display onto a large viewing surface for use in auditoriums, classrooms, and board rooms. There are four kinds of projectors: CRT (cathode ray tube), LCD (liquid crystal display), DLP (digital light processor), and PDP (plasma display panel). The best place to see all the different projectors in action is at the annual Infocomm conference, which has a projection shoot-out in which all the vendors line their projectors up around a huge auditorium where you can walk around and compare how well the different projectors display the same video signal. For more information, follow the *Multilit* Web site link to Infocomm and its parent organization, the International Communications Industry Association (ICIA), where you can follow the links to the Projection Encounter for a very highly produced multimedia tutorial on projection technology.

Printers

No list of computer accessories would be complete without mentioning printers. The quality of the printed output is largely determined by how many dots per inch (dpi) the printer can produce. Printers that print at 300 dpi produce acceptable graphics, but 600 dpi looks a lot better. This book was produced on a printer with 2400 dpi.

Because color is important in multimedia applications, you would ideally like to have a color printer. Happily, the cost of color printers has been declining steadily. If you do not have a color printer, however, your computer's printer driver will automatically convert color bitmaps to grayscale images that look surprisingly good when printed on a monochrome printer.

Laser printers produce the best and fastest prints, but they also cost the most. Inkjet printers are an alternative that costs less yet looks almost as good so long as you do not smear the ink before it dries. Some inks run when you get them wet, which is another reason why laser printers are preferred over inkjets.

For the latest information about printers, follow the *Multilit* Web site link to CNET or the Computer Shopper and search for printers.

e x e r c i s e s

1. Define the following terms and explain the role they play in a multimedia computer:

   - Central processor

   - RAM

   - Hard disk

   - Modem

2. Run through the multimedia components discussed in this chapter and make a list of which ones your computer has, which ones it does not have, and, of the latter, which ones you would like it to have.

3. Have you ever used a trackball? If not, go to your local video arcade and play a game that uses one. What advantages does the trackball have over a mouse? What are the disadvantages? Which do you prefer?

4. Have you ever used an optical mouse? If not, go to your local computer store and try out the Microsoft IntelliMouse Explorer. How does the optical mouse compare to the kind of mouse that has a rolling ball? Which kind of mouse would you rather use, an optical mouse, or a rolling ball mouse?

5. Go to www.kodak.com and search for digital cameras. When this book went to press, the highest-resolution camera being marketed by Kodak had a pixel grid of 3060×2036. What is the pixel grid of the highest-resolution camera Kodak is marketing now?

12

Multimedia Computer Buyer's Checklists

After completing this chapter, you will be able to:

■ **Use multimedia computer buyer checklists that clarify what you need to buy and why**

■ **Assess the multimedia PC you are using now and decide what upgrade(s) it needs next**

■ **Realize how rapidly prices are falling and how to get the best buys**

■ **Know where to find comparison-shopping advice for buying hardware on the Internet**

● This chapter contains three checklists. The first one lists the equipment in an affordable, low-budget system that will get you started without a large cash outlay. The second checklist describes a midrange system that is the most strategic buy if you can afford it. The third list is for a multimedia dream machine with all the bells and whistles. Though few readers will ever buy all the components that this chapter enumerates, a checklist is useful because it shows you all the options and lets you consider which items you really need.

Low-Budget System

System Unit

☐ 400 MHz central processor

☐ 64 MB RAM

☐ 15- to 17-inch color display

☐ 800 600 pixel resolution

☐ 24-bit color depth

☐ USB port

☐ Mouse or other pointing device

☐ Surge protector

Multimedia Accessories

☐ CD-ROM or DVD

☐ 16-bit waveform digital audio

☐ 2 self-powered speakers

Read/Write Storage

☐   4 GB hard disk

Communication Options

☐   36,600 baud modem

Printer

☐   Inkjet printer

Midrange System

System Unit

☐   600 MHz central processor

☐   128 MB RAM

☐   19-inch color display

☐   1024 × 768 pixel resolution

☐   24-bit color depth

☐   2 USB ports

☐   2 empty expansion slots

☐   Mouse or other pointing device

☐   Surge protector with 5-minute battery backup

Multimedia Accessories

☐   DVD

☐   16-bit waveform digital audio

☐   Stereo speakers with subwoofer

☐   16 MB graphics accelerator

☐   Video overlay with:

    ☐   TV tuner

    ☐   Full-motion video capture

Read/Write Storage

☐   10 GB hard disk

☐   Zip disk (USB port version)

☐   CD-ROM recorder (CD-R)

Communication Options

☐ 56 Kbps baud modem

   or

☐ Network card with ISDN, DSL, or cable modem

Auxiliary Input

☐ WebCam

☐ Flatbed scanner

☐ Digital camera

☐ DV camcorder

Printer

☐ Laser printer

High-End System

System Unit

☐ 800 MHz central processor

☐ 256 MB RAM

☐ 21-inch color display

☐ 1600 × 1200 pixel resolution

☐ 32-bit color depth

☐ 2 USB ports

☐ USB splitter hub

☐ 4 empty expansion slots

☐ Mouse or other pointing device

☐ Surge protector with 10-minute battery backup

Multimedia Accessories

☐ DVD

☐ 16-bit waveform digital audio

☐ 5.1 digital surround sound speakers

☐ 32 MB graphics accelerator

☐ Video overlay with:

    ☐ TV tuner

    ☐ Full-motion video capture

☐ MIDI IN and MIDI OUT

☐ MIDI keyboard

☐ MPEG capture board

Read/Write Storage

☐ 30 GB hard disk

☐ External SCSI connector

☐ Jaz disk

☐ CD-ROM Read/Write (CD-RW)

Communication Options

☐ 56 Kbps baud modem

    or

☐ Network card with ISDN, DSL, or cable modem

Auxiliary Input

☐ WebCam

☐ Flatbed scanner

☐ Hi-Res digital camera

☐ DV camcorder

Printer

☐ Color laser printer

How to Get the Best Buy

Anyone purchasing a multimedia computer should realize how fast costs are declining and where to get the best buy. Prices are falling due to advances in technology and because the multimedia PC has become a mass-market consumer item. Major retailers such as CompUSA, Best Buy, Staples, Sears, Radio Shack, and Circuit City sell multimedia computers in a broad range of prices.

When you purchase a multimedia PC, use the checklists in this chapter to help decide what features you want, then visit the retailers and find the best buy you can on the computer that comes closest to having these features. Make sure it is possible to buy and install any peripherals you may want in addition to those that come with the machine. For example, if you want more RAM than what comes with the machine, make sure the extra RAM is available at a reasonable price, and find out how difficult it will be to install. Check the number of slots and make sure there are empty slots of the type you need for installing extra hardware such as a SCSI board.

Online stores let you configure and purchase computers over the Web. The major retailers and manufacturers have Web sites where you can compare prices, specifications,

Figure 12-1   The Gateway site lets you configure your own PC when you click the option to customize it. By the time you read this, the prices will be lower, and the computers will be faster.

Figure 12-2   The strategic buy is the hard drive before the one that jumps too far in price. By the time you read this, the drives will be larger, and the prices will be lower.

and technical support. The author likes to shop online at Gateway, for example. Figure 12-1 shows how the Gateway site gives you the option to configure your own PC. To get the most strategic buy, you pull down the menus and see where the price breaks are. In Figure 12-2, for example, the author pulled down the hard drive menu to find the most economical buy. Notice how the 27.3 GB hard drive costs $165, while a 34 GB drive costs almost twice as much. The most economical buy is the 27.3 GB drive, because it falls right before the price jump. By the time you read this, the drives will be larger and the prices will be lower, but the principle is the same: To get the most strategic buy, choose the option right before the one that jumps a lot in price.

For more information about configuring and purchasing computers online, follow the *Multilit* Web site links to multimedia PC manufacturers and online computer stores.

exercises

1. What brand and model of multimedia computer do you use? Which one of the three checklists provided in this chapter most closely matches your multimedia PC? What features does your multimedia computer have in addition to those listed? What features does it lack?

2. Do you think any of the items listed in the high-end checklist are not needed in a multimedia computer? If so, list the items and explain why they are unnecessary.

3. Take the three checklists to your local computer store and price the equipment. Create an itemized list that shows what each component costs, and compute the total cost of each system.

4. Does your local computer store sell any multimedia peripherals not listed in the high-end checklist? If so, what are they? Do you feel they should be added to the checklist? Why or why not?

13

Configuring a Multimedia Computer

After completing this chapter, you will be able to:

- Connect the audio and video components of a multimedia computer in order to optimize functionality and minimize the complexity of the cabling

- Save slots by combining multiple features onto a single circuit board

- Use a low-cost audio/video switch that can increase the number of devices connected to your computer

- Mix volume levels to keep the audio from getting too loud or too soft when the sound source changes

● Sometimes computers have so many peripherals connected that it becomes difficult to add more devices due to the hopelessly entangled snare of cables. This chapter provides you with a better strategy for connecting the audio and video components of a multimedia computer. When you configure your multimedia PC, you can minimize the number of wires that can become entangled by integrating multiple features onto a single circuit board. If you still have more devices than your computer has input jacks, you can get a low-cost switch that lets you connect more audio/video sources without having to plug and unplug cables repeatedly. With your computer's mixing software, you can adjust the input levels to balance the volume of the incoming sound. This chapter teaches you how to perform all three tasks, namely, integrating, switching, and mixing.

Integrating

The place to begin simplifying your computer's configuration is to minimize the number of expansion boards by getting cards that integrate multiple features into one device. If you are installing a video overlay board, for example, and you also want a TV tuner card, consider purchasing an overlay board that also has a TV tuner on it, such as the Win/TV board shown in Figure 13-1. Not only will you save an expansion slot in your computer, but you will need fewer cables due to the on-board connection between the TV tuner and the overlay board.

Figure 13-1   The Win/TV-pci board has jacks for plugging in a TV cable, video input, and left and right audio channels.

Figure 13-2   The MIDI adapter from Creative Labs plugs into the game port of the SoundBlaster card and provides MIDI IN and OUT jacks for connecting a MIDI keyboard to your computer.

Another opportunity to save a slot is if you are planning to connect a MIDI keyboard to your computer. To connect a MIDI keyboard, your computer needs MIDI IN and OUT ports. You could purchase a MIDI card that has these ports, but why take up another slot inside your computer when you can get a waveform audio card that also lets you connect external MIDI devices? If you are planning to connect a MIDI keyboard, therefore, try to get an audio card that lets you plug in your MIDI IN and OUT cables without having to devote an expansion slot to a separate MIDI card. Chances are good that, if your computer has a Soundblaster-compatible sound card, you can use the adapter shown in Figure 13-2 to plug in a MIDI keyboard without needing another circuit board.

For more information about the latest advances in multimedia expansion card technology, follow the *Multilit* Web site links to Creative Labs, Hauppauge Computer Works, Diamond Multimedia, ATI Technologies, and 3Com. For a list of available feature cards, follow the links to CNET and the Computer Shopper and search for the key word Cards.

Switching

No matter how well you plan, eventually you may encounter a situation in which you need to connect to your computer more audio or video sources than you have jacks in which to plug them. Radio Shack makes a low-cost but highly useful switch that comes in handy in this kind of situation. Pictured in Figure 13-3, the Radio Shack switch costs less than $25. You can connect up to four devices to it.

Suppose you need to be able to record sound from different audio sources, such as a CD player, a cassette tape deck, a VCR, and a radio station. You can connect the audio outputs from all four of these devices to the Radio Shack switch, which in turn connects to your computer's line input audio jack. When you want to record sound from one of these four audio devices, you simply press the corresponding button on the Radio Shack switch, which connects the device to your computer's audio input jack.

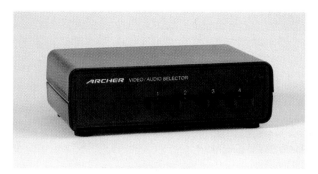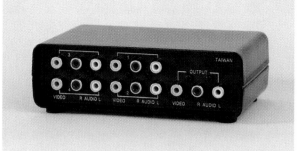

Figure 13-3 Radio Shack's Stereo Audio/Video Selector Switch lets you connect up to four devices and select any one of them by simply pressing a button.

You can connect video as well as audio to the Radio Shack switch. Suppose your video capture card lacks multiple inputs, for example, and you want to be able to capture video from several sources, such as a camera, a VCR, a satellite receiver, and a videodisc player. Without a switch, you would have to keep disconnecting and plugging in different wires each time you decided to record from a different video source. Happily, you can connect all four of these video sources to the Radio Shack switch. Instead of unplugging cables, you just press one button, and its video source instantly gets switched into your computer's video input jack.

For ordering information, follow the *Multilit* Web site link to Radio Shack and search for product number 15-1956.

Mixing

As you learned in Chapter 2, multimedia computers can play back several kinds of sound recordings, including waveform audio, MIDI songs, and CD audio tracks. A common problem encountered on multimedia PCs is that one of these kinds of audio sounds too much louder than the others, and you find yourself adjusting the volume knob to keep the audio from getting too loud or too soft when the sound source changes. Figure 13-4 shows how you can solve this problem by using your computer's audio mixer software to adjust the relative volume settings of the sound sources. In Chapter 25, which teaches you how to record sound on your computer, you will receive detailed instructions on using your computer's audio mixer.

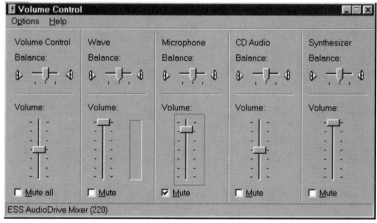

Figure 13-4 The Windows audio mixer.

1. This chapter told how you can save a slot in your computer by combining onto a single circuit card the video-recording and TV-tuner functions that might otherwise come on separate feature cards. Can you think of another way to save a slot in your computer?

2. Do you think you will ever need to connect to your computer a switching device such as the Radio Shack switch featured in this chapter? Explain why or why not. If you answer yes, describe the situation that would require such a switch. What specific devices would you plug into the Radio Shack switch?

3. How does the mixing screen for your digital audio board compare to the one illustrated in this chapter? Does your computer's mixing software let you control the volume of your microphone input? Of your waveform audio? Of your MIDI synthesizer? Of your CD audio playback? Do you have separate left and right volume controls, or is there a balance control that lets you adjust how much volume goes to your left and right speakers?

Part Four
Looking Into the Future of Multimedia

We must make sure the Information Superhighway is not a toll road for the rich.

—Linda Roberts, as White House Education Adviser

We shouldn't be looking for ways to subject new technologies to old rules.

—Reed Hundt, as Federal Communications Commission Chairman

Technology is one of the most difficult areas in which to make predictions, because new inventions occur at such a fast pace that the future changes before it gets here. How can the future change before it gets here? Big companies invest millions of dollars promoting new products, leading the consumer to believe that their products will be the mainstream of the future, but shortly after coming to market, the products get abandoned because the vendors pursue newer technologies that promise bigger profits. This has happened so often during the past two decades that almost anyone involved with multimedia has been frustrated by purchasing so-called mainstream technologies that quickly go out-of-date and are abandoned by their manufacturers.

Knowledge is the best strategy for coping with fast-paced change. The more you know about the issues and technologies, the better prepared you will be to make strategic choices. Specifically, you can:

- Identify the frontiers that multimedia researchers are investigating

- Study technologies that are emerging

- Identify societal issues raised by the manner in which multimedia technologies are used

- Find out about and even contribute to new knowledge in this exciting field

The next four chapters consider these topics.

14

Multimedia Frontiers

After completing this chapter, you will be able to:

- Understand how researchers invent new uses for multimedia and use multimedia technology to find new methods for solving problems

- Consider what kinds of printed books can be or should be replaced by electronic books

- Know what is meant by the term *rural datafication*

- Explore how virtual reality will improve the multimedia user interface

- Dream about the multimedia possibilities of appliance-based computing

- Consider whether there are other frontiers of multimedia that ought to be explored

- Join and participate in the Electronic Frontier Foundation

● A **multimedia frontier** is a field of technological research and development in which investigators invent new uses for multimedia or determine the extent to which multimedia can solve problems by finding better ways of doing things. This chapter discusses how multimedia is being used to improve and transform publishing, provide better access to networked information, enhance rural communication, simplify the user interface, and extend the network to everyday appliances.

Electronic Publishing

How much longer will books, magazines, and newspapers continue to be printed on paper? Anyone who has used hypertext knows how printed manuscripts pale by comparison. Printed manuscripts do not contain links that let you expand the text and navigate to related information; hot words that let you trigger explanatory sound tracks, videos, or animations; or full-text Boolean (AND, OR, NOT) searching that lets you locate quickly the material you need. Printed music does not let you scroll the score back and forth to locate and hear precisely the theme you want to study. Mathemathics and economics textbooks do not allow you to manipulate formulas and visualize your changes through dynamic real-time graphs.

The publishing industry knows this very well. Book publishers realize that their entire way of doing business is undergoing rapid and fundamental change, but they are not sure how it will emerge. Take this book for example. It includes a CD-ROM. How much of the text in this book would you have preferred to read on the CD-ROM instead? As Chapter 39 demonstrates, you can produce a CD-ROM for much less than a book, and you do not need a publisher to do so.

Knowing this, Microsoft has targeted electronic publishing as a strategic market opportunity. VP for technology development Dick Brass made the following prediction (ABCNews.com, October 1999, *Multilit* Web site) regarding how the new *Microsoft Reader* technology will unfold: By the year 2006, electronic news kiosks will allow people to download newspapers and magazines onto electronic reading devices. By the year 2010, the devices will be lightweight, have flexible screens and run off 24-hour batteries. By the year 2018, the newspaper on paper could become extinct. The future is electronic, the past is paper.

By the time you read this, a thousand classic titles from Penguin Books will be available on *Microsoft Reader,* which uses ClearType font-rendering technology to improve the readability of text on computer screens. Italian publisher Mondadori Editore Spa and the online Paris-based Editions 00h00.com have also adopted the *Microsoft Reader.* Brass predicts that printed books which normally cost $30 will fall in price to $5 for electronic versions.

To learn more about the scheduled rollout of *Microsoft Reader* products, follow the *Multilit* Web site link to *Microsoft Reader.* See especially the *Microsoft Reader* timeline, which predicts that by 2020, 90% of all book titles will be sold in electronic rather than paper form, and *Webster's Dictionary* will have changed its first definition of *book* to "a substantial piece of writing commonly displayed on a computer or other personal viewing device."

The Information Superhighway

In 1993, then Vice President Al Gore issued a report entitled *The National Information Infrastructure: Agenda for Action.* The report describes how the private sector would build, operate, and maintain the Information Superhighway, while the government was going to develop policies to ensure that all Americans have access to it, encourage private sector investment in building the network, and create a competitive market for telecommunications and information services. Concerned about how these policies would control what happens on the network, Farber (1993) explained the formation of an organization called the Electronic Frontier Foundation:

> In July 1990, the Electronic Frontier Foundation (EFF) was founded by John Perry Barlow and Mitch Kapor (who also founded Lotus Development Corporation) to help civilize the frontier more rapidly. It has the aim of trying to assure freedom of expression in digital media with emphasis on applying the principles embodied in the Constitution and the Bill of Rights to computer-based communication. From the beginning, EFF was determined to become an organization that would combine technical, legal, and public policy expertise. It would then apply these skills to the large number of complex issues and concerns that arise whenever a new communications medium is born. To paraphrase John Perry Barlow, it will take years to civilize the electronic frontier and bring law and order to it. And to quote Mitch Kapor, "There's a new world coming. Let's make sure it has rules we can live with."

So many people are concerned about these issues that the Electronic Frontier Foundation has become one of the most frequently visited sites on the Web. To see for yourself, follow the *Multilit* Web site link to the EFF, where you will find instructions on how to join.

Another organization working to represent public interests in the emerging communications infrastructure is the Benton Foundation. Among its many services is *The Digital Beat,* a free online news service supported by the Open Society Institute. As Benton states, "Our aim is to equip you to be engaged in the public debate on the public interest in digital television and the Internet. We will chronicle the action at the Federal Communications Commission and in Congress, the efforts of public interest advocates, the work of nonprofit organizations and government agencies to create new public services, technology developments, and communications trends." To read *The Digital Beat,* follow the *Multilit* Web site link to the Benton Foundation.

Rural Datafication

Rural America has traditionally lagged behind the rest of the country in gaining access to technological innovations. Telephones, radio, and television came first to big cities. To provide access to the rest of the country, the Department of Commerce made capital funding available through its Public Telecommunications Facilities Program for rural communities to install modern telecommunications equipment. These funds are still available and have recently been used to provide rural communities access to satellites. The process of extending the Information Superhighway to rural America is called **rural datafication**.

AeRie, the Applied Rural Telecommunications Online Clearinghouse, has a resource guide on the Web containing examples of how rural communities throughout the world are using telecommunications for economic development. To visit the Clearinghouse, follow the *Multilit* Web site link to the AeRie project, which in turn links to the resource guide.

Virtual Reality

As you are aware from using this book and its CD, multimedia computers can show any picture, play any sound, and link any word of any document or any part of any picture to any object on your computer. What is missing? A better human interface. We need better ways for users to communicate with multimedia computers. As you learned in Chapter 5, researchers in virtual reality (VR) are actively working on this, and as new input and output devices get invented, multimedia computers will benefit.

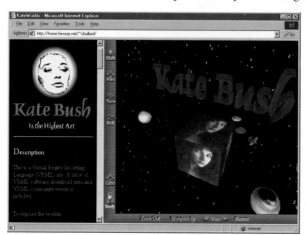

Figure 14-1   A VRML screen from Len Bullard's tribute to Kate Bush. A static picture does not do this justice; use a VRML-enabled browser to visit this site and use your mouse to explore this 3-D world, which you will find at http://home.hiwaay.net/~cbullard/.

The Web3D Consortium is working to bring virtual reality to the Web. The consortium spearheaded the development of the Virtual Reality Modeling Language (VRML), which is an object-oriented language that lets you create navigable 3-D spaces for the Web. Figure 14-1 shows how Web page designers use VRML to add dimensions, texture, and "lighting" specifications to Web sites. For more examples, follow the *Multilit* Web site link to the Web3D Consortium, where you will find more information on VRML, viewers and authoring clients, mailing lists, newsgroups, and documentation. See especially the VRML Repository, which contains demos of VRML worlds in architecture, art, astronomy, biomedical sciences, chemistry, commercial applications, computer science, entertainment, environmental science, history, maps, mathematics, music, physics, and scientific visualization.

Appliance-based Computing

Imagine tiny computers embedded in everyday appliances, such as your microwave oven, refrigerator, dishwasher, telephone, video camera, TV, stove, swimming pool, garage door opener, thermostat, heater, air-conditioner, humidifier, and water softener. Now imagine a way to connect these devices to the network so they can communicate and stream data complete with multimedia sound, graphics, and video.

The computer industry is working hard to make this happen. Appliance-based computing is one of the most important frontiers in multimedia today, because it will make it possible for you to do things such as:

- Configure your stove to page you or send you an e-mail message if someone leaves a burner on too long.

- Monitor your home when you are out dining or attending a show and a babysitter is watching the kids.

- Instruct your garage door opener to phone you if it is opened while you are away on vacation.

- Be informed if someone jumps or falls into your swimming pool when you are not using it.

Sun's Jini technology is the early leader in appliance-based computing. Jini is a connection technology that already is appearing in some commercial products. Hewlett-Packard has adopted Jini in its JetSend network, enabling a camera to send an image, for example, to a remotely located printer. Jini enables the camera to locate the printer, and JetSend gets the picture there in a format the printer can understand. For the latest news, follow the *Multilit* Web site link to Jini Connection Technology and Hewlett-Packard's JetSend.

e x e r c i s e s

1. Do you think electronic book technologies such as the *Microsoft Reader* will ever replace printed books? Are some kinds of books more likely to be replaced than others? Give an example of a kind of printed book that should be replaced by an electronic version and explain why. Then give an example of a book that should not be so replaced and explain why not.

2. Follow the *Multilit* Web site link to *Microsoft Reader* to check the status of the rollout of Microsoft's electronic book technology. Is Microsoft on schedule? Is there a link for you to follow if you want to purchase one of the new electronic book titles? If so, how many electronic books are available for purchase now in the *Microsoft Reader* format?

3. To what extent has your local community become "datafied"? Are your schools connected to the Internet? Do teachers have access to it, or just the administrators? How about students? Is your local library connected? What about homes in your area: Does a cable TV franchise, telephone company, or Internet Service Provider make Information Superhighway connections available to homes? If so, at what speeds? What online services are provided?

4. View the classic VR movie *Lawnmower Man,* which you can rent from your local video store. Do you believe multimedia computers will ever enable users to experience VR immersion to the extent Jobe Smith (Jeff Fahey) does in the movie?

5. If you could invent anything you could think of, what kind of devices would you create for improving your computer's user interface? How would the devices help you communicate with your computer better than you can now? How would they make it easier to use? How would they make the simulated environments you experience seem more real? How would they get you more involved in the interaction?

6. This chapter listed several possible applications of appliance-based computing. Try to think of some more. List three additional ways you could use appliance-based computing to solve problems or improve your quality of life.

15

Emerging Technology

After completing this chapter, you will be able to:

■ Recognize emerging multimedia technologies

■ Understand the role that MPEG and HDTV will play in the future of digital video

■ See how Intercasting is creating a new form of enhanced TV

■ Realize how holography promises to reduce substantially the size and increase the density of optical storage media

■ Consider the challenge of pen computing and the promise of speech recognition

■ Imagine how ubiquitous Teledesic will make the Internet when the wireless satellite network encircles the globe

■ Understand what knowbots can do for you on the Information Superhighway

■ Recognize the extent to which multimedia is an emerging technology, and question whether multimedia is just a fad or an important life skill

● New technologies follow a cycle that includes invention, prototyping, proof of concept, productizing, and manufacture. Throughout this process the inventions are called **emerging technologies**. It often takes many years for an emerging technology to achieve widespread use in the marketplace.

This chapter discusses multimedia technologies that are in the process of emerging. Some of them could get canceled prior to manufacture, and others may fail in the marketplace. Only technologies that succeed really belong here, because inventions that fail to emerge are by definition not emerging.

Digital Video

There is little doubt that digital video will emerge as the primary way in which movies will be recorded and transmitted in the twenty-first century. As this book goes to press, for example, DVD has become one of the most popular mass-market consumer items, surpassing CD-ROM in its growth rate. Movies are stored on DVD in the MPEG format. MPEG stands for Motion Pictures Experts Group, the name of the ISO standards committee that created it. Endorsed by more than 70 companies including IBM, Apple, JVC, Philips, Sony, and Matsushita, MPEG compresses video by using a discrete cosine transform algorithm to eliminate redundant data in blocks of pixels on the screen.

Figure 15-1 RCA DirecTV uses MPEG to deliver more than 175 channels of digital TV programming over the nation's first high-power direct broadcast satellite (DBS) service using 18-inch satellite dishes. For more information, go to http://www.directv.com.

MPEG compresses the video further by recording only changes from frame to frame; this is known as **delta-frame encoding**. MPEG is the digital video standard for high-definition television (HDTV) and direct satellite broadcast, such as the RCA DirecTV system advertised in Figure 15-1.

HDTV

HDTV stands for high-definition television. It is being developed to replace NTSC as the television standard for the United States. HDTV is based on four technologies:

- MPEG digital video compression

- Transmission in packets that will permit any combination of video, audio, and data

- Progressive scanning for computer interoperability up to 60 frames per second at 1920 × 1080 pixels

- CD-quality digital surround sound using Dolby AC-3 audio technology

During the 1990s, the major television studios began recording shows in HDTV so reruns can be broadcast in HDTV when the standard changes. To find out how many television stations are broadcasting in HDTV today, follow the *Multilit* Web site link to HDTV Group—Links—HDTV Stations.

Intercasting in TV's Vertical-Blanking Interval

The vertical-blanking interval is the gap between the frames of a television picture. You see the vertical-blanking interval if your television is out of horizontal adjustment, causing the frames to scroll down the screen. Ever since the invention of television, the vertical-blanking interval has had the capability of carrying additional information, but no one has used it effectively. Until now. Intel has trademarked the term **Intercast**, which means to transmit Web pages and other digital information in the vertical-blanking interval. Partnering with Intel in the Intercast venture are NBC, CNN, Viacom, WGBH, QVC, Comcast, America Online, Asymetrix, En Technology, Netscape, Gateway, and Packard Bell. NBC did its first Intercast during the 1996 Summer Olympic Games. In 1998, Microsoft built Intercasting into the operating system in the form of WebTV for Windows, which provides TV capabilities on the PC and supports a wide variety of services, including data broadcasting, an electronic program guide, and interactive TV programming. Television programming that has Intercast content is known as **enhanced TV**. For more information, follow the *Multilit* Web site link to Intercast.

Holography

Most people think of holograms as 3-D photographs. But holograms can also store huge amounts of data. For example, IBM scientists predict that holographic technology will make it possible to store the entire *Encyclopaedia Britannica* in a space the size and thickness of a penny. Holographic memory systems can stack data 40 layers deep, as opposed to computer disk and magnetic tape, which line up data on flat, single-layer tracks. The deeper layers can be read by tilting the angle of the laser beam that reads the data (*Investor's Business Daily* 1/20/94: 4). Scientists believe that by 2004, 5 gigabytes of data will fit in 2 cubic centimeters at a cost of 4 cents per megabyte. For technical details, follow the *Multilit* Web site link to holographic memory design.

Pen Computing

Pen computing is an emerging technology that Apple's handheld Newton computer first brought to public attention back in the twentieth century. As depicted in Figure 15-2, the need for a bulky keyboard to input characters was avoided by writing on the screen with a pen. Apple claimed that Newton was trainable, that it could learn to recognize your handwriting. But in practice, Newton trained the user, who ended up learning how to write in a format Newton could understand. Research continues, as does the popularity of the pen. For news and reviews of the latest pen computers, follow the *Multilit* Web site link to Pen Computing.

Figure 15-2   Pen computers use a stylus instead of a keyboard to input characters.

Speech Recognition

Figure 15-3 Voice recognition software enables the user to speak words into a word-processor document.

With pen computers crying out for a better handwriting algorithm, **speech recognition** is rapidly emerging across a broad range of applications and platforms. The Macintosh, for example, now comes with Apple Speech Recognition built in. Microsoft offers a Direct Speech Recognition Control for Windows users. SoundBlaster boards from Creative Labs come with ViaVoice speech recognition and Prody Parrot, who can play games with you and obey your spoken commands. Dragon Systems offers a product called NaturallySpeaking in versions for teens, professionals, medical, legal, and mobile users. You talk to your PC, and your words appear on the screen and in your document, as shown in Figure 15-3. To learn more about these emerging speech recognition products, follow the *Multilit* Web site links to Apple Speech Recognition, Microsoft Speech Research, Creative Labs, and Dragon Systems.

Internet Phone Services

Anyone with an Internet connection, a full-duplex sound card, and a microphone can use one of the newly emerging Internet phone services. First to market were VocalTec's Internet Phone for Windows and Electric Magic's NetPhone for Macs. The obvious advantage is cost savings on long-distance phone calls. For example, you can talk with someone overseas without having to pay for a long-distance call; the calling parties connect to their local networks, and the Internet makes the long-distance connection for free. There are several disadvantages, however. If your Internet connection is slow, delays can be significant, leading to jerky, stuttering conversations. This is a problem especially during times of high Internet traffic. Also, if the person you are calling is not logged on to the Net with their phone software running, they cannot answer your call.

Not all sound boards have the full-duplex capability required for Internet phone services. For many years the SoundBlaster was available only in a half-duplex version. With a half-duplex sound card, only one party can talk at a time. Now the SoundBlaster comes in full-duplex versions. Almost all Macintoshes produced since 1990 have full-duplex audio. For more information, follow the *Multilit* Web site link to Yahoo and search for Internet Phone.

Wireless Communications

Wireless communication technologies are enabling users to access telecommunication systems from almost anywhere. No longer must your computer be tethered to the nearest telephone line.

Developing nations are using wireless technologies to avoid the high cost of wiring their countries physically. Cellular networks in Malaysia, Thailand, and the Philippines are expanding so fast that they may leapfrog traditional networks to become the most common form of telephone service. In South America, so many Venezuelans are carrying cellular phones that some restaurants require customers to check them at the door to control the noise level (*St. Petersburg Times* 5/16/94 Business: 2). In Brazil, cellular

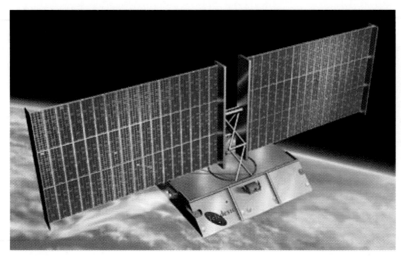

Figure 15-4   A computer rendering of a Teledesic satellite.

Figure 15-5   The Teledesic Network will consist of 288 operational satellites, divided into 12 planes, each with 24 satellites.

phones have become such a highway safety hazard that it is illegal to talk on a handheld cellular phone and drive at the same time (*Miami Herald* 5/18/94: C1).

Technology prophet George Gilder envisions wireless systems that will eventually offer worldwide bandwidth on demand, buffering and transmitting information whenever there is room (*Forbes ASAP* 4/11/94: 98). Microsoft chairman Bill Gates is teaming up with Craig McCaw of McCaw Cellular Communications to create such a network, a $9 billion wireless "global Internet." Known as Teledesic, it will use low earth-orbit satellites to provide wireless interactive voice, data, and video services. The system will have 288 refrigerator-sized satellites to connect handheld phones and other electronic devices to telephone networks all over the world (*Wall Street Journal* 3/21/94: A3). Figure 15-4 shows one of the satellites, and Figure 15-5 shows how they will encompass the globe. For the latest information on the status of their deployment, follow the *Multilit* Web site link to Teledesic.

Knowbots

Knowbots are software applications programmed to act as intelligent agents that go out on the network to find things for you. You tell a knowbot what you want, and it winds its way through the Internet, finding all the relevant information, digesting it, and reporting it to you succinctly.

Likening them to robotic librarians, Krol (1996: 418) refers to knowbots as ". . . software worms that crawl from source to source, looking for answers to your question. As a knowbot looks, it may discover more sources. If it does, it checks the new sources too. When it has exhausted all sources, it comes crawling home with whatever it found."

The *Multilit* Web site links to several knowbot repositories. At FerretSoft, for example, you'll find search utilities for locating Web pages, utilities, e-mail addresses, files, chatters' channels, phone numbers, and news. At BotSpot you'll find knowbots that can help you shop, invest, learn, research, and game. CompareNet, priceline, mySimon, and bottomdollar are online shopping sites that use agents to help you find the best prices. Also linked to the *Multilit* Web site are the Software Agents Group, the Multi-Agent Systems Laboratory, and the Agent Society.

Multimedia

In what sense is multimedia itself an emerging technology? Will the craze fade or evolve into something else, like when the term *multimedia* was invented and people began using it to describe preexisting technology?

The author believes that the ability to use multimedia will emerge as a life skill in the twenty-first century. Citizens who do not know how to use multimedia will become disenfranchised. Cut off from the Information Superhighway, they will end up watching life go by instead of living it fully.

exercises

1. It seems like it is taking forever for HDTV to come on the market. Did you know about HDTV before you read this book? If so, how did you first find out about it? Have you ever seen an HDTV demonstration? If so, what was your impression of it? If you have never seen high-definition television, contact your local video store and ask where you can see an HDTV demo in your area.

2. Follow the *Multilit* Web site link to Teledesic and check on the deployment of the Teledesic satellite network. Have any of the satellites launched yet? What is the latest news about the network?

3. If you could program a knowbot to go out on the Internet and do your bidding, what would you want the knowbot to do?

4. Do you believe multimedia is just a fad, or is its use emerging as a life skill for the twenty-first century? Give reasons for your belief.

16 Societal Issues

After completing this chapter, you will be able to:

▨ Question the potentially negative impact of multimedia on violence, game addiction, sexual exploitation, pornography, and obscenity

▨ Know what the V-chip is and how it works in conjunction with the TV Parental Guidelines

▨ Understand the regulatory nightmare facing lawmakers on issues of privacy, encryption, censorship, and protectionism

▨ Realize how fortune seekers have tried to profit from the legal system's lack of experience by patenting basic multimedia technologies that were already widely used

▨ Consider the copyright law and a teacher's right to fair use of multimedia

▨ Understand the issues of entitlement, equity, cost, usability, and universal access, and then question whether the building of the Information Superhighway will create a technological underclass in our society

● Until now this book has touted the great advantages of multimedia. But will its true potential be reached? Who will control access? Almost any good thing can be misused; how can multimedia harm society?

Human Impact

A lot of people worry about graphic violence in video games. Is it right to have laser shooting games in video arcades, which can train young people how to aim and fire weapons at people, when the leading cause of death among urban youth is gunshot wounds? Sex CDs let men exploit women virtually. With more than 60% of families reporting problems of marital violence, should CDs and DVDs in which men can torture women on-screen be legal? Research shows that virtual reality is even more addictive than conventional video games. What effect will this have on humankind?

Violence and Game Addiction

In her review of violence in video games, Stefanac (1994) reports that there were more than 10,000 murders involving handguns in the United States in 1990. During the same year, only 10 such murders occurred in Australia, 13 in Sweden, 22 in Great Britain, and 87 in Japan. In 1991, 55% of those arrested for murder in the United States were under the age of 25. According to federal crime reports, the number of children arrested for murder during the past decade has risen by 55%.

The author suggests that you visit your local arcade and try one of the video games that have laser-targeting firearms. As you hold the weapon, people appear on the screen in front of you. They are not mere "pixellated" computer graphics that only suggest human forms, but real live video recordings of street scenes. You must aim accurately and fire quickly to avoid being shot. Now go outside and walk down the street. Someone appears from around the corner in front of you. What is your basic instinct after playing the game?

Not everyone agrees that video game violence provokes street crime. According to popular culture Professor Christopher Geist (Stefanac 1994):

> People often assume that findings for one medium apply necessarily to the next. Some people are saying that interactive games will have more impact. That's a guess. It could turn out that the interactivity in some of these combat games actually lessens the negative impact; it could serve a cathartic effect. Much more research needs to be done before we start drawing absolute conclusions.

Sex

Sex is very important to most people. Traffic on the Internet reflects this: The newsgroup *alt.sex* has more than 350,000 readers with more than 10 MB of new messages per month; that is the equivalent of three Bibles. But multimedia is being used for more than just distributing erotic stories and pictures. Interactivity is letting users live out their fantasies virtually. For example, *NightWatch* allows the voyeur/player to snoop around a plush singles resort via a bank of security monitors. *Virtual Valerie* lets users roam about and explore Valerie's apartment and have cybersex with her in the bedroom. Linea Jacobson, editor of *CyberArts*, has a warning about the dangers of these applications (Stefanac 1994):

> What's wonderful about interactive media is also what's reprehensible about this kind of application: the idea of handing control over to the user. Smut on paper or video is much more benign than interactive stroke books. These products show men that they can have control over women. You can force them to do your bidding and they do it willingly. I am absolutely opposed to censorship, but I think men have to be made aware that this kind of thing can make women feel very uncomfortable.

Pornography and Obscenity

Mike Godwin (1994), online counsel for the Electronic Frontier Foundation, also has concerns about the risks of putting graphic sexual materials on the Internet. The GIF, JPG, and PNG file formats are capable of reproducing over the Net full-color photos of explicit "hardcore" pornography and child pornography. The federal government has been searching and seizing servers that contain such material. These are so popular that Delft University in the Netherlands has had to limit each user to eight downloads per day from its erotic image file server.

The Supreme Court's 1973 *Miller* ruling gave communities the right to legislate obscenity. To help interpret the laws, Godwin (1994: 58) developed the following four-part test, based on the Supreme Court's 1966 definition of obscenity:

1. Is the work designed to be sexually arousing?

2. Is it arousing in a way that one's local community would consider unhealthy or immoral?

3. Does it picture acts whose depictions are specifically prohibited by state law?

4. Does the work, when taken as a whole, lack sufficient literary, artistic, scientific, or social value?

Distributing such materials over the Internet raises some difficult issues. For example, while an erotic picture might not be immoral in the community where it was uploaded, it may very well be considered obscene in the place it gets downloaded. Internet resources like e-mail, FTP, and the Web make it very easy to take things out of context; who can prevent users from circulating an image devoid of the supplementary material that made it legitimate? Moreover, children can easily access over the Internet materials that were intended for adults.

The U.S. child protection laws forbid any pornographic images that use children, whether or not the images meet Godwin's obscenity test. Individuals convicted can be fined up to $100,000 and imprisoned up to 10 years. As the result of a nationwide FBI investigation of online porn, for example, a distributor of child pornography was sentenced to five years in prison for sending sexually explicit photos of children via his America Online account (*Tampa Tribune* 2/24/96: A6).

Canada's best-known computer science school, the University of Waterloo, banned from its campus five Internet bulletin boards dealing with violent sex out of concern that their contents break laws on pornography and obscenity (*Toronto Globe & Mail* 2/5/94: A1).

The Recreational Software Advisory Council on the Internet (RSACi) has created an open, objective, content rating system called RSACi. It provides users with information about the level of sex, nudity, violence, vulgarity, or hate-motivated language in software games and Web sites. Parents and teachers can set the level at which to block offensive content. To learn how to set the level at which content will be blocked, follow the *Multilit* Web site link to RSACi.

Multi-User Domains

In her fascinating book *Life on the Screen,* Sherry Turkle (1995) describes what it is like to participate in **Multi-User Domains**, or **MUDs**, which are virtual spaces in which you can navigate, strategize, and converse with other users. Turkle views MUDs as a new kind of parlor game and a new form of community that lets people generate experiences, relationships, identities, and living spaces that arise only through interaction with technology. One of the dangerous aspects is how men can stalk women in MUDs. For example, Turkle tells of a virtual rape:

> One MUD player had used his skill with the system to seize control of another player's character. In this way the aggressor was able to direct the seized character to submit to a violent sexual encounter. He did all this against the will and over the distraught objections of the player usually "behind" this character, the player to whom this character "belonged." Although some made light of the offender's actions by saying that the episode was just words, in text-based virtual realities such as MUDs, words *are* deeds (Turkle 1995: 15).

Parents need to be aware of the dangers of MUDs, because young people are especially susceptible. Discussing childhood encounters with "netsex," Turkle warns:

> Parents need to be able to talk to their children about where they are going and what they are doing. This same commonsense rule applies to their children's lives on the screen. Parents don't have to become technical experts, but they do need to learn enough about computer networks to discuss with their children what and who is out there and lay down some basic safety rules. The children who do best after a bad experience on the Internet (who are harassed, perhaps even propositioned) are those who can talk to their parents, just as children who best handle bad experiences in real life are those who can talk to an elder without shame or fear of blame (Turkle 1995: 227).

To find Multi-User Domains online, follow the *Multilit* Web site link to the MUD Connector. For the latest MUD research, follow the link to the *Journal of Virtual Environments*. The *Multilit* Web site also links to *Cybersociology Magazine,* which is a webzine dedicated to the critical discussion of the Internet, cyberspace, online culture, and life online. In an article dealing with online relationships, for example, Sannicolas (*Cybersociology,* 1997, *Multilit* Web site) observed that 40% of the chatrooms open on the network at 7 p.m. were advertised as having sexual content and also being chats appropriate for teenagers. Sannicolas worries about the effect that adults entering these rooms to have virtual sex with teenagers may have on the development, socialization, and sexual behavior of adolescents.

Internet Addiction Disorder

The Internet can be addicting, so much so that the term **Internet Addiction Disorder (IAD)** has entered the medical lexicon. University of Pittsburgh researcher Kimberly Young maintains that IAD is as real as alcoholism, characterized by loss of control, cravings and withdrawal symptoms, social isolation, marital discord, academic failure, excessive financial debt, and job termination (*Toronto Globe & Mail* 6/15/96: A1).

At the 1999 meeting of the American Psychological Association, researcher David Greenfield reported the findings of the largest study of Internet use conducted to date. According to the report, nearly 6% (i.e., more than 11 million users) suffer from some form of addiction to the World Wide Web. As Greenfield (1999, ABCNEWS.com, *Multilit* Web site) states, "Marriages are being disrupted, kids are getting into trouble, people are committing illegal acts, people are spending too much money. As someone who treats patients, I see it." Arguing that the number of Internet addicts will grow, Greenfield pointed out that just as a drug is most addictive when absorbed directly into the bloodstream, the Internet's potential for abuse will grow with modem speeds and ease of access. For the complete story, follow the *Multilit* Web site link to Internet Addiction.

To borrow from the title of Sherry Turkle's book, there is "life on the screen," and certain kinds of people may prefer cyberlife to real life. If you feel yourself becoming addicted, set a time limit for how long you spend on the Internet each day, and try to stay focused on the task at hand. Many Web pages contain enticing ads intended to draw you away from your original purpose. You can reduce the amount of time you spend online if you stay focused on accomplishing your intent instead of surfing off in other directions.

For more information about Internet Addiction Disorder, follow the *Multilit* Web site links to Virtual Addiction and the Center for Online Addiction.

Regulation

With the broadcast television, cable TV, telephone, and computer network industries all jockeying for position, the Information Superhighway presents a regulatory nightmare. With Regional Bell telephone companies wanting to compete in the long distance marketplace, cable companies hoping both to offer local phone service and keep local phone companies from providing video services, and TV broadcasters demanding the right to provide data services along with their regular programming, Congress faces a legislative quagmire. To avoid endless delay in the construction of the Information Superhighway, the White House proposed to deregulate the telecommunications industry to a point where any company can offer any services to any set of consumers. According to a survey by the National Consumers League, the public sided with the administration on this issue by a two-thirds majority (*BNA Daily Report for Executives* 2/1/94: A12).

On February 8, 1996, the Telecommunications Deregulation Act was signed into law. To read the provisions of the Act, follow the *Multilit* Web site link to the Telecommunications Act of 1996. To find out how America's local phone companies have been working hard to realize the promise of the Act, follow the *Multilit* link to TelecommPolicy.net.

Privacy

Do you realize that many employers claim the legal right to read all of the e-mail and other electronic correspondence that flows through their company's computer network? While the Federal Electronic Communications Privacy Act of 1986 protects the privacy of messages sent over public networks like MCI Mail and CompuServe, it does not cover a company's internal e-mail (*New York Times* 12/6/93: A8). The author believes this infringes upon freedom of speech and should be changed. Even though your employer pays for the telephone line in your office, your employer cannot listen in on your telephone conversations without having a court order. How then can it be legal to eavesdrop on your electronic conversations? As Neal J. Friedman, a specialist in online computer law, explains: "Employees are under the misapprehension that the First Amendment applies in the workplace—it doesn't. Employees need to know they have no right of privacy and no right of free speech using company resources" (*Computerworld* 2/5/96: 55). Beware of this: Do not ever communicate anything electronically that you would not want read by your employer or network administrators.

You should also be aware that when you send e-mail on the Information Superhighway, it passes through one or more **gateways**. Each gateway is a computer that can (and often does for backup and reliability purposes) retain a copy of your communications. Any computer systems analyst with access to that network can read your messages. It is also possible to write sophisticated snooper software that can monitor all of your electronic communications and alert the eavesdropper when your messages contain certain key words or phrases. The Canadian Security Intelligence Service, for example, contracted with a Montreal firm for a system that can quickly isolate key words and phrases from millions of airborne phone, fax, and radio signals (*CTV National News* 1/31/94: 11:00 P.M.).

Do you write messages in Internet newsgroups? If you do not set the x-no-archive flag on your messages, anyone on the Internet can find your messages via the *DejaNews* newsgroup search engine at www.deja.com. Imagine the implications of this kind of technology for job seekers. Sometimes young people do foolish things. Suppose that when you were young, you got on the Internet and wrote immature messages in newsgroups. Later on, when you apply for a job, your potential employer can look you up in *DejaNews* and obtain an indexed list of everything you have ever written in newsgroups. Is this an invasion of privacy? As you attempt to answer this question, keep in mind that *DejaNews* did not exist prior to its invention in 1995; suddenly, a search engine appears that makes it possible for anyone to search through newsgroups in which you may have expressed your feelings and orientations on sensitive topics and issues.

While it is possible to remove a message from the Deja archives, it is usually not possible to remove it from the Usenet at large. To learn how to remove a message from the Deja archives, follow the *Multilit* Web site link to Deja Nuke. For more tips on safeguarding your online privacy, follow the *Multilit* Web site link to the Electronic Frontier Foundation (EFF) and read the EFF's "Top 12 Ways to Protect Your Online Privacy."

Encryption and the Clipper Chip

To prevent people from reading electronic correspondence, many firms encrypt their messages. The government is concerned that this prevents law enforcement agencies who have court orders from eavesdropping on digital communications. For many years, the White House wanted to control the encryption process by requiring that every government computer contain a **Clipper chip**, which is an encryption device with a "back door" that allows detectives with the proper access to decipher the messages. In opposition to the White House plan, more than 250 members of Congress cosponsored legislation that would prohibit requiring such back-door devices on computers. The Clipper chip has been denounced by industry groups as well as civil liberties groups concerned about privacy (*New York Times* 2/5/94: A1). The Computer Professionals for Social Responsibility (CPSR) organized a protest; to learn more about civil liberties and privacy, follow the *Multilit* Web site link to CPSR.

In 1999, the White House revised its policy and proposed legislation entitled the Cyberspace Electronic Security Act, which limits government use of decryption keys obtained by the courts. According to the Center for Democracy and Technology, however, the proposed policy would give the government access to decryption keys without adequate Fourth Amendment privacy protections. According to the Fourth Amendment to the U.S. Constitution, "The right of the people to be secure in their persons, houses, papers and effects, against unreasonable searches and seizures, shall not be violated . . ." In defense of this right, Americans for Computer Privacy (ACP) endorsed the Security and Freedom Through Encryption (SAFE) Act, which protects the right of the American citizen to use the strongest possible encryption and prevents the government from building in back-door access to private online communications. For more information about privacy legislation and online activism, follow the *Multilit* Web site link to Americans for Computer Privacy. To study the details of the proposed Cyberspace Electronic Security Act, follow the link to The Center for Democracy and Technology.

InfoWorld publisher Bob Metcalfe opposes back doors for technological reasons: "I am against Clipper simply because it will not work, and it will cost an unnecessary amount of tax money to outfit government computers with the chips. . . . Smart criminals can easily get around Clipper by using additional encryption. Stupid criminals will continue to do stupid things and get caught" (*Wall Street Journal* 3/22/94: A14).

Pretty Good Privacy (PGP) is an encryption program written by Phil Zimmerman. It is the kind of "additional encryption" to which Metcalfe refers. PGP runs on almost every brand of computer and is the most common way of encrypting e-mail messages. For example, there is a PGP plug-in for the popular Eudora e-mail package. For more information, follow the *Multilit* Web site link to PGP. Also written by Zimmerman is PGPfone, which uses a complex algorithm called Blowfish to scramble phone calls made through a computer modem. For details, follow the *Multilit* Web site link to PGPfone. You can download both PGP and PGPfone for free.

Censorship

Many people are concerned that in addition to being able to read electronic communications, network administrators also have the ability to censor them. To what extent and under what circumstances should the government act as a censor on the Information Superhighway?

Few would argue that the University of Waterloo erred in banning obscene bulletin boards from its network. But what prevents users from avoiding the ban by distributing the material through e-mail? During a well-publicized criminal trial in Toronto, the Canadian government exercised its right to ban any publicity about the case, lest prospective jurors become biased and the hearings end in mistrial. So the University of Toronto stopped carrying an Internet bulletin board that disclosed banned information about the case. But that did not stop people from distributing the information through e-mail. It has become virtually impossible to intercept the electronic exchange of such information (*Toronto Globe & Mail* 12/2/93: A4).

There has been a lot of controversy surrounding the Communications Decency Act of 1996 (CDA), which made it illegal to distribute indecent or offensive materials on the Internet. Ruling that the act violates free speech, a three-judge federal court blocked enforcement of the CDA, describing it as "a government-imposed content-based restriction on speech," in violation of the Constitution. In defense of the CDA, the Justice Department appealed to the Supreme Court. The Citizens Internet Empowerment Coalition (CIEC) lobbied hard, however, and the Supreme Court ruled that the CDA was unconstitutional because it violated the First Amendment right of free speech. For more on the Supreme Court decision, follow the *Multilit* Web site link to the Citizens Internet Empowerment Coalition.

For more information about freedom of speech and censorship, follow the *Multilit* Web site link to the American Communication Association (ACA). The ACA Center for Communication Law maintains an extensive list of organizations dedicated to opposing censorship and preserving the right of free speech. To learn about the Blue Ribbon Campaign for Online Free Speech, for example, follow the *Multilit* Web site link to the Electronic Frontier Foundation.

Violence and the V-Chip

To provide a way for parents to censor TV programs containing adult content, the Federal Communications Commission invented the V-chip, which is a technology for blocking the display of television programming based upon its rating. The *V* stands for violence, but the V-chip also blocks other kinds of adult content, such as erotic, obscene, and profane materials. As of January 1, 2000, all television sets with picture screens 13 inches or larger must contain the V-chip. Set-top boxes permit parents to set the level at which the programs will be blocked.

The rating system is called TV Parental Guidelines. It was established in conjunction with the National Association of Broadcasters, the National Cable Television Association, and the Motion Picture Association of America. Ratings are displayed on the TV screen for the first 15 seconds of rated programming. To see the ratings, follow the *Multilit* Web site link to the FCC's V-Chip home page. For a parent's guide to the TV ratings, follow the link to the Kaiser Foundation's V-Chip Education Project.

Protectionism

Some countries view multimedia technology as a cultural threat and are taking steps to counteract it. To protect the French language, for example, France passed a law in 1996 requiring that all software sold in France must be provided in a French-language version. People who live in France should protest such a Machiavellian law.

China has a history of human rights abuses and denial of individual freedom. Continuing that tradition, China is building a centrally administered Internet backbone that will allow government monitoring of e-mail and other online activities (*Wall Street Journal* 1/31/96: A1).

Viewing the Internet as the end of civilization, Iraq has denied access to all of its citizens. An editorial in the Iraqi government newspaper *Al-Jumhuriya* says that the Internet is "the end of civilizations, cultures, interests, and ethics," and "one of the American means to enter every house in the world. They want to become the only source for controlling human beings in the new electronic village" (Associated Press 2/17/97). This viewpoint fails to realize that many of the key Internet inventions came from outside the United States. Packet switching originated in Great Britain, for example, and the Web was invented in Switzerland.

The Internet is a worldwide resource in which every country should participate and become a co-inventor. Restricting or denying access to the Internet will severely retard a nation's status in the twenty-first century. Every citizen in the world should have the right to unrestricted Internet access.

Internet Taxes

Taxation is a tricky problem on the Internet because any company can establish a storefront on the Web and sell products to anyone in the world. The White House and Congress have lobbied with the World Trade Organization to impose a moratorium on Internet tariffs and taxes. Several European countries have objected, however, because they want to collect their value-added tax (VAT) for goods purchased over the Internet. In France, for example, the value-added tax on goods exceeds 20% of the purchase price. Of particular concern is the bit tax that the United Nations is considering. Bit, which stands for binary digit, is a unit of measure for computer files. The larger the file, the more bits it has in it. Anderson tells how the bit tax would increase based on the size of the file being transferred (*ABC News* 1999, *Multilit* Web site).

A law which banned new U.S. Internet taxes for three years has also established an Advisory Commission on Electronic Commerce. Members of the commission are divided on the issue of the ban, with conservatives fearing the loss of government revenue to tax-free Internet business, and liberals arguing that sales taxes or bit taxes would hamper the network's growth. To learn more about electronic commerce and tax policy, follow the *Multilit* Web site link to the Advisory Commission on Electronic Commerce.

Multimedia and the Law

Multimedia is putting new pressures on the legal system. Initially slow to learn about new media, the patent office was tricked into granting some patents too broad in scope. Misinterpretations of the copyright law have prevented fair use of multimedia by teachers and students. Lawmakers and enforcers need to be multiliterate so they can bolster the use of new media on the Information Superhighway instead of retarding its progress through lack of understanding. *Note:* This chapter is not intended as a substitute for legal advice. You should consult a lawyer or a campus copyright official before taking action in specific cases, because your circumstances may differ from what is described here.

Patents

The U.S. Patent and Trademark Office granted two multimedia patents so broad in scope that the awardees blatantly announced all other vendors owed them royalties on all past, present, and future products. This created an industrywide protest so severe that one of the vendors withdrew its claim; the patent office overturned the other patent. In both cases, there was so much prior art that for people in the industry these claims were likened to trying to patent sunlight (*Wall Street Journal* 3/25/94: B2).

THE OPTICAL DATA PATENT

The first case involved a patent awarded to Optical Data Corporation for the syllabus-based curriculum outlining method used in the *Windows on Science* program. The syllabus is so basic to the teaching process that many other products already used it. Kinnaman (1993) describes how Videodiscovery filed a lawsuit seeking a declaratory judgment finding the patent invalid because of prior art and the obviousness of the claims. The Interactive Multimedia Association (IMA) supported the Videodiscovery complaint; as IMA president Philip Dodds politely stated, "Patents such as these, which require nearly every company involved in interactive multimedia and education to license an idea and application that have a long history and are widely known, are not in the best interest of the industry or educators" (Kinnaman 1993).

To stop the flow of negative publicity stemming from the patent, Optical Data dedicated the patent permanently to the public. According to Optical Data chair William Clark, "It was never our intent to use this patent to inhibit the development of multimedia based interactive teaching methods. A tremendous amount of concern—including a lawsuit by one of our competitors—arose from this patent award. We hope that by voluntarily dedicating this patent to the public, we will end any unfounded fears that Optical Data, or any other company, might try to limit the diversity of interactive, multimedia programs available to educators" (Kinnaman 1994).

But Foremski (1994) reports another company attempting to do just that. Compton's caused an uproar by claiming at COMDEX/Fall '93 that they had been awarded a patent that would require all multimedia developers to pay them royalties. As Compton's CEO Stanley Frank said, "We helped kick start this industry. We now ask to be compensated for our investments. We will do whatever it takes to defend our patent."

THE COMPTON'S PATENT

The Compton's patent is very broad. It covers any type of computer-controlled database system that allows a user to search for mixed media that includes text with graphics, sound, or animation. Compton's did not limit their claims to CD-ROM products; they also claimed rights to any type of database involving interactive TV or the Information Superhighway.

The title of the Compton's patent is "Multimedia search system using a plurality of entry path means which indicate interrelatedness of information." It claims:

> A computer search system for retrieving information, comprising:
>
> means for storing interrelated textual information and graphical information;
>
> means for interrelating said textual and graphical information;
>
> a plurality of entry path means for searching said stored interrelated textual and graphical information, said entry path means comprising:
>
> textual search entry path means for searching said textual information and for retrieving interrelated graphical information to said searched text;
>
> graphics entry path means for searching said graphical information and for retrieving interrelated textual information to said searched graphical information;
>
> selecting means for providing a menu of said plurality of entry path means for selection;
>
> processing means for executing inquiries provided by a user in order to search said textual and graphical information through said selected entry path means;
>
> indicating means for indicating a pathway that accesses information related in one of said entry path means to information accessible in another one of said entry path means;
>
> accessing means for providing access to said related information in said another entry path means; and
>
> output means for receiving search results from said processing means and said related information from said accessing means and for providing said search results and received information to such user.

Compton's presented all multimedia developers with four patent royalty payment options. Kinnaman (1994) explains how they included "entering into a joint venture with Compton's; distributing products through the company's Affiliated Label Program; licensing Compton's SmarTrieve technology; or paying royalties." Compton's had the audacity to require back royalties of 1% of net receipts from sales before June 30, 1994, and 3% thereafter.

To say the least, developers reacted negatively to Compton's demands. Some suggested that users should burn all Compton's CD-ROMs and refuse to purchase future titles from any company that would try to force such a Machiavellian proviso on the multimedia industry. As a result of public hearings held by the U.S. Patent and Trademark Office to review its handling of software patents, the Compton's patent was rescinded.

The furor over Optical Data's and Compton's patents caused the patent office to initiate reforms that include publicizing patent applications, hiring seven software specialists as examiners, revamping the examiner bonus program so it does not encourage superficial review, and requiring more information about patent applications before decisions are made (*Wall Street Journal* 4/11/94: B6). In fairness to the government, industry leaders like Optical Data and Compton's (who know better) should stop trying to profit from patenting prior art; instead, they should concentrate on improving their products and moving the industry forward.

UNISYS GIF PATENT

Unisys owns the patent on the compression scheme used in the GIF file format, which is one of the most popular image formats in the world. In 1994, Unisys decided to begin charging developers a licensing fee for using the GIF file format. This resulted in a backlash of harsh opposition from developers and users who felt Unisys had acted unfairly, and Unisys backed down. Recently, Unisys began to try again to charge for the use of GIF images. This time, Unisys is asking WebMasters to pay $5,000 if their Web site uses one or more GIF images created by a program that is not licensed by Unisys to use GIF images.

By trying a second time to make users pay for something they thought was free, Unisys has caused another uproar among GIF users and developers who, instead of paying the $5,000 fee, have begun converting their graphics to the PNG format. *PNG* stands for Portable Network Graphics. It is a format created largely in response to the Unisys patent fiasco. As this book goes to press, however, the PNG format cannot do animated GIFs, and an MNG format that can is not yet supported by browsers. To learn the latest on this problem, follow the *Multilit* Web site link to the PNG Home Page and Burn All GIFs.

To perform patent searches and read the latest news from the U.S. Patent and Trademark Office, follow the *Multilit* Web site link to PTO.

Copyright

Article I, section 8, of the U.S. Constitution grants Congress the power "to promote the progress of science and useful arts, by securing for limited times to authors and inventors the exclusive right to their respective writings and discoveries." Congress used this power to pass the Copyright Act of 1976, which defines and allocates rights associated with "original works of authorship fixed in any tangible medium of expression, now known or later developed, or otherwise communicated, either directly or with the aid of a machine or device" (U.S. Constitution, 17 § 102). This means that all of the elements presented in the taxonomy of multimedia in Chapter 2 of this book—including illustrations, text, movies, video clips, documentaries, animations, music, and software—are protected by copyright. There are stiff penalties for copyright offenders. For example, the Software Publishers Association took action in 1993 against 577 organizations for pirating commercial software, resulting in $3.6 million in fines (*Atlanta Journal-Constitution* 2/3/94: C2).

Whenever you plan to publish a multimedia work, whether on a CD, DVD, or the Information Superhighway, you must make sure you have the right to use every object in it. Similarly, you should register a copyright for your multimedia creations. On your application's home screen, and on the title page of any printed documentation, print the following copyright notice, replacing *xx* with the current year: **Copyright © 20*xx* by *your_name_goes_here*. All rights reserved.**

Although this notice legally suffices to protect your copyright, it is also a good idea to register the copyright with the U.S. Copyright Office. If someone infringes your copyright and you take legal action to defend it, copyright registration can help your case. To register a copyright, follow these steps:

1. Go to the U.S. Copyright Office Web page at http://www.loc.gov/copyright and choose Copyright Registration.

2. Choose Multimedia Works to display the policies and procedures for multimedia copyright registration. Read the policy to determine what form to use to register your copyright.

3. Go back to http://www.loc.gov/copyright and choose Copyright Application Forms. Download the form you need.

4. Complete the application form and make a copy to retain in your files.

5. Mail the application along with a copy of the work and the $20 registration fee to the Register of Copyrights, Copyright Office, Library of Congress, Washington, D.C. 20559.

If you want a receipt, have the post office mail your application "return receipt requested." It will take several weeks for the Library of Congress to process your application and send you the registration number. For more information, follow the links to Copyright at the *Multilit* Web site.

Fair Use

The **Fair Use** provision of the U.S. Copyright Act allows the use of copyrighted works in reporting news, conducting research, and teaching. The law states:

Notwithstanding the provisions of section 106 [which grants authors exclusive rights], the fair use of a copyrighted work, including such use by reproduction in copies or phonorecords or by any other means specified by that section, for purposes such as criticism, comment, news reporting, teaching (including multiple copies for classroom use), scholarship, or research, is not an infringement of copyright. In determining whether the use made of a work in any particular case is a fair use the factors to be considered shall include:

1. the purpose and character of the use, including whether such use is of a commercial nature or is for nonprofit educational purposes;

2. the nature of the copyrighted work;

3. the amount and substantiality of the portion used in relation to the copyrighted work as a whole; and

4. the effect of the use upon the potential market for, or value of, the copyrighted work.

INTERPRETING FAIR USE FOR EDUCATION

To summarize the Fair Use law for education, one may paraphrase its first paragraph as follows: "the fair use of a copyrighted work for . . . teaching (including multiple copies for classroom use) . . . is not an infringement of copyright." The difficulty arises from interpreting the four tests, which are intentionally left vague, as the law goes on to state: "Although the courts have considered and ruled upon the fair use doctrine over and over again, no real definition of the concept has ever emerged. Indeed, since the doctrine is an equitable rule of reason, no generally applicable definition is possible, and each case raising the question must be decided on its own facts."

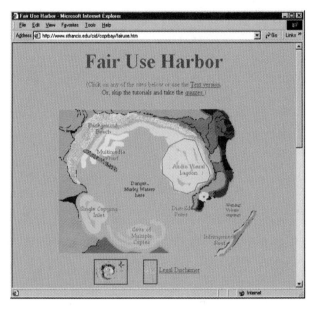

Figure 16-1 Copyright Bay is based on the metaphor of a Fair Use Harbor. The metaphor stems from the belief that the Fair Use guidelines provide a "safe harbor" within which multimedia users can exercise the right of Fair Use.

Courtesy of Gummess, Glen; Agnew, Janet; Hudson, Mike. Artwork: Gummess, Glen. University of St. Francis.

THE FAIR USE GUIDELINES FOR EDUCATIONAL MULTIMEDIA

To help educational institutions interpret the Fair Use law with regard to multimedia, the CCUMC (Consortium of College and University Media Centers) spearheaded the creation of the "Fair Use Guidelines for Educational Multimedia." The committee that created these guidelines consisted of representatives from print, film, music, and multimedia publishing companies, who spent many months discussing and debating fair use issues with representatives from educational institutions. Professor Lisa Livingston, director of the Instructional Media Division of the City University of New York, chaired the committee, and well-known copyright attorney Ivan Bender was retained to advise on legal issues. As a member of this committee, the author can attest to the rigor of the process.

The "Fair Use Guidelines for Educational Multimedia" are linked to the *Multilit* Web site. They specify what is fair for students as well as for teachers. The author encourages you to study these guidelines carefully and use them to exercise your right of fair use. Also linked to the *Multilit* Web site is Copyright Bay, which uses the metaphor of a harbor, as pictured in Figure 16-1. Clicking the bay's links brings up tutorials on the Fair Use issues illustrated in the harbor.

THE DIGITAL MILLENNIUM COPYRIGHT ACT

In 1998, the Digital Millennium Copyright Act (DMCA) was enacted into law in the United States. One of the primary purposes of this complex act was to bring the United States into conformance with the World Intellectual Property Organization (WIPO) Treaty. The DMCA contains many new statutory provisions, including:

- New rules prohibiting the circumvention of Technological Protection Measures (TPM), with stiff penalties for infringers.

- Prohibition of the removal from a copyrighted work of information related to ownership, copyright, and licensing.

- Limitation of liability of Online Service Providers if someone using their service infringes a copyright.

- Promoting distance education over digital networks while maintaining an appropriate balance between the rights of copyright holders and the needs of teachers and students making fair use of copyrighted works.

The DMCA charges the Library of Congress to work toward the implementation of these measures by proposing appropriate policies and guidelines. A key issue is whether fair use can be made of a work protected by a TPM since the DMCA makes it illegal to bypass the TPM. For more information about the status and implications of the DMCA, follow the *Multilit* Web site links to the Digital Millennium Copyright Act, the Library of Congress, the DMCA Primer, and the WIPO treaties.

Ethics

Ethics is a two-way street. If the Information Superhighway is to succeed, users must both behave and be treated ethically and responsibly. Because the Internet is a frontier, new users need a way to find out the rules of the road. In 1990, American University Professor Frank Connolly recognized this need. He led a project at EDUCOM (now EDUCAUSE) to create "The Bill of Rights and Responsibilities for Electronic Learners." The goal was to create a computer network policy addressing the rights and responsibilities of individuals, schools, and colleges in the twenty-first century.

Published in 1993, the Bill of Rights has four sections. The first section recognizes the right of all individuals to access the Information Superhighway, to find out what kind of information is being collected about them, and to exercise the right of free speech on the Internet. The second section holds individuals accountable for honoring the intellectual property of other users, protecting the integrity and authenticity of information, respecting and valuing each user's right to privacy, and refraining from activities that waste resources or prevent others from using them. Section three gives institutions the right to access the Internet, protect intellectual resources mounted on the Net, and allocate resources. Section four holds institutions accountable for making sure that software has been legally acquired, maintaining security to protect the integrity of individual files, treating personal files as the confidential property of the user, and providing training in the effective use of information technology.

The complete text of "The Bill of Rights and Responsibilities for Electronic Learners" is linked to the *Multilit* Web site. Every user should abide by this Bill of Rights and Responsibilities.

Equity, Cost, and Universal Access

As this book goes to press, only one in four American households has regular access to the Internet. We have a long way to go before achieving universal access.

In 1996, Congress expanded the Universal Service program to cover information technologies. True to its name, the Universal Service program subsidizes the cost of telecommunications in remote and rural areas so the fees paid by end users are roughly compatible. A Link-Up America program helps low-income households pay installation costs, and a Lifeline Assistance program subsidizes their monthly service fees. The National Telecommunications and Information Administration (NTIA) monitors the success of these programs in a series of reports, entitled *Falling Through the Net*.

According to the reports, people with high incomes are 20 times more likely to have access to the Internet, and more than nine times as likely to have a computer at home. Only 10% of households earning less than $20,000 have Internet access, while 60% of households earning $75,000 or more are connected. Whites are more likely to have access to the Internet at home than Blacks or Hispanics from any location. Black and Hispanic households are one-third as likely to have home access as Asian/Pacific Islander households, and roughly two-fifths as likely as White households. Rural Americans lag behind regardless of income level. City dwellers are twice as likely to have Internet access than rural Americans earning the same income. Only 18.9% of Native Americans have access, compared to the national average of 26.2%. In the Southwestern United States, 78% of the 56,000 homes on the Navajo Indian Reservation do not even have telephone service.

To understand what needs to be done to achieve universal access, follow the *Multilit* Web site links to the Universal Service Fund, the Digital Divide, and *Falling Through the Net.*

Multimedia Careers

As the growth charts presented in Chapter 1 demonstrate, multimedia is the fastest-growing industry in the world today, and as such, it is creating new job opportunities. Josephson and Gorman (1997) have written a book entitled *Careers in Multimedia: Roles and Resources* that can help you position yourself for a job in multimedia. You can order it online at amazon.com or barnesandnoble.com. The book covers multimedia industries, projects, work issues, roles, resources, and locations where most jobs are found. Dozens of successful professionals working in multimedia are profiled. Table 16-1 lists sample careers in multimedia.

Another strategy for finding work in multimedia, or any other field for that matter, is to put your résumé on the Web. McGraw-Hill's *Internet Literacy* textbook contains a step-by-step tutorial on creating Web résumés. Once your résumé is online, the Web crawlers will find it and make it accessible to potential employers who search the Net for talent. Several of the author's students have been invited to job interviews in this manner.

If you are looking for a job, or if you are an employer looking to fill a position opening, be sure to visit America's Job Bank (AJB) at www.ajb.org. Created by the U.S. Department

Table 16-1   Career Opportunities in Multimedia

Advertising	Online services
Animation	Presentations
CD recording	Public relations
Construction planning	Real estate marketing
Content design	Scientific modeling
Courtroom trial reenactment	Screen design
Electronic publishing	Scripting and storyboarding
Facilities design	Simulation
Front-Ending	Sound tracks
Games design	Special effects
Graphics production	Training
Instructional design	Travel systems
Interface design	Video production
Kiosking	Virtual reality
Landscape design	Webmaster

of Labor, America's Job Bank lists hundreds of thousands of job openings that you can search by occupation, location, qualifications, and salary. While you are visiting the AJB, also follow the links to America's Career Infonet and America's Learning Exchange, where you will find online career and job-training services, respectively.

Bandwidth

Traffic on the Information Superhighway is growing at a rate faster than the bandwidth needed to carry that traffic. The popularity of real-time audio and videoconferencing products has caused Web traffic to increase far beyond what Tim Berners-Lee envisioned when he invented the Web back in 1989.

When the amount of data exceeds the capacity of the routers and switches through which the data flow, a situation known as **Internet brownout** occurs. In an Internet brownout, packets of data sent over the network slow to a crawl and can be lost forever, never getting to their destinations. When your Web browser pops up an alert box telling you that a host is unreachable, brownout could be the culprit. NetStar's vice president for sales and marketing maintains that brownouts have caused the Internet to become "about as reliable these days as the phone system in Russia" (*Business Week* 4/8/96: 82).

The Internet Engineering Task Force (IETF) is working on these problems. Since the World Wide Web is the biggest culprit, the IETF is examining whether there is a way to streamline the transmission of data to and from Web servers. Another proposed solution would meter Internet usage, charging heavy users more and light users less. You can find out more by following the *Multilit* Web site link to the IETF.

Internet2

A consortium of research universities is conducting a project called **Internet2**. The goal is to create a higher speed version of the Internet that will revolve around a high-speed connection point called the Gigapop. Strategically placed throughout the network, Gigapops will guarantee high-speed bandwidth between universities implementing the Internet2 standards.

Internet2 uses three protocols to provide high-speed transmission and guaranteed bandwidth:

- RSVP permits a user to reserve bandwidth from the workstation to the network host computer.

- IPv6 is a packet delivery protocol that lets the user assign priority to certain kinds of information. You may want your Web search traffic to have a higher priority than your e-mail traffic, for example, so your searches get completed faster.

- Multicast will use IP tunneling and multithreading to increase multimedia throughput.

To find out the current status, follow the *Multilit* Web site link to Internet2.

e x e r c i s e s

1. If you have never played the *Mortal Kombat* video game, find a friend who has it and give it a try. Set it for the highest level of violence; if you cannot figure out how to do this, ask the kids who play it. Do you believe that this kind of graphic violence in video games is good for children to experience? What do you think should be done about it?

2. Visit your local video arcade and try the latest laser shooting games. Notice how real video footage is used to put you in a situation in which you must kill or be killed. See how realistic the interaction is, and how well you can learn to aim and fire the weapons. Do you believe these games should be available to the kind of crowd attracted to video arcades, especially when gunshot wounds are the leading cause of death among teenagers in our cities? What do you think should be done about this?

3. How do you feel about the use of multimedia for sex? Does virtual sex serve any useful role in our society? How can it be misused? Could it help solve any societal problems?

4. Do you believe software that lets men force women to do their bidding encourages men to believe they can and should have control over women in real life? If so, what should be done about this?

5. As explained earlier in this chapter, a lot of traffic on the Information Superhighway deals with sex. Do you believe this large amount of sexual traffic detracts from the goals and objectives of the Internet? Do you object to the use of public funds to transmit such material? Why or why not?

6. Do you agree that the University of Waterloo was justified in banning obscene bulletin boards from its network? Should obscene bulletin boards be banned from the Information Superhighway as a whole? Are obscene bulletin boards accessible from your connection to the network?

7. Has a government regulation ever prevented you from accessing services you felt you had a right to? For example, when the FCC ruled that cable companies cannot rebroadcast FM signals, the author's community lost its cable access to National Public Radio and several other FM stations. Since we live in an area too remote for good FM reception, we became disconnected from these important stations. And without any warning! This made the author wonder how the government will manage the Information Superhighway if it cannot regulate access to a simple FM radio station. Have you had a similar experience of being denied access to services you felt you had a right to? What service were you denied? Why did you feel you had a right to it?

8. How do you feel about encryption and Clipper chip technology? Since court-ordered wiretaps on the analog telephone lines of criminals will no longer be effective when all of the communication channels go digital, is the government justified in requiring that a back door be built into the system through which it can eavesdrop on digital communications? Why or why not?

9. The White House has promised the public that everyone will have equal access to the Information Superhighway. Do you believe this, or do you feel that its construction will create a technological underclass in our society? What do you see as the major obstacles that must be overcome to provide equal access for everyone?

10. Table 16-1 lists career opportunities in multimedia. Can you think of any multimedia careers that are not included in the table?

11. Go to America's Job Bank at www.ajb.org. When this book went to press, there were 1,521,306 available jobs. How many jobs are open now?

17

How to Keep Up

After completing this chapter, you will be able to:

- Keep up with the changes that are occurring in multimedia, Internet, and educational technology

- Join listservs that will e-mail you periodic summaries of the latest multimedia news

- Bookmark Web sites that will help you can stay current with new technology

- Subscribe to printed magazines that will help you keep up with the fast-paced field of multimedia

- Peruse catalogs for new products that may interest you

- Find out about conferences and exhibits where you can see the latest multimedia hardware and software products

There are many reasons why you need to keep up with what is happening in multimedia. Since the ability to use it is emerging as a life skill, you will continually need to develop your multimedia techniques to stay competitive in your profession and live life fully in the information society. As the technology changes and you upgrade your computer, you will need the latest information and advice on what to buy. By periodically checking the Web sites, joining the listservs, and subscribing to the periodicals listed in this chapter, you will be able to remain current and even contribute your own opinions and ideas about multimedia access to the Information Superhighway. Almost all of these resources are free; the only cost of reading the free ones is your time, which will be well spent.

Listservs

A listserv is an Internet resource consisting of an electronic mailing list that distributes e-mail to subscribers. When you subscribe to a listserv, your e-mail address gets added to the list. When someone sends a message to the list, everyone on the list gets served a copy. Hence the name listserv.

In Table 17-1, you will find the listservs that can help you keep up with what is happening in multimedia, Internet, and educational technology. Column 1 gives the name of the listserv, column 2 says what it does, and column 3 tells how to subscribe. The listservs listed here are moderated, meaning that the listserv administrator screens incoming messages before they get distributed to the list. You will not receive irrelevant or unwanted messages by joining these lists. At any time, however, you can unsubscribe, if you decide you do not want to receive the messages being sent to the list. All of the listservs in Table 17-1 are free; there is no cost to join.

Table 17-1 Recommended Listservs

Name of Listserv	What the Listserv Does	How to Subscribe
NewsScan	Summarizes news in multimedia and educational technology	Send e-mail to **NewsScan@NewsScan.com** with **subscribe** in the subject line
Seidman's Online Insider	Puts you on the inside track of what's happening on the Internet	To subscribe to the plain text version, send e-mail to **insider-text-on@seidman.infobeat.com** To get the HTML version, send e-mail to **insider-html-on@seidman.infobeat.com**
TOURBUS	Provides a virtual tour of the best Internet sites and tools	Send e-mail to **listserv@listserv.aol.com**; leave the subject line blank, and as your message, write **SUBSCRIBE TOURBUS firstname lastname**
Netsurfer Digest	Reviews the latest hot spots on the Internet	Send e-mail to **nsdigest-request@netsurf.com**. Leave the subject line blank, and as your message, write **Subscribe nsdigest-text**
AAHE	Lively discussion of current topics in educational technology	Send e-mail to **listproc@list.cren.net**. Leave the subject line blank and, as your message, write **SUBSCRIBE AAHESGIT firstname lastname**
DEOSNEWS	Distance education online symposium	Send e-mail to **listserv@lists.psu.edu**. Leave the subject line blank, and as your message, write **SUBSCRIBE DEOS-L firstname lastname**

Web Sites

Listed here are Web sites you can visit periodically to stay current with new technology. You will want to bookmark all of the Web sites listed here, because they are excellent places to keep up with what is happening in multimedia and the Internet.

NewMedia.com

THE MAGAZINE FOR CREATORS OF THE DIGITAL FUTURE

NewMedia.com is possibly the best single source for keeping up with what is new in multimedia. It is an enhanced, Web-based daily information service for professionals working on the cutting edge of Internet business, design, and technology. NewMedia.com has been designed to help the Internet architect develop the strategies, exploit the technologies, and build the business models that are leading the Internet revolution today. Be sure to visit www.newmedia.com and bookmark it in your Web browser.

CNET (www.CNET.com)

CNET is an online resource for the latest technology news and trend analysis, special reports, hardware and software reviews, and numerous download indexes that provide you with access to the Web's freeware and shareware programs. You will value the time you spend at www.cnet.com; be sure to bookmark it.

TERC (www.terc.edu)

TERC, a nonprofit organization founded in 1965, researches, develops, and disseminates innovative programs in science, mathematics, and technology for educators, schools, and other learning environments. TERC is organized into four project-based centers: Mathematics, Research, Science, and Tools for Learning. Some of the recent TERC projects include:

- **NGS Kids Network**. Developed by TERC and the National Geographic Society (NGS), this telecommunications-based science curriculum for elementary and middle-school students won the 1999 Golden Lamp award.

- **Science by Design**. A high school curriculum for successfully formulating and carrying out product design. Students apply concepts in science and technology to design and build a pair of insulated gloves, a model boat, a greenhouse, and a catapult.

- **The Global Laboratory Project**. A worldwide network of student scientists from more than 20 countries involved in collaborative environmental investigations.

- **New Directions in Science Playgrounds**. Creating a new type of playground equipment that facilitates the kinesthetic learning of elementary notions of physics in playground activities.

- **LabNet**. A telecomputing network of the science teaching community.

- **The Hub**. A World Wide Web link to a growing collection of educational resources and services for mathematics, science, and technology educators.

Printed Journals and Magazines

Listed here are printed journals and magazines that you can read to keep up with what is happening in multimedia and educational technology. All of these periodicals have Web sites where you can fill out a form to subscribe. Best of all, most of these magazines are free.

Internet World

A good source for the latest news about the Information Superhighway, *Internet World* features articles about new trends on the network, advertises Internet addresses of new online resources, reviews books about the Internet, and presents profiles of the key companies, people, and products that impact the Internet's growth and development. Penetrating analyses probe legal, social, and ethical issues. Labs educate users and buyers about important new Internet products and technologies for home and business. Job announcements list employment opportunities across a broad range of technologies. Subscriptions are free in the United States only for qualified individuals employed in the field of information technology. To apply for a subscription, follow the *Multilit* Web site link to *Internet World* and click Subscribe.

T.H.E. Journal

T.H.E. stands for Technological Horizons in Education. *T.H.E. Journal* appears monthly; each issue contains application highlights and dozens of new product announcements. Each year, *T.H.E. Journal* publishes the *Multimedia Source Guide,* which lists hundreds of multimedia products and tells how to order them. Subscribers also receive special multimedia supplements from vendors such as IBM, Apple, and Zenith.

T.H.E. Journal is free to qualified individuals in educational institutions and training departments in the United States and Canada. To subscribe, follow the *Multilit* Web site link to *T.H.E. Journal,* where you will also find an online version that lets you download product demos, search back issues, and read articles that did not appear in the printed journal. Online features include the Infrastructure Supplement, a Road Map to the Web for Educators, and a review of presentation products and a database of their manufactures.

Technology & Learning

Technology & Learning is published monthly, except in December and the summer months. Targeted primarily at precollege educators, it reviews software, advertises grants and contests, contains vendor supplements, articulates classroom needs, reviews authoring tools, and has a Q&A section to answer questions about technology and learning. Plus it has great cartoons.

To subscribe, follow the *Multilit* Web site link to *Technology & Learning*, where you will also find an online version that lets you search software reviews.

Wired

Wired is an award-winning monthly magazine that captures the excitement and the substance of the digital revolution. The best writers and designers in the world help you identify the people, companies, and ideas shaping our future. To subscribe, follow the *Multilit* Web site link to *Wired*.

Syllabus

Syllabus magazine informs educators on how technology can be used to support teaching, learning, and administrative activities. Each issue includes feature articles, case studies, product reviews, and profiles of technology use at the individual, departmental, and institutional level. Regular features cover multimedia, distance learning, the Internet, quantitative tools, publishing, and administrative technology. A variety of multi-platform technologies are covered, including computers, video, multimedia, and telecommunications. Special supplements to *Syllabus* are published on a regular basis, including Windows on Campus, Computer Science Edition, Engineering Edition, and Science and Medicine Edition. *Syllabus* is published nine times per year, following the academic calendar. In the United States, subscriptions are free to individuals who work in colleges, universities, and high schools. To subscribe, follow the *Multilit* Web site link to the SyllabusWeb.

Presenting Communications

Presenting Communications is the monthly magazine of presentation technology for the audio/video industry. It covers new developments, emerging standards, and analytical reports on video, multimedia, computers, audiovisuals, teleconferencing, industry trends, and government regulations and initiatives. Subcriptions are free to North American addresses. To subscribe, follow the *Multilit* Web site link to *Presenting Communications*.

Cinefex

If you are interested in cinematic special effects, *Cinefex* is the magazine for you. Since 1980, *Cinefex* has been the bible for special-effects enthusiasts. A profusely illustrated quarterly publication, *Cinefex* covers its subject comprehensively, from miniatures and matte paintings, to exotic makeup and animatronics, to computer-generated imagery and beyond. With each issue, the illusions in two or three major films are examined in detail via interviews with key effects artists. Shorter articles unveil technological advances in commercials, music videos, and theme park attractions. The articles identify the multimedia software packages used to create the special effects.

Cinefex Online lets you browse the current issue, preview the next issue, and explore back issues using a cross-referenced listing of all articles published in *Cinefex*. You can find out if a film or other effects-related project has been covered in the magazine, for example, and you can identify articles in which specific artists or multimedia production companies and products have appeared. To enjoy these capabilities, follow the *Multilit* Web site link to *Cinefex Online.*

Catalogs

Sometimes the broad array of different multimedia products on the market can be both dazzling and confusing. Catalogs allay the confusion by organizing the products into categories. Listed here are some of the catalogs the author has found useful.

Computer Shopper

One of the best catalogs for people considering computer purchases is *Computer Shopper.* It is filled with new product announcements, evaluations, advertisements, technology reviews, and shopper guides to multimedia peripherals, input/output devices, and modems. You can find *Computer Shopper* on the magazine rack of most newsstands. It is very popular, and new editions come out monthly. Although *Computer Shopper* is called a magazine, it looks and feels more like a catalog, which is why it is listed here as a catalog. To subscribe or to search the catalog online, follow the *Multilit* Web site link to *Computer Shopper.*

Multimedia Compendium

The *Multimedia Compendium* is a great way to find out about current CD, DVD, and multimedia-related software titles for use in education and training. The bound edition appears annually in September, and updates are published each January and July. A QuickSearch Index provides easy access to products by subject, title, company, and other topics in the listing. The *Compendium* provides detailed information on more than 5,000 products. To peruse the table of contents from the current edition, follow the *Multilit* Web site link to the *Multimedia Compendium* from Emerging Technology Consultants, where you will find ordering information.

Professional Associations

While most of the resources recommended in this chapter are free, you will have to pay to join the professional associations listed here. It is money well spent, however. Besides reaping the benefits afforded to the members, you will be supporting the organizations that are working to improve multimedia and the Internet.

AECT

AECT stands for Association for Educational Communications and Technology; it is the leading international organization representing instructional technology professionals working in schools, colleges, and universities, and the corporate, government, and military sectors. The mission of the AECT is to provide leadership in educational communications and technology by linking professionals holding a common interest in the use of educational technology and its application to the learning process. The association maintains an active publications program that includes *Tech Trends,* a magazine published six times during the academic year; *Educational Technology Research*

and Development, a research journal published four times a year; and a large number of books and videotapes. To join, follow the *Multilit* Web site link to AECT.

SALT

SALT stands for the Society for Applied Learning Technology. It sponsors educational conferences and exhibits as well as the publication of research journals. SALT covers a broad range of applications, with a special focus on education, training, and job performance improvement applications. SALT maintains a Web site at www.salt.org which contains information on conferences, newsworthy happenings, and links to other areas of interest. The Society-sponsored meetings are excellent for those who deal with media, regardless of industry or subject area.

Conferences and Exhibits

No matter how much reading you do, inevitably you will want to get hands-on experience with new multimedia hardware and software. Conferences and exhibits are the best place to do that. You can not only see the new products, but you will get to talk face-to-face with developers and users who are also attending the conference.

INFOCOMM

INFOCOMM is an annual exhibit of audiovisual and new media equipment sponsored by the International Communications Industries Association (ICIA). The exhibit occurs annually in the United States, Asia, Europe, and Japan. Cruising the aisles of the INFOCOMM exhibit is an excellent way to see the latest in audiovisual and multimedia presentation technology. For information on upcoming INFOCOMM exhibits, follow the *Multilit* Web site link to INFOCOMM.

COMDEX

SOFTBANK
COMDEX.

COMDEX is the world's leading producer of expositions and conferences for the information technology industry. COMDEX conferences are held all over the world. In the United States, COMDEX is held twice a year, once in the fall and again in the spring. The exhibit is so large that few cities have enough exhibition space to host it. COMDEX/ Fall is held in Las Vegas, and COMDEX/Spring is held in Atlanta or Chicago.

COMDEX used to be attended almost exclusively by remarketers looking for products to sell, but now the majority of those attending are end users in search of computing solutions. Vendors invest a small fortune on their COMDEX booths, giveaways, and promotions, and attending COMDEX at least once is an experience anyone working with multimedia will enjoy. For information about upcoming events, follow the *Multilit* Web site link to COMDEX.

CeBIT

CeBIT is the world's largest computer and communications show, with 600,000 attendees and more than 6,000 company exhibits from 56 countries. It is held annually each March in Hannover, Germany. Regarded as the most important show for introducing products in the German and European markets, the seven-day event features a USA Multimedia Pavilion in one of the show's busiest exhibit halls. For more information, follow the *Multilit* Web site link to CeBIT.

ED-MEDIA

ED-MEDIA is an international conference on educational multimedia and hypermedia. It includes papers, panels, tutorials, workshops, demonstrations, poster sessions, and tours. ED-MEDIA is sponsored by the Association for the Advancement of Computing in Education (AACE). For details about coming events, including the latest call for participation, follow the *Multilit* Web site link to ED-MEDIA.

NAB

The National Association of Broadcasters (NAB) holds an annual conference featuring multimedia presentations and exhibitions, computers, consumer electronics, telecommunications, publishing, and entertainment. NAB advertises the conference as the world's largest trade show focusing on all aspects of television, radio, video, film, entertainment, interactive media, satellite/telecommunications, and the Internet. For the latest news and information, follow the *Multilit* Web site link to the National Association of Broadcasters Web site.

NECC

If you're an educator, definitely try to attend the National Educational Computing Conference (NECC). Sponsored each year by the National Educational Computing Association (NECA), NECC is an annual meeting place to learn, exchange, and survey the latest advances in educational technology. Through hands-on workshops, discussions with key industry speakers, and the largest vendor exhibition of its kind, participants discover, share, and develop ideas about the appropriate use of technology in their classrooms, school districts, and universities. For more information about the National Educational Computing Conference, follow the *Multilit* Web site link to NECA's NECC Conference.

exercises

1. Following the instructions provided in the Listserv section of this chapter, join the *NewsScan* listserv. When the next issue of NewsScan arrives in your e-mail, read the news. In your opinion, what is the most significant news item in the current issue of *NewsScan?*

2. Following the instructions provided in the *Printed Journals and Magazines* section of this chapter, qualified individuals can apply for a free subscription to *Internet World, T.H.E. Journal, Syllabus,* and *Presenting Communications.* If you do not already subscribe, apply for your free subscription if you qualify. To find out if you are eligible for a free subscription, follow the *Multilit* Web site links to each magazine's Web site.

3. Are you aware of good sources for keeping up with multimedia that were not mentioned in this chapter? If so, what are they?

4. Of the many conferences and exhibits listed in this chapter, find out which one will occur nearest you during the coming year, and make plans to attend it. Do you know of other multimedia conferences or exhibits not listed in this chapter?

Part Five

Multimedia Tools and Techniques

It should be as easy to author in a medium as it is to experience works created in it.

—Ivan Illich, paraphrased by Brenda Laurel, *Edutopia* 1, no. 1 (Winter 1993): 6

This part of the book begins the hands-on tutorial that will prepare you to create your own multimedia applications. You will learn how to use a set of everyday multimedia tools and, through practice, develop techniques that will make you proficient in creating applications.

The tutorials in this book teach you how to use the following tools: Paint Shop Pro (Windows) and Graphic Converter (Macintosh) to capture and format graphics; QuickTime Pro to create and edit movies and animations on Windows and Macintosh computers; WS_FTP (Windows) and Fetch (Macintosh) to publish files to the Web; and a suite of tools in PowerPoint enabling you to record and play back waveform digital audio, make CD Audio clips, and link hypertext and hyperpicture triggers on the screen to multimedia objects. Thus, you will learn how to create multimedia applications.

PowerPoint is just one of many software packages you can use to create multimedia applications. The many alternatives to PowerPoint include presentation packages—such as Compel, Freelance, Harvard Graphics, ASAP WordPower, Aldus Persuasion, or WordPerfect Presentations—and authoring systems—such as Authorware, ToolBook, HyperStudio, Quest, TenCore, and IconAuthor. Many of these packages are discussed in Chapter 9.

PowerPoint was chosen for this book because it runs cross-platform on both Windows and Macintosh computers and is the most widely used multimedia program in the world. Users who are familiar with other packages will realize that many of the PowerPoint techniques taught in this book can be applied using other sets of tools. What is important here is not the choice of a specific tool but rather the concepts that are being presented. Later on, the student can apply these techniques using the tools available in different software packages.

18

Screen Design Principles

After completing this chapter, you will be able to:

- Arrange text in the proper size, color, and font on a multimedia screen

- Choose an appropriate background color and understand how foreground text colors interact with background screen colors

- Arrange pictures on the screen either as background images or design elements for text to flow around

- Make text stand out against a background photo

- Adopt a common look and feel for the screens in your application

● **The hands-on tutorial in this part of the book** will enable you to place text anywhere on the screen in any size, color, or font you want. You will learn how to put pictures on the screen, either as backgrounds that appear behind the text, or as design elements around which text flows. Then you will learn how to make your screens interactive by making hypertext links and placing buttons on the screen. Before you begin, it is important to understand a few principles of multimedia screen design that will help you make screens that have a good layout.

Layout

Multimedia screens consist of several design elements, including text, pictures, icons, triggers, and buttons. The relationships among these elements on the screen are called **layout**. When you create a multimedia screen, you should plan its layout so your content is presented with good balance. Think of dividing the screen into regions, of which some will be pictorial, with others consisting of blocks of text. You must also think about how the user will interact with your screen and include the appropriate navigational buttons and hypertext links.

Figures 18-1 through 18-6 analyze the screen layouts of some highly successful multimedia applications. Notice how some rely heavily on text, whereas others are more graphical. All of them provide intuitive ways to navigate that make these applications user-friendly.

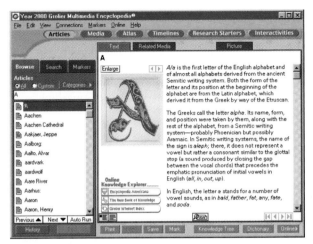

Figure 18-1 Textual screen design.

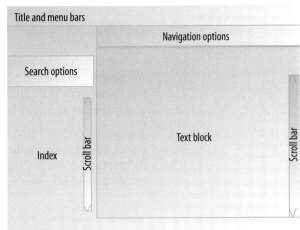

Figure 18-2 Layout analysis of Figure 18-1.

Figure 18-3 Graphical screen design.

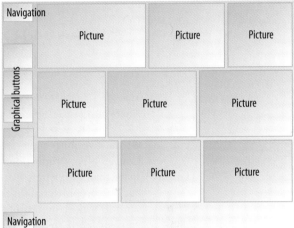

Figure 18-4 Layout analysis of Figure 18-3.

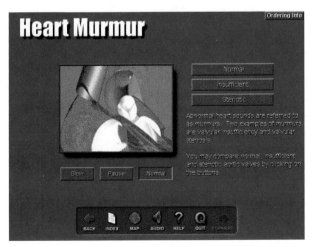

Figure 18-5 Mixed screen design.

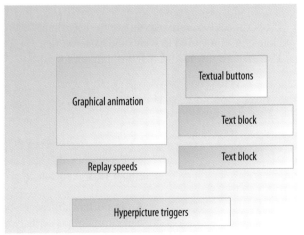

Figure 18-6 Layout analysis of Figure 18-5.

Font Selection

TrueType font technology enables you to place any font on the screen in any size and color you want. There are hundreds of different fonts available from vendors such as Adobe and Corel. But be careful when you choose a font for a multimedia application you intend to publish. If the font you choose is not installed on the user's machine, your screen will not appear as intended.

You can rely on all Windows and Macintosh users having the standard fonts listed in Figure 18-7. If your application uses a font your users do not have, you must publish that font along with your application. Most fonts are licensed and protected by copyright; make sure you have permission for any fonts you distribute.

Figure 18-7   Standard fonts.

Of the five fonts illustrated in Figure 18-7, all are proportionally spaced except for Courier New. **Proportional spacing** means that wide letters like *m* and *w* take up more space than thin letters like *l* and *i*. Normally, you will want to use a proportional font, because proportional fonts are easier to read than monospaced fonts. However, if you want to make columns of text line up precisely on the screen, such as in a spreadsheet, you will need to use the nonproportional Courier font. Figure 18-8 illustrates the difference between proportional and nonproportional spacing.

Times New Roman

Proportional fonts are pleasing to the eye; their characters are varied in width and easier to read. Use them in text blocks like this, but not for tables:

Sales:	$100,000	$85,000	$43,614
Taxes:	54,521	3,425	6,921
Fees:	231,947	41	324
Total:	$386,468	$88,466	$50,859

Courier New

Nonproportional, or monospaced, fonts are regimented and somewhat graceless, but make vertical alignment much easier:

```
Sales:   $100,000   $85,000   $43,614
Taxes:     54,521     3,425     6,921
Fees:     231,947        41       324
Total:   $386,468   $88,466   $50,859
```

Figure 18-8   Comparison of proportional and nonproportional spacing.

An important difference between the Times New Roman and Arial fonts is that Times New Roman has serifs, whereas Arial does not. A **serif** is a line stemming at an angle from the ends of the strokes of a letter. Typefaces without serifs are called **sans serif** fonts. Figure 18-9 compares a few characters from the Times New Roman and Arial fonts, pointing out the serifs in Times New Roman.

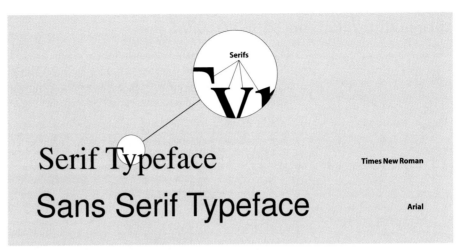

Figure 18-9   Comparison of Times New Roman and Arial fonts.

Text Sizing

Text size is measured in **points**, which tell how high the character is. TrueType fonts can be sized to any standard point size. They can also be stretched and squeezed to create a wide variety of nonstandard sizes. In print media a point is 1/72 inch. In multimedia a point is about the height of a single pixel on a 640 × 480 computer screen. Due to different-sized monitors, the actual size of the text will vary somewhat depending on the physical height of the screen. Figure 18-10 illustrates different point sizes.

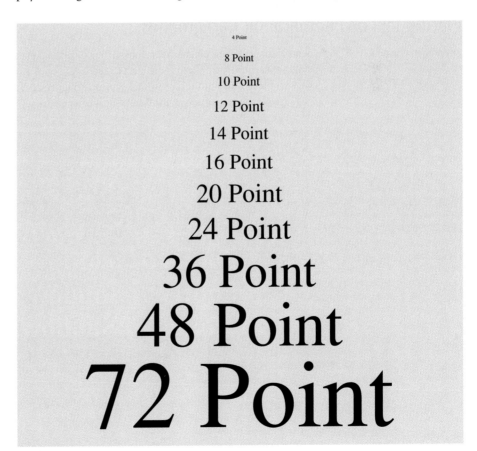

Figure 18-10   Comparison of different point sizes.

Foreground Versus Background Colors

In the next chapter, you will learn how to create colored backgrounds upon which you will place foreground text in different colors. The choice of the foreground and background colors is up to you. Some color combinations work better than others. Figure 18-11 illustrates recommended color combinations as well as colors to avoid.

Background Color	Recommended Foregrounds	Foregrounds to Avoid
White	Black, DarkBlue, Red	Yellow, Cyan, LightGray
Blue	White, Yellow, Cyan	Green,
Pink	Black, White, Yellow, Blue	Green, Red, Cyan
Red	Yellow, White, Black	Pink, Cyan, Blue, Green
Yellow	Red, Blue, Black	White, Cyan
Green	Black, Red, Blue	Cyan, Pink, Yellow
Cyan	Blue, Black, Red	Green, Yellow, White
LightGray	Black, DarkBlue, DarkPink	Green, Cyan, Yellow
Gray	Yellow, White, Blue	DarkGray, DarkRed
DarkGray	Cyan, Yellow, Green	Red, Gray
Black	White, Cyan, Green, Yellow	DarkCyan
DarkBlue	Yellow, White, Pink, Green	DarkGreen,
DarkPink	Green, Yellow, White	DarkCyan
DarkRed	White, LightGray, Yellow	
Brown	Yellow, Cyan, White	Red, Pink, DarkGreen
DarkGreen	Cyan, White, Yellow	DarkBlue, DarkRed
DarkCyan	White, Yellow, Cyan	Brown, Blue,

Figure 18-11　Recommended color combinations and colors to avoid.

Placing Text on Photographic Backgrounds

Exercise care when placing text on photographic backgrounds. Some photos are so busy that text placed atop them is difficult to read. A drop shadow can improve the readability of text placed on photographic backgrounds. Figure 18-12 illustrates text printed on top of a background photo with different amounts of drop shadow.

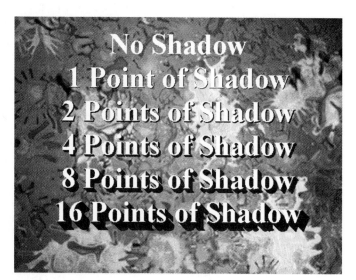

Figure 18-12　A drop shadow can improve the readability of text printed on top of a background photo.

Arranging Text and Pictures on the Screen

Although drop-shadowed text looks cool overlayed on pictures that are not too busy to detract from the readability of the text, you should not overuse text overlay. It is often better to position text above or below a picture, or to flow text around a picture, rather than overlay text on top of an image.

Navigational icons normally work best when they appear lined up in the same region of the screen instead of being scattered about the screen. Try to position the icons in a logical order. For example, it is logical to place the page-back icon in the lower left corner of the screen, and page-forward in the lower right. Here is a suggested sequence of icons that gives the user the option to page back, quit, return to the menu, print the screen, or page forward:

User Friendliness

It is important that multimedia screens be easy to use. When you plan your layout and decide where you will place pictures and text on your screen, make sure you include navigational buttons, icons, or hypertext to clarify what the navigational options are and where the user should click to navigate.

Because hypertext includes words, your hypertext can be self-documenting. For example, the phrases *Return to the Menu, Next Page, Previous Page, Stop, Print Screen,* and *Quit* can appear in hypertext which, when clicked, makes what they say happen. Iconic navigation is often more effective, takes up less screen space, and works better with international audiences because the icons can be understood regardless of what language the user speaks. For example, instead of the hypertext phrases, you can use icons like these:

Be consistent. If you adopt navigational icons, use them consistently throughout your application. If you use hypertext navigation, be consistent in how you word the directions.

Metaphors

In multimedia screen design, a **metaphor** is a way of thinking about new media in terms of something the user already knows. For example, when a multimedia application launches a series of images that the user will view sequentially, it may help to use the metaphor of a slide show. You might even use the icon of a slide projector to launch the slide show:

In addition to providing buttons to move back and forth through the slides, you could carry the slide projector metaphor a bit further and make a left mouse click show the next slide, and a right click back up a slide, just like the remote control buttons on a 35mm slide projector.

Other metaphors found in multimedia applications include the book (for paging through multimedia screens), a stack of cards (popularized by HyperCard), the tape recorder (for recording and playing back audio clips, as in Microsoft's Media Player), a television tuner (for selecting TV channels on multimedia PCs with TV tuners), and the jukebox (for selecting songs to play). Be creative and inventive in your use of metaphors. Think hard about the content of your application, imagine yourself as a user trying to navigate through it, and adopt a metaphor to help orient the user and make your application intuitive.

Adopting a Common Look and Feel

Avoid the temptation to demonstrate every trick you know when you design a multimedia application. Keep it simple. Do not make every screen look and work a different way. Rather, adopt a common look and feel so the user will be able to navigate intuitively after getting used to how your screens work.

It is frustrating to use an application that mixes metaphors and changes what icons mean on different screens. Be consistent. If users have to relearn how to use your application every time they run it, your design is not intuitive.

Successful designers develop the ability to think like a user and imagine themselves being a first-time user of the application. If you can learn to think like the user, look through the eyes of a novice at the screen you are designing, and imagine how the first-time user will interact with your application, you will become a good multimedia designer. Remember that most users are not as smart as you are. You cannot underestimate the skills of the average user. By definition of the term *average*, half of all users are below average. A successful design takes into account the needs of all potential users.

e x e r c i s e s

1. Suppose you have a photo, two paragraphs of text, a one-line title, and navigational icons for page forward, page back, home, and quit. Sketch three different ways of laying out these design elements on a multimedia screen. Assume that you have the capability to resize the photo, making it as large or as small as you want. Indeed, you will acquire that ability later on in this tutorial.

2. List three different ways you could write a hypertext instruction on the screen which, when clicked, takes the user to the application's home or startup screen.

3. Draw three different ways of providing an icon that moves forward to the next screen of an application.

4. In discussing the role of the metaphor in multimedia applications, this chapter cited the slide projector, the book, the card stack, the tape recorder, the TV tuner, and the jukebox. List three more metaphors and tell how they would be used in a multimedia application. Can you think of a metaphor you have never encountered on a computer screen before?

19

Creating Applications with PowerPoint

After completing this chapter, you will be able to:

- **Create the folders or directories that store multimedia applications on disk**

- **Start PowerPoint and understand its normal view, slide sorter view, slide show view, and outline view**

- **Turn on or off the PowerPoint toolbars and menus**

- **Make sense of IntelliSense**

- **Create a presentation with the AutoContent Wizard**

- **Create a presentation from a template or an outline**

- **Save a presentation on disk**

- **Get help from the Office Assistant and the PowerPoint Help window**

● **PowerPoint is one of the most widely used** computer applications in the world. Over the years, Microsoft has conducted considerable research on how to improve the user interface. You will benefit from these improvements as you work through this tutorial and learn how to create multimedia applications with PowerPoint.

Making a File Folder to Contain the Application

Before you create a multimedia application, you should make a file folder on your hard disk to put the application in. Think of your hard drive as a huge file cabinet that stores information. Each multimedia object you create will be stored in a file. To keep your files organized, you first create a file folder to hold the objects you are about to create.

Show-Me Movie:
"Creating a File Folder"

In this tutorial, you need to create a file folder called **multilit** in which you will place your first few PowerPoint screens. Table 19-1 shows how to create a file folder on Windows and Macintosh computers; follow the instructions for your brand of computer. If you have trouble creating a file folder, watch the Show-Me movie *Creating a File Folder* for your brand of computer. Throughout this tutorial, whenever you have trouble, look in the margin for the Show-Me Movie note, which tells you where to find the movies that illustrate the tutorial steps.

Table 19-1   How to Create a File Folder

Windows	Macintosh
To create a folder with Windows, use the Explorer. To get the Explorer started, use the Windows Start button. If the Start button is not visible on your screen, hold down Ctrl and press Esc, and the Start button will appear. Click the Start button and choose *Programs*. You will find the Explorer listed on the Programs menu. Click on the Explorer to get it running. Figure 19-1 shows how the Explorer provides a visual diagram of how all the files are organized on your computer. You can click on any folder to see a list of the files contained in it.	To create a folder on the Macintosh, use the New Folder command in the File menu of the Finder. If you have no programs running, then you are already in the Finder; if you have other programs running, select the icon in the upper right corner of the screen. This will vary depending on what programs you have running. When the menu drops down, select ▢ Finder. Figure 19-2 shows how the Finder provides a visual diagram of how all the files are organized on your computer. You can click on any folder to see a list of the files contained in it.

Figure 19-1   The Explorer provides a visual overview of all the files and folders on your computer.

To create a new folder, follow these steps:

▶ Click the icon that represents the hard disk drive on which you will create the folder.

▶ Pull down the File menu, select New, and select Folder. The new folder will appear with the name *New Folder*.

▶ For this tutorial, make the name of the new folder *multilit*. Since the name *New Folder* is already selected, you can change the name by simply typing: **multilit**

▶ Press ←Enter to complete the creation of the new folder.

▶ Close the Explorer by clicking on the ✕ in the upper right corner of the window.

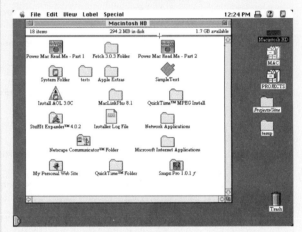

Figure 19-2   The Macintosh desktop.

To create a new folder, follow these steps:

▶ Select File from the menu bar, then select New Folder. The new folder will appear in whatever window is active or on the desktop if no windows are active. For this tutorial, select your hard drive so the folder will be opened there.

▶ The folder will be created with the name *untitled folder*. Select the name by clicking it once. Then type the new name. For this tutorial, make the name of the new folder *multilit*.

Starting Up PowerPoint

There are several ways to get PowerPoint running. If you have Windows, you can click the Start button, choose Programs, and choose Microsoft Powerpoint. On the Macintosh, double-click the PowerPoint icon on your desktop or in the Microsoft Office folder on your hard drive. When PowerPoint starts, the PowerPoint window will appear on-screen, and a dialog box will appear asking whether you want to create a new presentation or open an existing one. Choose the option to open an existing presentation. The Open File dialog appears. Put the *Multilit* CD that came with your textbook into your computer. Use the Open File dialog to open the presentation called *NeccKeynote,* which you will find in the *Necc* folder on the CD.

If you have an older version of PowerPoint, and the *NeccKeynote* presentation will not work, open instead the presentation called *NeccKeynote97* in the *Necc* folder on the *Multilit* CD.

The NECC keynote presentation was delivered by the author at the invitation of the National Educational Computing Conference (NECC). The topic of the presentation was Emerging Technology. This chapter uses the NECC keynote presentation to get you used to the PowerPoint window.

Getting Used to the PowerPoint Window

Depending on the version of PowerPoint you have, the window may look a little different. All versions of PowerPoint have a **Slide Sorter** view, an **Outline** view, and a **Slide Show** view. PowerPoint 2000 has a tri-pane view that displays the outline, the slide show, and the notes, all at once. At any time, you can use the View menu to change the view.

NORMAL VIEW

If your version of PowerPoint has the tri-pane view, your screen will appear as shown in Figure 19-3. Notice how it has three panes. On the left is an outline of the presentation. On the right is a view of the presentation slides. At the bottom, the lecture notes appear. If you have an older version of PowerPoint that does not have the tri-pane view, do not be concerned, because this tutorial does not require you to have the tri-pane view.

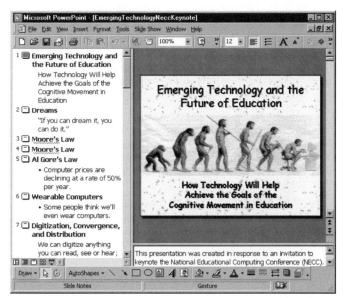

Figure 19-3 PowerPoint's normal view displays an outline of the presentation, a view of the presentation slides, and the author's notes.

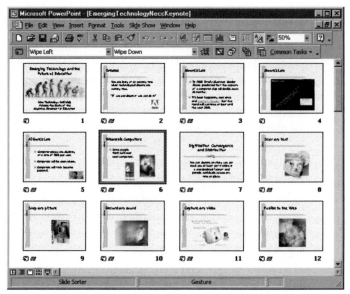

Figure 19-4   Slide Sorter view lets you go to any slide by double-clicking on the slide to which you want to go.

SLIDE SORTER VIEW

Pull down the View menu and choose Slide Sorter. Figure 19-4 shows how the presentation appears as a series of thumbnails, or miniaturized versions of each screen. You can go to any screen by double-clicking its thumbnail. You can even rearrange the order of the screens by clicking and dragging them to move them to a new location. Do not do that just yet because you will get plenty of practice doing that later. Read on to learn more about the PowerPoint window.

SLIDE SHOW VIEW

If you pull down the View menu and choose Slide Show, you will get just that! The presentation will launch, and you will be able to run the NECC keynote presentation just as it was presented at the conference. During the show, click your mouse to go from slide to slide. To back up to the previous slide, press ←, ↑, or ←Backspace. To return to Normal view, press Esc.

OUTLINE VIEW

To switch to Outline view, click the Outline icon at the lower left of the PowerPoint window. Next to the Outline icon, you'll find icons that let you switch to other views, depending on your version of PowerPoint. Figure 19-5 identifies what view the icons bring up when you click them. Try clicking the different icons to see what they do. If you click the icon to show the slide show, remember to click Escape to return to Normal view.

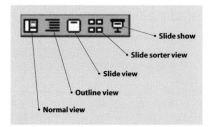

Figure 19-5   Clicking the View icons switches you to the different PowerPoint views.

The PowerPoint Toolbars and Menus

The toolbars and menus in PowerPoint are customizable. If your toolbars and menus do not look like the ones in this book, you might be running a different version of PowerPoint, or someone might have customized your toolbars and menus.

To turn the different toolbars on and off, pull down the View menu and choose Toolbars. Use your mouse to check the toolbars you want visible, or uncheck the toolbars you want hidden. Normally it is best to leave the Standard, Formatting, and Drawing toolbars checked.

To customize a toolbar, pull down the View menu, choose Toolbars, and choose Customize to make the Customize dialog appear. As illustrated in Figure 19-6, the Customize dialog lets you change the contents, appearance, and commands on the toolbars. You should not change these unless you are an advanced user. If someone has changed your toolbars and you want them reset to their factory settings, display the toolbar that contains the menu you want to restore. On the Tools menu, click Customize to make the Customize dialog appear. Click the menu you want to restore, and then click Reset on the Toolbars tab of the Customize dialog. If you do not see the toolbar you are looking for on the shortcut menu, click Customize on the Tools menu, click the Toolbars tab, and click the toolbar you want in the Toolbars list.

Figure 19-6   The three tabs (Toolbars, Commands, and Options) on the Customize dialog.

Making Sense of IntelliSense

If your version of PowerPoint has IntelliSense, you may notice the contents of the menus changing, depending on what you tend to do a lot. This is because PowerPoint customizes the menus according to your work habits by hiding items you do not use much so they do not clutter the menus. At first you may panic because an option you want has gone away. Not to worry, because if options have been hidden by IntelliSense, the bottoms of the menus will contain down-arrows that you can click to reveal the hidden options. Another way to show the hidden options is to just wait a few seconds. If you wait and do not choose anything, PowerPoint will automatically expand the menu to show you the hidden choices.

Creating a New Presentation with PowerPoint

PowerPoint gives you four ways to begin a new presentation. First, there is an AutoContent Wizard, which asks you questions and then creates a presentation based on how you answer the questions. Second, you can create a presentation from a template. You choose a template that has the look and feel you want, and then you fill in your content into the template. Third, you can create a presentation from an outline. You can even import an outline from a Microsoft Word document to create a presentation based on the outline of the document. Fourth, you can create an original presentation.

Creating a Presentation with the AutoContent Wizard

Show-Me Movie:
"Creating a Presentation with the AutoContent Wizard"

The AutoContent Wizard is for people who are on a fast track and want to create a presentation quickly, without paying too much attention to detail. The Wizard asks you a series of questions about the presentation you want to create, and then PowerPoint generates the presentation for you. After the presentation gets created, you can proceed to edit and fine-tune it using the text, graphics, and multimedia effects you will learn later on in this book.

There is no better way to learn how the AutoContent Wizard works than to try it! To create a presentation with the AutoContent Wizard, follow these steps:

▶ Pull down the PowerPoint File menu and choose New to make the New Presentation dialog appear.

▶ On the General tab of the New Presentation dialog, choose AutoContent Wizard.

▶ The AutoContent Wizard will appear as shown in Figure 19-7. Follow the instructions as the wizard steps you through the process. Click Next each time you finish a step until you get to the end of the process. Click Back if you want to back up a step, or click an icon in the wizard's flow diagram to go to a different part of the wizard.

▶ When you are done setting options with the wizard, click Finish. PowerPoint will create the presentation for you.

▶ To view the presentation, pull down the Slide Show menu and choose View Show, or click the Slide Show button.

▶ Click the mouse to move through the slides of the presentation. If you want to end the show before you get to the end, press [Esc].

▶ To change the text of the presentation, just select the text you want to change, and type the replacement text. If you don't know how to edit text yet, don't worry; the next chapter is devoted entirely to text entry and formatting.

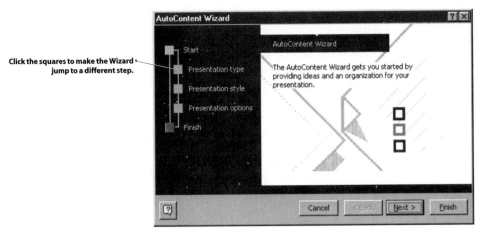

Click the squares to make the Wizard jump to a different step.

Figure 19-7   The AutoContent Wizard.

Creating a Presentation from a Template

PowerPoint has templates that give a presentation a predetermined look and feel. You choose a template, and then you fill in your presentation content, which flows onto the screen according to the template. To create a presentation from a template, follow these steps:

▶ Pull down the PowerPoint File menu and choose New to make the New Presentation dialog appear.

▶ Click the Design Templates tab; the menu of templates will appear. *Note:* Some versions of PowerPoint call this the Presentation Designs tab.

▶ You can preview the templates by clicking just once on the name of any template; Figure 19-8 shows how PowerPoint gives you a preview of what the template looks like.

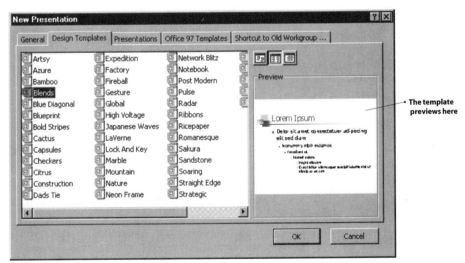

The template previews here

Figure 19-8   Previewing the Blends template on the Design Templates tab.

▷ After you find a template you want to try, double-click its name to select it, or click it once and then click OK.

▷ The New Slide dialog will give you a choice of layouts for the first slide in your presentation. Click the layout you want, then click OK.

▷ PowerPoint will prompt you where to click to modify the content of the slide; change the slide as you wish.

▷ To create a new slide, click the New Slide icon in the PowerPoint standard toolbar:

New slide icon

▷ The New Slide dialog will appear. As before, choose the layout you want for the next slide. Repeat this process for as many slides as you want to add to the presentation.

▷ To view the presentation, pull down the Slide Show menu and choose View Show, or click the Slide Show button.

▷ Click the mouse to move through the slides of the presentation. If you want to end the show before you get to the end, press Esc.

Creating a Presentation from an Outline

One of the author's favorite features in PowerPoint is its ability to create a presentation from an outline. Follow these steps:

▷ Use Microsoft Word to type the outline of your presentation. As you type each item in the outline, use the Style menu to give each item in the outline the appropriate heading, such as Heading 1, Heading 2, or Heading 3. *Note:* When you import the outline into PowerPoint, the Heading 1 style will always begin a new slide, and the other headings will cluster beneath it on the same slide, according to your outline.

▷ Save the outline in Microsoft Word.

▷ In PowerPoint, click your mouse in the Outline window at the spot where you want to insert the outline.

▷ Pull down the Insert menu and choose Slides from Outline. *Note:* If the Slides from Outline feature does not appear on the Insert menu, click the down-arrows on the menu to display the rest of the options.

▷ Follow the on-screen instructions to import the outline into your presentation.

▷ After the outline gets imported into PowerPoint, you may want to adjust the heading levels of one or more of the items in your outline. To demote an item, click the item in the Outline view, and press the Demote button in the PowerPoint formatting toolbar:

This is the Demote button

▷ Notice how the Demote button demoted the text and changed the slide.

▷ Now click the Promote button, which is the left-pointing arrow next to the Demote button. Notice how the text got promoted.

> You can also type new items directly into the outline, and click the Demote and Promote buttons to change the heading level. Notice how easily you can modify the outline, and how changes to the outline appear instantly in your presentation.

Stopping PowerPoint

When you're done viewing a presentation, you press [Esc] to stop it. To quit PowerPoint, you click the PowerPoint window's Close icon.

Saving Your Application

Show-Me Movie:
"Saving Your Application"

Whenever you want to save the application on which you are working, pull down the File menu, and choose Save. The Save dialog will appear. It will also pop out automatically if you try to quit PowerPoint before you have saved the application on which you are working. To save an application with the Save dialog, follow the steps in Table 19-2.

Table 19-2 How to Save a PowerPoint Application

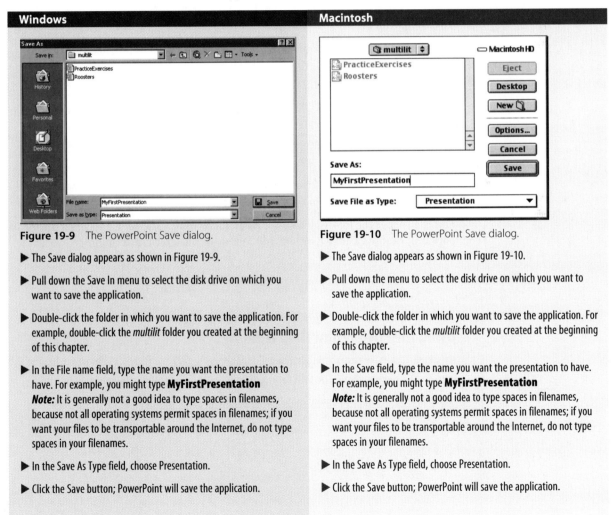

Windows	Macintosh
Figure 19-9 The PowerPoint Save dialog.	**Figure 19-10** The PowerPoint Save dialog.
▶ The Save dialog appears as shown in Figure 19-9.	▶ The Save dialog appears as shown in Figure 19-10.
▶ Pull down the Save In menu to select the disk drive on which you want to save the application.	▶ Pull down the menu to select the disk drive on which you want to save the application.
▶ Double-click the folder in which you want to save the application. For example, double-click the *multilit* folder you created at the beginning of this chapter.	▶ Double-click the folder in which you want to save the application. For example, double-click the *multilit* folder you created at the beginning of this chapter.
▶ In the File name field, type the name you want the presentation to have. For example, you might type **MyFirstPresentation** **Note:** It is generally not a good idea to type spaces in filenames, because not all operating systems permit spaces in filenames; if you want your files to be transportable around the Internet, do not type spaces in your filenames.	▶ In the Save field, type the name you want the presentation to have. For example, you might type **MyFirstPresentation** **Note:** It is generally not a good idea to type spaces in filenames, because not all operating systems permit spaces in filenames; if you want your files to be transportable around the Internet, do not type spaces in your filenames.
▶ In the Save As Type field, choose Presentation.	▶ In the Save As Type field, choose Presentation.
▶ Click the Save button; PowerPoint will save the application.	▶ Click the Save button; PowerPoint will save the application.

Getting Help

Although PowerPoint is very user-friendly, and its user interface is fairly intuitive, there will be times when you get stuck and need help figuring out how to do something. Happily, PowerPoint has a very complete Help system. There is an Office Assistant, of whom you can ask a question in ordinary English, or you can use the PowerPoint Help window and search through the Help system index and search by key word.

Asking the Office Assistant for Help

Show-Me Movie:
"Asking the Office Assistant for Help"

The Office Assistant is a cute little cartoonlike figure with a pleasant personality. When the Office Assistant is on-screen, it will sometimes smile or wink at you, or even frown if it sees you having trouble. Then it will suggest Help topics to get you the help you need. By default, the Office Assistant looks like this:

To ask the Office Assistant for help, follow these steps:

▶ Click the Office Assistant. If the Office Assistant is not already on-screen, pull down the Help menu, and choose the option to Show the Office Assistant. If that option is not available, skip to the next part of this tutorial, "Using the PowerPoint Help Window."

▶ The Office Assistant will ask what question you want to ask. Type your question into the Office Assistant's question box.

▶ The Office Assistant will scan your question for key words and display a menu of choices; click what you are interested in learning more about.

▶ If you want to put the Office Assistant away so it is no longer visible on-screen, pull down the Help menu and choose the option to Hide the Office Assistant.

You can change the look of the Office Assistant by right-clicking it, and when the menu pops out, choose Change Assistant and follow the on-screen instructions.

Macintosh reminder: Macintosh users right-click by holding down Ctrl during the click.

Using the PowerPoint Help Window

Show-Me Movie:
"Using the PowerPoint Help Window"

The PowerPoint Help window provides you with access to the entire PowerPoint Help system. To get the PowerPoint Help window on-screen, follow these steps:

▶ Pull down the Help menu and select Microsoft PowerPoint Help.

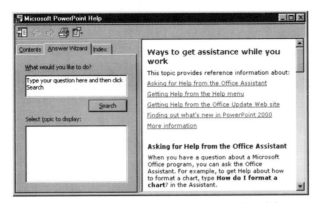

Figure 19-11   The Help window has an Answer Wizard that asks what you want to do. Type your question, then click the Search button.

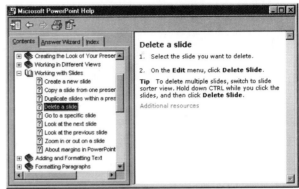

Figure 19-12   Click the Contents tab to display the Help system's contents, then click the plus signs to expand the topics you want.

▷   If the Office Assistant appears instead of the Help system window, click the Office Assistant's Options button, unclick the option to use the Office Assistant setting, and click OK. Then pull down the Help menu and select Microsoft PowerPoint Help.

As illustrated in Figure 19-11, the Help window has three tabs: Contents, Answer Wizard, and Index. Click the Contents tab to browse through the table of contents of the Help system. To expand a topic in the table of contents, click its plus sign to make the subtopics appear, as shown in Figure 19-12. If you want to search the index by key word, click the Index tab and follow the on-screen instructions.

exercises

1. How many slides are there in the NECC keynote show? To answer this question, use PowerPoint to open the presentation called *NeccKeynote*, which you will find in the *Necc* folder on the *Multilit* CD. Use Slide Sorter view to see thumbnails of all the slides in the show. The slides are numbered in Slide Sorter view. Scroll the window down to reveal the last slide, and see what its number is. That is how many slides are in the show.

2. Use PowerPoint's AutoContent Wizard to create a presentation. When the wizard asks you questions about the content, answer the questions based on a topic of your choice. Save the presentation; then run the show. Are you pleased with it? What changes would you like to make to it? *Note:* The remainder of this tutorial will teach you how to create customized presentations.

3. Use Microsoft Word to type an outline on a topic of your choice. Use the Style menu to make each item in the outline have a heading style (Heading 1, Heading 2, or Heading 3). Save the outline, then import it into PowerPoint by pulling down the Insert menu and choosing Slides from Outline. Save the presentation, then run the show. Compare this way of creating a presentation to the AutoContent wizard you practiced in Exercise 2. What are the advantages and disadvantages of creating a presentation from an outline as compared to the AutoContent wizard?

4. Get PowerPoint's Office Assistant on screen by pulling down the Help menu and choosing the option to show the Office Assistant. When the Office Assistant asks you to type a question, ask it something you've been wondering about PowerPoint. What question did you ask, and what answer did the Office Assistant give you? Did you find the Office Assistant responsive to your question? Why or why not?

20 WYSIWYG Text Editing

After completing this chapter, you will be able to:

- **Tell people what WYSIWYG means**

- **Create a new multimedia screen and position text on it**

- **Size, align, center, bold, italicize, underline, emboss, shadow, and color text**

- **Display text in any font installed on your computer**

- **Create superscripts and subscripts and insert special symbols**

- **Change foreground and background colors and effects**

- **Undo and redo text edits**

- **Create bulleted and numbered text**

- **Copy and paste text from one text object to another**

- **Correct mistakes via AutoCorrect, Spell Checking, and Find and Replace**

- **Use the Format Painter to copy attributes from one text object to another**

● Text is a key element of most multimedia applications, and a good working knowledge of how to enter, edit, and manipulate text is a basic requirement for anyone who wants to become multiliterate. This tutorial begins by showing you how to enter, position, size, color, shadow, copy, and edit text in a multimedia application.

Creating a Blank Presentation

Show-Me Movie:
"Creating a Blank
Presentation"

To practice working with text, you'll need a screen to type it on. To create a new presentation to hold the screens you'll create in this chapter, follow these steps:

▷ If you do not have PowerPoint running at the moment, get it started.

▷ Pull down the File menu and choose New to make the New Presentation dialog appear.

▷ On the General tab, choose the option to create a blank presentation and click OK.

> When the New Slide dialog appears and asks you to choose an AutoLayout, select the Title slide layout and click OK. *Note:* If the New Slide dialog does not appear, pull down the Format menu and choose Slide Layout.

Your screen should appear as illustrated in Figure 20-1. Read on to begin entering your text.

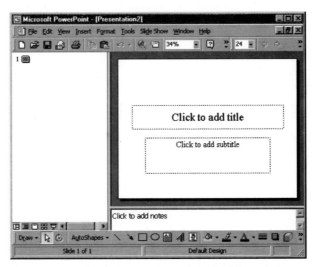

Figure 20-1   A blank presentation with a title slide ready for text entry.

Entering Text

Show-Me Movie:
"Entering Text"

Entering text is easy. Just click the box into which you want to type some text, and type away! For example, the title slide has a box that says "Click to add title." Click there, and type **Multimedia Literacy**

Now click the box that says "Click to add subtitle" and type **Integrating Media Across the Enterprise**

Notice how your text appears on the screen immediately, while you type it. This is known as WYSIWYG text entry; *WYSIWYG* stands for what-you-see-is-what-you-get.

Click in the white space at the top of the slide to end text entry mode. Your screen should now appear as shown in Figure 20-2.

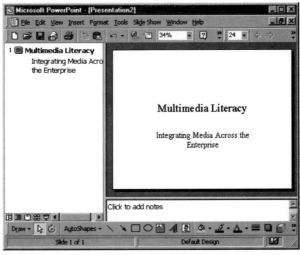

Figure 20-2   Text entry for the title slide.

Saving the Presentation

Show-Me Movie:
  "Saving the Practice
    Presentation"

From time to time as you work through this tutorial, you should save the presentation you are making, just in case you get interrupted. Later on, when you come back to work some more, you can open the presentation and resume working where you left off. Because the presentation contains the practice you will be doing as you complete the tutorial examples, the name of the practice presentation will be *Practice.* To save the *Practice* presentation, follow the steps in Table 20-1.

Table 20-1   How to Save the *Practice* Presentation

Windows	Macintosh
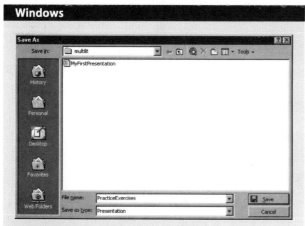	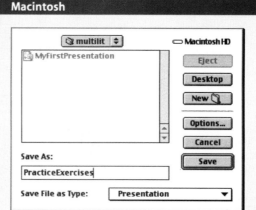
Figure 20-3 The PowerPoint Save dialog.	**Figure 20-4** The PowerPoint Save dialog.

▶ The Save dialog appears as shown in Figure 20-3.

▶ Pull down the Save In menu to select the disk drive on which you want to save the presentation.

▶ Double-click the folder in which you want to save the presentation. In this example, double-click the *multilit* folder you created in the previous chapter. *Note:* If you did not create the *multilit* folder yet, please return to Chapter 19 and follow the steps in Table 19-1, How to Create a File Folder.

▶ In the File name field, type the name you want the presentation to have. In this example, type **Practice**

▶ In the Save As Type field, choose Presentation.

▶ Click the Save button; PowerPoint will save the presentation.

▶ The Save dialog appears as shown in Figure 20-4.

▶ Pull down the menu to select the disk drive on which you want to save the presentation.

▶ Double-click the folder in which you want to save the presentation. In this example, double-click the *multilit* folder you created in the previous chapter. *Note:* If you did not create the *multilit* folder yet, please return to Chapter 19 and follow the steps in Table 19-1, How to Create a File Folder.

▶ In the Save field, type the name you want the presentation to have. In this example, type **Practice**

▶ In the Save As Type field, choose Presentation.

▶ Click the Save button; PowerPoint will save the presentation.

Positioning Text

Show-Me Movie:
"Positioning Text"

PowerPoint lets you move text anywhere on the screen. For example, suppose you want to move the title *Multimedia Literacy* further up on the screen. Follow these steps:

▷ Click on the text you want to move. In this example, click on Multimedia Literacy.

▷ Figure 20-5 shows how a selection box will appear around the text. The selection box consists of a shaded border and eight sizing handles.

▷ Position your mouse on the border of the selection box, anywhere except on the sizing handles, which are used to change the shape of the box. When your mouse is over the border, the cursor will have the shape of arrows pointing in four directions; this tells you that you have moused to a spot from which you can move the text.

▷ While your cursor is positioned over the border, click and drag your mouse. *Note:* To click and drag means to hold down the left mouse button while you move the mouse to another location on screen.

▷ Notice how the text box moves as you drag it with your mouse.

▷ Let the mouse button up to stop moving the text.

▷ If the text is not where you want it, repeat these steps.

▷ To constrain an object so it moves only horizontally or vertically, hold down ⇧ Shift as you drag the object. You can also move an object short distances by selecting it and pressing the arrow keys.

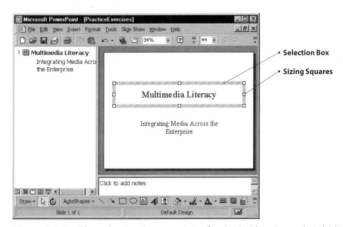

Figure 20-5 The selection box consists of a shaded border and eight little sizing squares, one in each corner, and one in the middle of each side of the square.

Finding the Formatting Toolbar

The next part of this chapter will teach you how to use the text formatting tools. Depending on how your toolbars are set up, the Formatting toolbar may not be visible. Check your toolbars to see if the following tools are visible:

If none of these tools are visible, your Formatting toolbar is off. To get it back on, pull down the View menu, choose Toolbars, and select Formatting. If some but not all of these tools are visible, there are three ways to reveal more of them. First, click the window's Maximize button to make the window as large as possible. Second, click the little down-arrow at the right end of the toolbar to reveal more buttons. Third, click and drag the toolbar to position it underneath your other toolbars, giving the Formatting toolbar its own unique row in your PowerPoint window.

Sizing Text

Show-Me Movie:
"Sizing Text"

Sometimes you want your text to be larger or smaller than the default size. For example, suppose you want to make the title bigger. Follow these steps:

▷   Select the text you want to size. In this example, click and drag your mouse to select the words *Multimedia Literacy*.

▷   The words *Multimedia Literacy* should now be inversed to indicate that you've selected them, as illustrated in Figure 20-6.

▷   Pull down the Font Size menu and select the point size you want. In this example, choose 72 points.

▷   Click in the white space outside the selection box to deselect it. Your screen should now appear as shown in Figure 20-7, which illustrates the result of enlarging the text.

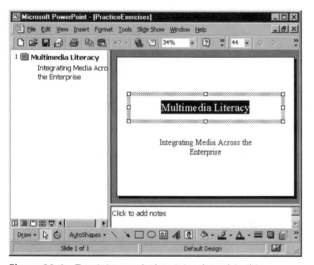

Figure 20-6   Text is inversed when it is selected. In this example, the text *Multimedia Literacy* has been selected.

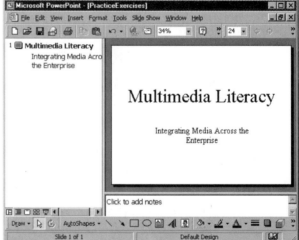

Figure 20-7   The result of increasing the font size of *Multimedia Literacy* to 72 points.

Another way to size text is to use the Text Sizing buttons on the Formatting toolbar. Simply click your mouse over the text you want sized, then click the appropriate button to make the text larger or smaller:

Aligning and Centering Text

Text can be aligned left, centered, or aligned right. To align or center text, you simply click the text you want to align or center, then click one of the alignment buttons on the Formatting toolbar. The alignment buttons are pictured in the Formatting toolbar as follows:

The best way to find out what these settings do is to try them. Follow these steps:

▷ Click once over the text *Integrating Media Across the Enterprise*

▷ Click the Align Left button; the text aligns to the left:

**Integrating Media Across the
Enterprise**

▷ Click the Align Right button; the text aligns to the right:

**Integrating Media Across the
Enterprise**

▷ Click the Center button; the text centers:

**Integrating Media Across the
Enterprise**

Bolding Text

The Bold button is the one that looks like a **B** on the Formatting toolbar:

To bold text, follow these steps:

▷ Use your mouse to select the text you want bolded. *Note:* To select text, click and drag your mouse over it.

▷ Click the Bold button on the Formatting toolbar.

▷ If you want to remove the bolding, repeat these steps.

Italicizing Text

The italics button is the one that looks like *I* on the Formatting toolbar:

Suppose you want the title of your presentation to be in italics. Follow these steps:

▷ Use your mouse to select the text you want italicized. In this example, click and drag your mouse over the words *Multimedia Literacy*.

▷ Click the Italics button on the Formatting toolbar.

▷ If you want to remove the italicizing, repeat these steps.

Underlining Text

The underline button is the one that looks like <u>U</u> on the Formatting toolbar:

This is the Underline button

Suppose you want the title of your presentation to be underlined. Follow these steps:

▷ Use your mouse to select the text you want underlined. In this example, click and drag your mouse over the words *Multimedia Literacy*.

▷ Click the Underline button on the Formatting toolbar.

▷ If you want to remove the underlining, repeat these steps.

Selecting Fonts

Show-Me Movie:
"Selecting Fonts"

To change the font, use the Font menu, which drops down from the Formatting toolbar when you pull down the Font menu:

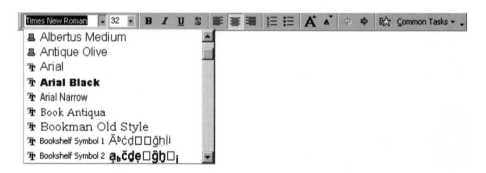

Suppose you want the title of your presentation to appear in the Arial font. Follow these steps:

▷ Use your mouse to select the text you want changed. In this example, click and drag your mouse over the words *Multimedia Literacy*.

▷ Pull down the Font menu and select Arial.

More fonts are available for download at the *Multilit* Web site. Be aware, however, that many commercial fonts have copyright restrictions. PowerPoint's Pack and Go Wizard, which you will learn how to use in Chapter 39, will not permit you to pack fonts that have copyright restrictions, for example.

Superscripts and Subscripts

To insert superscripted or subscripted characters, follow these steps:

▷ Click your mouse in a line of text at the spot where you want to insert a superscript or a subscript.

▷ Pull down the Format menu and choose Font; the Font dialog appears, as illustrated in Figure 20-8.

▷ In the Effects group of the Font dialog, select Superscript or Subscript, then click OK.

▷ Type the text you want superscripted or subscripted.

▷ To return to normal typing, pull down the Format menu, choose Font, unselect the Superscript or Subscript setting, and click OK.

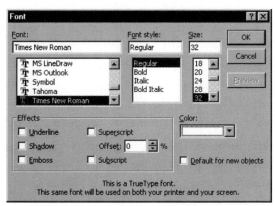

Figure 20-8   The Font dialog contains an Effects group that lets you make text that's superscripted, subscripted, embossed, underlined, and shadowed.

Embossing and Shadowing

Other special effects include embossing and shadowing. **Embossing** makes text look like it is chiseled into the screen. **Shadowing** creates a drop shadow, which can enhance the readability of text overlaid on a pictorial background. To create embossed or shadowed text, follow these steps:

▷ Click and drag your mouse to select the text you want embossed or shadowed.

▷ Pull down the Format menu and choose Font; the Font dialog appears.

▷ In the Effects group of the Font dialog, select Emboss or Shadow, then click OK.

▷ Type the text you want embossed or shadowed.

▷ To return to normal typing, pull down the Format menu, choose Font, unselect the embossed or shadowed setting, and click OK.

Coloring Text

Show-Me Movie:
"Coloring Text"

You can make text any color you want. You can select a color from a palette, or you can mix your own custom color. To color text, follow these steps:

▷ Click and drag your mouse to select the text you want colored. In this example, select the text *Multimedia Literacy*.

▷   Pull down the Format menu and choose Font; the Font dialog appears.

▷   In the Font dialog, pull down the Color menu. Several suggested colors appear.

▷   If you see the color you want, click it to select it. If you do not see the color you want, click More Colors to bring up the Colors dialog, and choose one of those colors. Figure 20-9 shows how you can choose from a selection of premixed colors, or you can create your own custom color as illustrated in Figure 20-10.

▷   Click OK to close the Color dialog, and click OK to close the Font dialog. Your text now appears in the selected color.

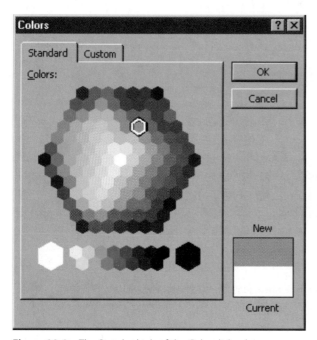

Figure 20-9   The Standard tab of the Color dialog lets you choose a premixed color.

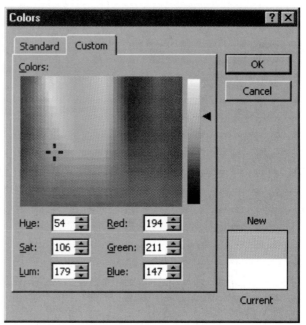

Figure 20-10   The Custom tab lets you mix your own color by manipulating RGB (red, green, blue) color values.

Changing the Background Color

Show-Me Movie:
"Changing the
Background Color"

Before learning how to change the background color, remember that it is not generally a good idea to make frequent color changes in your presentation. You should adopt a consistent color scheme and use it throughout your application. Change the background color only when you need to do so for emphasis or some special effect. If you make every screen have a different color, you will overwhelm your users.

That said, whenever you want to change the background color, follow these steps:

▷   Pull down the Format menu and choose Slide Color Scheme; the Color Scheme appears.

▷   As illustrated in Figure 20-11, the Color Scheme dialog has two tabs: Standard and Custom.

▷   Click the Custom tab to reveal the custom scheme colors, as shown in Figure 20-12.

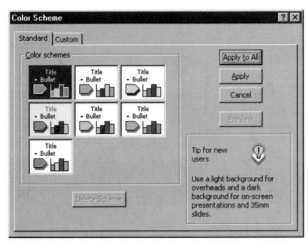

Figure 20-11 The Standard tab of the Color Scheme dialog lets you select from standard color schemes designed to look good on-screen.

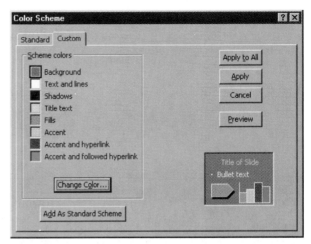

Figure 20-12 The Custom tab lets you customize the color of individual components of the color scheme.

▷ Click Background, then click Change Color to make the Color dialog appear.

▷ Choose the color you want, then click OK.

▷ Click the Apply button to make the current slide have that color, or click Apply to All to apply that color to all your slides.

Inserting More Text Boxes

Show-Me Movie:
"Inserting More Text Boxes"

Sometimes you will want to insert another text box to add more information on-screen. You can insert another text box via the Text Box button on the Drawing toolbar:

The Text Box button

For example, suppose you want to enter some copyright information at the bottom of your title slide. Follow these steps:

▷ To insert a new text box, click the Text Box button on the Drawing toolbar, or pull down the Insert menu and choose Text box.

▷ Move your mouse to position the cursor at the spot where you want the new text box to appear, and click the mouse button; the new text box appears on-screen, as illustrated in Figure 20-13.

▷ Type the text you want the new box to contain. In this example, type **Copyright © 2000 by McGraw-Hill**

Figure 20-14 shows how the text box resizes automatically as you type the text. *Note:* To type the copyright symbol, simply type a *c* in parentheses; PowerPoint will automatically replace the (c) with a © sign.

▷ Using the techniques taught earlier in this chapter, use the formatting tools to make the text have the font, point size, and color you want.

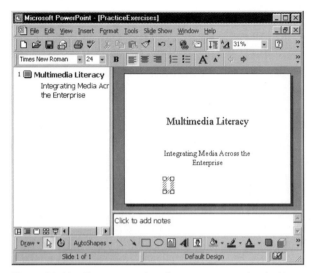

Figure 20-13   The new text box first appears as a placeholder, which is an empty box that will hold the text you type.

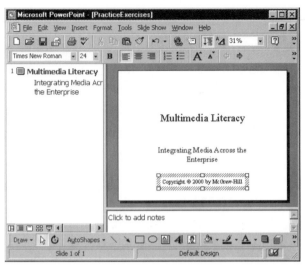

Figure 20-14   As you type your text, the text box automatically resizes to fit the text.

Background Fill Colors and Effects

Each text box on your screen can be filled with a unique background color. To change the background fill color of a text box, follow these steps:

▶   Click the text box whose background you want to fill with a color.

▶   Pull down the Format menu and choose Colors and Lines. If this choice is not visible, click the menu's down-arrow to reveal more choices, or just wait for the rest of the menu to appear automatically.

▶   The Format dialog appears. In the Fill portion of the Format dialog, pull down the Color menu and select the color you want, as illustrated in Figure 20-15.

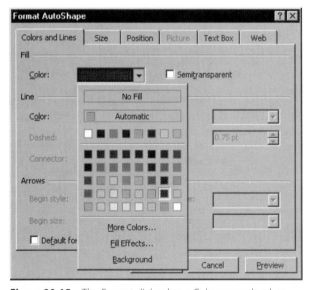

Figure 20-15   The Format dialog has a Color menu that lets you set the fill color.

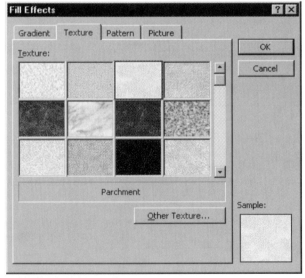

Figure 20-16   Clicking the Color menu's Fill Effects option brings up the Fill Effects dialog.

▷ If you want to get creative, pull down the Format dialog's Color menu and select the Fill Effects to bring up the Fill Effects dialog shown in Figure 20-16. It lets you fill the background with a gradient, a texture, a pattern, or a picture. Remember not to get carried away and dazzle your user with too many special effects.

Undo and Redo

While creating a multimedia application, you will occasionally make a mistake you will wish you could undo. PowerPoint lets you do that, via the Undo button. Moreover, if you decide you want to redo what you undid, you can redo it via the Redo button. The Undo and Redo buttons are found on the Standard toolbar:

Click here to Redo the previous Undo
Click here to Undo the previous action

You can also do an Undo or a Redo by pulling down the Edit menu and choosing Undo or Redo. Undo will only be available after you have done something that can be undone, and Redo will be active only when something has been undone that can be redone.

Bulleted Text and Numbered Text

You can make text with bullets or numbers via the Bullet and Number buttons on the Formatting toolbar:

Click here for bulleted text
Click here to make text be numbered

To create bulleted text on the title slide on which you've been working in this chapter, follow these steps:

▷ Click the text at the bottom of the title slide that says *Copyright © 2000 by McGraw-Hill*. (Clicking the text selects it.)

▷ Click the Bullet button on the Formatting toolbar. Notice how the text becomes bulleted.

▷ Cursor to the end of the text, press Enter, and type **All rights reserved**

▷ Notice how the text *All rights reserved* also is bulleted.

▷ If you want some practice using the Undo button, click the Undo button to undo the bulleting just created.

▷ If you want some practice using the Redo button, click the Redo button to redo the bulleting.

▷ Click the text *Copyright © 2000 by McGraw-Hill* to select it, and click the Number button on the Formatting toolbar. Do likewise for the text *All rights reserved*. Notice how the bulleting changes to numbering.

Formatting Bullets and Numbers

The bullets and numbers you saw in the exercise just completed are the defaults for the current style in PowerPoint. If you want to change the appearance of the bullets and numbers, follow these steps:

▶ Use your mouse to select the text whose bulleting or numbering you want to customize.

▶ Click your right mouse button to make the Choice menu pop out.

▶ When the choice menu pops out, choose Bullets and Numbering to make the Bullets and Numbering dialog appear.

▶ Modify the settings as you wish, then click OK to close the dialog.

▶ If you want to undo the changes, click the Undo button, or pull down the Edit menu and click Undo.

Macintosh reminder: Macintosh users right-click by holding down Ctrl during the click.

Using the Clipboard to Copy and Paste Text

Show-Me Movie:
"Copying and Pasting Text"

The Clipboard is a special place in your computer's memory where you can temporarily store things you want to copy from one place to another. At any time during your use of PowerPoint, you can use the Clipboard to copy and paste text from one place to another. To copy and paste text via the Clipboard, follow these steps:

▶ Click and drag your mouse to select the text you want to copy. The selected text will appear highlighted.

▶ To copy the selected text to your Clipboard, press Ctrl-C on Windows or ⌘-C on the Macintosh. The c stands for copy.

▶ Click your mouse in a text object at exactly the spot where you want the copy to go. Make sure the cursor is positioned where you want the copy to go.

▶ Click Ctrl-V on Windows or ⌘-V on the Macintosh. This pastes the copied text from the Clipboard.

To cut text, click and drag your mouse to select the text you want to cut, then press Ctrl-X on Windows or ⌘-X on the Macintosh.

Inserting Special Symbols

Show-Me Movie:
"Inserting Special Symbols"

As you noted earlier in this tutorial when you learned how to type the copyright sign, PowerPoint has shortcut ways of creating special symbols. For example, if you want to make a registered trademark symbol, you can just type (r) and PowerPoint will automatically replace that with the ® sign. Sometimes you will want other symbols, however, for which there are no shortcuts. To insert special symbols, follow these steps:

▶ Click your mouse at the spot in a text box where you want to insert a special symbol.

▶ Pull down the Insert menu and choose Symbol. If the Symbol choice is not visible, click the menu's down-arrow to display the rest of the choices.

▶ The Symbol dialog appears as illustrated in Figure 20-17.

▶ If the symbol you want is not visible, use the scroll bar to reveal more symbols. If the symbol still is not visible, use the Symbol dialog's Font menu to select a different font in which you think the symbol might be found. The Symbol font contains a lot of special symbols, for example.

▶ Click the symbol you want to insert, and click Insert.

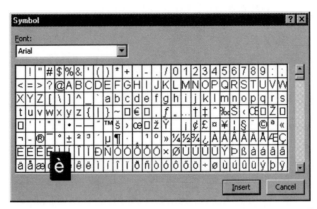

Figure 20-17 The Symbol dialog lets you insert special symbols from any font on your computer.

Editing Text in the Outline View

One of the author's favorite PowerPoint features is the one that lets you edit your text in the Outline view; this can be a timesaver when you want to make a small text change in the midst of a large application. To find out how easy it is to edit a presentation in Outline view, follow these steps:

▶ In the bottom-left corner of the PowerPoint window, click the Outline view button to put PowerPoint into Outline view.

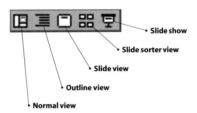

▶ In the Outline window, click your mouse on the text you want to change, and modify it as you wish. For example, change *Integrating Media* to *Integrating Multimedia*.

▶ Switch back to Normal view, and notice how the change you made in Outline view affected your presentation.

Correcting Mistakes

It's only human to make mistakes. The only person who never makes a mistake is the person who does not do anything. If you are a doer, you need a way to correct mistakes. Happily, PowerPoint gives you three ways to do that: AutoCorrect, Spell Checking, and Find and Replace.

AutoCorrect

True to its name, AutoCorrect looks for certain kinds of errors and automatically corrects them. Most users like this feature. AutoCorrect automatically capitalizes the first word of a sentence, for example, and corrects capitalization errors caused by accidental use of the ⌐Caps Lock⌐ key. You can also personalize the AutoCorrect feature by creating a list of common errors you want corrected as you type. If you tend to type the word *separate* as *seperate,* for example, you can add this entry to the AutoCorrect list.

To control how the AutoCorrect feature works as you use PowerPoint, pull down the Tools menu and click AutoCorrect.

Spell Checking

PowerPoint has a spell-checker built in. To spell check the text of your application, click the A-B-C spell-check icon on the standard toolbar, or pull down the Tools menu and choose Spelling.

If you notice PowerPoint underlining misspelled words automatically, your automatic spell-checking option is on. Most authors like this feature, but you can turn it off if you want. To turn automatic spell checking on or off, pull down the Tools menu, choose Options, click the Spelling and Style tab, and use your mouse to select or unselect the options you want.

Find and Replace

Especially useful in lengthy applications, the Find option can search for any word or phrase in your presentation, and the Replace option can replace it with any other word or phrase you specify. To use the Find option, pull down the Edit menu, and choose Find. To use the Find and Replace option, pull down the Edit menu, and choose Replace. If the Replace option is not visible, click the Edit menu's down-arrow to reveal the rest of the options.

Using the Format Painter

As a final touch to learning how to edit text, consider using a timesaver called the Format Painter. Suppose you have spent a lot of time getting some text to have exactly the size, font, and color you want. You want another line of text to have those same attributes. Do you have to go through the time-consuming process of sizing, typefacing, and coloring the new text? Not if you use the Format Painter, which you will find on the standard toolbar:

The Format Painter

To use the Format Painter, follow these steps:

▷ Select the text object with the attributes you want to copy. In this example, click the copyright notice to select it.

▷ Click the Format Painter, and then click the object to which you want to copy the attributes. In this example, click the words *Multimedia Literacy*.

▷ Notice how the words *Multimedia Literacy* now have the same attributes as the copyright notice.

▷ To undo the results of this experiment, click the Undo button, or pull down the Edit menu and choose Undo.

exercises

1. Experiment with different font sizes on the title screen of the *Practice* application you created in this chapter. How large can you make the title *Multimedia Literacy* before it is too large to fit on one line of the screen? What do you feel is the optimal font and point size for the title?

2. Experiment with different foreground and background colors on the title screen. What is your favorite foreground/background color combination?

3. Run the spell-checker on your *Practice* application. Did the spell-checker find any spelling mistakes?

4. Pull down the File menu and click Properties. If the Properties choice is not visible, click the down-arrow to reveal the rest of the choices. When the Properties dialog appears, click the Statistics tab. How many paragraphs, and how many words are in your *Practice* application so far? How many minutes do the statistics say you have spent editing the *Practice* application?

Graphics

After completing this chapter, you will be able to:

- ▓ **Create a new screen in a multimedia application**

- ▓ **Insert clip art onto the screen**

- ▓ **Insert an image file onto the screen**

- ▓ **Resize graphics**

- ▓ **Position graphics anywhere on the screen**

- ▓ **Find additional clip art online**

- ▓ **Use WordArt to create special graphics effects in text**

- ▓ **Draw on-screen while showing a presentation**

● The tutorial exercises in this chapter continue to use the PowerPoint application you began making in the previous chapter. As you will recall, the name of that application is *Practice*, and you saved it in the *multilit* file folder on your hard drive.

If you do not already have PowerPoint running, start PowerPoint now and choose the option to open an existing file. If you have PowerPoint running, click the Open File icon on the Standard toolbar. When the Open File dialog appears, use it to open the *Practice* application in your *multilit* file folder.

↱ **Open File**

Creating a New Screen

Show-Me Movie:
"Creating a New Screen"

At the moment, your PowerPoint window should be displaying the title screen you created in the last chapter. Let's create a new screen to use in this chapter. To create a new screen, click the New Slide button on the Standard toolbar.

↱ **New Slide**

Follow these steps to create the new screen:

▶ Click the New Slide button; the New Slide dialog appears as illustrated in Figure 21-1.

▶ The New Slide dialog asks you to choose a layout; click the layout that is totally blank, so you'll get a screen that has nothing on it yet.

▶ Click OK to close the dialog.

▶ Your screen should appear as illustrated in Figure 21-2.

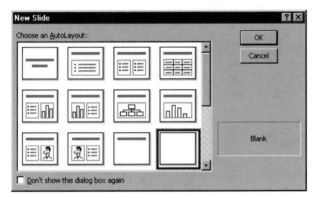

Figure 21-1 The New Slide dialog. In this exercise, choose the layout that is totally blank.

Figure 21-2 The newly created blank slide appears on-screen.

Inserting Clip Art

Now comes the fun part, inserting clip art on the screen. There are thousands of clip-art images from which to choose. You insert clip art with the Insert Clip Art button on the Drawing toolbar. If the Drawing toolbar isn't visible, pull down the View menu, choose Toolbars, and select the Drawing toolbar.

↳ **Insert Clip Art**

To insert clip art, follow these steps:

▶ Click the Insert Clip Art button; the Insert Clip Art dialog appears as shown in Figure 21-3.

▶ Notice how the Insert Clip Art library is organized according to subject areas, such as Academic, Business, Communications, and Entertainment.

▶ Click the Academic area; the academic clip art appears, as illustrated in Figure 21-4.

▶ One of the choices is a diploma. Click the diploma to select it. A menu will pop up giving you the option to insert the clip, preview the clip, add the clip to your favorites, or find similar clips. Choose the option to insert the clip. *Note:* If the diploma is not in your clip art library, follow these steps to import it from the *Multilit* CD:

▪ Click the Import Clips button near the top of the Insert ClipArt dialog; the Add Clip to Clip Gallery dialog appears.

Figure 21-3   The Insert Clip Art dialog.

Figure 21-4   Clip art in the Academic category.

◼ Use the Look In menu to look in the *Diploma* folder on the *Multilit* CD.

◼ Click the Diploma to select it, then click the Import button to import it.

◼ When the Clip Properties dialog asks you to type a description of the imported image, type Diploma, then click OK.

◼ The Diploma now appears in your ClipArt library. Click the Diploma to select it, and when the menu pops up, click the option to insert the clip.

▷ Close the Insert Clip Art dialog and notice what has happened to your screen: The image you selected appears on it, surrounded by little sizing squares called **handles**. Read on to learn how to use the handles to resize images.

Sizing and Positioning Graphics

Show-Me Movie:
"Sizing and Positioning Graphics"

After you have inserted an image on-screen, you will want to know how to position and size it so you can make it appear just the way you want. Let's practice on the diploma you just placed on-screen. Follow these steps:

▷ To move the diploma to different places on the screen, click and drag it with your mouse. Try this now. Move it up, down, left, and right. Then move it to the middle of the screen.

▷ When you click on the image, handles appear, as illustrated in Figure 21-5. These are the sizing handles, which you can use to change the size of the image.

▷ To resize the image and keep its aspect ratio the same, click and drag the handles in the corners of the image. Try that now.

▷ To change only the width of the image, drag the handles in the middle left or middle right of the image. Try that now. Notice how the image gets fatter or thinner when you do this.

▷ To change only the height of the image, drag the handles in the middle top or middle bottom of the image. Notice how the image gets taller or shorter when you do this.

▷ Having learned all this, make the diploma big, so it nearly fills the screen, and center the diploma on-screen.

▷ Use the text box button to put a text box near the top of the diploma. Type into the text box the name of the academic institution granting this diploma, such as **College of the North Pole**.

▷ Now use the text box button to insert a second text box on the diploma. Type into the text box an appropriate message to appear on a diploma. For example, if your name is Santa Claus, type **Santa Claus passed Multimedia Literacy with a grade of A+**. Use the text editing techniques you learned in the previous chapter to make your diploma look really cool. Figure 21-6 may give you some ideas; notice the text box containing a large A+, for example, in the lower left corner of the diploma.

▷ Save your application by clicking the Save button, or pull down the File menu and choose Save.

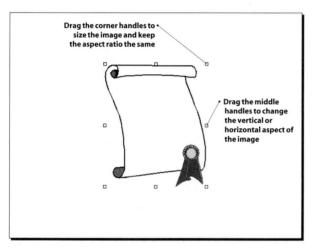

Figure 21-5 To adjust the size of a graphic, click and drag the handles that appear around the border of the graphic.

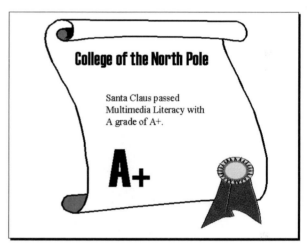

Figure 21-6 The diploma graphic with three text boxes written on it.

Inserting an Image File

An image file is a bitmapped graphic residing somewhere on your computer's disk drive, CD-ROM, DVD, or network. PowerPoint makes it easy to put image files on your computer screen. Follow these steps:

▷ You can insert an image file on any screen of your application. For this example, let's create a fresh screen on which to place the image. To create a new screen, click the New Slide button, or pull down the Insert menu and choose New Slide. When the New Slide dialog asks you to choose a layout, click the layout that is totally blank.

▷ Pull down the Insert menu, choose Picture, then choose From File; the Insert Picture dialog appears.

▷ The Insert Picture dialog has controls that let you find pictures anywhere on your computer. If you have a picture of yourself somewhere on your computer, use the Look In menu to locate it. Otherwise, you can use the picture of the author on your *Multilit* CD by following these steps:

1. Put the *Multilit* CD into your CD-ROM drive.

2. Pull down the Look In menu at the top of the Insert Picture dialog, and set it to look at the root directory of your CD.

3. Double-click the Photos folder, and click the image named *Author*.

▷ The Preview window shows the image you selected, as illustrated in Figure 21-7.

▷ Click the Insert button on the Insert Picture dialog to insert the picture.

▷ The picture now appears on your screen. Use the corner handles to stretch the picture and make it fill the screen.

▷ Click the Slide Show button to run your application, and click through it.

▷ Save your application by clicking the Save button, or pull down the File menu and choose Save.

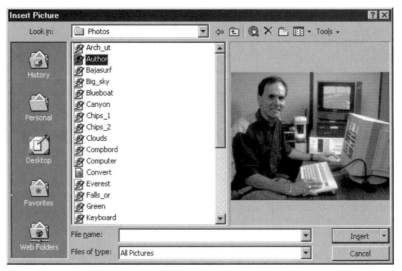

Figure 21-7   The Insert Picture dialog has a preview window that shows the images you click.

Linking to an Image File

If you look more closely at the Insert button on the Insert Picture dialog in Figure 21-7, you will see that there is a down-arrow that lets you reveal more choices. If you click the down-arrow, you will get the option to Link to a file. When you Link to an image file, PowerPoint does not insert and save the picture as part of your application. Instead, when you run the application, PowerPoint follows the link and displays the linked file from its original location on your computer's disk or network.

Unless you are sure that the linked files will always be in the same places on your computer, you should choose the option to Insert instead of Link to a file. This is especially important if you are planning to publish your application as a PowerPoint (.ppt) file and distribute the file to others. In the case of the author's picture, for example, if you Link it, your users would need to have their own copy of the *Multilit* CD in the same CD-ROM location yours was when you linked it. If you Insert the author's picture, on the other hand, a copy of it will be inserted into, and distributed along with, the .ppt file.

You will learn more about multimedia publishing in the last part of this book. For now, unless you really know what you are doing, choose the option to Insert instead of Link to image files.

Finding More Clip Art Online

A powerful feature of the PowerPoint Clip Art library is the way it links to the Internet and provides you with access to thousands of additional images online. If your computer is connected to the Internet, and you want to peruse the online clip art, follow these steps:

▷ You can insert online clip art on any screen of your application. For this example, create a fresh screen on which to put the image. Click the New Slide button, or pull down the Insert menu and choose New Slide. When the New Slide dialog asks you to choose a layout, click the layout that is totally blank.

▷ Click the Insert Clip Art button, or pull down the Insert menu, choose Picture, then choose Clip Art.

▷ When the Clip Art dialog appears, click the Clips Online button, as illustrated in Figure 21-8.

▷ Your Web browser will launch, and you may see a screen or two of licensing and copyright information. Follow the on-screen instructions.

▷ Eventually, you'll come to the online clip library, as illustrated in Figure 21-9. Follow the on-screen instructions to find the kind of clip art you want.

▷ Click any thumbnail-sized clip to see a larger version. If you like the image and want to use it, click the download button beneath the thumbnail.

▷ After the image downloads, if you have the Microsoft Internet Explorer, the image will appear in the Picture window of your Insert Clip Art dialog. Click the image and choose Insert Clip to insert it into your presentation.

▷ If you have Netscape, follow the on-screen instructions to save the downloaded image to disk, from which you can insert it by following the steps in the section above on Inserting an Image File.

For even more clip art, follow the *Multilit* Web site links to clip art you can find online.

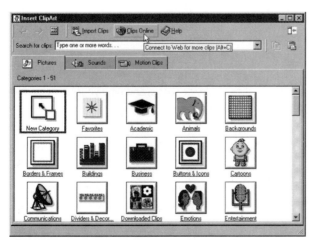

Figure 21-8   The Clips Online button connects you to the Web to look for more clip art.

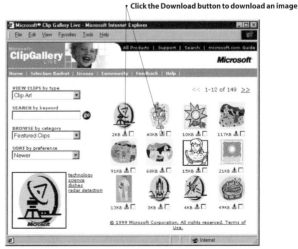

Figure 21-9   Microsoft's Online ClipGallery lets you download clip art into your presentation.

AutoShapes

Show-Me Movie:
"AutoShapes"

PowerPoint comes with a set of ready-made shapes, called **AutoShapes**, which you can use in your presentations. The shapes can be sized, moved, rotated, flipped, colored, and combined with other shapes to make more complex shapes. To see the kinds of AutoShapes that are available, click the AutoShapes menu on the Drawing toolbar. If the Drawing toolbar is not visible, pull down the View menu, choose Toolbars, and choose Drawing. The AutoShapes menu contains lines, connectors, basic shapes, flowchart elements, stars and banners, and callouts.

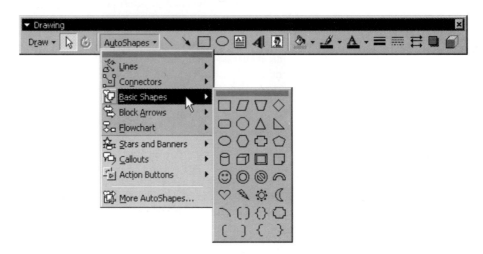

You can add text to AutoShapes by clicking in the shape and typing. Text you add becomes part of the shape; if you rotate or flip the shape, the text rotates or flips with it. There is no better way to learn how to use AutoShapes than to try some. Follow these steps:

▶ You can put an AutoShape on any screen of your application. For this example, let's create a fresh screen on which to put the shape. To create a new screen, click the New Slide button, or pull down the Insert menu and choose New Slide. When the New Slide dialog asks you to choose a layout, click the layout that is totally blank.

▶ Pull down the AutoShape menu, choose Basic Shapes, and click the heart shape.

▶ Move your mouse to the place on your slide where you want the shape to go, and click; the shape appears on-screen.

▶ Use the handles to size the heart; make it big enough to write a message inside of it.

▶ If you need to move the heart, position your mouse anywhere inside the shape, and click and drag it where you want it.

▶ To type a message inside the shape, click inside the shape, and type your message; for example, type **Santa Loves You!**

▶ To change attributes of the shape, such as its fill color, right-click the shape, and when the menu pops out, choose Format AutoShape, and modify the fill color as you like.

▶ To rotate the shape, right-click it, and when the menu pops out, choose Format AutoShape, click the Size tab, and use the rotate menu to set the rotation, such as 45 degrees. Notice how the text you typed into the AutoShape also rotates.

Macintosh reminder: Macintosh users right-click by holding down Ctrl during the click.

WordArt

You create WordArt by clicking the WordArt button on the Drawing toolbar.

Once again, there is no better way to learn than by doing. Follow these steps:

▷ You can put WordArt on any screen of your application. In this example, you will add WordArt to the heart screen you just created.

▷ On the Drawing toolbar, click the WordArt button; the WordArt gallery appears as illustrated in Figure 21-10.

▷ Click the WordArt effect you want, and then click OK.

▷ In the Edit WordArt Text dialog box, type your text, select any other options you want, and then click OK. In this example, type **Happy Valentine's Day!**

▷ To add or change effects to the text, use the tools on the WordArt and Drawing toolbars. The WordArt toolbar will pop up automatically any time you click the WordArt to edit it.

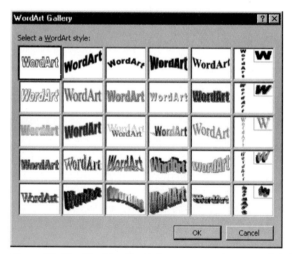

Figure 21-10 The WordArt Gallery appears when you click the WordArt button.

Drawing On-Screen During a Show

Pointer Options let you draw on-screen to annotate things while you are giving a presentation. To draw on-screen during a show, follow these steps:

▷ Get your presentation running by pulling down the Slide Show menu and choosing View Show, or click the Slide Show button to begin the presentation.

▷ On any screen of your presentation, right-click, choose Pointer Options, and then click Pen.

▷ Hold down the mouse button as you write or draw on your slide.

▷ If you want to erase the drawing, press E (*E* stands for erase).

▷ To change the drawing color, right-click, choose Pointer Options, and click Pen Color.

▷ To put the pen away, right-click, choose Pointer Options, and click Arrow to switch back from the pen to an arrow, or choose Hidden if you want the pointer to be hidden.

If you prefer not to have the menu pop up when you change the pointer options, you can press function keys instead. Table 21-1 lists the slide show controls you can use to control the show and write on slides while running your slide show in full-screen mode.

Table 21-1   Slide Show Controls and Pointer Options for Annotating Slides

Press:	To:
Ctrl - P (Macintosh ⌘- P)	Change the pointer to a pen
Ctrl - A (Macintosh ⌘- A)	Change the pointer to an arrow
Ctrl - H (Macintosh ⌘- H)	Hide the pointer
E	Erase on-screen annotations
N , ↵Enter , Page Down , → , ↓ , or Spacebar (or click the mouse)	Perform the next animation or advance to the next slide
P , Page Up , ← , ↑ , or ←Backspace	Perform the previous animation or return to the previous slide
\<number\> + ↵Enter	Go to slide *\<number\>*
⇧Shift - F10 (or right-click)	Display the shortcut menu
F1	See a more complete list of slide show controls

e x e r c i s e s

1. Decorate the title screen of your *Practice* application with some clip art. Click the Insert Clip Art button and use the Clip Art dialog to find a graphic appropriate for communicating the idea of multimedia literacy. Click the Entertainment category, for example, and peruse the clip art you'll find there. Several of the entertainment images conjure the idea of multimedia. Select the image that appeals most to you. When it appears on-screen, size and position the image so it looks good among the other objects on the title screen.

2. There is a picture of a little flower in the Images folder on the *Multilit* CD. The name of the image is *LittleFlower*. Create a new screen, and insert the *LittleFlower* on it. Right-click the image, choose Format Picture, click the Size tab, and use the Scale controls to increase the size of the picture. How large can you make it before the picture begins to pixellate, meaning that the picture elements (i.e., dots) in the picture become unacceptably visible?

    Macintosh reminder: Macintosh users right-click by holding down Ctrl during the click.

3. Run your *Practice* application and experiment with the Pointer options. Press Ctrl - P (Windows) or ⌘- P (Macintosh) to change the pointer into a pen, and use the pen to draw on top of your slide. Press E to erase the drawing. Use the pen to try underlining or circling things. Write something on-screen with the pen. How well does the pen work for annotating slides during a presentation? What suggestions would you give to Microsoft for improving the pointer options?

22

Manipulating Objects

After completing this chapter, you will be able to:

- ▓ **Understand the object-oriented nature of PowerPoint**

- ▓ **Manipulate an object's border**

- ▓ **Create 3-D effects**

- ▓ **Align and distribute objects**

- ▓ **Flip, rotate, size, and scale objects**

- ▓ **Anchor text, adjust margins, and wrap text in text objects**

- ▓ **Crop graphics and adjust the brightness and contrast of graphics objects**

- ▓ **Group and ungroup objects**

- ▓ **Change an object's stacking order**

- ▓ **Delete objects**

● In PowerPoint, an object is an element of a slide you can select and manipulate while editing your presentation. If you think about the screens you have created for your *Practice* application, each slide consists of text boxes and graphics that you placed on-screen. Each text box and each graphic is an object. While editing a slide, you can click a graphic or click a text to select it. Handles appear around the object you click. The handles show you which object you selected. The text or graphic inside the handles is the object.

Objects have two important roles in PowerPoint. First, objects can be selected and manipulated. In the last two chapters, you learned how to select a text or graphics object and move it or resize it. In this chapter, you will learn how to change an object's borders, fills, and shadows; add 3-D effects; flip, rotate, and scale objects; anchor text, wrap text, and adjust margins in text objects; and crop and adjust the brightness and contrast of graphics objects.

The second role objects play is to determine the order in which PowerPoint displays things on-screen. PowerPoint keeps track of the order in which you created the objects. This order is called the stack order. When a slide appears, the objects appear on-screen in the order of the stack. Sometimes, you will want to change the stack order to make a text appear on top of a graphic, instead of getting buried beneath it, for example. PowerPoint also lets you group objects. This comes in handy, for example, when you want two or more objects to dissolve onto the screen simultaneously. If you group the objects, they will appear all at once, as a group.

This chapter introduces these concepts in order from simple to complex. We begin by learning how to manipulate an object's border.

Borders

Show-Me Movie:
"Manipulating an Object's Borders"

Every object has a border. Often the borders are invisible, and you do not see them on-screen. Text objects normally have invisible borders, for example, because you normally do not want users to see the borders around your text.

To learn how to manipulate an object's borders, follow these steps:

▷ If you do not already have your *Practice* application open, use PowerPoint to open it now.

▷ Go to the first slide, which is the title slide.

▷ Click the words *Multimedia Literacy* to select them. Handles appear, indicating that the text object has been selected.

▷ Right-click your mouse anywhere on the text object to make the menu pop up, and choose the option called Format Placeholder or Format Text Box; the Format dialog appears, as illustrated in Figure 22-1. *Note:* A Placeholder is the outline that appears around an object when you select it.

▷ In the Line group of the Format dialog, pull down the Color menu, and set the color you want the border to be.

▷ Click OK to close the dialog. The border now appears around the text object.

▷ To see the border clearly, you may want to make the placeholder around the object disappear. To do this, deselect the object by clicking somewhere on the slide outside of the object.

▷ If you want the border to be thicker, simply repeat these steps, and when the Format dialog appears, increase the Weight of the line to make it thicker.

▷ If you make the border thicker, you may also want to create a pattern in it. If so, click the Patterned Lines option on the Color dialog, as illustrated in Figure 22-2.

Macintosh reminder: Macintosh users right-click by holding down Ctrl during the click.

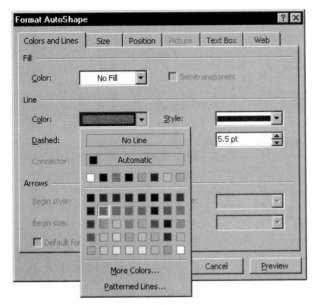

Figure 22-1 The Format dialog has a Color menu that lets you set the line color of the border.

Figure 22-2 Clicking the Color menu's Patterned Lines option brings up the Fill Effects dialog.

3-D Effects

Show-Me Movie:
"3-D Effects"

PowerPoint has 3-D effects that you can use on AutoShape objects and WordArt objects to create some really cool special effects. The 3-D button is located on the Drawing toolbar. If your Drawing toolbar is not visible, pull down the View menu, choose Toolbars, and select the Drawing toolbar.

The 3-D Effects button

To learn how to make 3-D effects, follow these steps:

▷ Use PowerPoint to edit the screen on which you placed the heart in your *Practice* application. *Note:* The quickest way to get to a specific slide is to click Slide Sorter view and then double-click the slide to which you want to go.

▷ Click your mouse over the heart to select it; handles will appear, indicating that the heart object has been selected.

▷ Click the 3-D button on the Drawing toolbar; the 3-D menu pops up as illustrated in Figure 22-3.

▷ The quickest way to get a 3-D effect is to click one of the choices on the 3-D menu; go ahead and do that now. Observe the change in the heart shape as the 3-D effect is applied.

▷ Experiment with more 3-D effects: Click the 3-D button, and try other choices.

▷ When you are ready to learn more advanced 3-D effects, click the 3-D button, and choose the 3-D Settings; the 3-D Settings toolbar appears, as illustrated in Figure 22-4.

▷ The 3-D Settings toolbar has lots of cool settings with which you can play. Click the Lighting button, as an example, and experiment with changing the lighting perspective.

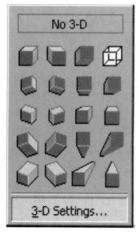

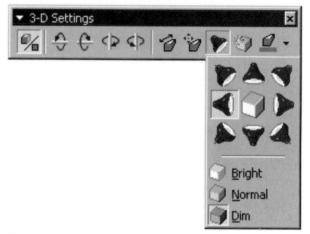

Figure 22-3   The 3-D menu.

Figure 22-4   The 3-D Settings Toolbar with the Lighting button selected.

Align and Distribute

Sometimes you want objects to line up on the screen so their left or right edges are aligned. Other times, you want to distribute objects evenly on the screen, so there is equal space around them. The title screen of your *Practice* application is a good place to practice this. Get your title slide into the PowerPoint window's normal view, and follow these steps:

▷ To align two or more objects, select them with your mouse. Remember that in order to select more than one object, you must hold down the Shift key when you click the other objects to select them. In this example, select the title text *(Multimedia Literacy)* and the subtitle *(Integrating Media Across the Enterprise)*.

▷ Pull down the Draw menu, select Align or Distribute, and choose Align Left. The placeholders immediately line up at the left of the screen.

▷ With the title and the subtitle still selected, pull down the Draw menu, select Align or Distribute, and choose Align Right. The placeholders line up at the right.

▷ With the title and the subtitle still selected, pull down the Draw menu, select Align or Distribute, and choose Align Center. The placeholders will center on-screen.

Distributing objects is just as easy. To distribute evenly the objects on your title screen, follow these steps:

▷ To align three or more objects, select them with your mouse. In this example, select the title text *(Multimedia Literacy)*, the subtitle *(Integrating Media Across the Enterprise)*, and the copyright notice.

▷ Pull down the Draw menu, select Align or Distribute, and choose Distribute Vertically.

▷ Study the results. If you liked the way you had the text before, when you positioned it by hand, click the Undo button to undo the change.

Flip and Rotate

Show-Me Movie:
"Flipping & Rotating Objects"

Objects can be flipped and rotated. Once again, the title screen of your *Practice* is a good place to learn how to do this. Get your title slide into the PowerPoint window's normal view, and follow these steps:

▶ Click the title text *(Multimedia Literacy)* to select it.

▶ On the Drawing toolbar, click Draw, and point to Rotate or Flip; the menu shown in Figure 22-5 appears.

▶ Choose the rotation or flip you want; the change takes effect on-screen immediately.

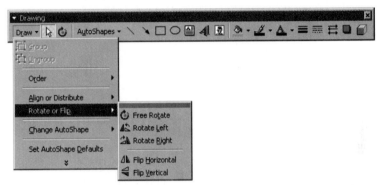

Figure 22-5 The Rotate or Flip menu pulls down from the Draw menu on the Drawing toolbar.

The Rotate menu's rotations are in 90-degree increments. If you want to make a finer rotation, you can use Free Rotate. Follow these steps:

▶ Select the object you want to rotate. In this example, click the title text *(Multimedia Literacy)*.

▶ On the Drawing toolbar, click Free Rotate.

▶ Drag a corner of the object in the direction you want it to rotate.

▶ If you want to constrain the rotation of the object to 15-degree angles, hold down ⇧Shift while you use the Free Rotate tool.

▶ If you want to rotate the object around the handle opposite the handle you are using, hold down Ctrl while you use the Free Rotate tool.

▶ Click outside the object to set the rotation.

Size and Scale

Show-Me Movie:
"Sizing & Scaling Objects"

Earlier in this tutorial, you learned how to size an object by dragging its handles. You can also resize an object by scaling it by a specific percentage. Follow these steps:

▶ Select the object you want to resize. In this example, click any object in your presentation.

> ▶ On the Format menu, click the command for the type of object you selected (AutoShape, Text Box, Object, or Picture).

> ▶ When the Format dialog appears, click the Size tab.

> ▶ Under Scale, enter the percentages you want in the Height and Width boxes.

> ▶ To maintain the ratio between the object's height and width whenever you resize it, select the Lock aspect ratio check box on the Size tab. This is especially important when you resize a photograph, for example, because pictures will appear too thin or too fat if the aspect ratio is off.

Text Objects

When you choose to format a text object, the Format dialog has a Text Box tab that lets you set the anchor, internal margin, and word wrap of the object.

Anchor

The Anchor helps you position text inside a text object. You can anchor the text to the top, middle, or bottom of the object. Follow these steps:

> ▶ Select the text object you want to adjust. In this example, click any text object in your presentation.

> ▶ On the Format menu, click the command for the type of object you selected (AutoShape or Text Box).

> ▶ When the Format dialog appears, click the Text Box tab.

> ▶ In the Text Anchor point box, click the position where you want the text to start.

> ▶ The text moves to the position selected unless the *Resize AutoShape to fit text* check box is selected. In that case, the text does not move but expands in the opposite direction of the position selected.

Internal Margin

The Internal Margin setting lets you change the margins around the text of the text object. Follow these steps:

> ▶ Select the object containing the text whose margins you want to adjust. In this example, click any text object in your presentation.

> ▶ On the Format menu, click the command for the type of object you selected (AutoShape or Text Box).

> ▶ When the Format dialog appears, click its Text Box tab.

> ▶ Select the Resize AutoShape to fit text check box.

> ▶ Under Internal Margin, adjust the measurements to increase or decrease the distance between the text and the object.

> ▶ Click the Preview tab to rehearse the change; when you get it the way you want it, click OK to close the Format dialog.

Word Wrap

The Word Wrap setting lets you turn word wrap on or off. When a text object's word wrap is off, all of the words in the object appear on a single line. To experiment with the Word Wrap setting, follow these steps:

▷ Select the object containing the text whose Word Wrap setting you want to change. In this example, click one of your longer text objects, such as the text on your diploma screen.

▷ On the Format menu, click the command for the type of object you selected (AutoShape or Text Box).

▷ When the Format dialog appears, click its Text Box tab.

▷ Click the Word wrap text in AutoShape check box.

▷ Click the Preview tab to rehearse the change; when you get it the way you want it, click OK to close the Format dialog.

Graphics Objects

PowerPoint lets you adjust the brightness, contrast, and color of a picture object. You can also crop the object, if you do not want all of it to appear.

Brightness and Contrast

Show-Me Movie:
"Adjusting Brightness and Contrast"

To adjust the brightness and contrast of a picture, follow these steps:

▷ Right-click the picture you want to adjust. In this example, select one of the photographs in your *Practice* application.

▷ When the menu pops up, choose the option to Format Picture.

▷ When the Format dialog appears, click the Picture tab.

▷ Use the scroll bars to adjust the brightness and contrast.

▷ Click the Preview tab to rehearse the change; when you get it the way you want it, click OK to close the Format dialog.

Another way to adjust brightness and contrast is to use the Picture toolbar. Right-click the picture you want to adjust, and when the menu pops up, choose Show Picture toolbar. Click the Brightness and Contrast controls to adjust the picture.

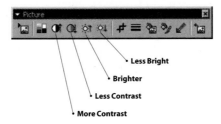

Image Control

You can use Image Control on the Picture toolbar to make your picture black and white, shades of gray, or a watermark. Follow these steps:

▷ Right-click the picture you want to adjust. In this example, select one of the photographs in your *Practice* application.

▷ When the menu pops up, choose the option to Show Picture Toolbar.

▷ When the Picture toolbar appears, click Image Control; the image control choices appear, as shown in Figure 22-6.

▷ Click the option you want; the change takes effect immediately.

▷ Watermark is a really cool effect; make sure you try Watermark to see what it does. See Figure 22-7 for an example.

▷ The image control options are also available from the Format menu; choose the option to Format the Picture, and the Format dialog will appear. Pull down the menu under Image Control, and choose the option you want.

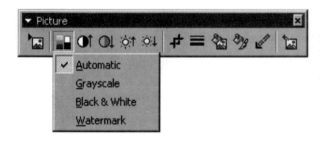

Figure 22-6   The image control choices appear when you click Image Control on the Picture toolbar.

Figure 22-7   The effect of the image control choices on the author's photo.

Set Transparent Color

Show-Me Movie:
"Setting the Transparent Color"

A situation may arise in which the background color of a picture does not match the color scheme of the slide to which you are adding the picture. You can often solve this problem by making the background a transparent color. When a color is transparent, it does not paint the screen; instead, whatever color is on the slide beneath will show through. To set the transparent color, follow these steps:

▷ Right-click the picture; when the menu pops up, choose the option to Show Picture Toolbar.

▷ When the Picture toolbar appears, click the Set Transparent Color button.

Set Transparent Color

> Move your mouse over the picture; notice how the cursor takes the shape of the Transparent Color icon.

> Position the cursor over a pixel that has the color you want to make transparent, and click; all of the pixels of that color in the picture will immediately become transparent.

Crop

To crop a picture means to cut a strip off of one or more sides of the picture so that not all of the original photograph gets displayed. To crop a picture, follow these steps:

> Right-click the picture; when the menu pops up, choose the option to Show Picture Toolbar.

> When the Picture toolbar appears, click the Crop button.

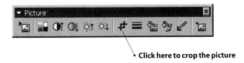

▸ **Click here to crop the picture**

> Drag the corners of the picture to crop it as you like.

> If you really mess things up, click the Reset button.

▸ **Click here to reset the picture**

Group and Ungroup

Show-Me Movie:
"Grouping & Ungrouping Objects"

Objects automatically stack in individual layers as you add them to a slide. Sometimes you will want two or more objects to be grouped, however. Suppose you have a screen that builds as you click your mouse, displaying more information with each mouse click. On one of those mouse clicks, you might want more than one object to come on-screen simultaneously. You can make that happen by grouping the objects. When objects are grouped, they will appear on-screen simultaneously.

To learn how to group and ungroup objects, use PowerPoint to get your *Practice* application on-screen, and go to the screen that has the diploma on it. Your diploma screen should have several objects on it: the diploma graphic, the name of the college, the name of the person getting the diploma, and whatever else you might have written on the diploma. Suppose you want the diploma graphic and the name of the college to appear on-screen first, followed by the rest of the information. Follow these steps to group the objects accordingly and make that happen:

> Click the name of the college to select it; the placeholder appears around the text, indicating that it has been selected, as illustrated in Figure 22-8.

> Hold down [⇧ Shift], and click the diploma graphic to select it as well. Now both objects are selected simultaneously, as illustrated in Figure 22-9.

> Pull down the Draw menu on the Drawing toolbar, and choose Group. This causes the objects to become grouped.

▷ Right-click the diploma, and when the menu pops up, choose the Custom Animation option. The Custom Animation dialog will appear. Notice how there is a group in the list of objects to animate.

▷ Click the check box next to the group to select it, then click the Effects tab, and set the animation effects you want; set it to fly from the left, for example.

▷ Click the check boxes next to the other objects, and set the effects you want them to have as they come on-screen.

▷ Click the Order and Timing tab. Since you want the diploma to appear on-screen first, make sure the diploma is first in order. If it is not, click to select it, then click the Move arrows to move it up to the first position in the order. Click OK to close the Custom Animation dialog.

▷ Click the Slide Show button to run your presentation. Notice how the grouped objects come on-screen together; that is because they are grouped! It is possible that one or more of your text objects may have slid under instead of on top of your diploma. Not to worry, just read on to learn how to modify the stacking order.

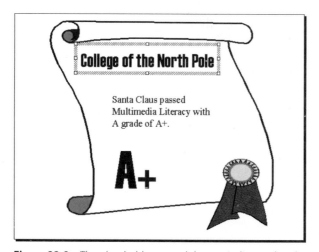

Figure 22-8   The placeholder around the text indicates that the text object has been selected.

Figure 22-9   Selecting another object while holding down your Shift key causes multiple objects to be selected.

Stacking Order

Show-Me Movie:
"Stacking Order"

Objects automatically stack in individual layers as you add them to a slide. You see the stacking order when objects overlap, because the top object covers a portion of the objects beneath it. If an object disappears because you lose track of it in a stack, you can press [Tab ↹] to cycle forward (or [⇧ Shift]+[Tab ↹] to cycle backward) through the objects until the lost object is selected.

You can move individual objects or groups of objects in a stack. Objects can move up or down within a stack one layer at a time, or you can move them to the top or bottom of a stack in one move. The best way to learn how to stack objects is to just do it. If you do not already have the diploma slide in your PowerPoint window, use PowerPoint to get your *Practice* application on-screen, and go to the screen that has the diploma on it. Then follow these steps:

▷ To bring an object or group to the front of the stack, click the object or group once to select it, then pull down the Draw menu, select Order, and choose Bring to Front. Try that now with the diploma group.

▷ The diploma graphic probably covers some of the text objects you entered on top of it previously. That is because you have made the diploma first in the stack. To make the other text visible, just keep following the rest of these steps until you have made it all visible.

▷ Click your mouse button on the diploma slide.

▷ Press Tab ⇆ repeatedly until one of the hidden objects is selected.

▷ Pull down the Draw menu, select Order, and choose the option to bring that object to the front.

▷ When you think all of your objects are visible, click the Slide Show button and rehearse the diploma screen. If anything that should be visible is covered up by the diploma graphic, press Esc to stop the show. Repeat the steps to select the hidden object and bring it closer to the front. If you keep having trouble, a surefire way to fix the problem is to select the diploma graphic and send it to the back.

Deleting Objects

You probably know how to delete objects already, but no chapter about object manipulation would be complete if it did not tell you explicitly how to delete an object. Anytime you want to delete an object, follow these steps:

▷ Click the object to select it.

▷ Press Del.

e x e r c i s e s

1. Go to the screen in your *Practice* application in which you placed a full-screen photo. Click the picture to select it, then right-click it. When the menu pops up, choose Format Picture. Click the Colors and Lines tab. Create a border around the picture by selecting a line color. Click the Preview button to preview the border. What color looks best around your photo? Use the Weight control to make the line thicker. How many points of thickness looks best around your photo?

2. Go to the heart screen in your *Practice* application. Select the heart, click the 3-D tool, and choose 3-D options to make the 3-D toolbar appear. Use the 3-D options to make the heart look as cool as you can. What settings did you modify? How many points of depth are there? In what direction? How did you set the lighting? What kind of surface did you use? *Hint:* Pull down the menus on the toolbar to see what the current settings are.

3. Create a new screen and put a photo on it four times, so the same photo appears on-screen four times. It is all right if the photos overlap. Right-click each picture, and when the Picture toolbar appears, click Image Control. Make each instance of the photo have one of the four Image Control choices: Automatic, Grayscale, Black and White, and Watermark. Observe the differences among these effects, and think of ways you can use them in a multimedia application. For what purpose could you use the Watermark effect, for example?

    Macintosh reminder: Macintosh users right-click by holding down Ctrl during the click.

23

Triggers and Hyperlinks

After completing this chapter, you will be able to:

▨ **Understand the concept of hyperlinking**

▨ **Create hypertext and link the hypertext to one or more multimedia objects on your computer**

▨ **Create hyperpictures and link them to multimedia objects**

▨ **Edit the links to hypertext and hyperpictures, changing what will happen when the user clicks the mouse**

▨ **Add sound to a hyperlink**

▨ **Put action buttons anywhere on the screen and link them to any multimedia object**

▨ **Link to other applications as objects**

● Triggers let you make multimedia applications interactive by linking objects to words or pictures on the screen. When you mouse over a trigger, the cursor changes shape to indicate that you are on a hot spot; if you then click the mouse, the link gets triggered, and whatever you linked there will happen. In PowerPoint, this process is called **hyperlinking**. As you learned in Chapter 2, the prefix *hyper* signifies that the process of linking adds a new dimension to the object that is linked. The most common kind of hyper object is hypertext. This chapter begins by teaching you how to make hypertext.

Hypertext

Show-Me Movie:
"Creating Hypertext Triggers"

As you learned in Part One, linked text is called **hypertext**. To prepare for making your first hypertext, follow these steps:

▷ Use PowerPoint to bring up your *Practice* application in normal view.

▷ Check to make sure you are editing the first slide (i.e., the title slide) of the presentation; if not, drag the scrollbar up to reveal the first slide.

▷ If you haven't already inserted the *Multilit* CD into your computer, please do so now.

To learn how to create hypertext, follow these steps:

▷ Drag your mouse over the words *Multimedia Literacy* to select them.

▷ Pull down the Insert menu and choose HyperLink; the Insert Hyperlink dialog appears as illustrated in Figure 23-1.

▷ Click the option to browse for a file; the Link to File dialog appears.

▷ Pull down the Files of Type menu and set it to look for files of all types.

▷ Use the Look In menu to look in the Audio folder of the *Multilit* CD, as illustrated in Figure 23-2.

▷ Select the file called *greeting.wav* and click OK to close the dialog.

▷ *Greeting.wav* now appears as the "link to" file in the HyperLink dialog; click OK to close the dialog.

▷ Click the Slide Show button to run your application. When the title screen appears, you will notice that the words *Multimedia Literacy* are underlined, indicating that they are hyperlinked.

▷ Click the underlined words. You should hear a waveform audio recording of the author welcoming you to *Multimedia Literacy*. If you did not hear the greeting, check your computer's audio setup to make sure your audio playback is working properly.

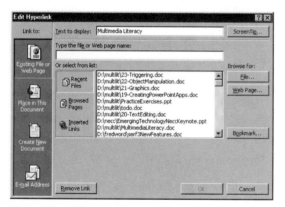

Figure 23-1 The Insert Hyperlink dialog.

Figure 23-2 Using the Look In menu to look in the Audio folder of the *Multilit* CD.

You can link to anything that is available on your computer or its network. For example, if your computer is connected to the Internet, you can create hyperlinks to Web sites. Follow these steps:

▷ While editing the title screen of the *Practice* application, drag your mouse over the words *McGraw-Hill* to select them.

▷ Pull down the Insert menu, and choose HyperLink; the Insert Hyperlink dialog appears.

▷ In the box where the dialog tells you to type the file or Web page name, type **http://www.mcgraw-hill.com**

▷ Click OK to close the dialog; the link is created.

▷ Click the Slide Show button to run your application. When the title screen appears, you will notice that the words *McGraw-Hill* are underlined, indicating that they are hyperlinked.

▷ Click the underlined words *McGraw-Hill*. If your computer is connected to the Internet, you will be taken to the McGraw-Hill Web site.

Hyperpictures

Show-Me Movie:
"Creating Hyperpicture Triggers"

Just as hypertext is text that has been linked, so is a **hyperpicture** a picture that has been linked. You can link any picture to any file or Web resource on your computer or its network. To learn how to create a hyperpicture, follow these steps:

▶ While editing the title screen of the *Practice* application, pull down the Insert menu, choose Picture, and click From File.

▶ When the Insert Picture dialog appears, use it to look in the Logo folder on the *Multilit* CD; select the logo named *McGraw-Hill*, and click the Insert button to insert the logo on your screen.

▶ Resize or reposition the logo on-screen as you like.

▶ Click the picture to select it, if it is not already selected.

▶ Pull down the Insert menu and choose Hyperlink; the Insert Hyperlink dialog appears.

▶ In the box where the dialog tells you to type the file or Web page name, type **http://www.mcgraw-hill.com**

▶ Click OK to close the dialog; the link is created.

▶ Click the Slide Show button to run your application. When the title screen appears, you will notice that the cursor changes shape when you mouse over the McGraw-Hill logo; the change of cursor shape indicates that the picture is linked, and if you click there, something will happen.

▶ Go ahead and click the picture to trigger the link. If your computer is connected to the Internet, you will be taken to the McGraw-Hill Web site.

Editing and Removing Links

Show-Me Movie:
"Editing and Removing Hyperlinks"

Sometimes you will need to change a hyperlink. For example, if a Web address changes, you will need to edit the hyperlink to update it. If a Web site goes out of business altogether, you will need to remove the link. To edit or remove a link, follow these steps:

▶ Use PowerPoint's Slide View to locate quickly the screen you want to modify. Double-click the slide to go to it.

▶ Click the hypertext or hyperpicture whose link you wish to change or delete.

▶ Pull down the Insert menu and choose the Hyperlink option.

▶ To delete the hyperlink, choose Remove Link, and you are done.

▶ To edit the hyperlink, update the link as you like, then click OK to close the dialog.

Action Buttons

PowerPoint has a set of **action buttons** that you can place anywhere on any screen to make a wide variety of things happen. You can link buttons to the beginning or end of your presentation, for example, to provide a quick way for users to restart or exit your application. You can link to individual screens, to provide a way for users to navigate their way through your application. If you are connected to the Internet, you can link to Web pages all over the world. You can either use built-in shapes or create your own custom action buttons. You can even add audio so the action buttons make sound when clicked or moused over.

Suppose you want to put an action button on the last screen of your application, which, when clicked, will return the user to the startup screen. Follow these steps:

▶ In Slide Sorter view, click the last slide in your application; the last slide now appears in Normal view.

▶ Click the AutoShapes button on the Drawing toolbar, and when the menu pops up, choose Action Buttons.

▶ The Action Buttons menu appears as illustrated in Figure 23-3.

▶ As you mouse over the action buttons in the menu, screen tips pop up telling you the name of the button you are on. Look around for the button called Beginning, and select it.

▶ Move your mouse to the spot on your slide where you want the button to be, and click; the Action Settings dialog appears.

▶ Since you clicked the button intended to take you back to the beginning, the mouse click setting is preset to take you to the beginning. It is possible to make the button take you to other places, however; Figure 23-4 shows the choices you get when you pull down the Hyperlink menu.

Figure 23-3 The Action Buttons menu.

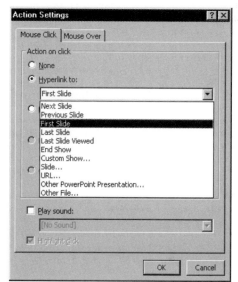

Figure 23-4 The Hyperlink menu.

▷ Leave the settings alone for now, and just click OK to close the dialog.

▷ If the button is not where you want it, drag it to where you want it on-screen. You can also use the handles to make it larger or smaller, as you like.

▷ Click the Slide Show button to run your show. Click through to the end of your presentation; the button appears on your last slide, right where you put it.

▷ Click the button, and it will return you to the first slide of your application.

Imagine the power the action buttons give you. By using them judiciously, you can provide ways for the user to navigate anywhere in your application. You can even create custom buttons, by clicking the blank button called Custom and putting other text or graphics inside it to indicate what clicking it will do.

Applications as Objects

So far, you have learned how to link text, pictures, and buttons to sounds, Web pages, and locations within your presentation. Applications can also be the object of a link. Any executable file, such as Microsoft Word, Netscape Navigator, or PaintShop Pro can be the object of a link. To learn how to create a link to an application, let's work through an example. Suppose you want to put a button on-screen which, when clicked, pops up a calculator. To do that, follow these steps:

▷ Use PowerPoint's Slide View to locate the screen on which you want to put the calculator. Double-click the slide to go to it. In this example, choose the last screen in your *Practice* application.

▷ The *Multilit* CD contains an icon of a calculator that you can make trigger the calculator. To get the calculator icon on-screen, pull down the Insert menu, choose Picture, then choose From File.

▷ When the Insert Picture dialog appears, use it to look in the Icons folder on your *Multilit* CD, and choose the calculator icon. When the calculator icon comes on-screen, position and size it as you like.

▷ To make the calculator icon become a trigger, click it to select it.

▷ Pull down the Insert menu and choose Hyperlink.

▷ When the Insert Hyperlink dialog appears, in the *Type the file or Web page name* field, type:

Windows NT: **C:\winnt\system32\calc.exe**

Windows 98:   **C:\windows\calc.exe**

Macintosh: **File:///Macintosh HD/System Folder/Apple Menu Items/Calculator**

Note: Instead of typing all this, you can click the hyperlink dialog's Select button and use the menus to find the calculator application.

▷ Click OK to close the Insert Hyperlink dialog.

▷ Click the Slide Show button to run the application, and click through to the screen on which the calculator icon appears.

▷ Mouse over the calculator, and notice how the cursor changes shape to indicate something has been linked to the calculator icon.

▷ Click the calculator icon; if the application launches, congratulate yourself, because you have succeeded in learning how to link to applications as objects.

Adding a Default Sound to a Hyperlink

Show-Me Movie:

"Adding Sound to a Hyperlink"

A cute effect used in some applications is to have the mouse clicks create sound effects when the user clicks the mouse to trigger a link. You can have the mouse make a clicking sound, for example, or you could have a link to a document make the sound of someone opening a book and flipping through its pages.

PowerPoint comes with a library full of default sounds that you can add to your hyperlinks. To add a default sound to a hyperlink, follow these steps:

▶ Use PowerPoint's Slide View to locate the screen containing the hyperlink on which you want a sound effect. Double-click the slide to go to it. In this example, choose a slide on which you placed an action button.

▶ Right-click on the action button (or any hyperlinked object); when the menu pops up, choose Action Settings.

▶ Figure 23-5 shows how the Action Settings dialog has two tabs called Mouse Click and Mouse Over. In this example, you will use the Mouse Click tab to play a sound effect when the user clicks the mouse.

▶ Click the Play Sound check box to check it; the pull-down menu of sound effects choices becomes active.

▶ Pull down the menu and peruse the sound effects that are available. To make a clicking sound, choose Camera.

▶ Click OK to close the Action Settings dialog.

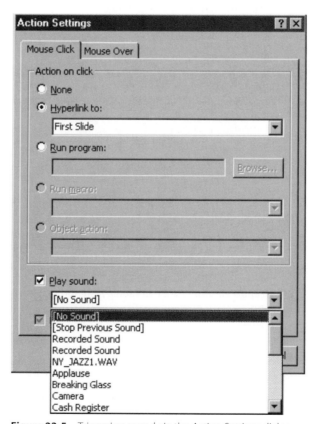

Figure 23-5   Triggering sound via the Action Settings dialog.

▷   Click the Slide Show button to run your application, and click through to the slide containing the hyperlink to which you added the sound effect. Click the hyperlink to trigger it; notice how your sound effect plays.

▷   To experiment with other sound effects, press Escape to stop the presentation, right-click the hyperlink, and when the menu pops up, choose Action Settings, and use the Action Settings dialog to select a different sound.

Remember not to dazzle your user with too many special effects. Use the sound effects in good taste. Do not use special effects merely for the sake of effect, because you can overload the senses.

Macintosh reminder: Macintosh users right-click by holding down [Ctrl] during the click.

Adding a Custom Sound to a Hyperlink

In case you do not find the sound you want on the default sound effects menu, you can make a hyperlink trigger any audio file on your computer, CD-ROM, or network. To do this, follow the same steps you took when you added a default sound to a hyperlink, except that when you pull down the sound effects menu, instead of choosing one of the effects listed there, you scroll down to the bottom of the menu and choose Other Sound. The Add Sound menu will pop up and let you browse to find other sound files on your computer. In Chapter 25, you will learn how to make custom waveform audio recordings and link them to mouse clicks, so you can really make your slides talk to people and explain things as they mouse over things.

e x e r c i s e s

1. There is a file folder full of music recordings on the *Multilit* CD. The name of the folder is Audio\Aris_wav. In your *Practice* application, make a jukebox screen that lists these songs and lets the user play them by clicking them. Use the *Jukebox* image in the *Backdrop* folder to make the screen appear musical.

2. Add to the screen you created in exercise 1 a silence button that makes the sound stop. *Hint:* The sound effects menu in the Action Settings dialog contains an option to silence the previous sound.

3. Add to the screens of your *Practice* application action buttons that the user can click to go forward to the next screen or back to the previous screen. *Hint:* You can save time if you copy and paste the next and back buttons instead of creating them anew on each screen.

4. Make the buttons you created in exercise 3 make a camera-click sound when the user clicks them. *Hint:* Camera is one of the action button default sounds.

5. On the last screen of your *Practice* application, insert the CD audio icon from the Icons folder of the *Multilit* CD. Link to the CD audio icon the *cdplayer.exe* application (Windows) or the Apple CD Audio Player (Macintosh) so that, when the user clicks the CD audio icon, a CD player pops up on-screen. *Hint:* The Apple CD Audio Player is in the Applications folder on the Macintosh HD. The Windows *cdplayer.exe* file should be in the i386 folder. If you cannot find it, use the Start button's Find option to locate it.

24 Multimedia Effects

After completing this chapter, you will be able to:

- Understand the concept of slide transitions and create transition effects from screen to screen

- Add sound effects to slide transitions and control the timing of transition effects

- Understand how animation effects can make any text or graphics object move onto the screen with a variety of special effects

- Know the difference between preset and custom animations

- Animate text, build text, and dim previously animated text

- Animate images and coordinate the animation of multiple objects

- Insert sound and video from the clip library

- Find and insert sound and video from other sources beyond the clip library

- Make sound and movies autostart

- Create movie special effects including loops, animations, autoplay, crop, resize, brightness, and contrast

- Insert automated GIF images onto the screen

- Use audio CDs to play sound in your application from any track or minute-and-second location on the CD

● Remember in Chapter 1 how the definition of multimedia encompassed the use of a computer to present and combine text, graphics, audio, and video? Now it is time to learn how to use multimedia effects that enable you to do just that. In this chapter, you will learn how to create transitions and animations that combine text, graphics, audio, and video in powerful and interesting ways. Remember that the goal is to use the special effects to enhance your presentation, not draw the audience's attention to the effects themselves. If your audience begins to focus on the effects instead of your message, you have gotten carried away and need to scale back your special effects.

Transition Effects

A **transition** is a special effect used to bring a slide onto the screen. You can choose from a variety of transitions and vary their speed. You can dissolve the screen from one slide into another, for example, or you can fade to black in between your slides.

Slide Transitions

Show-Me Movie:
"Slide Transitions"

PowerPoint lets you make a wide variety of slide transitions. You need to be careful not to overuse them. You do not want to put a different kind of transition on each screen of your application. Instead, you can change the transition effect to indicate the beginning of a new section of a presentation, or to emphasize a certain slide.

To learn how to make slide transitions, use PowerPoint to open your *Practice* application. Then follow these steps:

▶ In Slide or Slide Sorter view, select the slide or slides to which you want to add a transition. In this example, select the diploma slide.

▶ On the Slide Show menu, click Slide Transition; the Slide Transition dialog appears, as illustrated in Figure 24-1.

▶ In the Effect box, pull down the menu and click the transition you want.

▶ Set the speed to slow, medium, or fast; PowerPoint previews the dissolve so you can see what it is going to do.

▶ If you want the slide to advance automatically to the next screen, click the Automatically After check box and set the number of seconds. Normally it is not a good idea to have screens advancing automatically, however, so be careful how you use this feature.

▶ To apply the transition to the selected slide, click Apply.

▶ To preview animation and transition effects in a slide, display the slide you want to preview, pull down the Slide Show menu, and click Animation Preview. The Animation Preview window plays the transition. To replay it, click the Animation Preview window.

▶ To see the slide transitions full-screen, click the Slide Show button to run your presentation full-screen.

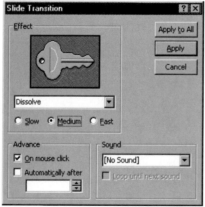

Figure 24-1   The Slide Transition dialog.

Transitional Sound Effects

Show-Me Movie:
"Transitional Sound Effects"

When you learned how to make a slide transition, you may have noticed the option to make a sound effect play during the transition. Be careful not to overuse this feature because it is quite acceptable and often preferable for a slide to dissolve silently. When you do want a transitional sound effect, follow these steps:

▶ In Slide or Slide Sorter view, select the slide or slides to which you want to add the transitional sound effect. In this example, select one of your photograph slides.

▶ On the Slide Show menu, click Slide Transition; the Slide Transition dialog appears.

▶ In the Effect box, pull down the menu and click the transition you want.

▶ Use the Sound menu to select the sound you want.

▶ To apply the transition to the selected slide, click Apply.

▶ To preview animation and transition effects in a slide, display the slide you want to preview, pull down the Slide Show menu, and click Animation Preview.

▶ To preview animations on multiple slides, switch to Slide Sorter view, select the slides you want to preview, and then click Animation Preview on the Slide Show menu.

Animation Effects

The transition effects you learned in the first part of this chapter apply to the screen as a whole. Sometimes, you will want to be able to animate an individual object on the screen, such as a text box or a picture. PowerPoint has animation effects that enable you to do so. You can set up the way you want an object to appear on your slide—to fly in from the left, for example—and you can set text to appear by the letter, word, or paragraph. You can also choose whether you want text or other objects to dim or change color when you bring a new element on-screen. There are two kinds of animations: preset and custom.

Preset Animations

Show-Me Movie:
"Preset Animations"

The quickest way to create an animation is to use one of the preset methods. Follow these steps:

▶ Go to the slide on which you want to animate an object. The quickest way to do this is to click Slide Sorter view and double-click the slide to which you want to go. In this example, choose the heart slide.

▶ Select the object you want to animate by clicking it with your mouse; handles appear around the object you selected. In this example, select the action button.

▶ Click the Slide Show menu and point to Preset Animation; the Preset Animation menu appears as shown in Figure 24-2. Depending on whether you selected a text object or a picture, different choices will be active.

▶ Click the kind of animation you want.

▶ To preview the animation, pull down the Slide Show menu, and click Animation Preview.

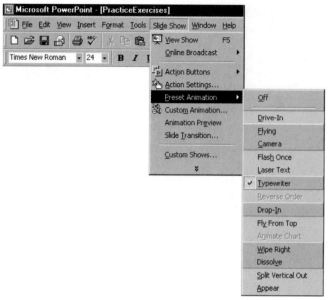

Figure 24-2   The Preset Animation menu pops up from the Slide Show menu.

Custom Animations

If you want to get more creative and do a little more work, you can create a custom animation, which lets you customize the animation variables that are preselected in the Preset animations. You can use custom animations to animate text, dim previously animated text, animate images, and coordinate multiple animations.

ANIMATING TEXT

Show-Me Movie:
"Custom Text Animations"

PowerPoint lets you create some intricate custom text animations. You can set up the way you want the text to appear on your slide, such as to fly in from the left, for example, and you can set the text to appear by the letter, word, or paragraph. To create a custom animated text, follow these steps:

▶ Go to the slide on which you want to animate text. The quickest way to do this is to click Slide Sorter view and double-click the slide to which you want to go. In this example, go to the title screen in your *Practice* application.

▶ Pull down the Slide Show menu and choose Custom Animation. If the Custom Animation option is not visible, click the Slide Show menu's down-arrows to reveal the rest of the options.

▶ The Custom Animation dialog appears as illustrated in Figure 24-3.

▶ Notice how each of the text objects on the screen has a check box. Check the boxes for the items you want to animate.

▶ Notice how the Order and Timing box became filled in automatically as you clicked the check boxes. This determines the order in which the items will appear on-screen. You can change the order if you want by clicking the Move buttons alongside the Order and Timing box.

▶ If you want the text to open on-screen automatically, without waiting for a mouse click, set the Start Animation option to Automatically; otherwise, set it to On Mouse Click.

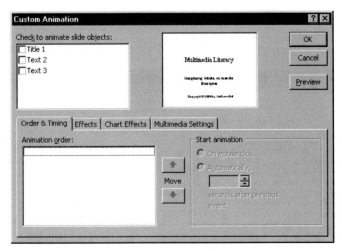

Figure 24-3 The Custom Animation dialog.

▷ Click the Preview button to preview your animation at any time.

▷ There are many kinds of animation effects. To try the different kinds of animation, click the Effects tab. Remember to click the Preview button to rehearse your animation.

▷ When you are done animating, click the OK button to close the Custom Animation dialog.

BUILDING TEXT

To **build text** means to make the text objects on your screen appear sequentially, instead of all at once. When you are making a lot of points on a single screen, for example, it is a good idea to display the items one by one instead of all at once to keep from overwhelming your audience. It is easy to build text with PowerPoint animations. Simply set the Start animation option in the Custom Animation dialog to On Mouse Click for each text object you want to build.

The *Keynote* presentation contains many examples of text that builds as you click your mouse. If you use Powerpoint to run the *Keynote* presentation in the *Necc* folder of the *Multilit* CD, you will notice how the author adopted a style in which the first paragraph of a slide appears on-screen automatically; then you click your mouse to reveal the rest of the text.

If you have a text object consisting of several bullets, you can make the bullets within the text object build by following these steps:

▷ Use Slide Sorter view to locate the slide containing the bullets, and double-click the slide to go to it.

▷ Pull down the Slide Show menu and select Custom Animation.

▷ When the Custom Animation dialog pops up, click the check box next to the text object you want to build.

▷ Click the Effects tab to make the effects settings appear, as illustrated in Figure 24-4.

▷ Under the Introduce Text settings, choose the option to introduce the text grouped by first level paragraphs.

▷ Click OK to close the dialog.

▷ Click the slide show icon to rehearse the slide. Notice how the bullets inside the text box build as you click the mouse.

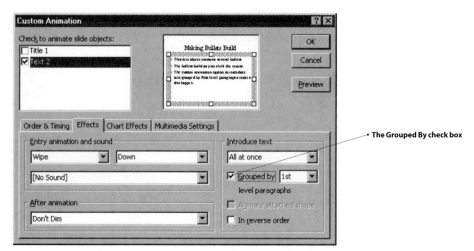

Figure 24-4   The custom animation option to introduce text grouped by first level paragraphs makes a text object's bullets build as you click the mouse.

DIMMING PREVIOUSLY ANIMATED TEXT

To draw the user's attention to text newly written onto the screen, you can make previously animated text dim or change color when the new text comes on-screen. The setting that lets you do this is called After Animation, which you will find on the Effects tab of the Custom Animation dialog. To make text dim, use the After Animation menu to choose the dim color, as illustrated in Figure 24-5.

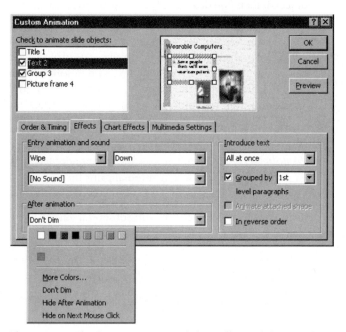

Figure 24-5   The Custom Animation dialog's Effects tab has an After Animation menu you can use to dim text.

Animating Images

Just as text can be moved onto the screen in a wide variety of styles, so also can you create custom animations for images. You will be happy to know that the process for creating custom image animations is the same as for text. Simply select the image object you want to animate, then pull down the Slide Show menu, select Custom Animation, and use the Effects tab to set the style. Use the Order and Timing tab to adjust the order if necessary.

Coordinating Multiple Animations

Sometimes you will want two or more objects to animate onto the screen simultaneously. There is an example of this in the NECC keynote presentation. To view it, open the *Keynote* application in the *Necc* folder of the *Multilit* CD. In Slide Sorter view, click the screen entitled *Multi Multimedia*. Pull down the Slide Show menu and choose Animation Preview. You will see six corporate logos come on as a group and spin together.

To see how this effect was achieved, double-click the slide to edit it, then pull down the Slide Show menu and choose Custom Animation. You will see how this effect was created by grouping the objects that needed to appear on-screen simultaneously. When objects are grouped, the Custom Animation dialog lets you set animation effects that apply to all of the objects in the group simultaneously.

As you learned in Chapter 22, you group objects via the Group command on the Draw menu. Use your mouse to select the objects (hold down the Shift key to select multiple objects), then pull down the Draw menu and select Group. To undo the grouping, select the group, pull down the Draw menu, and select Ungroup.

Audio Clips

You can insert an audio clip on any screen where you want it to play during a slide show. You can choose either to have the sound start automatically when you move to the slide, or you can have the sound play only when you click its icon during a slide show. To change how the sound starts or to add a hyperlink to the clip, click Action Settings on the Slide Show menu. You can change play settings by clicking Custom Animation on the Slide Show menu. For example, you can set a sound to play automatically in an animation sequence.

Inserting Sound Files from the Clip Gallery

Show-Me Movie:
"Inserting Sound Files"

A wide variety of sound files are available to you from the clip gallery. To insert a sound file from the clip gallery onto a slide, follow these steps:

▶ You can insert a sound file on any screen of your application. For this example, let's put a sound file on the heart screen of your *Practice* application. Use Slide view to move to the heart screen.

▶ Pull down the Insert menu and choose Movies and Sounds; Figure 24-6 shows how a menu pops up giving you the choice of inserting a sound from the Gallery or from a file.

▶ Choose the option to insert a sound from the Gallery; the Insert Sound dialog appears.

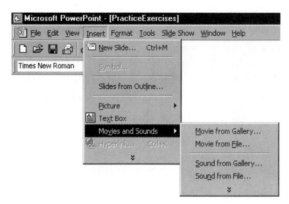

Figure 24-6 Pulling down the Insert menu and choosing Movies and Sounds gives you the choices to insert movies or sounds from the gallery or from a file.

▷ If you are connected to the Internet, click the Clips Online option to look for music clips online. When the clip gallery comes up, follow the on-screen instructions to search for sound files.

▷ Click one or more of the sound files to download them. When the file appears in your Insert Sound dialog, click it, and a menu will pop out letting you insert the sound, play it, or file it in your computer's clip library. Choose the option to insert the sound into your presentation.

▷ PowerPoint will ask whether you want the sound to start playing automatically when this slide appears; say no. You'll learn how to change this setting later on.

▷ Close the Insert Sound dialog and notice what has happened to your screen: A sound icon appears on it. When a user clicks the sound icon, the sound will play. If you right-click the sound icon to make the menu pop up, you will get choices that let you play the sound, edit the sound object, or change the animation effects. In the animation effects, you can make the sound start to play automatically, or you can leave it set to play only when the user clicks it or make it play when the user mouses over it.

Macintosh reminder: Macintosh users right-click by holding down [Ctrl] during the click.

Inserting Other Sound Files

In addition to inserting sound files from the clip gallery, you can also insert sound files from any place on your computer's hard drive, CD-ROM or DVD drive, or network. Follow these steps:

▷ Use Slide view to bring up the slide on which you want to insert the sound file.

▷ For this exercise, make sure the *Multilit* CD is inserted in your CD-ROM drive.

▷ Pull down the Insert menu, choose Movies and Sounds, and choose the option to insert a sound from a file; the Insert Sound dialog appears.

▷ Use the Look In menu to look to your *Multilit* CD's Audio folder.

▷ Choose the sound of your choice and click OK to select it.

▷ PowerPoint will ask whether you want the sound to start playing automatically when the slide appears; answer as you like. You can change this later by right-clicking the sound icon and choosing Custom Animation, which lets you set the sound to autoplay or not.

Movie Clips

You can insert a movie clip and size and position it on any screen where you want it to play during a slide show. You can choose either to have the movie start automatically when you move to the slide, or to have the movie play only when you click its icon during a slide show. You can choose whether you want the user to have slider controls and buttons to control the movie while it plays.

Inserting Movie Files

Show-Me Movie:
"Inserting Movie Files"

The *Multilit* CD contains movies that you can insert into your application. To insert a movie file onto a slide, follow these steps:

▶ You can insert a movie on any screen of your application. In this example, go to the last screen of your *Practice* application, and click the New Screen button to create a fresh screen.

▶ Pull down the Insert menu and choose Movies and Sounds. When the menu pops up, choose the option to insert a movie from a file; the Insert Movie dialog appears.

▶ Use the Look In menu to look in the Movies folder of the *Multilit* CD.

▶ Select the file of your choice and click OK to close the dialog.

▶ PowerPoint will ask whether you want the movie to start playing automatically when this slide appears; say no. You will learn how to change this setting later on.

▶ When you close the Insert Movie dialog, notice what has happened to your screen: The first frame of the movie appears on it. Click the Slide Show button to run the show. Click the movie, and it will begin to play. Click the movie again, and it will stop playing.

▶ Switch to Normal view. If you right-click the movie to make the menu pop up, you will get choices that let you play the movie, edit the movie object, or change the animation effects. In the animation effects, you can make the movie start to play automatically, or you can leave it set to play only when the user clicks it or make it play when the user mouses over it.

Movie Effects

Once you have a movie on a PowerPoint screen in Normal view, you can manipulate it like any other object. You can resize the movie, for example, by dragging the handles that appear around the movie when you click it to select it. Sizing the movie via the corner handles preserves the movie's aspect ratio; sizing the movie with the side handles, on the other hand, will stretch or squeeze the movie, making it appear thinner, fatter, shorter, or taller than usual.

If you right-click the movie to pop out the menu, and choose the option to edit the movie object, you will get the Movie Options shown in Figure 24-7. These options let you set the movie to loop (i.e., repeat) until stopped, and rewind automatically when it stops.

If you right-click the movie and choose the Custom Animation option, you will get controls that let you make the movie play as part of an animation. As illustrated in Figure 24-8, you can pause or continue the slide show during the movie, and you can even keep the movie playing on-screen while you continue showing slides. There is also an option to hide the movie while it is not playing.

Figure 24-7   The Movie
Options dialog.

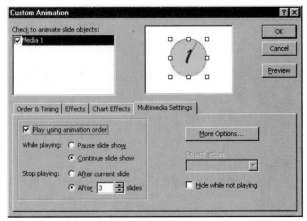

Figure 24-8   Multimedia Movie Settings in the Custom
Animation dialog.

If you would like to set the movie to play when the user mouses over it, right-click the movie in Normal view, and when the menu pops up, choose Action Settings. When the Action Settings dialog appears, click the Mouse Over tab, then click the object action and set it to play, as illustrated in Figure 24-9.

Finally, if you right-click the movie and choose the option to Format Picture, you can crop the movie, change its brightness and contrast, or make it play in black and white instead of color. You should recall having learned how to use the Format Picture dialog in Chapter 21, when you learned how to make special effects for graphics. You will be happy to discover that the Format Picture controls work the same way for movies, as illustrated in Figure 24-10.

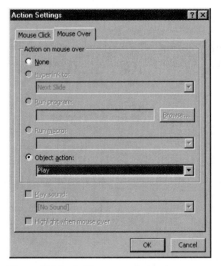

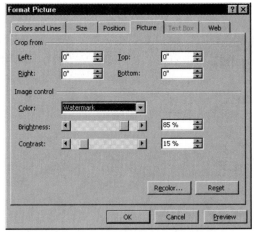

Figure 24-10   Use the Format Picture dialog to crop
a movie and alter its brightness and contrast.

Figure 24-9   Setting a movie to play on
Mouse Over in the Action Settings dialog.

Animated GIF Images

Show-Me Movie:
"Animated GIF Images"

As you learned in Chapter 2, animated GIF images are one of the simplest yet most effective means of getting motion on-screen. It is easy to insert animated GIFs anyplace on a PowerPoint screen. Just be careful not to overuse them. Too much movement will bombard the senses and overwhelm the user. Avoid the temptation of the novice to have animated GIFs on every screen. Unless there is a good reason for the animation, use a still image. That said, you will be happy to learn how easy it is to insert an animated GIF on-screen. Follow these steps:

▷ You can insert an animated GIF on any screen of your application. For this example, let's put an animated GIF on the heart screen of your *Practice* application. Use Slide Sorter view to find the heart screen, and double-click the heart screen to select it for editing.

▷ Pull down the Insert menu, choose Picture, then choose From File; the Insert Picture dialog will appear.

▷ If the *Multilit* CD is not in your computer right now, put the *Multilit* CD into your CD-ROM drive.

▷ Pull down the Look In menu at the top of the Insert Picture dialog, and set it to look at the root directory of your CD.

▷ Double-click the AnimatedGIFs folder, and click the image of your choice.

▷ Click the Insert button on the Insert Picture dialog to insert the picture.

▷ Click the Slide Show button to run the show. You should see the animation.

▷ Press Escape to stop the show and go back to Normal view. If you right-click the animated GIF to make the menu pop up, you will get choices that let you create a custom animation, alter the action settings, or format the picture. These work the same way for animated GIFs as they do for still pictures.

Audio CD

As you learned in Chapter 2, we are fortunate that practically all recorded music is available on commercially produced audio CDs. You can insert any audio CD into your computer's CD-ROM or DVD drive, and use PowerPoint to play music from the CD during your presentation. You can make any track play at any time, depending on how you decide to synchronize it with your presentation. Be aware, however, that the audio CD must be in the drive in order for the music to play. If you are planning to publish your application and distribute it to other users, audio CD may not be the preferred medium for playing the audio. If copyright and fair use laws permit, it may be better to use one of the ripper programs discussed in Chapter 9 to create an MP3 file, for example, and insert the audio as a file instead of requiring users to have the CD. With that caveat, if you want to use an audio CD in a PowerPoint presentation, follow these steps:

▷ You can make an audio CD play on any screen of your application. In this example, let's put some CD audio on the heart screen of your *Practice* application. Use Slide view to move to the heart screen.

▷ Insert an audio CD into your CD-ROM or DVD drive. It does not matter what audio CD you use; insert your favorite audio CD, for example. The CD may start playing automatically when you insert it; use your computer's CD player to stop it if you want, or you can let it play, especially if it is your favorite CD!

▷ Pull down the Insert menu and choose Movies and Sounds. If the menu does not show the option to play sound from a CD audio track, click the down-arrows to reveal that choice, as illustrated in Figure 24-11.

▷ Click the option to play a sound from a CD audio track. The Movies and Sounds dialog appears as illustrated in Figure 24-12.

▷ Click the arrows next to the track settings to choose the start and end track. If you want to play just one track, set the start and end tracks to the same number.

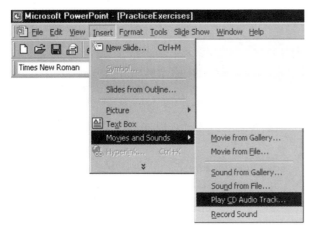

Figure 24-11   The expanded Insert Movies and Sounds menu gives you the choice to play a sound from a CD audio track.

Figure 24-12   The Movies and Sounds dialog lets you set the track and the minute:second location of a CD audio clip.

▷ Beneath the track fields are two At fields, which let you set the minute:second address at which to start and stop playing. When you clicked the track controls to choose your track, the At fields got set automatically to the beginning minute:second (00:00) of the start track, and the last minute:second of the end track (02:20 in this example). If you want the clip to start or stop playing at a different minute:second location, click the arrows of the At field you want to change. You can also type the minute:second location directly into the At field by clicking the field to edit it.

▷ When you are done setting up the clip, PowerPoint will ask whether you want the sound to start playing automatically when this slide appears; say no for now.

▷ Click OK to close the dialog and notice what has happened to your screen: A sound icon appears on it. When a user clicks the sound icon, the sound will play. If you right-click the sound icon to make the menu pop out, you will get choices that let you play the sound, edit the sound object, or change the animation effects. In the animation effects, you can make the sound start to play automatically or when the user mouses over it, or you can leave it set to play only when the user clicks it.

e x e r c i s e s

1. Run through your *Practice* application and study the transition effects you have put into it. Revise the effects and rehearse the show until you get the transitions you like best. Which transitions are your favorites?

2. Run the *Keynote* presentation from the *Necc* folder of the *Multilit* CD. Make note of the slide transitions the NECC keynote uses. Notice how there are just a few well-chosen dissolve patterns and animation techniques. What dissolve patterns do you find the NECC keynote using most?

3. Create a new screen in your *Practice* application. Make the heading "Text Building Demonstration." Put three or four text objects on-screen. Type whatever text you want into the text boxes. Use custom animation effects to make the text objects build onto the screen, one by one, as the user clicks the mouse.

4. Make the text you created in exercise 3 dim each time the user clicks to bring a new text object on-screen. What dim color works best for the background color you are using? What background color, foreground text color, and dimmed text color work best on this slide?

25 Waveform Audio Recording

After completing this chapter, you will be able to:

▓ **Create a waveform audio recording of your voice or any other sound source**

▓ **Set recording levels to ensure a good signal-to-noise ratio**

▓ **Make narrated slide shows that tell a story as the user clicks through them**

▓ **Understand the concept of ambient sound and learn how to use it to give a sense of realism to your multimedia screens**

▓ **Record sound bites that play when the user mouses over a trigger**

▓ **Edit a waveform audio recording to remove unwanted sound**

▓ **Experience how the sampling rate and bits-per-sample settings affect the quality of the sound and the size (required bandwidth) of the waveform audio file**

● By definition, every multimedia PC has the capability to record and play back waveform audio. In this chapter you will learn how to record waveform audio, trigger its playback, and create narrated slide shows. You will also learn how to record ambient sound to create a sense of realism on a multimedia screen.

Preparing to Make Your First Waveform Audio Recording

In order to complete the exercises in this chapter, you are going to need a microphone. Some computers have the microphone built in. If your computer does not have a built-in microphone, you will need to plug in a microphone of your own. If you do not have a microphone, you can buy one inexpensively at any Radio Shack store. If the connector on your microphone does not fit the microphone jack on your computer, you can purchase the necessary adapter from Radio Shack.

Show-Me Movie:
"How to Select the Record Sound Source"

Once your microphone is connected, you need to make sure it is selected as the source in the recording section of your computer's sound mixing software. Follow the steps in Table 25-1 to do that.

Table 25-1 How to Select the Record Sound Source

Windows	Macintosh
▶ If there is a sound icon on your Windows taskbar, double-click it to bring up your sound mixer controls. Otherwise, look on your Windows Start menu for a group related to sound, in which you should be able to find your sound mixer software.	▶ Pull down the Apple menu, choose Control panels, and choose Monitors and Sound. When the control panel opens, choose Sound. You will get a Sound Control panel similar to the one shown in Figure 25-4.

▶ Pull down the Options menu and choose Properties; the Properties dialog appears as shown in Figure 25-1.

Click here to see Playback settings

Click here to see Record settings

Make sure these boxes are all checked

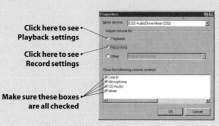

Figure 25-1 The Sound Properties dialog.

▶ Click the Recording button, if it is not already selected.

▶ The listbox identifies the different recording controls on your computer. Make sure they are all selected, so they will show up in the Recording Control window in the next step.

▶ Click OK; the Recording Control window appears as shown in Figure 25-2.

The slider adjusts the record level; it should be up about 90% of the way; increase this if the recording sounds too faint; decrease this if you get distortion

This box must be checked in order to record from a microphone

Figure 25-2 The Recording Control window.

▶ Make sure the check box for the source you're recording is selected. In this example, check the microphone source.

▶ Pull down the Options menu and choose Properties to make the Properties dialog shown in Figure 25-1 reappear.

▶ Click the Playback button.

▶ The listbox identifies the different playback controls on your computer. Make sure they are all selected, so they will show up in the Volume Control window in the next step.

▶ Click OK; the Volume Control window appears as shown in Figure 25-3.

Microphone Control; mute this to avoid feedback while you're recording from a microphone

Master volume control

The slider adjusts the playback volume

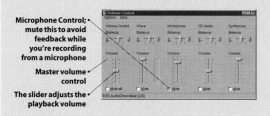

Figure 25-3 The Volume Control window.

▶ If you are recording from a microphone, you will probably want to mute the microphone; otherwise, sound from the microphone will feed back through your speakers. Feedback can cause distortion, but it can also create an interesting depth effect if your microphone is not positioned too close to the speakers. The author recommends you mute the mike setting your first time through; later on, you can try making depth effects.

▶ Make sure the master volume control is turned up.

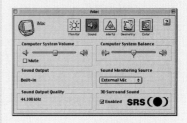

Figure 25-4 The Sound Control Panel.

▶ Pull down the Sound Monitoring Source menu; it lets you set the sound source to external mike, audio CD, sound in, or built-in mike, as illustrated in Figure 25-5.

Figure 25-5 The Sound Monitoring Source menu.

▶ In this example, click the built-in mike to select it as your input source, unless you happen to have an external mike, in which case you should select it instead.

▶ Click the Close icon in the upper left corner of the control panel to close it.

Making Your First Recording

PowerPoint has a simple waveform audio recorder built in that makes it easy for you to record a simple narration for a slide. The tool does not let you edit the recording, so it is limited in that respect, but it is so easy to make your first recording that we will start with it before learning a more complete tool later on in this chapter. Not to belittle the PowerPoint audio recording tool, however; even experienced professionals use it to record short narrations called **sound bites** because it is so quick and easy to do. Follow these steps to make your first recording:

▷ Go to the PowerPoint screen on which you want to record some waveform audio. In this example, let's create a new screen on which to place your first recording. Go to the last screen of your *Practice* application, and click the New Slide icon or pull down Insert and choose New Slide to create a new blank screen.

▷ To make your first recording, pull down the Insert menu, choose Movies and Sounds, and select the option to Record Sound, as illustrated in Figure 25-6. If the Record Sound option is not visible, click the down-arrows to expand the menu and reveal the rest of the choices.

▷ The Record Sound dialog will appear, as illustrated in Figure 25-7.

▷ Into the Name field, type the name you want the recorded sound to have. In this example, type **My First Narration**

▷ To begin recording, hold the microphone close to your mouth so you will get a good presence on mike; then click the Record button, which is the button with the solid red circle inside it. Start talking immediately, and say anything you want. For example, you might say: "This is my first recorded narration."

▷ Click the Stop button as soon as you are done, so you do not record unwanted silence at the end of the recording. The Stop button is the one with the square in it. The square is blue when the button is active, or gray when it is inactive.

▷ To rehearse your recording, click the Play button, which is the one with the arrow in it. Listen as the recording plays back.

▷ If you do not like the recording, click Cancel. Then repeat these steps to try it again.

If you like the recording, click OK. An audio icon appears on your slide. When you run the presentation, the recording will play when you click on this audio icon.

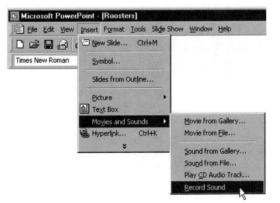

Figure 25-6   Selecting the option to Record Sound from the Movies and Sounds section of the Insert menu.

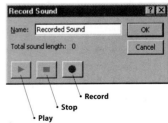

Figure 25-7   The Record Sound dialog.

Checking Record Levels

If the recording sounds faint, it is possible that the record level is turned down too low on your computer. You may be tempted to turn up the volume on your amplifier, but that is not the proper solution, because doing that will also amplify background noises due to the recording level having been set too low. Instead, use your Recording Control window to check the record level and adjust it if necessary. Refer back to Table 25-1 if you need help getting the recording controls to appear on-screen.

Recording Narrations

The simple technique you have just learned for making voice recordings with PowerPoint's built-in audio recorder can be used to narrate any slide or object in a presentation. An effective technique in training, for example, is to use audio narration to explain things as they appear on-screen. Let's create a simple example that shows you how to do this. We will make an example that has three slides, so you can practice the technique three times. Follow these steps:

SLIDE 1: THE EGG

▷ Pull down the PowerPoint File menu and choose New to create a new presentation to hold this example. When the New Presentation dialog appears, choose the option to create a Blank presentation. When the New Slide dialog appears, choose the option to create a Blank slide.

▷ Pull down the Insert menu, choose Picture, then choose From File. When the Insert Picture dialog appears, use the Look In menu to go to the Images folder of the *Multilit* CD, and choose the image called Egg.

▷ Click and drag the corners of the picture of the egg to make it fill the screen.

▷ Pull down the Insert menu, choose Movies and Sounds, then Record sound. When the Record Sound dialog appears, use it to record the following narration: "Roosters grow through several interesting stages. Here you see how they get born: in eggs!"

▷ Click the Play button to make sure the recording sounds good. If not, click Cancel, and repeat the previous step. If the recording is OK, use the Name field to make its name *Eggs,* then click OK.

▷ The audio icon appears on top of the Egg slide. Right-click the audio icon, choose Order, and choose Send to Back.

▷ Right-click the Egg slide and choose Custom Animation. Use the Custom Animation's Order and Timing tab to make the audio recording start automatically.

▷ Click the Slide Show button to rehearse the show so far. As soon as the egg appears on-screen, the narration should play automatically. If there is a problem, go back and fix it.

▷ Pull down the File menu, choose Save, and when the Save dialog appears, use the Save In menu to choose the *multilit* folder on your hard drive, and save the presentation under the filename: *Roosters*

SLIDE 2: THE CHICK

▷ Click the New Slide icon to add a blank slide after the Egg.

▷ Pull down the Insert menu, choose Picture, then choose From File. When the Insert Picture dialog appears, choose the image called Chick from the Images folder on the *Multilit* CD.

▷ Click and drag the corners of the picture of the chick to make it fill the screen.

▷ Pull down the Insert menu, choose Movies and Sounds, then Record Sound. When the Record Sound dialog appears, use it to record this narration: "Then they hatch into little chicks."

▷ Click the Play button to make sure the recording sounds good. If not, click Cancel, and repeat the previous step. If the recording is OK, use the Name field to name it *Chick*, then click OK.

▷ The audio icon appears on top of the Chick slide. Right-click the audio icon, choose Order, and choose Send to Back.

▷ Right-click the Chick slide and choose Custom Animation. Use the Custom Animation's Order and Timing tab to make the audio recording start automatically.

▷ Click the Slide Show button to rehearse the show so far; the audio on each slide should begin automatically soon as the slide appears.

▷ Pull down the File menu and choose Save, or click the Save icon, to save your work so far.

SLIDE 3: THE ROOSTER

▷ Click the New Slide icon to add a blank slide after the Chick.

▷ Pull down the Insert menu, choose Picture, then choose From File. When the Insert Picture dialog appears, choose the image called Rooster from the Images folder on the *Multilit* CD.

▷ Click and drag the corners of the picture of the rooster to make it fill the screen.

▷ Pull down the Insert menu, choose Movies and Sounds, then Record Sound. When the Record Sound dialog appears, use it to record the following narration: "Eventually, they grow up and look like this. And then they start to crow!"

▷ Click the Play button to make sure the recording sounds good. If not, click Cancel, and repeat the previous step. If the recording is OK, use the Name field to name it *Rooster*, then click OK.

▷ The audio icon appears on top of the Rooster slide. Right-click the audio icon, choose Order, and choose Send to Back.

▷ Right-click the Rooster slide and choose Custom Animation. Use the Custom Animation's Order and Timing tab to make the audio recording start automatically.

▷ Click the Slide Show button to rehearse the show so far; the audio on each slide should begin automatically soon as the slide appears.

▷ Click the Save icon to save the presentation.

Ambient Sound

Ambient sound is a multimedia technique in which a waveform audio file keeps repeating to create the aural illusion that the user is in the place or situation where the sound was recorded. PowerPoint makes it easy to put ambient sound on any multimedia screen. Follow these steps:

▷   Go to the slide on which you want to insert some ambient sound. In this example, go to the last screen of the Rooster application, and click the New Slide icon to create a new blank screen.

▷   Pull down the Insert menu, choose Picture, then choose From File. When the Insert Picture dialog appears, choose the image called Rooster from the Images folder on the *Multilit* CD.

▷   Pull down the Insert menu, choose Movies and Sounds, then choose Sound from File.

▷   When the Insert Sound dialog appears, look in the Ambient folder of the *Multilit* CD, and choose the ambient sound of your choice. In this example, choose Rooster.

▷   When PowerPoint asks if you want the sound to play automatically, answer Yes. The sound's audio icon appears on-screen.

▷   Right-click the audio icon, and choose the option to edit the sound object. When the Sound Options dialog appears, choose the option to Loop until stopped.

▷   Click the Slide Show button to rehearse the application. When you get to the slide that has the ambient sound, listen how it loops continually.

In the next section of this book, when you create the History of Flight application, you will use ambient sound to make it sound like your users are standing in an airport lobby.

Adding Custom Sound to a Hyperlink

Show-Me Movie:
"Adding Custom Sound to a Hyperlink"

You can add custom sound to a hyperlink to give the user an audible hint about what will happen if the user triggers the link. For example, suppose you want to insert a hyperlink at the end of your *Practice* application that will trigger the Rooster application you created in this chapter. When the user mouses over the hyperlink, you will play a narration telling what will happen if the user clicks there. Follow these steps:

▷   Use PowerPoint to open the *Practice* application and scroll down to the last screen.

▷   Pull down the Insert menu, choose Movies and Sounds, and choose Record Sound. When the Record Sound dialog appears, record the following narration: "Click here to find out what came first: the chicken or the egg?"

▷   Make the name of the recorded narration *RoosterLink,* then click OK to close the Record Sound dialog. The audio icon for the narration you recorded should now appear on-screen.

▷   Pull down the Insert menu, choose Picture, then choose From File. When the Insert Picture dialog appears, choose the image called Rooster from the Images folder on the *Multilit* CD.

▷ Resize the picture of the rooster so it appears as a little icon on your screen.

▷ Right-click the rooster icon, and when the menu appears, choose Hyperlink.

▷ When the Hyperlink dialog appears, choose the option to browse for a file, and in the *multilit* folder on your hard drive, choose the Rooster application and click OK to close the dialog.

▷ Right-click the hyperlink you just created, and choose Action Settings to make the Action Settings dialog appear.

▷ Click the Mouse Over tab, check the Play Sound check box, pull down the menu, and choose the RoosterLink audio you just recorded, as illustrated in Figure 25-8.

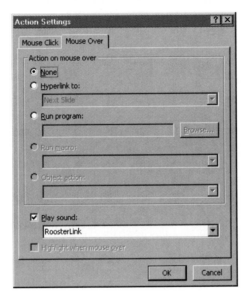

Figure 25-8 Making the Action Settings trigger a sound when the user mouses over a hyperlink.

▷ Click the Slide Show button to run the application. When you get to the screen on which you put the hyperlink, mouse over it, but do not click. Notice how mousing over it causes the narration you recorded to play: "Click here to find out what came first: the chicken or the egg."

Waveform Audio Recording and Editing

Although PowerPoint's built-in waveform audio tool is quick and easy to use for brief narrations, it does not let you edit the audio if you make a mistake or if you need to update something that goes out of date. Windows comes with a program called the Sound Recorder that enables you to create and edit waveform audio recordings. The remainder of this chapter shows Windows users how to record and edit waveform audio with the Sound Recorder. Macintosh users can edit audio with the QuickTime Pro software featured in Chapter 35.

Get the Windows Sound Recorder running by following these steps:

▷ Click the Windows Start button.

▷ Choose Programs—Accessories—Multimedia—Sound Recorder.

▷ The Sound Recorder appears as shown in Figure 25-9. The green line in the black window is an oscilloscope that shows you the incoming sound wave. When you press the Record button to begin recording, the green line should oscillate as the sound comes in. If the line does not move, your sound source is not active. Review the instructions in Table 25-1 to fix the problem.

▷ To begin recording, click the Record button. If you are using a microphone, hold the mike close to your mouth, so your recording will have good presence of sound. Speak in a loud, clear voice.

▷ To stop recording, click the Stop button.

▷ To hear the recording, click the Play button. If you do not hear anything, your sound source is probably not connected properly. Make sure your microphone or line input is plugged in to the proper jack, and follow the steps in Table 25-1 to select it as the recording source.

▷ To rewind the recording, click the Rewind button.

▷ To save the recording, pull down the File menu and click Save As; the Save As dialog appears. Save the recording in the folder of your choice, such as your *multilit* folder.

▷ If the recording sounds too faint, you need to adjust the record level; pull down the Edit menu, choose Audio Properties, and turn up the recording level.

▷ If you hear distortion, you need to turn the record level down; pull down the Edit menu, choose Audio Properties, and turn down the recording level.

▷ It may take you several tries to get a good recording. Keep adjusting the settings and rerecord until you get the result you want.

▷ To rerecord, pull down the File menu and choose New to empty the waveform buffer. If you do not choose New, what you record next will get inserted into what has already been recorded.

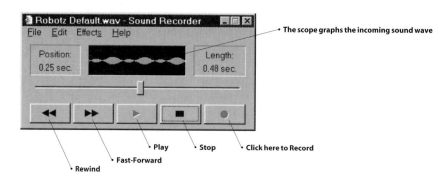

Figure 25-9   The Windows Sound Recorder.

Editing Waveform Audio Recordings

In addition to letting you record waveform audio, the Sound Recorder enables you to edit the audio. For example, if you pressed the Record button too soon, there is extra sound at the beginning of the recording that you need to delete. Similarly, if you pressed the stop button too late, there is extra sound at the end that you will want to remove. To edit a waveform audio recording, follow these steps:

▷ Get the Sound Recorder running if it is not already on-screen.

▷ Pull down the File menu, choose Open, and open the waveform audio file you want to edit. If the file is already open, you can skip this step.

▷ Play the file, and make note of the spots at which you want to delete the sound. You can drag the slider to move quickly to different positions in the recording. The Position counter shows where you are in hundredths of seconds.

▷ To delete the first part of a recording, position the slider at the spot where the good stuff starts, then pull down the Edit menu and choose Delete Before Current Position.

▷ To delete the last part of a recording, position the slider at the end of the good stuff, then pull down the Edit menu and choose Delete After Current Position.

▷ Play the file to make sure you have what you wanted.

▷ Save the file.

Adjusting the Quality of Waveform Audio Recordings

Most waveform audio recording software lets you adjust two parameters that govern the quality of a waveform audio recording: sampling rate and bits per sample. Be aware that the higher you set these parameters, the larger your waveform audio file will be.

SAMPLING RATE

The **sampling rate** determines the frequency response of the recorded sound. To record frequencies faithfully, your sampling rate must be at least two times greater than the highest frequency you want to record. However, the higher you set the sampling rate, the larger your waveform audio file will be. Since the size of the file increases, you should not choose a higher sampling rate than you need because of the increased bandwidth required to transfer the file over the Internet. To help you grasp the relationship between sampling rate and sound quality, Table 25-2 compares different sampling rates to real-world audio devices of differing fidelities.

Table 25-2   The Relationship Between Sound Quality and Sampling Rate

Samples per Second	Sonic Equivalent
6,000	Telephone
15,000	AM radio
37,500	FM radio
40,000	Phonograph records
44,100	Compact disc

BITS PER SAMPLE

Table 25-3 illustrates how the number of **bits per sample** determines the dynamic range, which determines how much of a volume change you will hear between the loudest and softest sounds in a recording. Waveform audio devices typically give you a choice of 8 or 16 bits-per-sample.

Since file size is determined by multiplying the bits per sample by the sampling rate, you do not want to choose a higher bits-per-sample setting than required. Try recording at 8 bits per sample first. Only if that does not provide adequate sound quality should you increase the setting to 16 bits. To help you grasp the relationship between bits per sample and sound quality, Table 25-4 shows the dynamic range equivalents of some real-world sound sources.

Table 25-3   The Relationship Between Bits per Sample and Dynamic Range

Bits per Sample	Dynamic Range	Bits per Sample	Dynamic Range
1	8 dB*	10	62 dB
2	14 dB	11	68 dB
3	20 dB	12	74 dB
4	26 dB	13	80 dB
5	32 dB	14	86 dB
6	38 dB	15	92 dB
7	44 dB	16	98 dB
8	50 dB	17	104 dB
9	56 dB	18	110 dB

*dB is the abbreviation for decibel

Table 25-4   Bits-per-Sample Equivalents of Traditional Sound Sources

Sound Source	Bits-per-Sample Equivalent
AM radio	6 bits
Telephone	8 bits
FM radio	9 bits
Phonograph records	10 bits
Reel-to-reel Tape	11 bits
Compact Disc	16 bits

Bandwidth Considerations

If you are using the Windows Sound Recorder, you can modify the sound quality settings by pulling down the Edit menu and choosing Audio Properties to make the Audio Properties dialog appear as shown in Figure 25-10. To adjust the quality, pull down the Preferred Quality menu, and choose the setting you want. If you understand how bits per sample and dynamic range affect sound, you can click the Customize button to create your own custom settings. Be careful to keep bandwidth in mind, however, because the higher you set the quality adjustments, the larger the file will become, and the more space it will take up on your computer. If you are planning to publish your application on the Internet, bandwidth may also be a consideration, because larger audio files take longer to download and play from the Web.

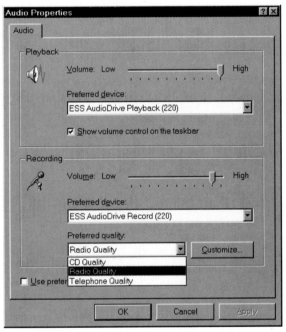

Figure 25-10 The Audio Properties dialog.

exercises

1. If you completed the *Rooster* application that you created while working through this chapter, the rooster crows incessantly when the user gets to the final screen on which you inserted the ambient sound. Some users might want to silence that screen. Put a Silence button there. *Hint:* One of the options on the Action Settings dialog's Play Sound menu is to stop the previous sound.

2. After you complete exercise 1, add a button that makes the ambient sound resume. Try the buttons and make sure the user can press your Silence button to stop the sound, then press Resume to restart it.

3. If you have Windows, use the Windows Sound Recorder to record 10 seconds of your voice at 8 bits and then at 16 bits per sample. Save the first recording as *c:\multilit\8bit.wav,* and save the second recording as *c:\multilit\16bit.wav.* Play the files back repeatedly and compare them. Can you hear a difference between the two recordings? Use the Windows Explorer to inspect the size of these files. How much larger is the 16-bit recording?

4. If you have Windows, use the Windows Sound Recorder to record music at different sampling rates. Can you hear how the higher sampling rates result in a brighter recording? This is because lower sampling rates cannot record high frequencies, effectively filtering them out.

Part Six
Creating a Multimedia Application

*If you can **dream** it, you can **do** it.*

—Adobe Systems Incorporated

Having learned the basic tools and techniques of multimedia, you will now use them to create an actual application. Your topic, the History of Flight, was chosen for several reasons. First, almost everyone is fascinated by aircraft and the subject of flight. Second, the history of aviation can be broken down into a few well-defined historical periods that lend themselves to the design of a simple, beginning-level application. Third, Aris Entertainment was kind enough to license materials from its *MediaClips* CD-ROMs for inclusion on the *Multilit* CD. These *MediaClips* CDs contain clip art, music, and digital videos of both jets and propeller aircraft. Finally, DuPont granted permission for us to digitize clips of historical aircraft featured in the IMAX video *To Fly!,* which was created for the IMAX theater in the Smithsonian Institution's National Air and Space Museum under a grant from Conoco, a subsidiary of DuPont.

> *Note:* There are no end-of-chapter exercises until the very end of Part Six because of the progressive nature of the tutorial in which you build the *History of Flight* application.

CHAPTER 26

The History of Flight Picture Menu

After completing this chapter, you will be able to:

- Create the opening or "home" screen for the History of Flight application

- Save the Flight application in your *Multilit* file folder

- Title the home screen and give it a backdrop

- Position the text on the History of Flight home screen

- Use ambient sound to provide a sense of realism for the home screen

● The simplest way to design a multimedia application is to have it begin with a screen that provides the user with a menu. When the user chooses an item from the menu, the application launches the object(s) linked to it. Then the application returns to the menu, and the user can make another choice. In Chapters 26 to 31, you learn how to create an application that uses a menu to teach about the history of flight.

The *Multilit* CD contains a History of Flight bitmap consisting of four buttons that represent different eras in aviation history: biplanes from the 1920s, military aircraft from World War II, jet age Blue Angels, and a contemporary Boeing 747 jumbo jet. Figure 26-1 shows the buttons bitmap. In this chapter you will use the buttons bitmap to create the History of Flight menu. In subsequent chapters you will learn how to link to the buttons to multimedia screens that describe and illustrate each era in the history of flight.

Figure 26-1   The History of Flight bitmap consists of four buttons representing different eras in the history of flight. Photos by David K. Brunn.

Copyright © 1994 Aris Multimedia Entertainment, Inc.

Creating the Home Screen

The home screen of the *History of Flight* application consists of four buttons that the user can click to go to information about different eras in the history of flight. To begin creating the home screen, follow these steps:

▷ If you do not have PowerPoint running at the moment, get it started.

▷ Pull down the File menu and choose New to make the New Presentation dialog appear.

▷ On the General tab, choose the option to create a blank presentation and click OK.

▷ When the New Slide dialog appears and asks you to choose an AutoLayout, select the Blank layout and click OK. *Note:* If the New Slide dialog does not appear, pull down the Format menu and choose Slide Layout.

▷ Pull down the Insert menu, choose Picture, then choose From File; the Insert Picture dialog appears.

▷ As illustrated in Figure 26-2, use the Insert Picture dialog to look in the *Aircraft* folder on the *Multilit* CD, and insert the picture called Buttons.

▷ Drag the picture's handles to make the picture fill the slide.

▷ Pull down the File menu and choose Save; when the Save dialog appears, use it to save the application in your *Multilit* folder under the name: **Flight**

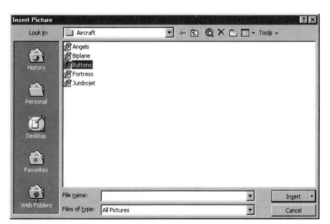

Figure 26-2 Use the controls in the Insert Picture dialog to look in the *Aircraft* folder, click Buttons to select it, then click Insert.

Titling the Home Screen

The title of the home screen is "The History of Flight." To title the home screen, follow these steps:

▷ If your version of PowerPoint has the tri-pane view, click in the outline pane to position your cursor there; otherwise, click the Outline icon to bring up the Outline view.

▷ In the outline, alongside the icon that represents the first slide, type:
The History of Flight

Entering the Subtitle

The subtitle of the home screen is "From Props to Jets." To type this title onto the home screen, follow these steps:

▶ If your version of PowerPoint has the tri-pane view, click in the slide pane to position your cursor there; otherwise, click the Slide view icon to bring up the Slide view.

▶ Pull down the Insert menu and choose Text Box, or click the Text Box icon on the Drawing toolbar.

▶ Click the spot on the slide beneath the title where you want to type the subtitle.

▶ Type the text: **From Props to Jets**

Entering the Rest of the Text

To tell the user what to do, you need to type some instructions at the bottom of the home screen, right below the buttons. Follow these steps:

▶ Pull down the Insert menu and choose Text Box, or click the Text Box icon on the Drawing toolbar.

▶ Click the spot on the slide beneath the buttons where you want to type the instructions.

▶ Type the text: **Click an Airplane to Study an Era of Flight**

Arranging the Text

Following the text-editing procedures you learned in Chapter 20, arrange the text and make it look good on the screen. Screen design is a matter of personal taste. Figure 26-3 shows one way of arranging this screen. Here are some suggestions for how to arrange the text on your screen:

▶ Use the Increase and Decrease Font Size tools to adjust the size of the text.

▶ Drag the text boxes to move each line where you want it on the screen.

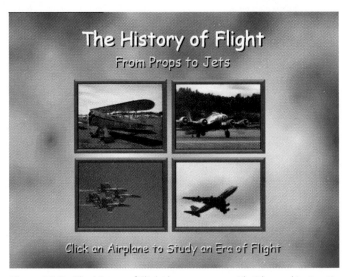

Figure 26-3   The History of Flight home screen with titles and instructions.
Photos by David K. Brunn. Copyright © 1994 Aris Multimedia Entertainment, Inc.

> Use the Font Color tool to make the first line white, the second line yellow, and the bottom line white.

> Use the Shadow tool to create drop shadow.

> Use the Font tool if you want to change the font.

> Use the Align tool to center all three lines on the screen.

Creating the Ambient Sound

There is a waveform audio file in the *Ambient* folder of the *Multilit* CD that makes airport sounds. The name of the file is *Airport*. To create the ambient Airport sound for the History of Flight home screen, follow these steps:

> Pull down the Insert menu, choose Movies and Sounds, then choose Sound from File; the Insert Sound dialog appears.

> As illustrated in Figure 26-4, use the Insert Sound dialog to look in the *Ambient* folder on the *Multilit* CD, and insert the sound called *Airport*.

> If PowerPoint asks whether you want the sound to play automatically, answer Yes.

> Pull down the Edit menu and choose Sound Object, or right-click the sound icon and choose Edit Sound Object. When the Sound Options dialog appears, check the box to make the sound loop until stopped.

> Drag the sound icon to an unobtrusive place on the slide, such as the lower right corner.

> Pull down the File menu and choose Save; when the Save dialog appears, use it to save the application in your *Multilit* folder under the name: **Flight**

> Press F5 to run the application. The ambient sound should start playing. If it does not, click the audio icon. Notice how the ambient sound creates the illusion that the user is in an airport lobby.

Figure 26-4   Use the controls in the Insert Sound dialog to look in the *Ambient* folder, click Airport to select it, then click OK.

27

1920s
Barnstorming

After completing this chapter, you will be able to:

▨ **Create a multimedia screen that presents the 1920s barnstorming era in the History of Flight**

▨ **Provide realism with the ambient sound of a biplane in flight**

▨ **Show the user a movie of a biplane in motion**

▨ **Link the Biplane button on the History of Flight menu to the biplane screen**

▨ **Use action buttons to enable the user to navigate**

● The home screen you just created serves as a menu. When the user clicks one of the four aircraft buttons, the application branches to materials that describe the corresponding period in aviation history. In this chapter you will create multimedia screens describing the barnstorming era of the 1920s and link them to the Biplane button on the History of Flight home screen.

Creating the Biplane Screen

If you do not already have PowerPoint running the Flight application, start PowerPoint and open the Flight application you began creating in the previous chapter. Follow these steps to create the biplane screen:

▷ Click the New Slide button to create a new slide, or pull down the Insert menu and choose New Slide.

▷ When the New Slide dialog appears and asks you to choose an AutoLayout, select the Blank layout and click OK. *Note:* If the New Slide dialog does not appear, pull down the Format menu and choose Slide Layout.

▷ Pull down the Insert menu, choose Picture, then choose From File; the Insert Picture dialog appears.

▷ Use the Insert Picture dialog to look in the *Aircraft* folder on the *Multilit* CD, and insert the picture called Biplane.

▷ Drag the picture's handles to make the picture fill the slide.

▷ Pull down the File menu and choose Save. Remember to save your application periodically as you work on it.

Titling the Biplane Screen

The title of the biplane screen is "Barnstorming Biplanes." To title the biplane screen, follow these steps:

▶ If your version of PowerPoint has the tri-pane view, click in the Outline pane to position your cursor there; otherwise, click the Outline icon to bring up the Outline view.

▶ In the outline, alongside the icon that represents the second slide, type: **Barnstorming Biplanes**

Entering the Biplane Text

Printed below are the text objects for you to type onto the Biplane screen. For each text object, create a separate text box by pulling down the Insert menu and choosing Text Box, or by clicking the Text Box icon on the Drawing toolbar. Then click the spot on the slide where you want the text to appear, and type the text. The text objects to type are listed as follows:

Biplanes were popularized by barnstormers who used them to dazzle onlookers during the 1920s.

Pictured here is the Waco Taperwing, a very acrobatic biplane.

In the 1940s, biplanes were used heavily to train civilian pilots during World War II.

Click anywhere to continue.

Adjusting the Text

Following the text-editing procedures you learned in Chapter 20, arrange the text and make it look good on the screen. Use the Font Size tools to make the text large or small. Drag the text boxes to move each line where you want it on the screen. Use the Font Color tool to colorize the text. Use the Shadow tool to create drop shadow. Use the Font tool to adjust the fonts. Figure 27-1 shows one way of arranging the biplane screen.

Creating the Ambient Sound

There is a waveform audio file called *Biplane* in the *Ambient* folder of the *Multilit* CD. Use the Insert Sound tool to make *Biplane.wav* be the ambient sound for your biplane screen. Try to do this on your own, but if you need help, follow these steps:

▶ Pull down the Insert menu, choose Movies and Sounds, then choose Sound from File; the Insert Sound dialog appears.

▶ Use the Insert Sound dialog to look in the *Ambient* folder on the *Multilit* CD, and insert the sound called *Biplane*.

▶ If PowerPoint asks whether you want the sound to play automatically, answer Yes.

▶ Pull down the Edit menu and choose Sound Object, or right-click the sound icon and choose Edit Sound Object; when the Sound Options dialog appears, check the box to make the sound loop until stopped.

Figure 27-1   The completed biplane screen. Photo by David K. Brunn.
Copyright © 1994 Aris Multimedia Entertainment, Inc.

▷   Drag the sound icon to an unobtrusive place on the slide, such as the lower right corner.

▷   Pull down the File menu and choose Save.

▷   Click the Slide Show icon to rehearse the application. The ambient sound should start playing. If it does not, click the Audio icon. Notice how the ambient sound creates the illusion that a biplane is flying overhead.

Linking the Biplane Screen to the Biplane Button

Now that you have created the biplane screen, you can link it to the Biplane button on the History of Flight home screen. The way to do this is to draw a rectangle over the Biplane button, turn the rectangle transparent, and then link the rectangle to the biplane screen. Follow these steps:

▷   In PowerPoint, select the home screen for editing. To do this, either use the scrollbar to move back to the home screen or click the Slide Sorter icon and then double-click the home screen to go to it.

▷   Click the Rectangle tool on the Drawing toolbar.

▷   Click and hold down the mouse button on the upper left corner of the Biplane button, then drag the mouse to the lower right corner and release the button.

▷   A solid rectangle now appears over the Biplane button. If the rectangle is not where you want it, drag its handles to adjust it.

▷   To turn the rectangle transparent, right-click it, and when the menu pops up, choose Format AutoShape.

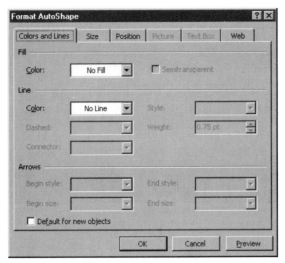

Figure 27-2 To turn the rectangle invisible, set its Fill Color to No Fill, and set the Line Color to No Line.

▷ When the Format AutoShape dialog appears, set the Fill Color to No Fill, and set the Line Color to No Line, as illustrated in Figure 27-2. Then click OK to close the dialog.

▷ To create the link, pull down the Insert menu and choose Hyperlink; the Hyperlink dialog appears as illustrated in Figure 27-3.

▷ In the left column of the Hyperlink dialog, click the option to link to a place in this document.

▷ As illustrated in Figure 27-4, click the slide you want to link to. In this example, click slide 2, which is your biplane slide. Notice how the dialog previews the slide to make sure you selected the one you wanted.

▷ Click OK to close the dialog. The link has been created.

▷ Remember to save your application by pulling down the File menu and choosing Save, or click the Save icon.

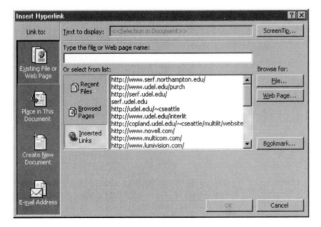

Figure 27-3 The left-hand column of the Hyperlink dialog has an option that lets you link to places in the current document.

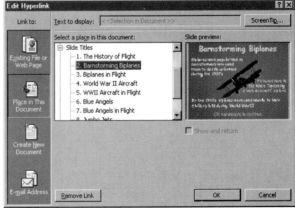

Figure 27-4 Linking to slide 2, which is the Biplane slide in the *History of Flight* application. Notice how the dialog previews the slide to make sure you link to the one you want.

Triggering the Link

To trigger the link and find out if it works, click the Slide Show icon to run your application. Move your mouse over the Biplane button. The cursor should change shape as you move over the button, indicating there is a link at that spot. Click that spot, and your biplane screen appears. The ambient sound of the biplane will begin to make it sound like a biplane is flying overhead. Read on to learn how to show the user a movie of a real biplane flying through the air.

Creating the Movie Screen

To bring your application to life, you can add a full-motion video clip of a barnstorming biplane in action! Follow these steps:

▷ In PowerPoint, select the biplane screen for editing. To do this, either use the scrollbar to move to the biplane screen or click the Slide Sorter icon and then double-click the biplane screen to go to it.

▷ Click the New Slide button to create a new slide, or pull down the Insert menu and choose New Slide.

▷ When the New Slide dialog appears and asks you to choose an AutoLayout, select the Blank layout and click OK. *Note:* If the New Slide dialog does not appear, pull down the Format menu and choose Slide Layout.

▷ Pull down the Insert menu, choose Picture, then choose From File; the Insert Picture dialog appears.

▷ Use the Insert Picture dialog to look in the *Aircraft* folder on the *Multilit* CD, and insert the picture called Biplane.

▷ Drag the picture's handles to make the picture fill the slide.

▷ If your version of PowerPoint has a tri-pane view, click in the outline pane to position your cursor there; otherwise, click the Outline icon to bring up the Outline view.

▷ In the outline, alongside the icon that represents the biplane movie slide, type the title of this slide: **Biplanes in Flight**

▷ Switch back to Normal view or Slide view. Notice how the picture covers up the title. Press ⎀Tab⎀ until the title is selected, then pull down the Draw menu, choose Order, and bring the title to the Front. Adjust the title's font, color, size, and shadow to suit your taste.

▷ Pull down the Insert menu and choose Movies and Sounds, then choose Movie from File. The Insert Movie dialog appears.

▷ Use the Insert Movie dialog to look in the *Aircraft* folder on the *Multilit* CD, and insert the movie called *Biplane*.

▷ If PowerPoint asks whether you want the movie to start playing automatically, say Yes.

▷ Use your computer's arrow keys to place the movie at the spot where you want it to appear on-screen.

▷ Save your application by clicking the Save icon, or pull down the File menu and choose Save.

Rehearsing the Movie Screen

To rehearse the movie and make sure it will play well, click the Slide Show icon to get your application running. When the movie screen appears, the movie should start playing. If it does not autostart, click the movie to play it. Each time you click the movie, its play state will change. Click to stop, click to play, and enjoy.

Creating a Home Button

The last step in producing the biplane slides is to create some action buttons that will provide the user with navigation options. To create a Home button that will return the user to the History of Flight home screen, follow these steps:

▷ In PowerPoint, select the biplane movie screen for editing. To do this, either use the scrollbar to move to the biplane movie screen, or click the Slide Sorter icon and then double-click the biplane movie screen to go to it.

▷ Pull down the AutoShapes menu, select Action Buttons, and click the Home button.

▷ Click the spot on the screen (probably near the bottom) where you want the Home button to appear. The Action Settings dialog appears, as illustrated in Figure 27-5.

▷ Notice how the Action on Click is automatically set to hyperlink to the first slide. Leave that setting alone, because that is what you want.

▷ Click OK to close the dialog. The Home button has been created.

Since the background picture on the screen is primarily blue, you may want to right-click the Home button, choose Format AutoShape, and change the fill color to a shade of blue. If the button appears too large on-screen, you can click and drag its handles to adjust the size of the button, as you like.

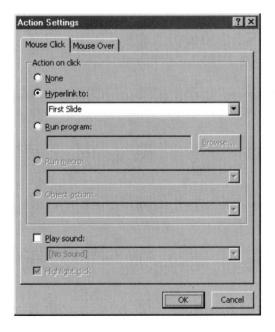

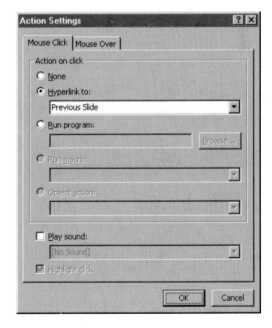

Figure 27-5 When you create a Home button, the Action Settings dialog is preset to hyperlink to the first slide.

Figure 27-6 When you create a Back button, the Action Settings dialog is preset to hyperlink to the previous slide.

Creating a Back Button

To create a Back button that will take the user back to the previous screen, follow these steps:

▶ In PowerPoint, select the biplane movie screen for editing.

▶ Pull down the AutoShapes menu, select Action Buttons, and click the Back button.

▶ Click the spot on the screen (probably near the bottom) where you want the Back button to appear. The Action Settings dialog appears, as illustrated in Figure 27-6.

▶ Notice how the Action on Click is automatically set to hyperlink to the previous slide. Leave that setting alone, because that is what you want.

▶ Click OK to close the Action Settings dialog. The Back button has been created. As you did with the Home button, adjust the Back button's color and size as you like.

Rehearsing the Action Buttons

To rehearse the application and make sure the action buttons work well, pull down the Slide Show menu and choose View Show. When the History of Flight menu appears, click the Biplane button. When the biplane screen appears, click through to the screen that plays the biplane movie. Now comes the test: Click the Home button, and the home screen should reappear.

Click the Biplane button again, and click through to the screen that plays the biplane movie. Then click the Back button. This should take you back to the biplane screen.

If this worked, congratulate yourself—you are well on your way to becoming a multimedia application developer. If you had trouble, try repeating the previous steps. With practice, you can master this process.

28

The Flying Fortress

After completing this chapter, you will be able to:

▨ **Create a multimedia screen that presents the World War II era in the history of flight**

▨ **Provide realism with the ambient sound of a Flying Fortress in flight**

▨ **Show the user a movie that illustrates the history of aircraft development during World War II**

▨ **Link the Flying Fortress button on the History of Flight menu to the Flying Fortress screen**

▨ **Use action buttons to enable the user to navigate**

▨ **Create this multimedia sequence with a little less hand-holding than in the previous chapter**

● This chapter is very similar to the one you just completed. In fact, all four of the historical aircraft chapters in this tutorial have the same design. The goal is to make you so familiar with the process of linking buttons to multimedia materials that you can do it without referring to the instructions. Accordingly, each chapter will provide less hand-holding than the previous chapter until you can make these linkages without looking in the book. Then, you will be ready to create original multimedia applications on your own.

The second button on the History of Flight menu pictures the Boeing-17G "Flying Fortress," one of the most famous World War II aircraft. This chapter shows you how to create multimedia screens describing World War II aircraft and link them to the Flying Fortress button on the History of Flight home screen.

Creating the Flying Fortress Screen

If you do not already have PowerPoint running the *Flight* application, start PowerPoint and open the *Flight* application you began creating in the previous chapter. Follow these steps to create the Flying Fortress screen:

▷ Select the Biplane Movie screen for editing. To do this, either use the scrollbar to move down to the Biplane Movie screen, or click the Slide Sorter icon and then double-click the Biplane Movie screen to go to it.

▷ Create a new slide either by clicking the New Slide button, or pull down the Insert menu and choose New Slide.

▷ When the New Slide dialog appears and asks you to choose an AutoLayout, select the Blank layout and click OK. *Note:* If the New Slide dialog does not appear, pull down the Format menu and choose Slide Layout.

▷ Pull down the Insert menu, choose Picture, then choose From File; the Insert Picture dialog appears.

▷ Use the Insert Picture dialog to look in the *Aircraft* folder on the *Multilit* CD, and insert the picture called Fortress.

▷ Drag the picture's handles to make the picture fill the slide.

▷ Pull down the File menu and choose Save. Remember to save your application periodically as you work on it.

Titling the Flying Fortress Screen

The title of the Flying Fortress screen is "World War II Aircraft." To title the Flying Fortress screen, follow these steps:

▷ If your version of PowerPoint has the tri-pane view, click in the outline pane to position your cursor there; otherwise, click the Outline icon to bring up the Outline view.

▷ In the outline alongside the icon that represents the Flying Fortress slide, type: **World War II Aircraft**

Entering the Flying Fortress Text

Printed below are the text objects for you to type onto the Flying Fortress screen. For each text object, create a separate text box by pulling down the Insert menu and choosing Text Box, or by clicking the Text Box icon on the Drawing toolbar. Then click the spot on the slide where you want the text to appear, and type the text. The text objects to type are listed as follows:

The Allies relied on aircraft to help win World War II.

Pictured here is the famous Boeing B-17 bomber, which was nicknamed the Flying Fortress due to its heavy armament.

Click anywhere to continue.

Adjusting the Text

Following the text-editing procedures you learned in Chapter 20, arrange the text and make it look good on the screen. Use the Font Size tools to make the text large or small. Drag the text boxes to move each line where you want it on the screen. Use the Font Color tool to colorize the text. Use the Shadow tool to create drop shadow. Use the Font tool to adjust the fonts. Figure 28-1 shows one way of arranging the Flying Fortress screen.

Figure 28-1   The completed Flying Fortress screen.

Photo by David K. Brunn. Copyright © 1994 Aris Multimedia Entertainment, Inc.

Creating the Ambient Sound

There is a waveform audio file called *Fortress* in the *Ambient* folder of the *Multilit* CD. Use the Insert Sound tool to make *Fortress* be the ambient sound for your Flying Fortress screen. By now, you should be able to do this on your own, but if you need help, follow these steps:

▷   Pull down the Insert menu, choose Movies and Sounds, then choose Sound from File; the Insert Sound dialog appears.

▷   Use the Insert Sound dialog to look in the *Ambient* folder on the *Multilit* CD, and insert the sound called *Fortress*.

▷   If PowerPoint asks whether you want the sound to play automatically, answer Yes.

▷   Pull down the Edit menu and choose Sound Object, or right-click the Sound icon and choose Edit Sound Object; when the Sound Options dialog appears, check the box to make the sound loop until stopped.

▷   Drag the Sound icon to an unobtrusive place on the slide, such as the lower right corner.

▷   Pull down the File menu and choose Save.

▷   Click the Slide Show icon to rehearse the application. The ambient sound should start playing. If it does not, click the Audio icon. Notice how the ambient sound creates the illusion that a Flying Fortress is flying overhead.

Linking the Flying Fortress Screen to the Flying Fortress Button

Now that you have created the Flying Fortress screen, you can link it to the Flying Fortress button on the History of Flight home screen. The way to do this is to draw a rectangle over the Flying Fortress button, turn the rectangle transparent, and then link the rectangle to the Flying Fortress screen. Try to do this without looking at the instructions, but if you need help, follow these steps:

▷ In PowerPoint, select the home screen for editing. To do this, either use the scrollbar to move back to the home screen, or click the Slide Sorter icon and then double-click the home screen to go to it.

▷ Click the Rectangle tool on the Drawing toolbar.

▷ Click and hold down the mouse button on the upper left corner of the Flying Fortress button, then drag the mouse to the lower right corner and release the button.

▷ A solid rectangle now appears over the Flying Fortress button. If the rectangle is not where you want it, drag its handles to reposition it.

▷ To turn the rectangle transparent, right-click it, and when the menu pops out, choose Format AutoShape.

▷ When the Format AutoShape dialog appears, set the Fill Color to No Fill, and set the Line Color to No Line, as illustrated in Figure 28-2. Then click OK to close the dialog.

Figure 28-2   To turn the rectangle invisible, set its Fill Color to No Fill, and set the Line Color to No Line.

▷ To create the link, pull down the Insert menu and choose Hyperlink; the Hyperlink dialog appears as illustrated in Figure 28-3.

▷ In the left column of the Hyperlink dialog, click the option to link to a place in this document.

▷ As illustrated in Figure 28-4, click the slide to which you want to link. In this example, click slide 4, which is your Flying Fortress slide. Notice how the dialog previews the slide to make sure you selected the one you wanted.

▷ Click OK to close the dialog. The link has been created.

▷ Remember to save your application by pulling down the File menu and choosing Save, or click the Save icon.

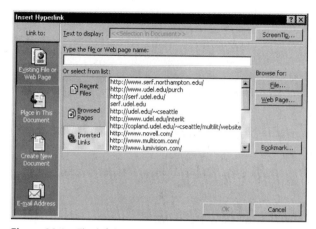

Figure 28-3   The left-hand column of the Hyperlink dialog has an option that lets you link to places in the current document.

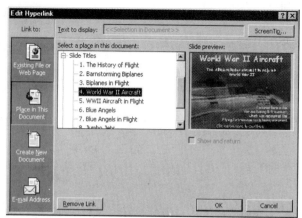

Figure 28-4   Linking to slide 4, which is the Flying Fortress slide in the *History of Flight* application. Notice how the dialog previews the slide to make sure you link to the one you want.

Triggering the Link

To trigger the link and find out if it works, click the Slide Show icon to run your application. Move your mouse over the Flying Fortress button. The cursor should change shape as you move over the button, indicating there is a link at that spot. Click that spot, and your Flying Fortress screen appears. The ambient sound of the Flying Fortress will begin to make it sound as if a Flying Fortress is flying overhead. Read on to learn how to show the user a movie that illustrates the history of aircraft development during World War II.

Creating the Movie Screen

Many aircraft participated in the Allied fight to win World War II. You can add a full-motion video clip to chronicle the history of the development of these airplanes. Follow these steps:

▶ In PowerPoint, select the Flying Fortress screen for editing. To do this, either use the scrollbar to move to the Flying Fortress screen, or click the Slide Sorter icon and then double-click the Flying Fortress screen to go to it.

▶ Click the New Slide button to create a new slide, or pull down the Insert menu and choose New Slide.

▶ When the New Slide dialog appears and asks you to choose an AutoLayout, select the Blank layout and click OK. *Note:* If the New Slide dialog does not appear, pull down the Format menu and choose Slide Layout.

▶ Pull down the Insert menu, choose Picture, then choose From File; the Insert Picture dialog appears.

▶ Use the Insert Picture dialog to look in the *Aircraft* folder on the *Multilit* CD, and insert the picture called Fortress.

▶ Drag the picture's handles to make the picture fill the slide.

▶ If your version of PowerPoint has the tri-pane view, click in the outline pane to position your cursor there; otherwise, click the Outline icon to bring up the Outline view.

▷ In the outline, alongside the icon that represents the biplane movie slide, type the title of this slide: **WWII Aircraft in Flight**

▷ Switch back to Normal view or Slide view. Notice how the picture covers up the title. Press ⎄Tab⎄ until the title is selected, then pull down the Draw menu, choose Order, and bring the title to the front. Adjust the title's font, color, size, and shadow to suit your taste.

▷ Pull down the Insert menu and choose Movies and Sounds, then choose Movie from File. The Insert Movie dialog appears.

▷ Use the Insert Movie dialog to look in the *Aircraft* folder on the *Multilit* CD, and insert the movie called *Fortress*.

▷ If PowerPoint asks whether you want the movie to start playing automatically, say Yes.

▷ Use your computer's arrow keys to place the movie at the spot where you want it to appear on-screen.

▷ Save your application by clicking the Save icon, or pull down the File menu and choose Save.

Rehearsing the Movie Screen

To rehearse the movie and make sure it plays OK, click the Slide Show icon to get your application running. When the movie screen appears, the movie should start playing. If it does not autostart, click the movie to play it. Each time you click the movie, its play state will change from stopped to playing, or vice versa.

Creating a Home Button

The last step in producing the Flying Fortress slides is to create some action buttons that will provide the user with navigation options. To create a Home button that will return the user to the History of Flight home screen, follow these steps:

▷ In PowerPoint, select the Flying Fortress movie screen for editing. To do this, either use the scrollbar to move to the Flying Fortress movie screen, or click the Slide Sorter icon and then double-click the Flying Fortress movie screen to go to it.

▷ Pull down the AutoShapes menu, select Action Buttons, and click the Home button.

▷ Click the spot on the screen (probably near the bottom) where you want the Home button to appear. The Action Settings dialog appears, as illustrated in Figure 28-5.

▷ Notice how the Action on Click is automatically set to hyperlink to the first slide. Leave that setting alone, because that is what you want.

▷ Click OK to close the dialog. The Home button has been created.

▷ Since the background picture on the screen is primarily brown, you may want to right-click the Home button, choose Format AutoShape, and change the fill color to a shade of brown. If the button appears too large on screen, you can click and drag its handles to adjust the size of the button, as you like.

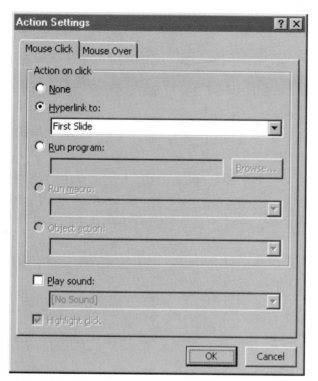

Figure 28-5 When you create a Home button, the Action Settings dialog is preset to hyperlink to the first slide.

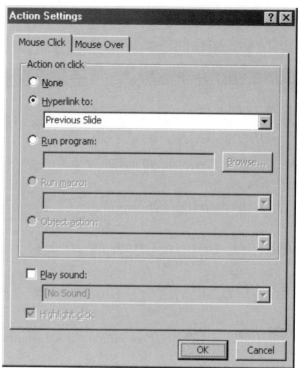

Figure 28-6 When you create a Back button, the Action Settings dialog is preset to hyperlink to the previous slide.

Creating a Back Button

To create a Back button that will take the user back to the previous screen, follow these steps:

▷ In PowerPoint, select the Flying Fortress movie screen for editing.

▷ Pull down the AutoShapes menu, select Action Buttons, and click the Back button.

▷ Click the spot on the screen (probably near the bottom) where you want the Back button to appear. The Action Settings dialog appears, as illustrated in Figure 28-6.

▷ Notice how the Action on Click is automatically set to hyperlink to the previous slide. Leave that setting alone, because that is what you want.

▷ Click OK to close the Action Settings dialog. The Back button has been created. As you did with the Home button, adjust the Back button's color and size as you wish.

Rehearsing the Action Buttons

To rehearse the application and make sure the action buttons work well, pull down the Slide Show menu and choose View Show. When the History of Flight menu appears, click the Flying Fortress button. When the Flying Fortress screen appears, click through to the screen that plays the Flying Fortress movie. Now comes the test: Click the Home button, and the home screen should reappear.

Click the Flying Fortress button again, and click through to the screen that plays the Flying Fortress movie. Then click the Back button. This should take you back to the Flying Fortress screen.

29

The Blue Angels

After completing this chapter, you will be able to:

▓ **Create a multimedia screen that presents the famous U.S. Navy Flight Demonstration Squadron known as the Blue Angels**

▓ **Provide realism with the ambient sound of the Blue Angels in flight**

▓ **Show a spectacular video of the Blue Angels in flight**

▓ **Link the Blue Angels button on the History of Flight menu to the Blue Angels screen**

▓ **Use action buttons to enable the user to navigate**

▓ **Create this multimedia sequence with very little hand-holding**

● This chapter provides less hand-holding than the previous ones. If you have trouble, go back to the previous chapter for more detailed instructions. The only difference is in the filenames of the multimedia objects.

The third button on the History of Flight menu depicts the Blue Angels, McDonnell Douglas F/A-18 Hornets, acrobatic jet aircraft that made their debut in 1978. This chapter shows you how to create multimedia screens describing these fascinating jets and link them to the Blue Angels button on the History of Flight home screen.

Creating the Blue Angels Screen

If you do not already have PowerPoint running the *Flight* application, start PowerPoint and open the *Flight* application you began creating in the previous chapter. Follow these steps to create the Blue Angels screen:

▷ Select the Flying Fortress Movie screen for editing. To do this, either use the scrollbar to move down to the Flying Fortress Movie screen, or click the Slide Sorter icon and then double-click the Flying Fortress Movie screen to go to it.

▷ Create a new slide either by clicking the New Slide button, or pull down the Insert menu and choose New Slide.

▷ When the New Slide dialog appears and asks you to choose an AutoLayout, select the Blank layout and click OK. *Note:* If the New Slide dialog does not appear, pull down the Format menu and choose Slide Layout.

▷ Pull down the Insert menu, choose Picture, then choose From File; the Insert Picture dialog appears.

> Use the Insert Picture dialog to look in the *Aircraft* folder on the *Multilit* CD, and insert the picture called Angels.

> Drag the picture's handles to make the picture fill the slide.

> Pull down the File menu and choose Save. Remember to save your application periodically as you work on it.

Titling the Blue Angels Screen

The title of the Blue Angels screen is "Blue Angels." To title the Blue Angels screen, follow these steps:

> If your version of PowerPoint has the tri-pane view, click in the outline pane to position your cursor there; otherwise, click the Outline icon to bring up the Outline view.

> In the outline, alongside the icon that represents the Blue Angels slide, type:
> **Blue Angels**

Entering the Blue Angels Text

Printed below are the text objects for you to type onto the Blue Angels screen. For each text object, create a separate text box by pulling down the Insert menu and choosing Text Box, or by clicking the Text Box icon on the Drawing toolbar. Then click the spot on the slide where you want the text to appear, and type the text. The text objects to type are listed as follows:

Pictured here is the U.S. Navy Blue Angels Flight Demonstration Squadron.

The Blue Angels are McDonnell Douglas F/A-18 Hornets.

Click anywhere to continue.

Adjusting the Text

Following the text-editing procedures you learned in Chapter 20, arrange the text and make it look good on the screen. Use the Font Size tools to make the text large or small. Drag the text boxes to move each line where you want it on the screen. Use the Font Color tool to colorize the text. Use the Shadow tool to create a drop shadow. Use the Font tool to adjust the fonts. Figure 29-1 shows one way of arranging the Blue Angels screen.

Creating the Ambient Sound

There is a waveform audio file called *Angels* in the *Ambient* folder of the *Multilit* CD. Use the Insert Sound tool to make *Angels* be the ambient sound for your Blue Angels screen. By now, you should be able to do this on your own, but if you need help, follow these steps:

> Pull down the Insert menu, choose Movies and Sounds, then choose Sound from File; the Insert Sound dialog appears.

> Use the Insert Sound dialog to look in the *Ambient* folder on the *Multilit* CD, and insert the sound called *Angels*.

Figure 29-1   The completed Blue Angels screen.

Photo by David K. Brunn. Copyright © 1994 Aris Multimedia Entertainment, Inc.

▷   If PowerPoint asks whether you want the sound to play automatically, answer Yes.

▷   Pull down the Edit menu and choose Sound Object, or right-click the Sound icon and choose Edit Sound Object; when the Sound Options dialog appears, check the box to make the sound loop until stopped.

▷   Drag the Sound icon to an unobtrusive place on the slide, such as the lower right corner.

▷   Pull down the File menu and choose Save.

▷   Click the Slide Show icon to rehearse the application. The ambient sound should start playing. If it does not, click the Audio icon. Notice how the ambient sound creates the illusion that the Blue Angels are flying overhead.

Linking the Blue Angels Screen to the Blue Angels Button

Now that you have created the Blue Angels screen, you can link it to the Blue Angels button on the History of Flight home screen. The way to do this is to draw a rectangle over the Blue Angels button, turn the rectangle transparent, and then link the rectangle to the Blue Angels screen. Try to do this without looking at the instructions, but if you need help, follow these steps:

▷   In PowerPoint, select the home screen for editing. To do this, either use the scrollbar to move back to the home screen, or click the Slide Sorter icon and then double-click the home screen to go to it.

▷   Click the Rectangle tool on the Drawing toolbar.

▷   Click and hold down the mouse button on the upper left corner of the Blue Angels button, then drag the mouse to the lower right corner and release the button.

▷   A solid rectangle now appears over the Blue Angels button. If the rectangle is not where you want it, drag its handles to reposition it.

> To turn the rectangle transparent, right-click it, and when the menu pops out, choose Format AutoShape.

> When the Format AutoShape dialog appears, set the Fill Color to No Fill, and set the Line Color to No Line. Then click OK to close the dialog.

> To create the link, pull down the Insert menu and choose Hyperlink; the Hyperlink dialog appears.

> In the left column of the Hyperlink dialog, click the option to link to a place in this document.

> In the Select a Place window, click the slide to which you want to link. In this example, click slide 6, which is your Blue Angels slide. Notice how the dialog previews the slide to make sure you've selected the one you wanted.

> Click OK to close the dialog. The link has been created.

> Remember to save your application by pulling down the File menu and choosing Save, or click the Save icon.

Triggering the Link

To trigger the link and find out if it works, pull down the Slide Show menu and choose View Show. Click the Blue Angels button, and your Blue Angels screen should appear. The ambient sound will make it sound like the Blue Angels are flying overhead.

Creating the Movie Screen

The *Multilit* CD contains a spectacular movie of the Blue Angels in flight. The video clip is called *Angels*, and it resides in the *Aircraft* folder on the *Multilit* CD. Try to link the video clip without looking at the instructions, but if you need help, follow these steps:

> In PowerPoint, select the Blue Angels screen for editing. To do this, either use the scrollbar to move to the Blue Angels screen, or click the Slide Sorter icon and then double-click the Blue Angels screen to go to it.

> Click the New Slide button to create a new slide, or pull down the Insert menu and choose New Slide.

> When the New Slide dialog appears and asks you to choose an AutoLayout, select the Blank layout and click OK. *Note:* If the New Slide dialog does not appear, pull down the Format menu and choose Slide Layout.

> Pull down the Insert menu, choose Picture, then choose From File; the Insert Picture dialog appears.

> Use the Insert Picture dialog to look in the *Aircraft* folder on the *Multilit* CD, and insert the picture called Angels.

> Drag the picture's handles to make the picture fill the slide.

> If your version of PowerPoint has the tri-pane view, click in the outline pane to position your cursor there; otherwise, click the Outline icon to bring up the Outline View.

> In the outline, alongside the icon that represents the biplane movie slide, type the title of this slide: **Blue Angels in Flight**

> Switch back to Normal view or Slide view. Notice how the picture covers up the title. Press Tab⇆ until the title is selected, then pull down the Draw menu, choose Order, and bring the title to the front. Adjust the title's font, color, size, and shadow to suit your taste.

> Pull down the Insert menu and choose Movies and Sounds, then choose Movie from File. The Insert Movie dialog appears.

> Use the Insert Movie dialog to look in the *Aircraft* folder on the *Multilit* CD, and insert the movie called *Angels*.

> If PowerPoint asks whether you want the movie to start playing automatically, say Yes.

> Use your computer's arrow keys to place the movie at the spot where you want it to appear on-screen.

> Save your application by clicking the Save icon, or pull down the File menu and choose Save.

Rehearsing the Movie Screen

To rehearse the movie and make sure it plays OK, click the Slide Show icon to get your application running. When the movie screen appears, the movie should start playing. If it does not autostart, click the movie to play it. Each time you click the movie, its play state will change from stopped to playing or vice versa.

Creating a Home Button

The last step in producing the Blue Angels slides is to create some action buttons that will provide the user with navigation options. To create a Home button that will return the user to the History of Flight home screen, follow these steps:

> In PowerPoint, select the Blue Angels movie screen for editing. To do this, either use the scrollbar to move to the Blue Angels movie screen, or click the Slide Sorter icon and then double-click the Blue Angels movie screen to go to it.

> Pull down the AutoShapes menu, select Action Buttons, and click the Home button.

> Click the spot on the screen (probably near the bottom) where you want the Home button to appear, and the Action Settings dialog will appear.

> Notice how the Action on Click is automatically set to hyperlink to the first slide. Leave that setting alone, because that is what you want.

> Click OK to close the dialog. The Home button has been created.

> Since the background picture on the screen is primarily blue, you may want to right-click the Home button, choose Format AutoShape, and change the fill color to a shade of blue. If the button appears too large on-screen, you can click and drag its handles to adjust the size of the button, as you like.

Creating a Back Button

To create a Back button that will take the user back to the previous screen, follow these steps:

▶ In PowerPoint, select the Blue Angels movie screen for editing.

▶ Pull down the AutoShapes menu, select Action Buttons, and click the Back button.

▶ Click the spot on the screen (probably near the bottom) where you'd like the back button to appear, and the Action Settings dialog will appear.

▶ Notice how the Action on Click is automatically set to hyperlink to the previous slide. Leave that setting alone, because that is what you want.

▶ Click OK to close the Action Settings dialog. The Back button has been created. As you did with the Home button, adjust the Back button's color and size as you wish.

Rehearsing the Action Buttons

To rehearse the application and make sure the action buttons work well, pull down the Slide Show menu and choose View Show. When the History of Flight menu appears, click the Blue Angels button. When the Blue Angels screen appears, click through to the screen that plays the Blue Angels movie. Now comes the test: Click the Home button, and the home screen should reappear.

Click the Blue Angels button again, and click through to the screen that plays the Blue Angels movie. Then click the Back button. This should take you back to the Blue Angels screen.

Jumbo Jets

After completing this chapter, you will be able to:

▨ Create a multimedia screen that introduces the age of passenger air travel via jumbo jet

▨ Provide realism with the ambient sound of a jumbo jet in flight

▨ Show a dramatic video of a Boeing 747 takeoff

▨ Link the Jumbo Jet button on the History of Flight menu to the Jumbo Jet screen

▨ Create the text and graphics on the Jumbo Jet screen without any hand-holding

● This chapter is the supreme test of your ability to create multimedia linkages, because it has no hand-holding! If you have trouble, refer to the previous chapters. The process is exactly the same; only the filenames and the historical information differ.

Creating the Jumbo Jet Screen

▷ Use PowerPoint to go to the Blue Angles movie screen of your *History of Flight* application.

▷ Choose the option to create a new screen, insert the picture called Jumbojet in the *Aircraft* folder on the *Multilit* CD, and make the picture fill the screen.

Titling the Jumbo Jet Screen

The title of the Jumbo Jet screen is "Jumbo Jets." In the application's outline, make the Jumbo Jet screen's title: **Jumbo Jets**

Entering the Jumbo Jet Text

Put the following text objects onto the Jumbo Jet screen in the order listed here.

The Boeing 747 passenger jet pictured here is the largest aircraft in commercial service.

Nicknamed the jumbo jet, it was the first wide-body passenger jet. It started flying in 1970.

Click anywhere to continue.

Adjusting the Text

Arrange the text and make it look good on the screen. Use the Font tools to size, color, and shadow the text. Figure 30-1 shows one way of arranging the Jumbo Jet screen.

Figure 30-1 The completed Jumbo Jet screen.
Photo by David K. Brunn. Copyright © 1994 Aris Multimedia Entertainment, Inc.

Creating the Ambient Sound

There is a waveform audio file called *Jumbojet* in the *Ambient* folder of the *Multilit* CD. Use the Insert Sound from File tool to make *Jumbojet* the ambient sound for your Jumbo Jet screen.

Linking the Jumbo Jet Screen to the Jumbo Jet Button

Now that you have created the Jumbo Jet screen, you can link it to the Jumbo Jet button on the History of Flight home screen. Draw a rectangle over the Jumbo Jet button, turn the rectangle transparent, and then link the rectangle to the Jumbo Jet screen.

To trigger the link and find out if it works, pull down the Slide Show menu and choose View Show. Click the Jumbo Jet button, and your Jumbo Jet screen should appear. The ambient sound will make it sound like the jumbo jet is flying overhead.

Creating the Movie Screen

The *Multilit* CD contains a spectacular movie of the jumbo jet in flight. The video clip is called *Jumbojet,* and it resides in the *Aircraft* folder on the *Multilit* CD. After the Jumbo Jet screen you just created, insert another screen that displays the same picture of the jumbo jet, on top of which the movie plays. Make the title of the screen: **Jumbo Jets in Flight**

Rehearsing the Movie Screen

To rehearse the movie and make sure it plays well, click the Slide Show icon to get your application running. When the movie screen appears, the movie should start playing. If it does not autostart, click the movie to play it.

Creating a Home Button

Onto the Jumbo Jet movie screen, insert an Action button that the user can click to return to the History of Flight home screen.

Creating a Back Button

Onto the Jumbo Jet movie screen, insert an Action button that the user can click to go back to the previous slide, which tells the history of the jumbo jet.

Rehearsing the Action Buttons

To rehearse the application and make sure the action buttons work properly, pull down the Slide Show menu and choose View Show. When the History of Flight menu appears, click the Jumbo Jet button. When the Jumbo Jet screen appears, click through to the screen that plays the Jumbo Jet movie. Click the Home button, and the home screen should reappear.

Click the Jumbo Jet button again, and click through to the screen that plays the Jumbo Jet movie. Then click the Back button. This should take you back to the Jumbo Jet screen.

Self-Assessment

If you were able to complete this chapter successfully without looking at any of the instructions provided in previous chapters, you really should congratulate yourself. You are well on your way to developing the skills needed to create multimedia applications.

31

Completing and Presenting the Application

After completing this chapter, you will be able to:

▦ Hang an Exit sign on the History of Flight home screen

▦ Link the Exit sign to the End Show command

▦ Create action buttons that let the user move back and forth to all the screens of the application

▦ Save the *History of Flight* application as a show so you can launch it from the Windows desktop without having the PowerPoint window open

▦ Use the rehearsal toolbar to time how long your presentation lasts and record the timings if you want the presentation to be self-running

▦ Set up the presentation so mouse clicks are ignored unless the user clicks on an action button or a hyperlink in your application

▦ Prepare speaker's notes and audience handouts

● When you complete an application, such as the *History of Flight* tutorial you created in Chapters 26 to 30, there are a few finishing touches you will want to make. This chapter steps you through the process of providing the user with a way to exit gracefully and navigate more completely. Then you learn how to save the application as a show, rehearse it thoroughly, and prepare speaker's notes and audience handouts.

Providing a Graceful Way to Exit

Although users can always pull down the Files menu and choose Quit to leave your application, it is better to provide a more graceful way to exit. This chapter shows how to hang a customized Exit sign on the History of Flight home screen. The customized Exit sign features a parachutist leaving the screen.

Creating the Exit Sign

The exit sign is located in the *Icons* folder on the *Multilit* CD. The name of the Exit sign is *exit2fly*. Use the Insert Picture from File tool to hang the Exit sign on your History of Flight home screen. Then drag the Exit sign to position it wherever you want it on the screen. Figure 31-1 shows one way of positioning the Exit sign. If you need help getting the Exit sign onto the History of Flight home screen, follow these steps:

▷　Use PowerPoint to bring up the History of Flight home screen in Normal view.

▷　Pull down the Insert menu, choose Picture and click From File.

▷　When the Insert Picture dialog appears, use it to look in the *Icons* folder on the *Multilit* CD, select the icon named *exit2fly*, and click the Insert button to insert the icon on your screen.

▷　Drag the icon to position it on-screen as you like. The lower right corner is probably the best place to put it.

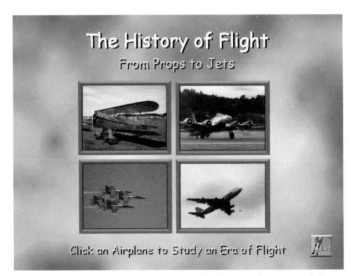

Figure 31-1　Positioning the Exit sign in the lower right corner of the History of Flight home screen.

Photo by David K. Brunn. Copyright © 1994 Aris Multimedia Entertainment, Inc.

Linking the Exit Sign to the End Show Command

▷　Right-click the Exit sign, and when the menu pops up, choose Action Settings; the Action Settings dialog appears.

▷　In the Action Settings dialog, check the Hyperlink option and set it to End show. Then click OK to close the dialog.

▷　Save your application by clicking PowerPoint's Save icon.

Testing the Exit Sign

To test the Exit sign and make sure it works, click the SlideShow button to run the show. When the home screen appears, move your mouse over the Exit icon. Notice how the cursor changes shape to indicate that the icon is hyperactive. Click the Exit icon, and the show should end. Now the user has a graceful way to exit your *History of Flight* application. *Note:* If the show did not end, go back and follow more carefully the steps for creating the Exit sign.

Customizing the Navigation

In the *History of Flight* tutorial, you put navigation buttons on the movie screens that enabled the user either to go back to the previous slide or go all the way back to the home screen. Some users may also want a way to step forward or backward through the entire presentation, without having to return to the home screen to select another airplane. You can provide this capability by placing on each screen of the application action buttons that let the user move forward to the next slide or back to the previous slide. You could also put a Home button on every screen if you want the user to have the option of returning to the home screen. If you put all of these buttons on-screen, the logical order in which to arrange them is:

After you customize the navigation in this manner, you should go back through your presentation screens and remove the instruction to "Click anywhere to continue" that you placed on the airplane screens earlier in this tutorial.

Presenting a Multimedia Application

PowerPoint enables you to present a multimedia application in a variety of ways, depending on your topic, the purpose of your presentation, and the audience. You can save the presentation as a show and launch it from the desktop. You can use the Slide navigator to go to any slide at any time. Using the rehearsal toolbar, you can find out how long your presentation will last, and make adjustments if it takes too long. You can set up the application to run in kiosk mode, and you can make it self-running. Read on to learn how to do these things.

Saving the Presentation as a Show

PowerPoint has an option to save the presentation as a show. When you save a presentation as a show, it will automatically start as a slide show when you open it from your desktop. If you start the show from within PowerPoint, the presentation opens and can be edited us usual. To save the presentation as a show, follow these steps:

▷ Open the presentation you want to save as a slide show. In this example, open the *History of Flight* application you created in this tutorial.

▷ Pull down the File menu and choose Save As; the Save As dialog appears.

▷ In the Save As Type menu, choose PowerPoint Show.

▷ Click the Save button to close the dialog and save the show.

The filename extension for a file saved as a slide show is *.pps*. Save a presentation as a show if you want to be able to launch it from your desktop without having the PowerPoint editing window open. At any time you can reverse this process. Should you decide you want an application to revert to the standard PowerPoint presentation format, simply open the *.pps* file with PowerPoint, pull down the File menu and choose Save As, and use the Save As Type menu to save it as a presentation. The filename extension for a file saved as a presentation is *.ppt*.

Starting a Multimedia Application from Your Desktop

It's easy to start a PowerPoint application from your desktop. Follow the steps in Table 31-1.

Table 31-1   Starting a PowerPoint Application from the Desktop

Windows	Macintosh
To start a PowerPoint application from the Windows desktop, follow these steps: ▶ In My Computer or Windows Explorer, locate the file you want to open as a slide show. ▶ Right-click the filename, and then click Show. To make it even quicker to start the show, you can place a shortcut to it on your desktop. Follow these steps: ▶ In My Computer or Windows Explorer, locate the file you want to put on your desktop. ▶ Use the right mouse button to drag the file to your desktop. When you release the mouse button, click the option to Create Shortcut Here. ▶ Any time you want to start the slow, double-click the shortcut.	To start a PowerPoint application from the Macintosh desktop, follow these steps: ▶ In the Finder, locate the show you want to open. ▶ Double-click the filename to open it. To make it even quicker to start the show, you can place an alias to it on your desktop. Follow these steps: ▶ In the Finder, locate the file you want to put on your desktop. ▶ Hold down the Control key while you click the file's name. ▶ Choose the option to Make Alias. ▶ Drag the alias to the desktop. ▶ Anytime you want to start the show, double-click the alias.

Going to a Specific Slide

While a PowerPoint show is running, you can go to any slide at any time. If you know the number of the slide you want to go to, just type the number and press ⏎Enter. If you do not know the number of the slide, you can use the slide navigator to find the slide.

Using the Slide Navigator

While running a PowerPoint presentation, right-click to make the navigation menu pop out, select Go, then click By Slide. In newer versions of PowerPoint, the navigation menu contains a Slide Navigator: Select it, then double-click the title of the slide you want.

Using the Rehearsal Toolbar

Speakers often wonder how long their presentation will last. It's rude to show up at a conference to speak in a 20-minute time slot and have your speech last an hour. PowerPoint has a rehearsal toolbar that lets you time the presentation so you will know how long it lasts. If it is too long, you can make adjustments prior to your talk. To use the rehearsal toolbar, follow these steps:

▶ Pull down the Slide Show menu and click Rehearse Timings to start the show in rehearsal mode. The Rehearsal toolbar appears as illustrated in Figure 31-2.

▶ Click the advance button when you are ready to go to the next slide.

> When you reach the end of the slide show, PowerPoint will ask whether you want to accept the timings. If you click Yes, PowerPoint will set the slides to advance automatically, just as you rehearsed them. You will probably want to click No, unless you really want the slides to advance automatically.

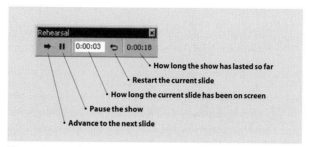

Figure 31-2   The Rehearsal toolbar lets you time how long your presentation lasts.

Setting Up a Self-Running Application

If you plan to run your presentation as a kiosk, where you let users come up and click the action buttons and hyperlinks, you can set it up to launch as a self-running application. To set up an application to be self-running, follow these steps:

> Use PowerPoint to open the presentation. In this example, open your *History of Flight* application.

> Pull down the Slide Show menu and choose Set Up Show; the Set Up Show dialog appears.

> Click the option to set up the application to be browsed at a kiosk, as illustrated in Figure 31-3.

> Click OK to close the dialog.

> Click the Save button to save your application.

One of the benefits of setting up a presentation as a self-running application is that mouse clicks are ignored unless they are on action buttons or objects you hyperlinked. The user can navigate only by clicking the navigation options and links you provided.

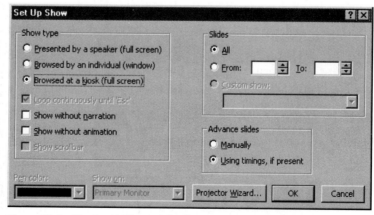

Figure 31-3   The Set Up Show dialog lets you run a presentation in kiosk mode.

Running a Show with Automatic Timings

If your kiosk application will run in an environment in which users do not have control, you will want to take advantage of PowerPoint's ability to advance from one screen to the next automatically. To set slide timings automatically while rehearsing, follow these steps:

▷   Pull down the Slide Show menu and click Rehearse Timings to start the show in rehearsal mode. The Rehearsal dialog was illustrated in Figure 31-2.

▷   Click the advance button when you are ready to progress to the next slide.

▷   When you reach the end of the slide show, PowerPoint will ask whether you want to accept the timings. Click Yes to accept the timings; PowerPoint sets the slides to advance automatically, just as you rehearsed them.

Preparing Speaker's Notes and Audience Handouts

PowerPoint enables you to type notes while working on a presentation. Each slide has a Notes pane into which you can type notes associated with that screen. You can create notes for yourself to help you remember key points during a presentation, or you can create notes intended for handouts you will print out for your audience. To type a note, follow these steps:

▷   Use the outline pane to move to the slide you want to annotate.

▷   Click the icon to put PowerPoint into the normal tri-pane view. If your version of PowerPoint does not have the tri-pane view, click the icon to put PowerPoint into Notes Page view.

▷   Click the notes pane and type your notes for the current slide. To see more of the notes pane, move the mouse to the top border of the notes pane until the pointer becomes a double-headed arrow, then drag the border until the pane is the size you want.

Notes have a special significance if you plan to save your presentation as a Web page. As you will see in Chapter 41 when you learn how to create Web sites with PowerPoint, the notes can be made to appear on the screen of the Web page with each slide. Thus, notes can give your audience the background and details that a speaker provides during a live presentation.

Printing Speaker's Notes and Audience Handouts

To print speaker's notes and audience handouts, pull down the File menu and choose Print. The Print dialog will appear. As illustrated in Figure 31-4, you can pull down the Print What menu to print slides, handouts, notes pages, or the outline. When you print handouts, the Slides per Page becomes active, enabling you to print handouts with two, three, four, six, or nine slides per page.

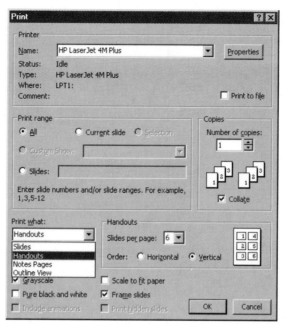

Figure 31-4   Use the Print What menu in the Print dialog to print slides, handouts, notes, or outlines.

Laying Out Speaker's Notes

The notes and handout pages have masters on which you can add items you want to appear on each page. For example, you can create headers and footers that contain the date, time, and page numbers. To add, change, or delete items on the notes master, follow these steps:

▶ Pull down the View menu, choose Master, then click Notes Master. The Notes Master is illustrated in Figure 31-5.

▶ Resize or move the slide image or notes box to suit your needs.

▶ Click the fields in the header, date, footer, and number areas to type the information you want there.

Items you add to the Notes Master will appear when you print the slides with notes. These items do not appear, however, in the notes pane or on the Web pages you create when you save your presentation as a Web page.

Laying Out Audience Handouts

To customize the layout of audience handouts, modify the Handout Master by following these steps:

▶ Pull down the View menu, choose Master, then click Handout Master. The Handout Master is illustrated in Figure 31-6.

▶ To preview the layout you want, click the buttons on the Handout Master toolbar.

▶ Click the fields in the header, date, footer, and number areas to type the information you want there.

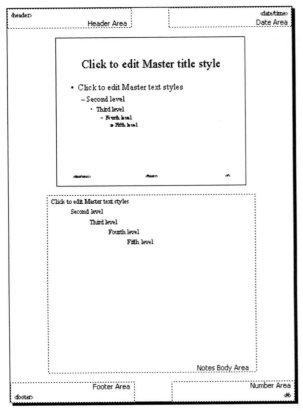

Figure 31-5   The Notes Master lets you customize the layout of printed speaker's notes.

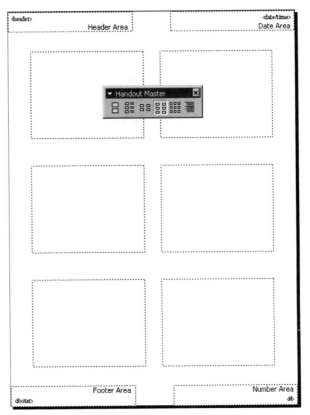

Figure 31-6   The Handout Master lets you customize the layout of audience handouts.

Practice Makes Perfect

The saying "practice makes perfect" never was more appropriate than when you are getting ready to present a multimedia show. Rehearse everything thoroughly. Ask a friend or business associate to act as an audience and give you suggestions for making your presentation better. Print handouts well in advance so you will have time to solve any formatting problems that may occur. The time you spend rehearsing will pay off when your presentation goes well, and you reach your goal.

32 Hypermedia Design Principles and Techniques

After completing this chapter, you will be able to:

▦ Know when to use a flowchart, a storyboard, and a script

▦ Recognize the five basic multimedia design paradigms

▦ Understand how the linear list design lets the user move back and forth in a sequence of multimedia objects

▦ Understand how the menu design provides users with a choice of items, and how the hierarchical design provides levels of choices by linking menus to menus

▦ Realize how the multiple linking in a network design provides the richest form of interactivity

▦ Visualize how hybrid designs can incorporate lists, menus, hierarchies, and networks

▦ Define the content of a multimedia application and adopt an appropriate navigational metaphor

● Now that you have completed the *History of Flight* tutorial, it is time for you to learn some techniques that will prepare you for creating more advanced applications in the future. It is not unusual for a multimedia application to contain hundreds or even thousands of multimedia screens. Your challenge is to present this material in such a way that the user will not get lost or confused. From the get-go, you must have a clear notion of how the material will be organized and how the user will navigate from screen to screen.

This chapter teaches hypermedia design techniques that will help you plan the development of a multimedia application. You will learn to visualize the flow of your application and imagine yourself running through it as a user. You will save time and money by learning to correct problems in the design before costly on-screen development begins.

Design Paradigms

There are five ways to design the flow of a multimedia application: the linear list, the menu, the hierarchy, the network, and the hybrid.

Linear List

The simplest design is the **linear list** you see in Figure 32-1. As the user clicks the mouse, the application presents the information, one item after the other. Each object in the list can be a text, a graphic, an audio clip, a video, or a compound object consisting of more than one medium playing at once, such as a text overlaid on a graphic accompanied by a sound track. The user can move back and forth through the list, moving forward to new materials or backward to review.

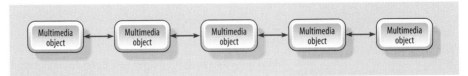

Figure 32-1   The linear list design lets the user move forward to see new materials or backward to review.

Menu

The second way to design an interaction is to create a **menu** such as the one shown in Figure 32-2. The items in the menu can appear as lines of hypertext, graphics in hyperpictures, or a combination of textual and graphical triggers. When the user chooses an item on the menu, the item linked to it appears and stays on the screen until the user clicks the mouse. Then the application returns to the menu, from which the user makes another choice. The home screen in the *History of Flight* application you created in Chapters 26 to 31 used a menu design.

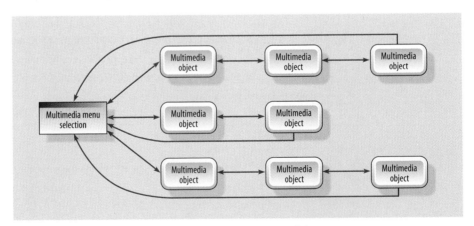

Figure 32-2   The menu design presents the user with a set of choices.

Hierarchy

The third kind of design is the **hierarchy** shown in Figure 32-3. Each object provides the user with a menu of choices that trigger more menus with more choices. There is no limit to the size or number of menus and submenus you can have in such a hierarchy.

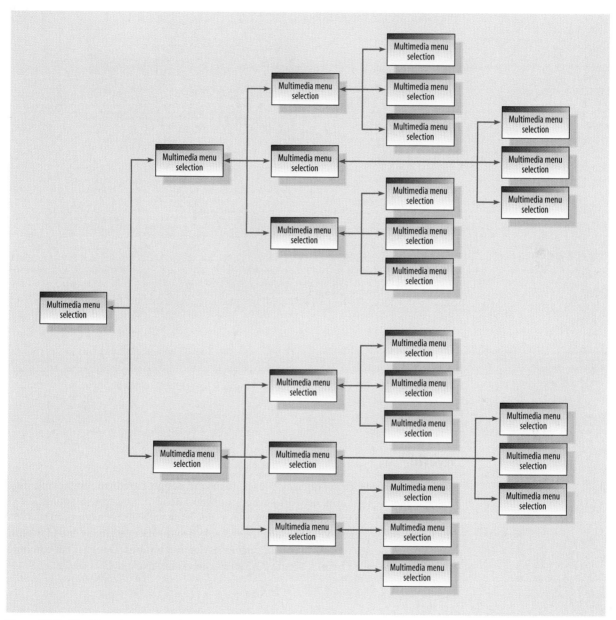

Figure 32-3 The hierarchy presents the user with menus of submenus.

Network

The most complex design is the **network** shown in Figure 32-4, in which objects can be multiply linked in any direction to any object in your application. Especially when a multimedia application is large, the network design enables the user to navigate to any screen with a minimum of mouse clicks. A tight design enables users to get where they want within three clicks.

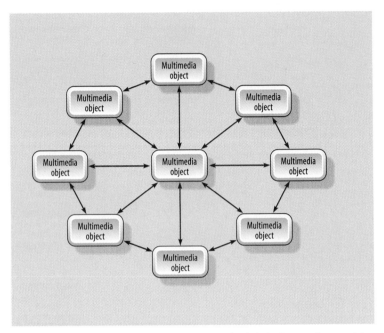

Figure 32-4   The network diagram contains multiply linked items that provide the richest kind of navigation.

Hybrid

Multimedia applications often use more than one design paradigm, employing lists, menus, hierarchies, and networks where appropriate. For example, a sophisticated network design can trigger a list of images in a slide bank with simple navigation that lets the user move back and forth through the slides. When the user gets to the end of the list, the network design returns to provide richer navigation options. Designs that combine paradigms are called **hybrid**. Figure 32-5 shows an example of a hybrid design.

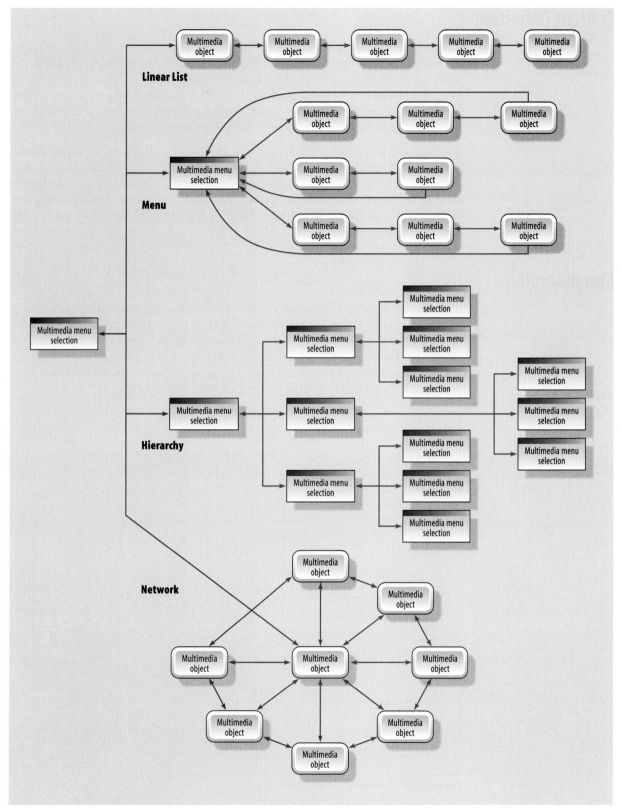

Figure 32-5 Hybrid designs employ linear lists, menus, hierarchies, and networks where appropriate.

Content Definition

To develop a good application, you must have a clear idea of what it is going to be about. **Content definition** is the act of specifying what a multimedia application is about. To define an application's content, make an outline of the topics you plan to cover. Think hard about the tasks involved and make sure you are not leaving out a topic that needs to be covered in order for the user to understand a subsequent topic. The process of hierarchically outlining an application's content is known as **task analysis.**

If you are not an expert in the content area, team with a subject matter expert (SME) who can work with you to make sure the task analysis is not missing an essential step. After you complete the task analysis, pretend you are a user: Imagine navigating through your application and ask whether anything the user needs to know is missing. A good, tight design will never skip a piece of information required to prevent the user from getting lost.

Storyboarding

A **storyboard** is a series of sketches that describe the content of a sequence of multimedia screens. Figure 32-6 shows a sample storyboarding form, which contains a frame for sketching the screen layout and a space below the frame for making comments. To create a storyboard, you fill out such a form for each screen in an application. Inside the frame, sketch the design elements that will appear on the screen. In the space below the frame, write comments describing the screen's function and purpose.

Module: _____ Strand:_____
Filename: _____
Screen No. _____ of _____
Images: _____
    _____
Audio: _____
    _____
Video: _____
    _____

N A V I G A T I O N
Next: _____
Back: _____
Menu: _____
Help: _____
Notes: _____

Figure 32-6   A multimedia storyboarding form.

Use the storyboard to reflect on the flow of your application. Spread out the sketches on the floor, tape them to a wall, or tack them onto a bulletin board. Arrange the sketches in their logical sequence—the order in which the user will view them. Seeing your screens all at once can help you visualize the form of your application and help you make design changes before proceeding to the more costly and time-consuming development stage.

Scripting

After you storyboard a project, you are ready to script it. A **script** is a complete specification of the text and narration in a multimedia application. Especially when you are using a team of people to develop an application, it is important to have a written script. Scriptwriting makes the team think through the project thoroughly. A written script helps team members communicate with each other, share comments on the design, and make adjustments prior to beginning the costly development stage. Having a script also helps you role-play the application from the viewpoint of a user and identify any missing elements.

Flowcharting

Multimedia applications often require users to make decisions. A **flowchart** is a logic diagram that illustrates the steps involved in an interactive decision-making process. Flowcharts are helpful when designing conditional branching and answer judging in a multimedia application. For example, you might present a test question and ask the user to select the correct answer. Depending on how the user responds, you will either give some positive reinforcement and proceed to the next question, or you will provide remedial feedback explaining why the answer was incorrect. Drawing a flowchart can help you visualize the answer-judging process.

Figure 32-7 shows the shapes designers use to create flowcharts. The most important shapes are the rectangular "process" box and the diamond-shaped "decision" symbol. The flowchart shown in Figure 32-8 uses these symbols to diagram the answer judging in a multiple-choice question. In the process box at the top of the diagram, the user is asked a question. If the user answers correctly, positive feedback will reinforce the correct answer. If the response is incorrect, the computer will provide a hint and repeat the question. If the user fails again, remedial action will be provided.

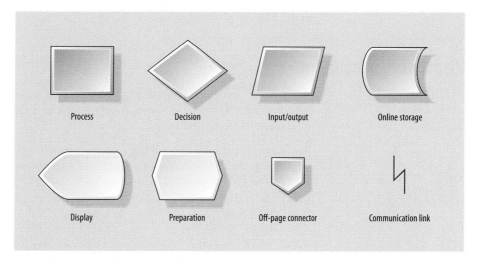

Figure 32-7   Flowcharting shapes and symbols.

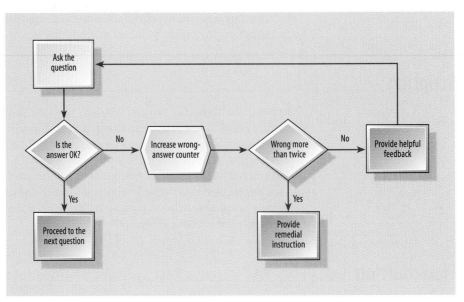

Figure 32-8　Flowchart of a multiple-choice question.

Navigational Metaphors and Icons

Designers often adopt a **metaphor** that makes it easy for the user to interact with an application. For example, the multimedia CD-ROM *Exploring America's National Parks* by Multicom uses a map metaphor to provide access to more than 230 parks. Charles F. Patten Middle School in Kennett Square, Pennsylvania, uses a Monopoly game board metaphor to provide links to different places at the school's Web site. The teacher/pathfinder Web site uses a metaphor of a village. The NewMedia Invision Festival uses a flipbook. The Macintosh version of Microsoft Internet Explorer uses a notebook metaphor. Follow the *Multilit* Web site links to metaphors to see some examples in action.

It's also common for multimedia developers to create navigational icons to fit the theme or style of an application. The *Multilit* CD contains a collection of icons that you can freely use in your applications. Table 32-1 shows you where to find active, inactive, and pressed versions of these icons.

Visualizing a Structure

Successful designers are so good at visualizing what an application will be like they can actually run it through in their minds before creating a single screen. With practice, you, too, can develop this ability.

For example, consider the billboard metaphor pictured in Figure 32-9. Think of the billboard as the home screen for a multimedia application about the Internet. Imagine how the words and pictures printed on the billboard could trigger the text, graphics, audio, and video in an application about the Internet. Pause for a few moments and think about how you could design such an application. Then turn the page and study Figure 32-10.

Table 32-1   Button Bitmaps on the *Multilit* CD*

Purpose	Shape	Directory	Active	Inactive	Pressed
Home	square	buttons\square\	home.bmp	ihome.bmp	phome.bmp
Done	square	buttons\square\	done.bmp	idone.bmp	pdone.bmp
Next	square	buttons\square\	next.bmp	inext.bmp	pnext.bmp
Back	square	buttons\square\	back.bmp	iback.bmp	pback.bmp
Quit	square	buttons\square\	quit.bmp	iquit.bmp	pquit.bmp
Page up	square	buttons\square\	pgup.bmp	ipgup.bmp	ppgup.bmp
Page down	square	buttons\square\	pgdown.bmp	ipgdown.bmp	ppgdown.bmp
Print	square	buttons\square\	print.bmp	iprint.bmp	pprint.bmp
Play	square	buttons\square\	play.bmp	iplay.bmp	pplay.bmp
Stop	square	buttons\square\	stop.bmp	istop.bmp	pstop.bmp
Home	round	buttons\round\	home.bmp	ihome.bmp	phome.bmp
Done	round	buttons\round\	done.bmp	idone.bmp	pdone.bmp
Next	round	buttons\round\	next.bmp	inext.bmp	pnext.bmp
Back	round	buttons\round\	back.bmp	iback.bmp	pback.bmp
Quit	round	buttons\round\	quit.bmp	iquit.bmp	pquit.bmp
Print	round	buttons\round\	print.bmp	iprint.bmp	pprint.bmp
Play	round	buttons\round\	play.bmp	iplay.bmp	pplay.bmp
Stop	round	buttons\round\	stop.bmp	istop.bmp	pstop.bmp
Calculator	square	buttons\square\	calc.bmp	icalc.bmp	pcalc.bmp
Notepad	square	buttons\square\	notepad.bmp	inotepad.bmp	pnotepad.bmp

*Even more buttons are found in the buttons folder.

Figure 32-9   A billboard metaphor for the *Information Superhighway* application.

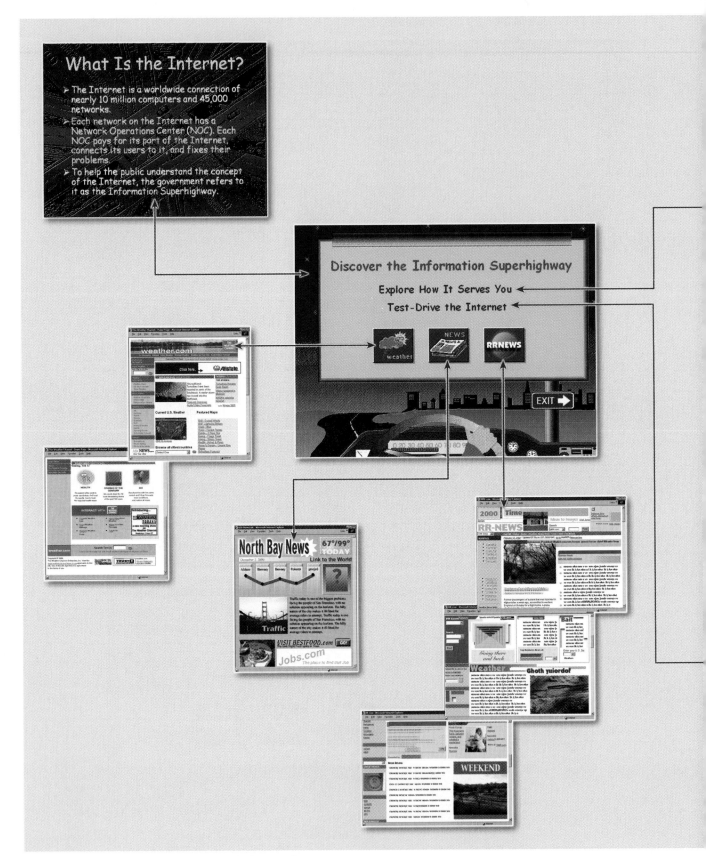

Figure 32-10   Design of the *Information Superhighway* application.

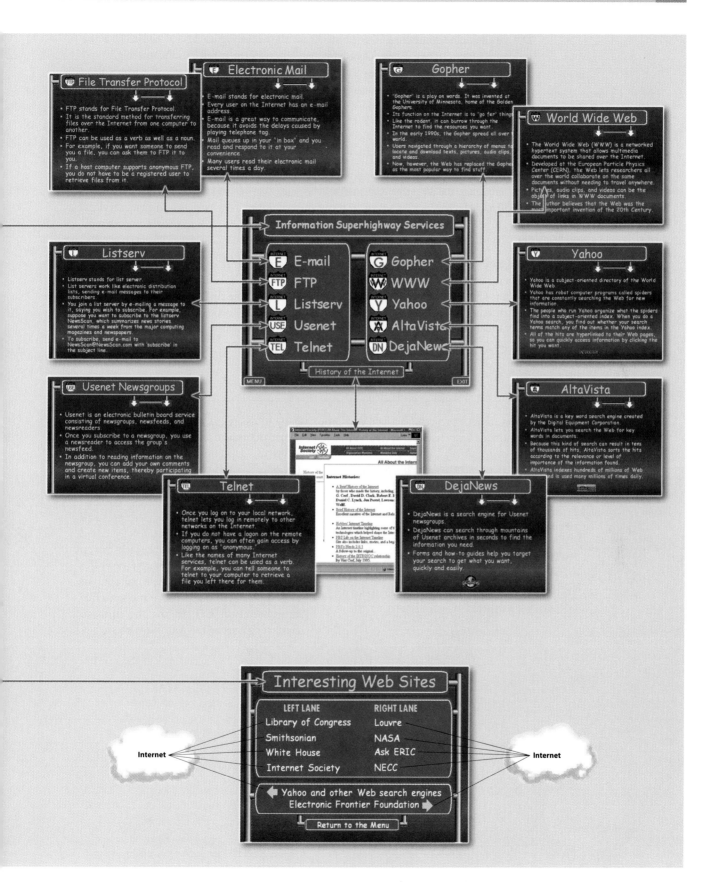

Did you imagine something like the structure shown in Figure 32-10? Notice how the billboard functions as a menu. The first item, "Discover the Information Superhighway," links to a screen that defines the Internet. Clicking the mouse returns the user to the billboard. This is the simplest part of the design. The second menu item, "Explore How It Serves You," launches a submenu listing the kinds of things you can do on the Internet; each submenu item triggers a screen explaining an Internet service. "Test-drive the Internet" lets the user select interesting places to visit on the Information Superhighway and, if a real Internet connection is present, takes the user to those places.

In addition to hypertext, the billboard also contains a few hyperpictures. The Weather icon launches the Weather Channel's Web site. The News icon is linked to the AJR Newslink, which provides access to thousands of online newspapers and news services. The globe icon links to the CNN newsroom. Finally, the Exit sign provides a graceful way for the user to leave the application.

You can run the *Information Superhighway* application on the *Multilit* CD. Use PowerPoint to open the presentation named *InfoHighway* in the *Highway* folder of the *Multilit* CD. Refer to the diagram in Figure 32-10 as you run the application. As you click the different buttons and hypertext options, keep track of where you are in the diagram. This will help you develop a feel for moving about the hyperspace that gets created when you trigger the links on a multimedia screen.

The Systems Approach

Development projects follow a continuous cycle of design, development, and evaluation that is known as the **systems approach** to instructional design. Figure 32-11 shows an artful depiction of the process from *Designer's Edge* by Allen Communication. *Designer's Edge* is an integrated set of preauthoring tools and wizards intended to accelerate the analysis, design, and evaluation of effective technology-based training materials. A visual, task-driven interface walks the user through the entire instructional design process from analysis to evaluation. To learn more and get a free demonstration CD, follow the links to *Designer's Edge* at the *Multilit* Web site.

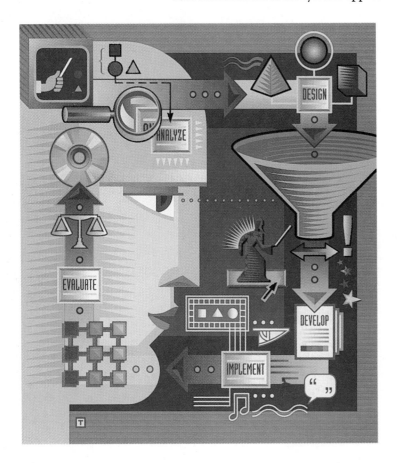

Figure 32-11 The project development cycle as depicted on the cover of *Designer's Edge* by Allen Communication.

exercises

1. Draw a diagram showing the structure of the *History of Flight* application you created in Chapters 26 to 31.

2. What design paradigm(s) does the *History of Flight* application use? To help answer this question, refer to the diagram you drew in response to the previous question.

Part Seven
More Multimedia Tools and Techniques

Now that you have completed the *History of Flight* tutorial, it is time to learn more multimedia tools and techniques that you can use to create advanced applications. Specific tools and techniques you will learn include:

- Downloading multimedia resources from the Internet, which enables you to take full advantage of the richest source on the planet for finding audiovisual material for use in multimedia productions.

- Image capture and manipulation, which enables you to grab images and prepare them for presentation in multimedia applications and Web pages. Windows users will learn how to use Paint Shop Pro, and Macintosh users will learn Graphic Converter.

- Video recording and editing, which enables you to produce video clips for use in multimedia applications. Both Windows and Macintosh users will learn how to use QuickTime Pro, which is available for both platforms.

- PowerPoint drawing tools, with which you can enhance the look and feel of multimedia screens.

- Master layout, which helps you create and apply a common user interface to a PowerPoint application.

- Charts, tables, and graphs, which extend the scope of the information you can communicate in a multimedia application.

33 Downloading Multimedia Resources from the Internet

After completing this chapter, you will be able to:

- Use Internet search engines to locate resources in specific application content areas

- Download text and graphics from the Internet

- Download audio and video resources from the Internet

- Use proper bibliographic style when citing sources from which Internet materials were downloaded

- Use good judgment in deciding what is a fair use, and what requires copyright clearance, when downloading materials from the Internet

● The richest source of multimedia materials on the planet is at your fingertips when you are connected to the World Wide Web. Never before have students had such a fantastic resource for scholarship and research. Millions of texts, images, audios, and videos await you on the Web.

This chapter teaches you how to use search engines to find materials that pertain to your application's content area. You will learn how to use Yahoo to perform subject-oriented searches, and AltaVista to perform key word searches that can locate specific documents, pictures, and sounds. You will be amazed how quickly you can have just the right multimedia resources on your screen.

After you learn how to locate resources on the Internet, this chapter proceeds to teach you how to download multimedia objects to your computer's hard drive. Before using a resource downloaded from the Internet, however, you need to determine whether your purpose falls within the Fair Use guidelines; if not, you must seek copyright clearance in order to obtain the legal right to use the material. Finally, you will learn the proper bibliographic form for citing electronic information.

Internet Search Engines

Figures 33-1 through 33-5 illustrate several search engines on the Internet that can help you locate resources in your application's content area. You access the search engines by pointing your World Wide Web browser at the addresses listed in Table 33-1. The search engine will provide you with a blank field into which you type one or more search terms or key words that indicate what you seek.

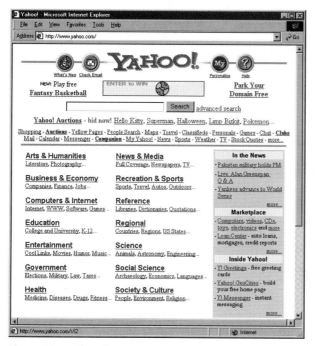

Figure 33-1 The Yahoo search engine.

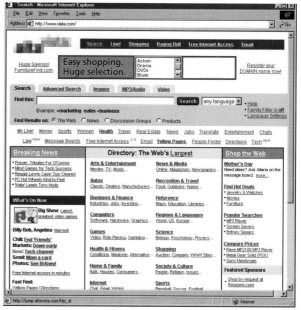

Figure 33-2 The AltaVista search engine.

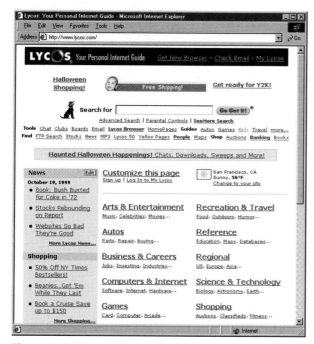

Figure 33-3 The Lycos search engine.

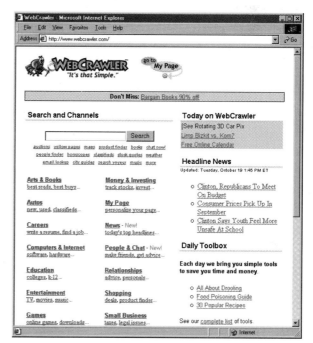

Figure 33-4 The WebCrawler search engine.

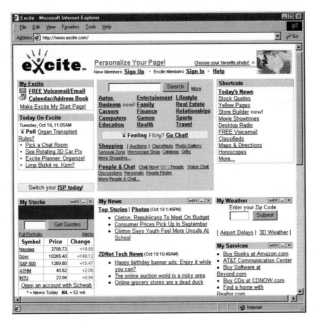

Figure 33-5   The Excite search engine.

Table 33-1   World Wide Web Addresses of Internet Search Engines

Search Engine	Kind of Search	Web Address
Yahoo	Subject-oriented search	http://www.yahoo.com
AltaVista	Searches for key words in documents	http://www.altavista.com
Lycos	Searches Carnegie Mellon University's Worldwide Internet Catalog	http://www.lycos.com
WebCrawler	Global Network Navigator search engine licensed by America Online; powered by Excite	http://www.webcrawler.com
Excite	Concept search or key word search	http://www.excite.com

How to Do a Yahoo Search

As this book goes to press, the most famous search engines are Yahoo and AltaVista. Yahoo is a good place to begin your search. Yahoo has robot computer programs called spiders that are constantly searching the Web for new information. The people who run Yahoo organize what the spiders find into a hierarchically organized directory of topics and subtopics. When you do a Yahoo search, you find out whether your search terms match any of the items in the Yahoo directory. All of the items listed are hyperlinked to their Web pages, so you can quickly access information by clicking its entry in the directory. A nice feature of Yahoo is that if you do not find what you want, Yahoo provides buttons you can click to try other search engines.

AltaVista is a search engine created by the Digital Equipment Corporation. Like Yahoo, AltaVista has spiders that are constantly combing the Web and feeding information into a database. Unlike Yahoo, AltaVista does not organize the Web according to subject areas; rather, AltaVista lets you search for key words in documents, regardless of the "subject" of the documents. AltaVista is, therefore, likely to produce more "hits" than Yahoo, but the hits may not be as relevant to your subject. AltaVista sorts the hits according to the relevance or level of importance of the information found. As this book goes to press, AltaVista indexes 140 million Web pages. According to Digital, AltaVista is the fastest search service available (0.4 to 0.5 seconds average response time), with the most up-to-date content (refreshed every 28 days). For the latest statistics, follow the Multilit Web site link to information about AltaVista.

Search engines are undergoing a lot of research and development on the Internet. By the time you read this, new search engines will have been announced that were not available when this book went to press. You can use Yahoo to find out the latest information about new search engines and what they do. Point your Web browser at http://www.yahoo.com, go to the Yahoo section on Computers and Internet, and do a search for the key word *search*. The search engine sites are also taking on more capabilities in addition to searching. In its competition to attract users from other search sites, for example, excite.com now offers free Web-based e-mail, instant messaging, chat, and online shopping.

To perform a Yahoo search, follow these steps:

▶ Point your Web browser at http://www.yahoo.com; the Yahoo home page appears.

▶ If you want to search all of Yahoo, type your key word(s) into the blank search field and click the Search button.

▶ If you want to search within a Yahoo subject area, scroll down through the subjects listed on the Yahoo home page and click on the subject area you want; the Yahoo subject area page appears.

▶ If subtopics are listed on the subject area page, scroll through the subtopics and select the one you want. Repeat this process until you have narrowed the subject area of your search.

▶ When you are ready to conduct a search, type your key word(s) into the blank search field.

▶ Click the option to search all of Yahoo, or just the subject area you have chosen.

▶ Click the Search button; Yahoo will perform the search and display the items that match your key word(s).

▶ Scroll through the matches to see what Yahoo found. All of the matches are hyperlinked; to see an item, click a highlighted word.

▶ If there are more matches to be displayed, you will find "Next 20 matches" printed at the bottom of the search results. Click "Next 20 matches" if you want to see more.

By default, Yahoo combines your search terms with the Boolean **AND**, which means that you will get a match only when all of the search terms are found together in an item. If you want a Boolean **OR** done instead, click the phrase *Advanced Search* next to the Search button, and the advanced search screen appears as shown in Figure 33-6. In addition to letting you set the Boolean OR option, the advanced options let you choose whether to search Usenet newsgroups or the Yahoo index. You can specify whether you want to search for exact phrases or do an intelligent search, which means that if the search term appears as part of a larger word, you want Yahoo to consider that a match. You can also change the number of entries that Yahoo will return on each Web page of your search results; the default number is 20 entries per page.

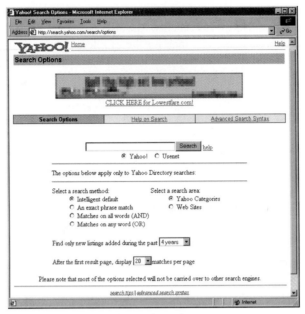

Figure 33-6   Yahoo's advanced search screen.

Reproduced with permission of Yahoo! Inc. ©2000 by YAHOO! Inc.
YAHOO! and the YAHOO! logo are trademarks of YAHOO! Inc.

How to Do an Advanced Search with AltaVista

To make the most effective use of AltaVista, you need to know how to do an advanced search. To perform an advanced search, follow these steps:

▶   Point your Web browser at http://www.altavista.com; the AltaVista home
page appears.

▶   Click the Advanced Text Search option; the advanced search screen appears as shown
in Figure 33-7.

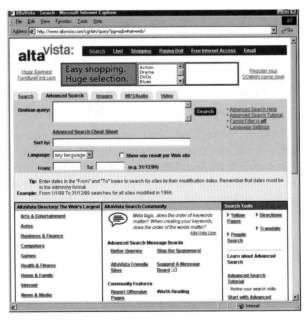

Figure 33-7   AltaVista's advanced search screen.

▶ In the Boolean Expression field, type your search terms using Advanced Search Syntax, which allows you to:

■ Put quote marks around phrases you want treated as search terms; for example, **"Martin Luther"** will search for the words *Martin* and *Luther* appearing next to each other

■ Use the operators AND, OR, NOT, and NEAR; for example, to search for *Martin Luther* but not *Martin Luther King,* you would enter **"Martin Luther" AND NOT "Martin Luther King"**

■ Use parentheses to group search terms, such as **"Martin Luther King" AND ("I Have a Dream" OR "Letter from a Birmingham Jail")**

▶ In the Ranking Keywords field, you have the option of specifying words for AltaVista to use in sorting the matches it finds; if you do not want the matches sorted, leave this field blank.

Almost anything in the world that you want to know is retrievable once you develop skill at using the Advanced Search Syntax. The exercises at the end of this chapter will help you develop this skill. For more information about advanced searching, click "Help" on the AltaVista advanced search screen.

Searching for Pictures, Sounds, and Movies

If you look closely at the AltaVista search screen pictured above in Figure 33-2, you will notice that AltaVista lets you search not only for text, but also for pictures, sounds, and movies, via the following radio buttons:

You may have also noticed that in Figure 33-3, the Lycos search screen lets you search for MP3 audio files and online radio stations. As this trend for search engines to include multimedia objects continues, multimedia authors will be able to use the Web as a worldwide source of audiovisual content for use in multimedia applications.

Suppose you are looking for pictures of Ludwig van Beethoven, for example. Figure 33-8 shows the result of clicking the Images button to search for his picture at AltaVista. If you move your mouse over one of the reduced images, a text box pops up explaining what the picture is about. When you find a picture that interests you, click the picture to retrieve it full size, as illustrated in Figure 33-9. Be sure to scroll down and read the licensing information that tells how you are permitted to use the picture.

Once you find a desired multimedia object on the Web, your next task is to download it to your computer. Read on to learn how to download text, graphics, audio, and video for use in your multimedia applications.

Figure 33-8 Moving the mouse over an image pops up a message box explaining what the picture is.

Figure 33-9 The result of clicking an image in Figure 33-8. Copyright © Corbis Corporation Archive Iconografico, S.A./Corbis.

Downloading Text from the Internet

The quickest way to download text from the Internet is to copy the text onto the Windows Clipboard, from which you can paste the text into any other window on your screen. Most Web browsers let you copy text onto the Clipboard. To download text this way, follow these steps:

▷   Use your Web browser to display the text you want to download.

▷   Drag the mouse over the text you want to copy; the selected text will appear highlighted. Or, if you want to select all of the text on the Web page, pull down the browser's Edit menu and choose Select All.

▷   Press the Copy key (Ctrl-C in Windows or ⌘-C on Macintosh) or pull down the browser's Edit menu and choose Copy.

▷   If the application into which you want to paste the text is not already running, get it running now.

▷   Position the cursor at the spot in the window to which you want to want to paste the text.

▷   Press the Paste key (Ctrl-V or ⌘-V) or pull down the application's Edit menu and choose Paste.

Most Web browsers permit you to download the HTML source code of the Web page on the screen. To download all of the HTML source code, follow these steps:

▷   Pull down the browser's File menu and choose Save As; the Save As dialog will appear.

▷   Type the path\filename under which you want the HTML to be saved.

▷   Click OK to save the HTML.

If you want to download only part of the HTML, pull down the browser's View menu and choose Document Source. When the HTML source code appears, drag the mouse to select the HTML codes you want and press the Copy key ([Ctrl]-[C] or [⌘]-[C]). Then position the cursor where you want to paste the HTML, and press the Paste key ([Ctrl]-[V] or [⌘]-[V]).

Downloading Graphics from the Internet

The quickest way to download a graphic from the Internet is to use your Web browser's option for saving the image to a file. For example, if you are using Microsoft Internet Explorer or Netscape, you can usually save a graphic to a file by right-clicking the graphic.

A popout menu will give you an option to "Save this image as . . ." or "Download Image to Disk." When you select that option, the Save As dialog appears. In the filename field, the name of the file will appear. If you change the name of the file before you save it, you must not change the filename extension. If the file has a *.gif* filename extension, for example, do not change it to *.jpg* or *.bmp* or some other type of file, because the Save As dialog cannot change the file's type.

If you want to change the file's type, you can grab the graphic with Paint Shop Pro (Windows) or Graphic Converter (Macintosh), which can convert graphics into a wide range of file types. You will learn how to use Paint Shop Pro and Graphic Converter in Chapter 34.

Downloading Audio and Video from the Internet

If your Web browser supports the option to download links, you can download any audio or video file that has been linked to a Web page. Follow these steps:

▷ Right-click the hot spot that you normally click with your left button to play the object. The Options menu will pop up.

▷ Choose the option to "Save this link as" or "Download this link to disk." The Save As dialog will appear.

▷ In the filename field, the name of the file will appear. If you change the name of the file before you save it, you must not change the filename extension. If the file has a *.mov* filename extension, for example, do not change it to *.avi* or *.mpg* or some other type of file, because the Save As dialog cannot convert files to different types.

▷ Press [←Enter] or click the Save button to save the file.

Bibliographic Style for Citing Internet Resources

Scholarly writing is not done in a vacuum. Rather than writing about your thoughts on a topic, you conduct research to find out what other people have discovered and documented. When you write your paper, you refer to this research to support your assertions, or to compare them to another point of view.

To provide a standard way of presenting and documenting references to scholarly material, style guides have been created. The three most popular style guides are the *Publication Manual of the American Psychology Association (APA)*, the *Modern Language Association (MLA) Handbook,* and the *Chicago Manual of Style (CMS)*. The APA style is normally used for papers written in psychology classes and the social sciences. MLA style is often used for papers written in English courses and the humanities. The CMS style is used across a broad range of disciplines; this book, for example, is written in CMS style.

At the *Multilit* Web site, you will find examples of term papers written in APA, MLA, and CMS styles. Unless your instructor, publisher, or employer tells you to use a specific style guide, it does not really matter whether you choose APA, MLA, or CMS style. What is important is that you follow an established style guide consistently to enable people who read your paper to locate the sources you cite.

Citing Internet Resources in APA Style

In the APA section of the *Multilit* Web site are resources related to APA style. Among them is a sample term paper written in APA style. If you study the sample term paper, you will notice that some of the references have been linked to other documents on the Web. When a reference that you cite is available online, you should link your citation of that reference to the online resource to provide someone reading your article quick and easy access to the online reference. Printed here are the guidelines for citing Web documents in APA style. Other aspects of the APA style are documented in the *Publication Manual of the American Psychology Association*. To obtain a copy, follow the links to APA Style Guidelines at the *Multilit* Web site.

The source of the guidelines printed here is University of Vermont librarians Xia Li and Nancy Crane, who have written a book entitled *Electronic Styles: An Expanded Guide to Citing Electronic Information*. For the latest information on the availability of the Li and Crane book, follow the *Multilit* Web site links to the Li and Crane Web site. The guidelines provided here were adapted from the Li and Crane Web site in the section on citing World Wide Web resources in the APA style.

INDIVIDUAL WORKS

Author/editor. (Year). *Title* (edition), [Type of medium]. Producer (optional). Available Protocol (if applicable): Site/Path/File [Access date].

Example:

Pritzker, T. J. (No date). *An early fragment from central Nepal* [Online]. Available: http://www.ingress.com/~astanart/pritzker/pritzker.html [1995, June 8].

PARTS OF WORKS

Author/editor. (Year). Title. In *Source* (edition), [Type of medium]. Producer (optional). Available Protocol (if applicable): Site/Path/File [Access date].

Example:

Daniel, R. T. (1995). The history of Western music. In *Britannica online: Macropaedia* [Online]. Available: http://www.eb.com:180/cgi-bin/g:DocF=macro/5004/45/0.html [1995, June 14].

JOURNAL ARTICLES

Author. (Year). Title. *Journal Title* [Type of medium], volume(issue), paging or indicator of length. Available Protocol (if applicable): Site/Path/File [Access date].

Examples:

Inada, K. (1995). A Buddhist response to the nature of human rights. *Journal of Buddhist Ethics* [Online], 2, 9 paragraphs. Available: http://www.cac.psu.edu/jbe/twocont.html [1995, June 21].

Johnson, T. (1994, December 5). Indigenous people are now more combative, organized. *Miami Herald* [Online], p. 29SA(22 paragraphs). Available: gopher://summit.fiu.edu/

Miami Herald—Summit-Related Articles/12/05/95—Indigenous People Now More Combative, Organized [1995, July 16].

OTHER FORMS OF ONLINE COMMUNICATION

For other forms of online communication such as newsgroups, Web sites, and listservs, you should provide as much of the following information as you can, in the order specified.

Author. (Year). Title. [Type of medium]. Available Protocol (if applicable): Site/Path/File [Access date].

Example:

Ritchie, Collin. Emulating PRINT & COPY in a JAVA Applet. [Newsgroup]. Available: news://msnews.microsoft.com/microsoft.public.java.visualj++ [1997, July 2].

Citing Internet Resources in MLA Style

MLA
Style

In the MLA section of the *Multilit* Web site are resources related to MLA style. Among them is a sample term paper written in MLA style. If you study that term paper, you will notice that some of the references have been linked to other documents on the Web. When a reference that you cite is available online, you should link your citation of that reference to the online resource, to provide someone reading your article quick and easy access to the online reference. Printed here are the guidelines for citing Internet resources in MLA style. Other aspects of the MLA style are documented in the *MLA Handbook for Writers of Research Papers*. To obtain a copy, follow the links to MLA Style Guidelines at the *Multilit* Web site.

The source of the guidelines printed here is University of Vermont librarians Xia Li and Nancy Crane, who have written a book entitled *Electronic Styles: An Expanded Guide to Citing Electronic Information*. For the latest information on the availability of the Li and Crane book, follow the *Multilit* Web site links to the Li and Crane Web site. The guidelines provided here were adapted from the Li and Crane Web site in the section on citing World Wide Web resources in the MLA style.

INDIVIDUAL WORKS

Author/editor. *Title of Print Version of Work.* Edition statement (if given). Publication information (Place of publication: publisher, date), if given. *Title of Electronic Work.* Medium. Information supplier. Available Protocol (if applicable): Site/Path/File. Access date.

Example:

Pritzker, Thomas J. *An Early Fragment from Central Nepal.* N.D. Online. Ingress Communications. Available: http://www.ingress.com/~astanart/pritzker/pritzker.html. 8 June 1995.

PARTS OF WORKS

Author/editor. "Part title." *Title of Print Version of Work.* Edition statement (if given). Publication information (Place of publication: publisher, date), if given. *Title of Electronic Work.* Medium. Information supplier. Available Protocol (if applicable): Site/Path/File. Access date.

Example:

Daniel, Ralph Thomas. "The History of Western Music." *Britannica Online: Macropaedia.* 1995. Online. Encyclopedia Britannica. Available: http://www.eb.com:180/cgi-bin/ g:DocF=macro/5004/45/0.html. 14 June 1995.

JOURNAL ARTICLES

Author. "Article Title." *Journal Title.* Volume. Issue (Year): paging or indicator or length. Medium. Available Protocol (if applicable): Site/Path/File. Access date.

Examples:

Inada, Kenneth. "A Buddhist Response to the Nature of Human Rights." *Journal of Buddhist Ethics* 2 (1995): 9 pars. Online. Available: http://www.cac.psu.edu/jbe/ twocont.html. 21 June 1995.

Johnson, Tim. "Indigenous People Are Now More Combative, Organized." *Miami Herald* 5 Dec. 1994: 29SA. Online. Available: gopher://summit.fiu.edu/Miami Herald— Summit-Related Articles/12/05/95—Indigenous People Now More Combative, Organized. 16 July 1995. 17 July 1995.

OTHER FORMS OF ONLINE COMMUNICATION

For other forms of online communication, such as newsgroups, Web sites, and listservs, provide as much of the following information as you can, in the order specified.

Author. Title. (Year). Medium. Available Protocol (if applicable): Site/Path/File. Access date.

Example:

Ritchie, Collin. Emulating PRINT & COPY in a JAVA Applet. 1997. Newsgroup. Available: news://msnews.microsoft.com/microsoft.public.java.visualj++. 2 July 1997.

Citing Internet Resources in CMS Style

In the CMS section of the *Multilit* Web site, you will find resources related to CMS style. Among them is a sample term paper written in CMS style. If you study that term paper, you will notice that some of the references have been linked to other documents on the Web. When a reference that you cite is available online, you should link your citation of that reference to the online resource to provide someone reading your article quick and easy access to the online resource.

Instead of issuing its own guidelines for citing electronic documents, the *Chicago Manual of Style* (1993:633-4) has adopted the International Standards Organization (ISO) system. Printed here are some examples of how to cite Internet resources in the ISO style. For complete documentation of the ISO style, follow the links to CMS/ISO at the *Multilit* Web site.

Printed here are the guidelines for citing Internet resources in CMS style. Other aspects of the CMS style are documented in the *Chicago Manual of Style.* To obtain a copy, follow the links to *Chicago Manual of Style* at the *Multilit* Web site.

INDIVIDUAL WORKS

Author/editor. *Title.* Type of medium. Subordinate responsibility (optional). Edition. Publication information (Place of publication: publisher, date, date of update/revision). Date of citation. Series (optional). Notes (optional). Availability and access. Standard number.

Example:

Pritzker, T. J. *An early fragment from central Nepal.* Available from http://www.ingress.com/~astanart/pritzker/pritzker.html [cited 8 June 1995].

PARTS OF WORKS

Author/editor (of host document). Title (of host document). Type of medium. Subordinate responsibility (of host document) (optional). Edition. Publication information (place of publication: publisher, date, date of update/revision), if given. Date of citation. Chapter or equivalent designation (of part). Title (of part). Location within host document. Notes (optional). Availability and access. Standard number.

Example:

Daniel, R. T. "The history of Western music." In Britannica online: Macropaedia [database online]. Available from http://www.eb.com:180/cgi-bin/g:DocF=macro/5004/45/0.html [cited 14 June 1995].

JOURNAL ARTICLES

Author. Article Title. *Journal Title.* Type of medium. Edition. Issue designations. Date of update/revision. Date of citation. Location within host document. Notes (optional). Availability and access. Standard number.

Example:

Inada, K. "A Buddhist Response to the Nature of Human Rights." *Journal of Buddhist Ethics* [journal online], vol. 2, 9 paragraphs. Available from http://www.cac.psu.edu/jbe/twocont.html [cited 21 June 1995].

OTHER FORMS OF ONLINE COMMUNICATION

For other forms of online communication such as newsgroups, Web sites, and listservs, provide as much of the following information as you can, in the order specified.

Author. Title. Type of Medium. Date of citation. Available Protocol (if applicable): Site/Path/File.

Example:

Ritchie, Collin. "Emulating PRINT & COPY in a JAVA Applet." In Visual J++ News [Newsgroup online]. [written 2 July 1997; cited 18 Aug 1997]. Available from news://msnews.microsoft.com/microsoft.public.java.visualj++.

Fair Use Guidelines for Downloading Internet Resources

The Internet is a brave new world in which debates about copyright and fair use are ongoing. Suppose you find a diagram or an illustration on the Internet that you would like to present on-screen. Are you permitted to put the picture into your multimedia application? What about poems and songs, animations and movies that you find on the Internet? Are you permitted to include them in your multimedia creations?

To provide guidance in what is fair, the Consortium of College and University Media Centers (CCUMC) has issued a set of guidelines for the educational fair use of new media. These guidelines have been endorsed by a broad range of publishers and educational institutions. The recommendations provided here are based on the CCUMC guidelines. The full text of the guidelines is available at the *Multilit* Web site; follow the links to the *Fair Use Guidelines.*

Downloading

According to the CCUMC guidelines, students are permitted to download into term papers certain portions of copyrighted works. These portions include:

- Up to 10% or 1,000 words of a text, whichever is less. Special rules apply to poetry; see section 4.2.2 of the guidelines for details.

- Not more than five images by an individual artist or photographer; for anthologies, not more than 10% or 15 images, whichever is less.

- Up to 10% but never more than 30 seconds of music, lyrics, and music video.

- Up to 10% of motion media or three minutes, whichever is less.

- Up to 10% or 2,500 fields or cell entries, whichever is less, from a copyrighted database or data table.

If you are not a student or an educator, however, or if you are engaging in a profit-making activity, you may not qualify for fair use. Refer to the CCUMC guidelines for detailed information on who qualifies. When in doubt, always request permission from the person or agency holding the copyright to the resource you wish to include.

Whenever you include a portion of a copyrighted work, you should always document the source with an in-text reference at the point where the object appears in your paper, and you must include a bibliographic citation at the end of the paper. If an image includes a copyright notice that is part of the bitmap of the image, it is unethical to remove the copyright notice from the image.

exercises

1. Perform a Yahoo search on the key words *set-top box*. How many matches did Yahoo find? Were the documents found appropriate to the topic? Now perform an AltaVista search on *set-top box*. How many matches did AltaVista find? Were the documents retrieved by AltaVista more informative than those found by Yahoo? How do you explain why AltaVista found more matches than Yahoo?

2. Use AltaVista to perform the following searches. How many matches does each search find? Can you explain why these particular searches find progressively fewer matches?

   - "Martin Luther"
   - "Martin Luther" AND NOT "Martin Luther King"
   - "Martin Luther King" AND ("I Have a Dream" OR "Letter from a Birmingham Jail")
   - "Martin Luther King" AND "Letter from a Birmingham Jail"

3. Choose one of the documents you found in exercise 1 and write a bibliographic citation for it in APA style. Use this chapter's examples of citing Internet resources as a guide to writing your set-top box citation.

4. Get your computer's Notepad running and practice copying text from your Web browser to the Notepad. If your Web browser does not support the copying of text from a Web page, you should get a browser that does, such as Microsoft Internet Explorer or Netscape.

5. Write a letter to your U.S. senators and congressional representatives, letting them know whether or not you support the notion of Fair Use, and whether you oppose any attempt to make fair use illegal on the Internet. Because the concept of Fair Use is being challenged on the Internet, it is important for you to take a stand on the issue and let your lawmakers know what you think about it. You can obtain the mailing addresses of all U.S. senators at http://www.senate.gov. Congressional representatives are at http://www.house.gov. The Senate and House agendas and committee assignments can also be reviewed at these sites.

Image Capture and Manipulation

After completing this chapter, you will be able to:

- Install the shareware version of Paint Shop Pro for Windows or Graphic Converter for the Macintosh

- Capture screens and import images from any software application

- Convert images from one file format into another, such as from BMP into GIF

- Resize images and make color adjustments

- Create special effects with image filters

Graphics come in a lot of different shapes, sizes, and formats. Developers such as you sometimes need to be able to manipulate an image to make it suitable for use in a multimedia application. An image might be too large or too small, for example, or you might want to grab part of an image instead of the whole picture. You may need to reduce the number of colors to save disk space or to make an image load more quickly over the Internet. You might want to apply some special effect to the image, such as emboss, chisel, bevel, weave, sharpen, or soften it.

This chapter teaches you how to do these things with two of the most popular graphics packages in the world: Paint Shop Pro for Windows and Graphic Converter for the Macintosh. Both are excellent, all-purpose image-editing programs that can import a picture in dozens of different image file formats, provide you with powerful tools for editing the image, and export it in any one of dozens of available image file formats. If you have lots of images to convert, there are batch-conversion capabilities that can convert multiple images automatically.

Installing the Imaging Software

Show-Me Movie:
"Creating a Blank Presentation"

Paint Shop Pro and Graphic Converter are **shareware**, which is software that you can try out before you buy it. If you continue using the programs for more than the free trial period, you must pay the license fee. Please respect the shareware license by paying the license fee if you continue using the programs beyond the free trial period.

Paint Shop Pro (Windows)

Show-Me Movie:

"Installing Paint Shop Pro"

The shareware version of Paint Shop Pro is on the *Multilit* CD in the *psp* directory. By the time you read this, a more advanced version of Paint Shop Pro will probably be available. Follow the *Multilit* Web site links to Paint Shop Pro to find out. For the tutorial printed here, however, you should use the version on the *Multilit* CD so the software matches the instructions in the tutorial. Once you master the basics, you can proceed to more sophisticated versions of Paint Shop Pro. To install Paint Shop Pro from the *Multilit* CD, follow these steps:

▷ Click the Start button and choose Run; the Run dialog appears.

▷ In the Run dialog, assuming your CD-ROM drive is D, type the following (if your CD-ROM drive is not D, use the letter of your CD-ROM): **d:\psp\setup.exe**

▷ Press (←Enter), and the Paint Shop Pro setup program will begin.

▷ Follow the on-screen instructions to install Paint Shop Pro.

The first time you run Paint Shop Pro, you must set up the hot key that you will use to capture graphics. Follow these steps:

▷ Double-click the Paint Shop Pro icon to run Paint Shop Pro.

▷ Pull down the Capture menu and choose Setup.

▷ Figure 34-1 shows how the Capture Setup dialog appears.

▷ Notice how the Capture group lets you set up to capture an area, the full screen, the client area of the current window, the entire current window, or an object. Set it to capture an area.

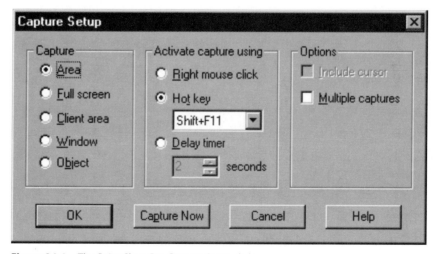

Figure 34-1 The Paint Shop Pro Capture Setup dialog.

▷ In the Activate Capture group, click the option to activate via Hot Key, and set the hot key to something you never use in any other application; the author recommends you set the hot key to ⇧Shift - F11 , which is the hot key this tutorial will use.

▷ Click OK to close the dialog.

Graphic Converter (Macintosh)

Show-Me Movie:
"Installing Graphic Converter"

Graphic Converter is a shareware program that you download from the Internet and then install onto your computer. If you have a Macintosh, follow these steps:

▷ Follow the *Multilit* Web site link to Graphic Converter.

▷ Click the Download option.

▷ Download the version appropriate for your computer (probably the U.S. version, which is in English).

▷ The download manager will transfer the program to your computer.

▷ When the download is finished, there will be a Graphic Converter icon on your desktop. Double-click the Graphic Converter icon. Stuffit Expander will expand the downloaded file and put a second Graphic Converter icon on your desktop. *Note:* If your computer tells you that it does not have Stuffit Expander, follow the *Multilit* Web site link to Stuffit Expander and download it. Then double-click the Graphic Converter icon to expand the downloaded file.

▷ Double-click the second Graphic Converter icon to install the software. When the Install dialog appears, set it to install the software to Macintosh HD, then click the Install button.

▷ To put a Graphic Converter launch icon on your desktop that will make it quick and easy to start Graphic Converter, double-click the Macintosh HD icon, and when the Macintosh HD contents appears, double-click Graphic Converter to open the Graphic Converter folder. Control-click the Graphic Converter launch icon and choose the option to Make Alias, then drag the alias to your desktop.

▷ To save disk space, at your option, you may drag the first two Graphic Converter icons into your trash can. Control-click the trash can and choose Empty Trash to free the disk space.

▷ Anytime you want to start Graphic Converter, double-click its alias on your desktop.

Capturing Images

Show-Me Movie:
"Capturing Images"

A basic skill important to all multimedia developers is the ability to capture an image, or part of an image, and get it into the window of Paint Shop Pro (Windows) or Graphic Converter (Macintosh). Follow the steps in Table 34-1.

Table 34-1 Capturing Images

Windows	Macintosh
▶ Run the program from which you want to capture a graphic. For example, suppose you want to capture one of the figures on the title screen of the NECC keynote presentation. Use the Windows Explorer to look in the *Necc* folder on the *Multilit* CD, and double-click the *NECCKeynote* to get it running.	▶ Run the program from which you want to capture a graphic. For example, suppose you want to capture one of the figures on the title screen of the NECC keynote presentation. Use the finder to look in the *Necc* folder on the *Multilit* CD, and double-click the *NECCKeynote* to get it running.
▶ Get Paint Shop Pro running, if it is not running already.	▶ To capture a rectangular area of an image, press ⌘-⇧Shift-4 and your cursor will change into a crosshair, indicating it is ready to capture something.
▶ Hold down Alt, and keep pressing Tab until Paint Shop Pro appears. Alt-Tab is a special Windows key for switching among programs running simultaneously on your computer.	▶ Drag the crosshair over the area you want to capture. As you drag, the rectangle expands or contracts to show what will be captured when you release the mouse button.
▶ Pull down Paint Shop Pro's Capture menu and select Start; immediately, Paint Shop Pro will disappear.	▶ When you release the mouse button, you will hear a clicking sound, indicating that you just grabbed an image.
▶ If the image you want to capture is not visible on your screen, hold down Alt, and keep pressing Tab until the screen you want to capture appears.	▶ Get Graphic Converter running, if it is not running already.
▶ Press the capture hot key (⇧Shift-F11); the cursor turns into a crosshair.	▶ Pull down the File menu, and choose Open.
▶ Click and drag to select the area of the screen you want to capture, then release the mouse button.	▶ When the Open dialog appears, use it to look on the Macintosh HD for the image you just captured; the image will be called something like Picture 1 or Picture 2, depending on how many images you captured so far. Double-click the name of the image to open it.
▶ The captured image will now appear in the Paint Shop Pro window. To save the image, pull down the File menu and choose Save As.	▶ The captured image will now appear in the Graphic Converter window. To save the image, pull down the File menu and choose Save As.
▶ In the Save as Type box, select the image format in which you want to save the image.	▶ Use the Format menu to select the image format in which you want to save the image.
▶ In the File Name field, type the name you want the image to have. You do not need to type a filename extension, because Paint Shop Pro will supply one automatically, based on the file type you set in the List Files of Type box.	▶ In the Name field, type the name you want the image to have. *Important:* Make sure the filename extension matches the type of file you selected via the Format menu.
▶ Click the Save button to save the file, then pull down the File menu and choose Exit to leave Paint Shop Pro.	▶ Click the Save button to save the file, then pull down the File menu and choose Quit to leave Graphic Converter.
Note: To capture the full screen or the contents of a window, pull down the Capture menu, choose Setup, and set the Capture option accordingly.	*Note:* In addition to the ⌘-⇧Shift-4 command that captures a rectangular region of an image, you can also use ⌘-⇧Shift-3 to capture the entire screen, or ⌘-⇧Shift-Caps Lock-4 to capture the contents of a window.

Converting Images

Sometimes you encounter situations in which you need to convert an image from one file format into another. If you plan to put an image on a Web page, for example, the best formats to use are *.gif* if the image has 256 colors or less, or *.jpg* for images with up to 16 million colors. To convert an image from one file format into another, follow the steps in Table 34-2.

Table 34-2   How to Convert Images from One File Format into Another

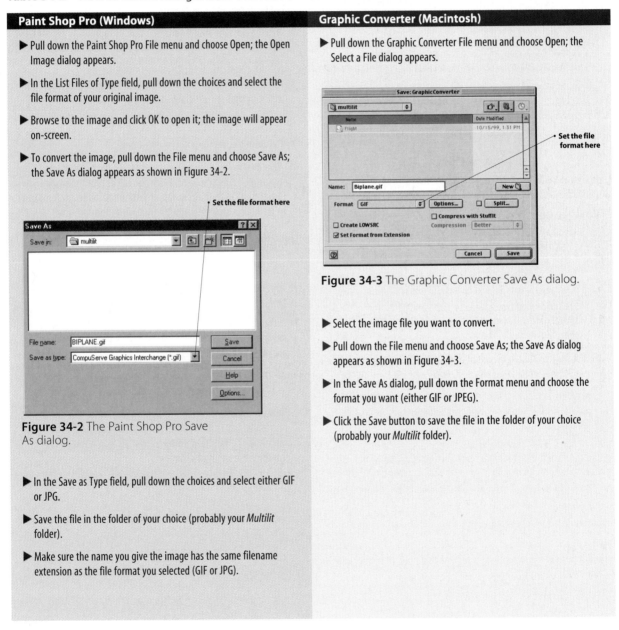

Paint Shop Pro (Windows)	Graphic Converter (Macintosh)
▶ Pull down the Paint Shop Pro File menu and choose Open; the Open Image dialog appears.	▶ Pull down the Graphic Converter File menu and choose Open; the Select a File dialog appears.
▶ In the List Files of Type field, pull down the choices and select the file format of your original image.	
▶ Browse to the image and click OK to open it; the image will appear on-screen.	
▶ To convert the image, pull down the File menu and choose Save As; the Save As dialog appears as shown in Figure 34-2.	

Figure 34-3 The Graphic Converter Save As dialog.

Figure 34-2 The Paint Shop Pro Save As dialog.

▶ Select the image file you want to convert.

▶ Pull down the File menu and choose Save As; the Save As dialog appears as shown in Figure 34-3.

▶ In the Save As dialog, pull down the Format menu and choose the format you want (either GIF or JPEG).

▶ Click the Save button to save the file in the folder of your choice (probably your *Multilit* folder).

▶ In the Save as Type field, pull down the choices and select either GIF or JPG.

▶ Save the file in the folder of your choice (probably your *Multilit* folder).

▶ Make sure the name you give the image has the same filename extension as the file format you selected (GIF or JPG).

Resizing Images

Show-Me Movie:
"Resizing Images"

Images may be the wrong size for placement on a multimedia screen or Web page. To resize an image, follow the steps in Table 34-3.

Table 34-3 How to Resize Images

Paint Shop Pro (Windows)	Graphic Converter (Macintosh)
▶ Pull down the Paint Shop Pro File menu and choose Open; the Open Image dialog appears	▶ Pull down the Graphic Converter File menu and choose Open; the Select a File dialog appears.
▶ In the List Files of Type field, pull down the choices and select the file format of your original image	▶ Select the image file you want to resize.
▶ Browse to the image and click OK to open it; the image will appear on-screen.	▶ Pull down the Picture menu and choose Size, then Scale; the Scale dialog appears as shown in Figure 34-5.
▶ To resize the image, pull down the Image menu and choose Resize; the Resize dialog appears as shown in Figure 34-4.	

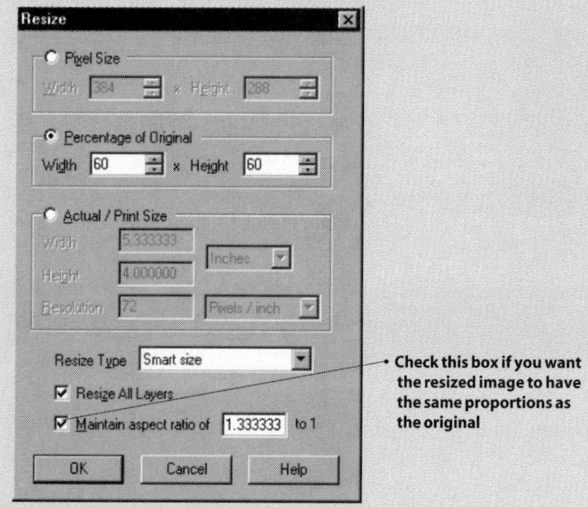

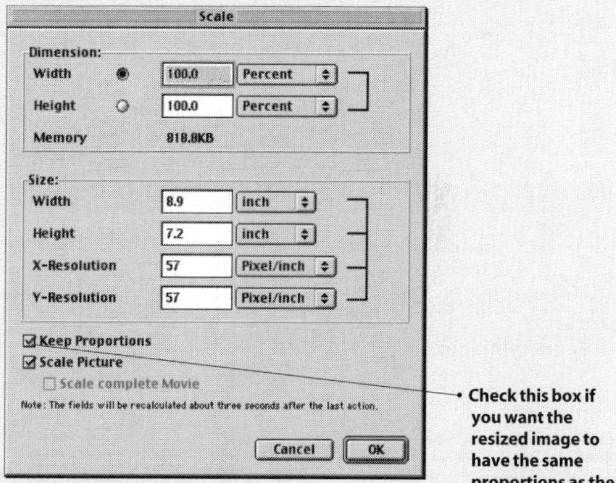

Figure 34-4 The Resize dialog in Paint Shop Pro.

Figure 34-5 The Scale dialog in Graphic Converter.

▶ Click a size option, such as Percentage of Original, then make the numbers larger or smaller, depending on whether you want the image to be larger or smaller. Check the Maintain Aspect Ratio box if you want the resized image to have the same proportions as the original.	▶ Set the width and height you want the resized image to be. You can do this by dimension or size.
▶ Click OK; the resized image appears.	▶ Check the Keep Proportions box if you want to maintain the aspect ratio.
▶ Pull down the File menu, and either choose Save to save this file under the same name as the original (this will replace the original file), or choose Save As to save it under another name.	▶ Click OK.
	▶ Pull down the File menu, and either choose Save to save this file under the same name as the original (this will replace the original file), or choose Save As to save it under another name.

Reducing the Color Depth

Unless you have a special reason for wanting to keep your images encoded in 16 million colors (24-bit), you should convert the images to 256 colors (8-bit), which will make them load faster and reduce considerably the file space occupied by the image. To convert a 24-bit image into an 8-bit image, follow the steps in Table 34-4.

Table 34-4   How to Reduce the Color Depth of an Image

Paint Shop Pro (Windows)	Graphic Converter (Macintosh)
▶ Pull down the Paint Shop Pro File menu, choose Open, and open the image, which will appear on-screen.	▶ Pull down the Graphic Converter File menu, choose Open, and open the image, which will appear on-screen.
▶ Pull down the Colors menu, choose Decrease Color Depth, and see if the 256-colors option is active. If it is not active, your image does not need to be reduced in color depth, so close the image and skip the rest of these instructions.	▶ Pull down the Picture menu, choose Colors, then Change to 256 Colors, as shown in Figure 34-7.
▶ If the 256-colors option is active, select it; the Decrease Color Depth dialog appears as shown in Figure 34-6.	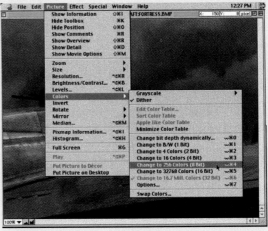
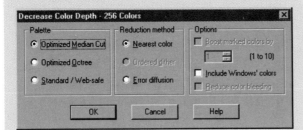 **Figure 34-6** The Decrease Color Depth dialog in Paint Shop Pro.	**Figure 34-7** Decreasing the color depth with Graphic Converter.
▶ If you choose one of the Optimized palette settings, click the option to Include Windows Colors. If you plan to publish this image to the Web, choose Standard/Web-safe.	▶ Pull down the File menu, and either choose Save to save this file under the same name as the original (this will replace the original file), or choose Save As to save it under another name.
▶ Whether to choose Nearest Color or Error Diffusion is up to you. Click OK to close the dialog.	
▶ Pull down the File menu, and either choose Save to save this file under the same name as the original (this will replace the original file), or choose Save As to save it under another name.	

Image Special Effects

Show-Me Movie:
"Image Special Effects"

Both Paint Shop Pro and Graphic Converter have a wide range of image special effects. You can sharpen or soften an image, for example, or emboss, chisel, weave, or bevel it. To apply special effects to an image, follow the steps in Table 34-5.

Table 34-5   How to Create Image Special Effects

Paint Shop Pro (Windows)	Graphic Converter (Macintosh)
▶ Open the image with Paint Shop Pro.	▶ Open the image with Graphic Converter.
▶ If the image is not already 16 million colors, pull down the Colors menu, choose Increase Color Depth, and increase the colors to 16 million. The special effects work only on 16-million-color images.	▶ Pull down the Effect menu and choose the kind of effect you want. On the menu, you will find deformation filters, gamma correction, and several kinds of dither.
▶ Pull down the Image menu and choose the kind of effect you want. On the menu, you will find deformation filters, edge effects, blur, sharpen, and so on.	▶ Depending on the effect you choose, a dialog box may appear. If you choose Effects, Gamma Correction, for example, the Gamma Correction dialog in Figure 34-9 will appear.
▶ Depending on the effect you choose, a dialog box may appear. If you choose Effects, Kaleidoscope, for example, the dialog in Figure 34-8 will appear.	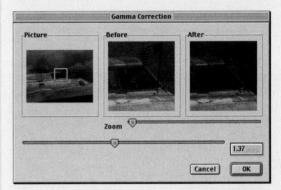 **Figure 34-9** The Gamma Correction dialog box.
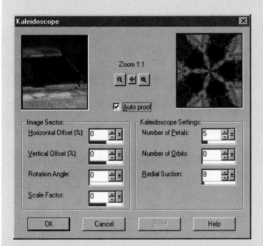 **Figure 34-8** The Kaleidoscope dialog box.	▶ Play with the settings in the dialog box until you achieve the desired effect. If you play with Gamma correction, for example, you should know that on a computer monitor, a small change in brightness at a low brightness level is not equal to the same change at a high level. Gamma correction compensates for this inequality.
▶ Play with the settings in the dialog box until you achieve the desired effect. If you have a fast computer and you want the full-size image to update automatically as you adjust the settings, click the Auto proof box.	▶ If a dialog box opened, click OK to close it, or click Cancel to cancel the effect.
▶ If a dialog box opened, click OK to close it, or click Cancel to cancel the effect.	▶ If you want to save the modified image, pull down the File menu and choose Save As to save the image under the filename you want it to have.
▶ If you want to save the modified image, pull down the File menu and choose Save As to save the image under the filename you want it to have.	

Figures 34-10 through 34-15 show the result of applying six different Paint Shop Pro image effects to the Flying Fortress image in the *Aircraft* folder of the *Multilit* CD. These are just a few of the special effects you will be able to create when you pull down the Effects menu and let your imagination be your guide.

Figure 34-10   Edge enhanced.

Figure 34-11   Rippled.

Figure 34-12   Sculptured.

Figure 34-13   Hot waxed.

Figure 34-14   Mirrored.

Figure 34-15   Framed in round wood.

exercises

1. If you have access to the World Wide Web, get on the Web and browse to a screen with an image you would like to capture. Otherwise, run the *NeccKeynote* presentation in the *Necc* folder on the *Multilit* CD, and go to a slide that shows an image you like. Get Paint Shop Pro running (Windows) or Graphic Converter (Macintosh). Following the steps in Table 34-1, try the different capture methods you learned in this chapter for grabbing rectangular areas of the screen, windows, or the full screen. Which method is most appropriate for capturing the images you decided to grab? Why does that method work better for you than the others?

2. The *photos* directory on the *Multilit* CD contains an image that is too dark. The name of the image is *toodark.bmp*. Use Paint Shop Pro (Windows) or Graphic Converter (Macintosh) to enhance the image. *Hint:* To achieve the best result, you must not only brighten this image but also increase its contrast. Brightness and contrast are two image parameters that interact with each other; with experience, you will learn how to make good contrast and brightness adjustments.

35 Digital Video Recording and Editing

After completing this chapter, you will be able to:

▨ **Understand how digital video recording works and realize why movies play back better on faster computers**

▨ **Consider the options available for recording and editing digital video with Windows or a Macintosh**

▨ **Know how to acquire the necessary hardware and/or software to setup your computer to record digital video**

▨ **Edit digital video using QuickTime Pro for Windows or QuickTime Pro for the Macintosh**

▨ **Conserve disk space by compressing the digital video recording**

● This chapter is a tutorial on recording and editing digital video clips on Windows and Macintosh computers. If your computer does not have a video capture device installed, you will not be able to make an actual recording; however, you will still be able to complete the digital-video-editing tutorial.

How Digital Video Works

Figure 35-1 An artistic impression of how microcomputers play digital video recordings.

Artwork provided courtesy of Intel, Inc.

Figure 35-1 shows an artist's impression of how video gets digitized. The basic process is fairly easy to understand. You connect a video source, such as a camera or a VCR, to your computer's video capture device. When you tell your computer to start recording, the video capture device converts the incoming video signal into a stream of numbers that represent the video signal digitally. The digital video stream contains an enormous amount of data. To conserve space on your hard disk when you save the movie, the video gets compressed, down to as little as 1/200 of its original size. One or more of the video compression schemes explained in Table 35-1 may be used.

On playback, the computer's microprocessor must read the encoded information, decode it, and route the video to the screen and the soundtrack to the waveform audio device. Because some computers are slower than others, the recording process uses a clever scheme in which audio frames are interleaved with the video. The soundtrack plays uninterrupted because the audio always takes priority. Then the computer shows as many frames of video as it has time to process. If it is too late to show a given frame, your computer just skips it and goes on to the next frame. Because the audio has priority, you get the aural illusion of uninterrupted playback. In this chapter, you will learn how to record and compress video for playback on slow as well as fast computers.

Table 35-1 Video Compression Schemes

Method	How It Works
YUV subsampling	Divides the screen into little squares and averages color values of the pixels in each square.
Delta frame encoding	Shrinks data by storing only the information that changes between frames; for example, if the background scene does not change, there is no need to store the scene again.
Run length encoding	Detects a "run" of identical pixels and encodes how many occur instead of recording each individual pixel.

Preparing Your Hard Drive

Before you can record video to your hard disk drive, you must make sure there is enough space to hold the recording. A rule of thumb is to have 15 MB of free disk space for every minute of video you plan to record. This will get compressed later on to save space, but you need enough free disk space to hold the raw video at first.

To complete the exercises in this chapter, you should have at least 20 MB of free disk space. If you do not have that much available, free some now.

Recording the Video

To make a digital video recording, you must first connect a video source, such as a camera or a VCR, to your computer's video capture device. Then you run the recording software that came with your video capture device. If your computer does not already have a video capture device, the author suggests that you consider purchasing one of the products recommended in the video capture section of Chapter 35 at the *Multilit* Web site.

One of the most popular video capture devices is Logitech's QuickCam, which comes in several versions ranging in price from $49.95 to $149.95. Figure 35-2 shows the USB

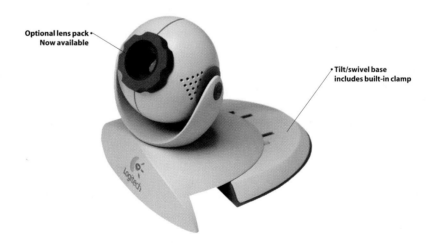

Figure 35-2 The Logitech QuickCam Pro.

version, which the author uses for videoconferencing and video capture on both Windows and Macintosh computers. The author purchased the USB version of the QuickCam because of the cross-platform capabilities that enable you to connect it to any Windows or Macintosh computer with a USB port. If your computer does not have a USB port, you can purchase a parallel port version of the Logitech QuickCam, or you can consider installing one of the video capture cards recommended at the *Multilit* Web site.

To record video with the QuickCam, you follow the steps in Table 35-2. If you have some other capture device, the process will be similar. If you do not have a video capture device, skip to the next part of this chapter, which will teach you how to create and edit digital video clips. You do not have to own a video capture device in order to edit digital video.

Table 35-2   How to Record Digital Video

Windows	Macintosh
▶ Connect your video source to your computer's video capture device; in this example, plug in the Logitech QuickCam.	▶ Connect your video source to your computer's video capture device; in this example, plug in the Logitech QuickCam.
▶ Get your computer's video recording software running; in this example, use the Start button's Programs menu to run the Logitech QuickCam software.	▶ Get your computer's video recording software running; in this example, use the Finder to go to the Logitech folder on Macintosh HD, and run the QuickMovie software.
▶ Click the movie camera icon to put the software into movie recording mode.	▶ When QuickMovie asks what filename to save the movie as, type in a filename, such as *MyFirstMovie*.
▶ Click the Settings tab, then click Format; the Format settings appear as illustrated in Figure 35-3.	▶ The record window will appear, as illustrated in Figure 35-5.

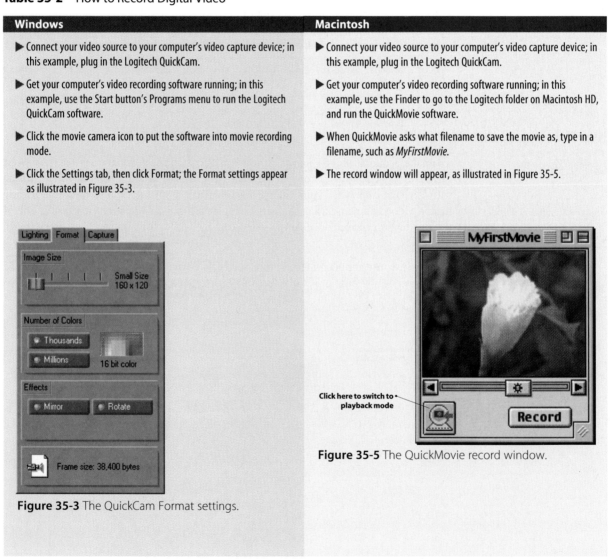

Figure 35-3 The QuickCam Format settings.

Figure 35-5 The QuickMovie record window.

Table 35-2 How to Record Digital Video *(continued)*

Windows	Macintosh
▶ For starters, choose the smallest image size, and set the number of colors to thousands. You can try increasing these settings later, if your computer is able to record at higher settings.	▶ To adjust the size of the recording window, pull down the Settings menu and choose Sizes. For starters, choose quarter screen. You can try increasing these settings later, if your computer is able to record at higher settings.
▶ If you want to record sound along with the movie, click the sound recording button on.	▶ To start recording, press the Record button.
▶ To start recording, press the Record Movie button.	▶ When you are done recording, press the Stop button.
▶ When you are done recording, press the Stop button.	▶ To play the movie back, click the button in the lower-left corner of the record window to switch the view to playback.
▶ After a few seconds, the recorded movie will appear in a QuickCam Viewer window, as illustrated in Figure 35-4.	▶ Playback controls will appear beneath the movie, as illustrated in Figure 35-6.

Figure 35-4 The QuickCam Viewer.	**Figure 35-6** The QuickMovie playback window.

Playing the Video

After you record the video, you will want to play it back. Click the Play button to rehearse the video. If the video plays back jerkily, you have problems. Here is what you can do about them:

▷ Try lowering the color depth. If you are trying to record millions of colors, for example, set the color depth to thousands of colors instead.

▷ Try reducing the dimensions of the recorded video. If you are recording at 640 by 480, for example, reduce the dimensions of the recorded video to 320 by 240 or 160 by 120. Your computer may not be fast enough to record larger screen sizes.

▷ Defragment your hard disk drive. Your computer may have come with its own defragmenting software; to find out, follow these steps:

▒ If you have Windows, click the Start button, choose Help, click the Index tab, and find the topic *defragment*.

▒ If you have a Macintosh, pull down the Finder's Help menu, choose Help Center, search for *Hard Disk,* and follow the links to repair or improve hard disk performance.

▒ If your computer does not contain a built-in defragmenter, follow the *Multilit* Web site links to the Norton Utilities, which contain hard disk maintenance software for both Windows and Macintosh computers.

Saving and Compressing the Video

After you play back the movie to make sure it recorded the way you want it, you need to save it. The QuickCam software gives you the option to compress the video when you save it. You can save the video in a wide range of formats, depending on its purpose and intended audience. To save and compress the video, follow the steps in Table 35-3.

Table 35-3   Saving and Compressing the Video

Windows	Macintosh
▶ If the QuickCam Viewer is not already displaying the video you want to compress, click the Images tab of the QuickCam window, then double-click the video to open it.	▶ If QuickMovie is not already displaying the video you want to compress, pull down the QuickMovie File menu, choose Open, and open the video you want to compress.
▶ Click the File icon in the QuickCam Viewer; the Save As dialog appears.	▶ Pull down the File menu and choose Compress Movie.
▶ In the File Name field, type the name you want the compressed video to have. For your first capture, assuming your hard drive is C, call the file **C:\multilit\MyMovie**	▶ Type the name you want to save the compressed movie as into the dialog box, then press the New button.
▶ Click the Compress button; the Video Compression dialog appears as illustrated in Figure 35-7.	▶ The Video Compression window appears, as illustrated in Figure 35-8.
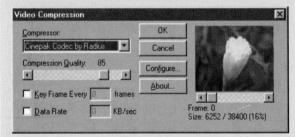 **Figure 35-7** The Video Compression dialog.	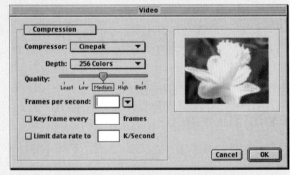 **Figure 35-8** The Video Compression window.
▶ Pull down the Compressor menu and click to select the compressor you want to use. For this example, choose Cinepak. For help selecting the compressor best suited to your application, consult Table 35-4 and follow the *Multilit* Web site links to Codec Central.	▶ Use the Compressor menu to select the compressor you want to use. In this example, choose Cinepak. For help selecting the compressor best suited to your application, consult Table 35-4 and follow the *Multilit* Web site links to Codec Central.
▶ If you are targeting a specific playback medium, check the Data Rate box, and enter the device's data rate. Enter 150 if you want the movie to be able to play back smoothly on slower computers as well as fast ones. Higher data rates will improve playback on faster computers, but beware that file sizes will be larger.	▶ If you are targeting a specific playback medium, check the Limit Data Rate box, and enter the device's data rate. Enter 150 if you want the movie to be able to play back smoothly on slower computers as well as fast ones. Higher data rates will improve playback on faster computers, but beware that file sizes will be larger.
▶ Click OK to close the Video Compression dialog.	
▶ Click SAVE to begin saving the compressed video. A status indicator will keep you informed as to the progress of the compressor.	▶ Click OK to begin saving the compressed video. A status indicator will keep you informed as to the progress of the compressor.

Choosing a codec may be your hardest decision. The comparison of codecs in Table 35-4 may make this decision a little easier. For more detailed information about video codecs, follow the *Multilit* Web site links to Codec Central.

Table 35-4 Video Compression Codecs

Name of Codec	Purpose of Codec
Apple Animation, Apple None	Lossless storage, but inefficient; see Photo JPEG
Cinepak	Medium-quality CD-ROM video, works on older computers; the most universal choice
H.261	Low-quality videoconferencing
H.263	Medium-quality videoconferencing
Intel Indeo 3	Medium-quality CD-ROM video, works on older computers
Intel Indeo Interactive	High-quality CD-ROM video; requires faster computers
Motion JPEG	General-purpose video editing and storage
Photo JPEG	When used at 100% as a storage/transfer format, it creates significantly smaller files than animation
MPEG-1	High-quality CD-ROM video; requires special hardware or fast computer
MPEG-2	High-quality DVD-ROM video; requires special hardware or fast computer
MPEG-4	High-quality Web-based video
Sorenson	High-quality video intended for publication on the Web and CD-ROM on newer computers

Editing the Video

Show-Me Movie:
"Digital Video Editing"

To edit video, you use a digital video editor. Video-editing software is available in a wide range of prices, from $29.99 for the Apple QuickTime Pro editor to thousands of dollars for more advanced editors that use special-purpose hardware to achieve a wide variety of video special effects. This tutorial teaches you how to edit video with the QuickTime Pro editor. Do not underestimate the power of QuickTime Pro, however; it can do a lot of your everyday video editing, even though it does not cost a lot. Follow the links at the *Multilit* Web site if you want to learn about other, more expensive editors.

QuickTime Pro is available for download from the Apple QuickTime Web site. If your computer does not already have a digital video editor installed and you want to download Apple QuickTime Pro, go to www.apple.com/quicktime and follow the links to download Apple QuickTime Pro. When this book went to press, the cost of purchasing a key to unlock QuickTime Pro's video-editing features was $29.99. Follow the on-screen instructions to pay this fee and unlock the powerful video-editing features in QuickTime Pro.

QuickTime Pro lets you cut, copy, and paste segments of video, much like you can cut, copy, and paste text with a word processor. Follow these steps:

▷ If you do not already have QuickTime Pro running, double-click its icon to get it running now.

▷ Pull down the File menu, choose Open Movie, and open the movie you want to edit. In this example, open the movie called Moonland in the Movies directory of the *Multilit* CD.

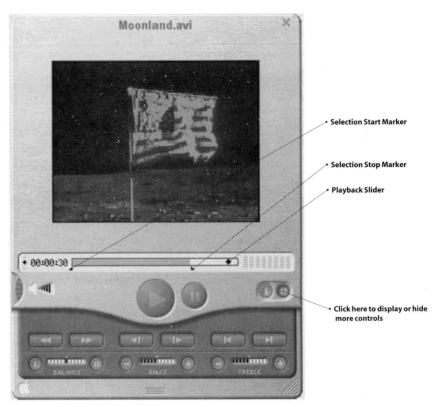

Figure 35-9   The QuickTime Pro Window.

▷ Click the Play button and listen carefully to the start of your recorded video. It probably contains frames you would like to cut out. You can do this with the slider and the Selection Start and Selection Stop markers, as illustrated in Figure 35-9.

▷ In this example, pretend that you want to cut out all of the video up to the point at which Neil Armstrong speaks his famous words, "That's one small step for man, one giant leap for mankind."

▷ Use your mouse to drag the slider to the very start of your video (it is probably there already, but check to make sure).

▷ Click the Play button to start the video, and play up to the point just after you hear the words "The eagle has landed."

▷ Drag the Selection Stop marker to the spot between "The eagle has landed" and "That's one small step." The spot you want is about 23 seconds past the start of the video.

▷ Leave the Selection Start marker at the beginning of the video. Notice how the slider is grayed out between the Selection Start and Stop markers. The gray area represents the video you are about to cut.

▷ Drag the slider to the Selection Stop marker you just set, click Play, and listen carefully. Does it start exactly where you want? If not, you marked too much or too little to cut. Adjust your Selection Stop marker accordingly. Repeat this step until you have the Stop marker exactly where you want it.

▷ Pull down the Edit menu and choose Cut, or press Ctrl-X or ⌘-X. Press the Play button, and you will find that the segment you marked has been cut out of the video.

If there is video at the end of the recording you want to cut, you can repeat this process by setting the Mark In and Mark Out points at the end of the clip. With practice, you will get very good at this. Later on, you can experiment with pasting sequences you have cut into different places in the video to make things happen in a different order than when you recorded them. When you are finished editing the video, pull down the File menu, choose Save As, and save the movie under the filename of your choice.

exercises

1. There is a movie in the *Video* directory on the *Multilit* CD called *clipvid*. When you play it, you will notice that it has material at the start and at the end that should be cut. Use your video-editing software, such as QuickTime Pro, to do that. Save the resulting file in your *Multilit* directory under the name *TrimmedClip*.

2. Use your video-recording software, such as Logitech QuickCam or QuickMovie, to record a 10-second video clip. Pull down the File menu, choose Compress File, and choose the option to save the file with no compression in your *Multilit* directory under the name *uncompressed*. Use the File Manager to find out how large the file is. Now use Logitech QuickCam or QuickMovie to compress the file with the Cinepak compressor at a color depth of 256 with medium quality. Save the file in your *Multilit* folder under the filename *compressed*. How large is the file now? By what percentage did the Cinepak compressor reduce the file in size, as compared to the size of the full framed version?

36 Drawing Lines, Arrows, Curves, and Freehand Shapes

After completing this chapter, you will be able to:

▨ **Draw lines and arrows on the screen**

▨ **Change the line color, style, and thickness**

▨ **Draw curves and reshape them by editing vertices**

▨ **Draw freehand and scribble on screen**

● Until now in this text, when you wanted to place a graphic on the screen you used the Insert Picture from File or Clip Art tool to bring up an image that had been created in advance. This works well for pictures, but if all you want is a simple line, curve, box, or circle, it is quicker to draw directly on the screen. This chapter teaches you how to use the drawing toolbar to draw simple graphics directly onto the screen.

Drawing Lines

Show-Me Movie:
"Drawing Lines"

To draw a line on the screen with PowerPoint, you use the Line tool. The Line tool appears about a third of the way over on the Drawing toolbar. If the Drawing toolbar is not visible, pull down the PowerPoint View menu, choose Toolbars, and select the Drawing toolbar. To draw a line, follow these steps:

▷ Use PowerPoint to go to the screen on which you want to draw the line. In this example, open your *Practice.ppt* file, go to the last slide, and click the New Slide icon to create a new slide. When PowerPoint asks you to choose a layout for the new slide, choose the blank layout.

▷ To draw a line, click the Line tool, then move your mouse to the spot at which you want to start drawing. Notice how your cursor has the shape of a cross; the cross means you are ready to draw.

▷ While holding down the left mouse button, drag the mouse to form the line. As you drag the mouse, the line will stretch to show where the line will go when you let up the button.

The Line tool ·

▷ When you release the mouse button, the line appears on screen, with handles on each end of it. The line is an object, and like any object in PowerPoint, you can drag the handles to manipulate the object.

▷ To practice manipulating the line, click and drag the handles. Notice how easily you can adjust the size of the line.

▷ To practice repositioning the line, click and drag on the line anywhere between the two endpoints. Notice how you can move the line anyplace on the slide.

▷ To modify the properties of the line, double-click it, or pull down the Format menu and choose AutoShape. The Format Autoshape dialog appears as illustrated in Figure 36-1. Pull down the menus if you want to change the color, style, or weight (i.e., thickness) of the line. Figure 36-2 shows the different styles you can choose.

▷ Right-click the line if you want to give it action settings, animate it, or hyperlink it.

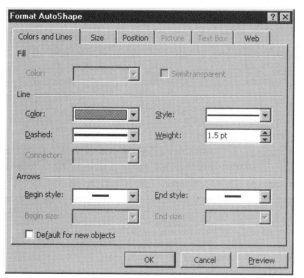

Figure 36-1 The Format Autoshape dialog lets you change the appearance of the line.

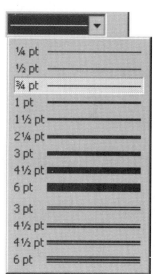

Figure 36-2 The Style menu in the Format Autoshape dialog.

Drawing Arrows

Show-Me Movie:
"Drawing Arrows"

To draw an arrow on the screen with PowerPoint, you use the Arrow tool. The Arrow tool appears alongside the Line tool about a third of the way from the left on the Drawing toolbar. To draw an arrow, follow the same steps as for drawing a line. The only difference is that you click the Arrow tool instead of the Line tool before you start drawing.

The Arrow tool

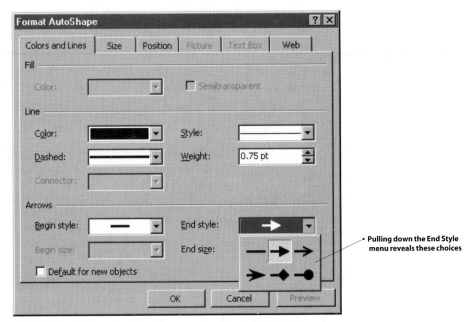

Figure 36-3   The Format AutoShape dialog lets you change the style of the arrow.

After you draw the arrow, you can modify the format and style that determines how the beginning and end of the arrow appear on-screen. After you draw the arrow, double-click it, or pull down the Format menu and choose AutoShape. When the Format Autoshape dialog appears, pull down the Begin Style or End Style menus and choose from the styles listed in Figure 36-3. To make the style you choose become the default for new arrows that you draw, click the box at the bottom of the dialog to make the current settings become the default for new objects.

Drawing Curves

Show-Me Movie:
"Drawing Curves"

To draw a curve on the screen with PowerPoint, use the Curve tool. The curve can have one or more vertices, around which you can bend the curve in a wide range of patterns. Follow these steps:

▷   Use PowerPoint to go to the screen on which you want to draw the curve. In this example, go to the last slide in your *Practice.ppt* file.

▷   On the Drawing toolbar, click AutoShapes, choose Lines, then click Curve.

▷   Move your mouse to the spot at which you want to start drawing. Notice how your cursor has the shape of a cross; the cross means you are ready to draw.

▷   Click where you want the curve to start, and then continue to move the mouse, and click wherever you want to add a curve.

▷   To end the shape, double-click it at any point. To close the shape, click near its starting point.

▷   When you are done drawing the curve, handles will appear around it. The handles mark the boundaries of the object you just drew. You can use the handles to resize the curve, or press the arrow keys to reposition it on-screen.

▷   Double-click the curve if you want to change its color, thickness, or style.

▷   Right-click the curve if you want to give it action settings, animate it, or hyperlink it.

Reshaping a Curve

Show-Me Movie:
"Reshaping a Curve"

Drawing curves freehand can be tricky. Often you will not get the shape you want on your first attempt. Happily, it is easy to reshape a curve and make it bend just the way you want. To change the shape of a curve after you have drawn it, follow these steps:

▷ Click to select the curve you want to reshape.

▷ On the Drawing toolbar, click Draw, then click Edit Points. *Note:* If Edit Points is not visible as a menu choice, click the down-arrow to expand the menu.

▷ To reshape the curve, drag one of the vertices that form its outline.

▷ To add a vertex to the curve, click where you want to add it, then drag.

▷ To delete a vertex, control-click the vertex you want to delete.

▷ To change the bend of a vertex, right-click the vertex and choose the option to smooth, straighten, or corner the curve, as illustrated in Figure 36-4.

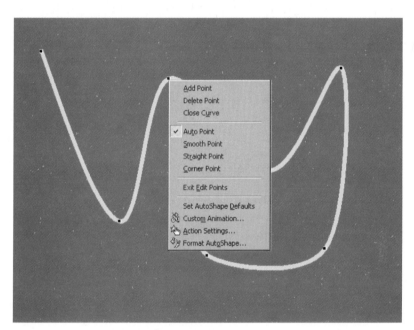

Figure 36-4   Right-clicking a vertex pops out a menu that lets you use any point to smooth, straighten, or corner a bend on the curve.

Freehand Drawing (Scribbling)

Freehand drawing, also known as scribbling, enables you to draw on-screen any movement you can create with your mouse. Follow these steps:

▷ Use PowerPoint to go to the screen on which you want to draw freehand or scribble. In this example, go to the last slide of your *Practice.ppt* file, and click the New Slide icon to create a new slide. When PowerPoint asks you to choose a layout for the new slide, choose the blank layout.

▷ On the Draw toolbar, click AutoShapes, choose Lines, and click the Scribble tool.

▷ Move your mouse to the point at which you want to begin scribbling. Notice that the cursor has the shape of a pencil, indicating that you are ready to draw.

▷ Hold down the mouse button, and draw. Scribble whatever you want. When you are done, release the mouse button.

▷ Handles appear around the scribbling. Like any object, you can use the handles to resize the scribbling, or you can use the arrow keys to reposition it on screen.

▷ If you want to reshape the scribbling, follow the steps above for reshaping a curve.

▷ Double-click the scribbling if you want to change its color, thickness, or style.

▷ Right-click the scribbling if you want to give it action settings, animate it, or hyperlink it.

e x e r c i s e s

1. In theory, freehand drawing lets you draw anything on-screen. The mouse can be limiting, however. To test the extent to which you can draw with the mouse, try to write your name on-screen. To do this, create a new screen at the end of your *Practice* application, and use the AutoShapes—Line—Scribble tool to sign your name. How closely does the scribbling resemble your signature?

2. To fix any abnormalities in the signature you created in exercise 1, try reshaping your signature. Right-click your signature, choose Edit Points, and try moving the points around to make the scribbling more closely resemble your signature. How closely does the reshaped scribbling resemble your signature?

37 Slide Masters and Design Templates

After completing this chapter, you will be able to:

- Control screen layout using slide masters and design templates

- Redesign the format and placement of a presentation's titles and text by modifying its slide master

- Create your own slide master

- Understand how design templates consist of a slide master, a title master, and a color scheme that work together to create a certain style

- Create a design template that expresses your own personal style

PowerPoint has a special kind of slide called the *slide master*. The slide master controls the default look and feel of the slides in a multimedia application. Changes you make to the font type, size, and color of the master text apply to screens throughout the presentation. If you want to make a global change to the font used in an application, for example, you can make the change on the slide master, and PowerPoint will automatically update all of the slides in your presentation.

As you gain experience creating multimedia applications, you will begin to develop your own style of screen layout and presentation. If you reflect on how you use PowerPoint, you will notice how you tend to make the same kinds of changes in fonts, colors, sizes, and screen locations. The patterns you tend to use a lot determine your style. You can save time if you create a design template that expresses your style. Instead of having to change each slide to match your style, you can simply apply the design template to your entire presentation.

In this chapter, you will learn how to create slide and title masters that define your style of authoring and export them into a style template that you can use to save time when you create a multimedia application.

Slide Masters

Show-Me Movie:
"Editing the Slide Master"

Every PowerPoint presentation has a slide master. Whether you use it or not, the slide master is there. You can use the slide master to make common elements appear on every screen of your presentation. Suppose you want a logo to appear at the bottom of every screen, for example; you can do that by adding a picture to the footer area of the master slide. Maybe you have designed a backdrop that you want to have appear behind the text of your presentation; you can make each screen have that backdrop by changing the background of the slide master. Suppose you have become fond of a certain font style, size, and color; by adjusting stylistic elements of the slide master text, you can apply them consistently throughout the screens of your application. To edit the slide master, follow these steps:

▷ Use PowerPoint to open the presentation whose slide master you want to edit. In this example, pull down the File menu, click New, and choose the option to create a blank presentation.

▷ When the New Slide dialog appears, choose the option to create a Bulleted list slide. If the New Slide dialog does not appear, pull down the Format menu, click Slide Layout, and choose the option to create a slide containing a bulleted list.

▷ When the bulleted list slide appears, click to type a title; in this example, type **Santa's Mailing Address**

▷ Click to type some bulleted text. In this example, type:

  ▪ **Mr. Santa Claus**
  ▪ **123 Reindeer Lane**
  ▪ **North Pole**

▷ Notice the font, color, and size in which the text you type appears. Do you know where the text style comes from? It comes from the slide master! You are seeing the style of the slide master, which controls the default style of the text you type.

▷ Pull down the View menu, choose Master, then click Slide Master. The slide master appears, as illustrated in Figure 37-1.

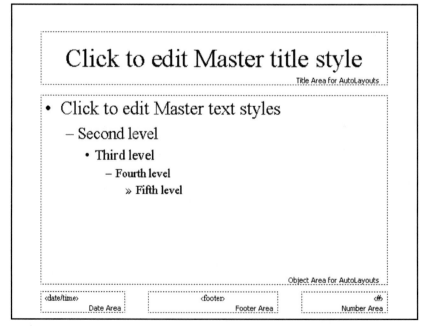

Figure 37-1   The Slide Master lets you edit the default style of a presentation.

Figure 37-2 The Slide Miniature window previews your style changes.

> Right-click the text of the slide master title, choose Font, and select the font Comic Sans MS.

> Click the Preview button to preview the change. Notice how the change takes effect in the slide miniature window, as illustrated in Figure 37-2.

> In like manner, you can change the master style of the different levels of bullets. Select them all, for example, and change the font to Arial Black. Click the Preview button to preview the change.

> Suppose you want to put a picture on every screen. Pull down the Insert menu, click Picture, choose Clip Art, go to Seasons, and choose a graphic appropriate for the season. Then click the Preview button to preview the change.

You can even set dissolve patterns and animation effects on the master slide. Remember that objects you place on the slide master will appear on every screen of your presentation. Normally, you put on the slide master only those elements you want on every screen. Later on, however, you can override the slide master on any screen. To override the slide master, simply go to the screen on which you want something different and edit the slide to make the change. Slides you modify in this way retain their uniqueness, even when you change the master slide.

Design Templates

Show-Me Movie:
"Previewing the Design Templates"

A design template contains a color scheme, a slide master, and a title master that combine to create a particular look and feel for a multimedia application. PowerPoint comes with dozens of professionally designed templates that create different looks. When you apply a design template to your presentation, the slide master, title master, and color scheme change. You can also create your own template. Anytime you create a special look that you would like to use as a design template for other applications, you can save your design as a template.

To preview the design templates that come with PowerPoint, follow these steps:

> Pull down the Format menu and choose Apply Design Template. *Note:* If the option to apply a design template is not visible, click the down-arrow to expand the menu.

> When the Apply Design Template dialog appears, click the name of a design template.

> As illustrated in Figure 37-3, PowerPoint shows you a preview of the design.

> Keep clicking designs until you find one you really like. To apply a design template you like to your presentation, double-click its name, or click the Apply button.

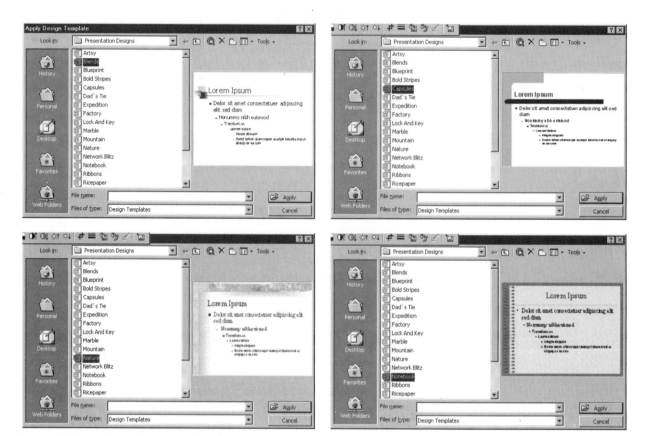

Figure 37-3   The Apply Design Template dialog previews the style of the selected design template.

Creating Your Own Design Template

As mentioned previously, one of the greatest advantages of design templates is how you can create your own custom template that can be used to create slides with your personal style. To create your own design template, follow these steps:

> Pull down the Format menu and choose Apply Design Template. *Note:* If the option to apply a design template is not visible, click the down-arrow to expand the menu.

> When the Apply Design Template dialog appears, double-click the design template that comes closest to matching your own personal style. If none of the templates even comes close, choose any one of them, because you can modify it by following the steps below.

> Pull down the View menu, choose Master, then click Slide Master. When the slide master appears, modify it to suit your style, as you learned to do at the start of this chapter.

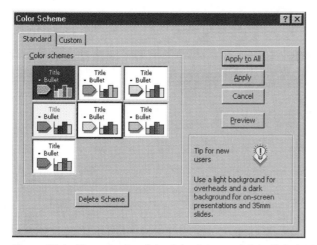

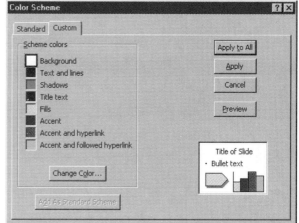

Figure 37-4 The two tabs of the Color Scheme dialog. Click the Standard tab to select a standard color scheme, or click the Custom tab to create your own custom color scheme.

▷ Pull down the View menu, choose Master, then click Title Master. When the title master appears, modify it to suit your style.

▷ Pull down the Format menu and choose Slide Color Scheme. *Note:* If the color scheme option is not visible, click the down-arrow to expand the menu.

▷ The Slide Color Scheme dialog appears. As illustrated in Figure 37-4, you can choose a set of standard colors, or you can totally customize the color elements in your color scheme.

▷ To save your design as a template, pull down the File menu, and click Save As.

▷ When the Save As dialog appears, set the Save as Type field to Design template.

▷ In the File name field, type the name you want the design template to have.

After you complete these steps, you can use your design template in any presentation. Simply open the presentation with PowerPoint, pull down the Format menu, and choose Apply Design Template. When the dialog appears, double-click your design template. New slides you create will be based on your template.

exercises

1. Pull down the Format menu and choose Apply Design Template. If the option to apply a design template is not visible, click the down-arrow to expand the menu. When the Apply Design Template dialog appears, click the names of the different design templates to preview them. Keep clicking the designs until you find one you really like. What is the name of the design template you like the best? Why do you like it the best? What design features does it have that contribute to its special look?

2. Repeat exercise 1, except this time, find a template that you think is poorly designed. What is the name of the poorly designed template? What are its deficiencies? State your reasons for not liking it. Refer specifically to its use of font, size, color, graphics, and positioning.

38 Creating Charts, Graphs, Tables, and Equations

After completing this chapter, you will be able to:

▨ **Use a datasheet to create a chart or graph some data you want to display on-screen**

▨ **Choose the proper type of chart for the kind of data you are presenting**

▨ **Use tables to display data neatly in columns and rows on the screen**

▨ **Display equations via the equation editor**

▨ **Understand the difference between object linking and embedding**

▨ **Link or embed objects created with other programs**

▨ **Animate charts, graphs, tables, and formulas**

● The ancient Greek mathematician Pythagoras claimed that all things are known by number. Sooner or later, in the midst of all your multimedia sound and graphics, you will inevitably encounter the need to display numerical data on the screen. You may want to display a graph showing how much something has grown during the past decade, for example, or you may need to forecast a future trend that requires you to graph numerical or financial projections. Happily, PowerPoint has a datasheet that makes it easy to create charts and graphs.

There will also be times when you need to display numerical or textual information in rows and columns on the screen. You may need to compare the features of two competing products, for example, or explain the relative advantages and disadvantages of different ways to solve a problem. PowerPoint's table feature can help you organize the screen into rows and columns that make side-by-side comparisons easy to present.

If the data you are presenting follows a numerical formula, you can use the Equation Editor to display the formula's equation on-screen. This chapter not only enables you to do all these things, but it also shows you how to use animation techniques to move the data on and off the screen in an engaging manner through multimedia sound and graphics.

Creating Charts and Graphs

Show-Me Movie:
"Creating a Chart"

To create a chart or graph some data, type or paste your numerical data into a special table called a datasheet. When the chart appears on-screen, you can alter its display settings to present your data in the most effective manner. Follow these steps:

▷ Go to the slide on which you want to create a chart or graph. In this example, open your *Practice* application, go to the last slide, and click the New Slide icon to create a new slide.

▷ Pull down the Insert menu and choose Chart; if the Chart option is not visible, click the down-arrow to reveal the rest of the menu.

▷ The chart appears on-screen with a sample set of data displayed in it, as illustrated in Figure 38-1. Beneath the chart is the datasheet, as illustrated in Figure 38-2. Compare these two figures, and notice how the chart graphs the numbers in the datasheet.

▷ The first row of the datasheet contains the data labels. Click each label and type the label for the corresponding column in your data. To delete a label, click it to select it, then press [Del]. To delete an entire column, right-click the label, and when the menu pops up, choose Delete, then choose Entire Column.

▷ The first column of the datasheet contains the series labels. Click each label and type the label for the corresponding row in your data. To delete a label, click it to select it, then press [Del]. To delete an entire row, right-click the label, and when the menu pops up, choose Delete, then choose Entire Row.

▷ The rest of the datasheet contains the data displayed in the chart. Click each cell and type the data you want displayed. To delete a cell, click it to select it, then press [Del]. To delete an entire row or column of data, right-click a cell, and when the menu pops out, choose Delete, then select Entire Column or Entire Row.

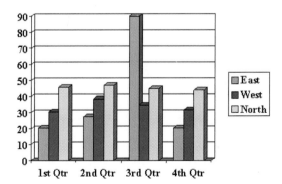

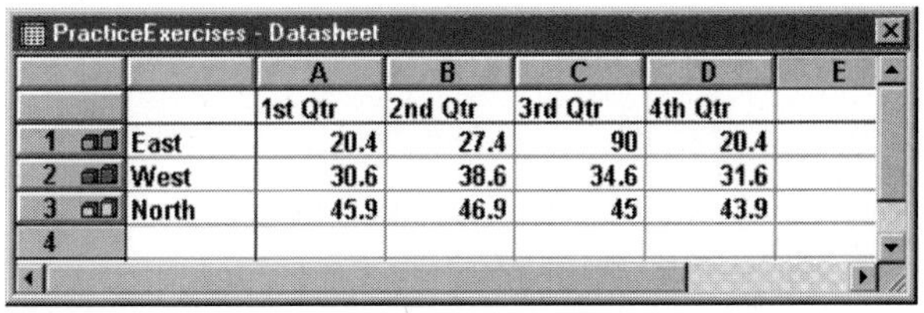

PracticeExercises - Datasheet		A	B	C	D	E
		1st Qtr	2nd Qtr	3rd Qtr	4th Qtr	
1	East	20.4	27.4	90	20.4	
2	West	30.6	38.6	34.6	31.6	
3	North	45.9	46.9	45	43.9	
4						

Figure 38-1   This chart appears when you pull down the Insert menu and choose Chart.

Figure 38-2   The datasheet table; this is the data that is displayed in Figure 38-1.

Choosing a Type of Chart Appropriate to Your Data

There are dozens of types of charts in which you can display your data. To change the chart style, right-click the white space between the chart and its placeholder; when the menu pops up, choose Chart Type. Figure 38-3 shows how the Chart Type dialog will appear. It lets you choose among the styles of charts listed in Table 38-1. Following the advice in Table 38-1, choose the charting style appropriate to your data.

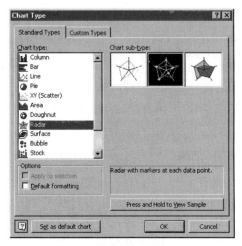

Figure 38-3   The Chart Type dialog.

Table 38-1   Chart Styles and When to Use Them

Type of Chart		When to Use This Type
	Column	Compares values across categories vertically
	Bar	Compares values across categories horizontally
	Line	Draws lines with markers displayed at each data point
	Pie	Displays the contribution of each value to a total
	X,Y (Scatter)	Compares pairs of values
	Area	Displays the trend of values over time or categories
	Doughnut	Functions like a pie chart, but can contain multiple series
	Radar	Displays changes in values relative to a center point
	Surface	Shows trends in values across two dimensions in a continuous curve
	Bubble	Compares sets of three values; a scatter plot in which the size of the bubble represents the third value
	Stock	Displays from three to five values of each label
	Cylinder	Compares values across categories with cylindrical columns or bars
	Cone	Compares values across categories with conical columns or bars
	Pyramid	Compares values across categories with pyramidal columns or bars

Importing a File to Create a Chart

If your chart has a lot of data in it, you can save time by importing the data from a file instead of typing it by hand. You can import data from a Lotus 1-2-3 file, a Microsoft Excel file, or a plain text file in which the data elements are defined by character position or are delimited by commas, spaces, or tab characters. To import data from a file, follow these steps:

▷ If you do not already have a chart on-screen, pull down the Insert menu and choose Chart.

▷ If the datasheet is not visible, right-click the white space just inside the chart's placeholder and when the menu pops up, choose Datasheet.

▷ Click the cell in which you want the imported data to begin; normally, you click the upper left cell on the datasheet.

▷ Pull down the Edit menu and click Import File. When the Import File dialog appears, use the Look In menu to switch to the folder containing the file you want to import.

▷ Use the Files of Type menu to look for the kind of file you are importing, as illustrated in Figure 38-4. After you have located the file, click the Open button, and follow the on-screen instructions to import the data. If you are importing a text file, for example, the Text Import Wizard appears. Answer the questions the Wizard asks, then click the Finish button to import the data into the datasheet.

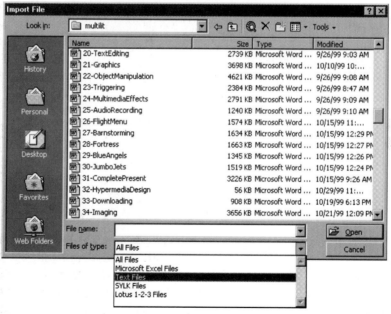

Figure 38-4   The Import File dialog lets you import data from a Lotus 1-2-3 file, a Microsoft Excel file, or a plain text file.

Inserting a Table

Whenever you want the user to make side-by-side comparisons of numerical or textual information, the best way to present the data is to create a table. A table consists of rows and columns that make side-by-side comparisons easy to present. To create a table, follow these steps:

▷   Go to the slide on which you want to create a table. In this example, open your *Practice* application, go to the last slide, and click the New Slide icon to create a new slide.

▷   Pull down the Insert menu and choose Table; if the Table option is not visible, click the down-arrow to reveal the rest of the menu.

▷   The Insert Table dialog appears as illustrated in Figure 38-5. Use this dialog to set the number of rows and columns your table will contain initially. In this example, designate two columns and seven rows. Click OK, and the table appears on-screen.

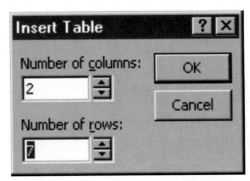

Figure 38-5   The Insert Table dialog sets the initial size of the table.

▷   To enter data into the table, click a cell to select it, then type the data. In this example, type the following data, which is the elevation of the world's highest mountains:

Mountain	Height
Everest	29,028
K2	28,250
Makalu	27,789
Dhaulagiri	26,810
Nanga Parbat	26,660
Annapurna	26,504

Drawing a Table

PowerPoint has a powerful table drawing capability. To unleash it, pull down the View menu, choose Toolbars, and select Tables and Borders. The Tables and Borders toolbar appears as follows:

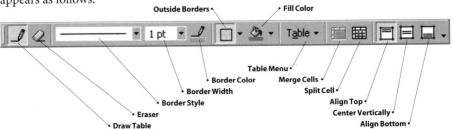

To create a table via the Tables and Borders toolbar, follow these steps:

▶ Go to the slide on which you want to create a table. In this example, open your *Practice* application, go to the last slide, and click the New Slide icon to create a new slide.

▶ If the Tables and Borders toolbar is not visible, pull down the View menu, choose Toolbars, and select the Tables and Borders toolbar.

▶ Click the Draw Table tool, which has the shape of a pencil.

▶ To create the table, click and drag from the spot where you want the table to begin to the place where you want it to end. Do not worry about being precise, because you can easily adjust the boundaries of the table later.

▶ Inside the table you drew in the previous step, click and drag to create the table cells.

▶ To erase a line in the table, click the Eraser tool, then drag over the line you want to erase.

▶ When you finish drawing the table, click a cell and begin typing to enter information into it.

▶ Use the Border Style, Border Width, and Border Color tools to change the default line drawing parameters.

▶ To change the outside border style, drag to select the cell(s) you want to modify, then pull down the Outside Borders menu and choose the border style you want.

▶ To change the fill color of any cell or cells, drag to select the cell(s), then pull down the Fill Color menu and choose the color or fill style you want.

▶ By default, the text you type will align to the top of the cell. To change that, click one of the align tools at the right end of the Tables and Borders toolbar.

▶ To insert or delete columns or rows above or below the current cell, pull down the Table menu and choose one of the options illustrated in Figure 38-6.

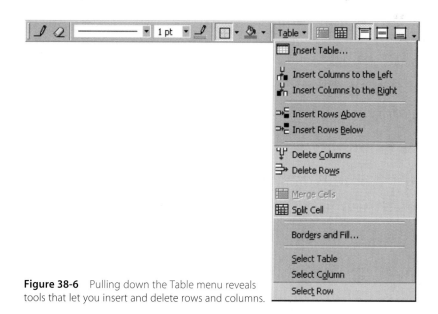

Figure 38-6 Pulling down the Table menu reveals tools that let you insert and delete rows and columns.

Inserting Equations

Show-Me Movie:
"Inserting Equations"

If you are involved in math, science, or statistics, there may come a time when you need to display a formula or an equation that you cannot create with PowerPoint's drawing tools. Happily, PowerPoint works in conjunction with a more powerful tool called the Microsoft Equation Editor, which lets you draw any conceivable type of mathematical equation or formula. To insert an equation onto a PowerPoint slide, follow these steps:

▶ Go to the slide on which you want to display an equation. In this example, open your *Practice* application, go to the last slide, and click the New Slide icon to create a new slide.

▶ Pull down the Insert menu and click Object; the Insert Object dialog appears.

▶ In the Object Type list, click Microsoft Equation 3.0 (or later) and click OK. If Microsoft Equation is not available in the Object Type list, follow these steps to get it there:

■ Pull down the View menu, select Toolbars, then click Customize; the Customize dialog appears.

■ Click the Commands tab, then select Insert in the Categories list.

■ In the Commands box, click Equation Editor, then drag it from the Commands box and put it onto a gray area on the toolbar of your choice.

■ Close the dialog box, then click the Equation Editor icon you put on the toolbar.

▶ Use the Equation Editor to create the equation. The Equation Editor is pretty intuitive, but if you need help, pull down the Equation Editor's Help menu and choose Equation Editor Help Topics.

▶ To return to PowerPoint, pull down the Equation Editor's File menu and choose Exit and Return to Presentation.

▶ The equation you drew with the Equation Editor now is an object on your PowerPoint slide.

Editing an Equation

To edit an equation that appears on a PowerPoint slide, follow these steps:

▶ Double-click the equation; the Equation Editor launches and displays your equation.

▶ Use the Equation Editor tools and menus to update your equation.

▶ To return to PowerPoint, pull down the Equation Editor's File menu and choose Exit and Return to Presentation.

Object Linking and Embedding

PowerPoint supports object linking and embedding (OLE), which is a process that lets you insert onto a PowerPoint slide an object that you created with another application that also supports OLE. All of the applications in the Microsoft Office suite support OLE, as do a lot of other programs. To insert an object onto a PowerPoint slide, follow these steps:

▶ Go to the slide on which you want to insert an object. In this example, open your *Practice* application, go to the last slide, and click the New Slide icon to create a new slide.

▶ Pull down the Insert menu and click Object; the Insert Object dialog appears.

▷ Click the option to Insert from file. A browse button appears. Use the browse button to locate the file that contains the object you want to insert. In this example, browse to the Midi folder on the *Multilit* CD, and choose one of the Midi songs you will find there.

▷ Now you decide whether to check the Link box on the Insert Object dialog. Figure 38-7 shows the location of this important setting. If you do not check the Link box, a copy of the object will be embedded in your presentation. If you check the Link box, PowerPoint will use the file you selected, from its current location, instead of copying it into the presentation.

▷ Click OK to close the dialog; the link appears on-screen.

▷ Click the Slide Show button to run your show, and when the link appears, click it and observe what happens.

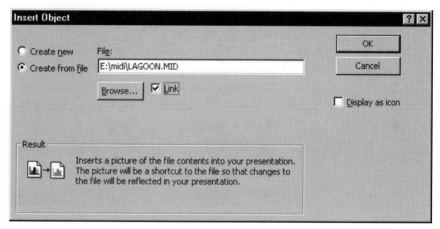

Figure 38-7   The Link box on the Insert Object dialog determines whether the object will be linked or embedded.

You might wonder how to decide whether to link or embed objects created with other applications. The answer depends on how disciplined you are in file management. Because when you publish an application, embedded files will get published as part of your PowerPoint show. Linked files must be published into folders that have the same relative positioning on the published medium as they did on your development machine.

The advantage of linking is that you conserve file space because there is only one copy of the file. This also makes applications easier to update. Since there is just one copy of the linked object, any change you make to it automatically takes place in the applications to which it is linked. The advantage of embedding an object is that you probably increase your chances of being able to publish your application reliably. You can also make changes to the embedded document apart from the original copy.

Animating Charts, Tables, Graphs, and OLE Objects

Show-Me Movie:
"Animating Charts"

All of the items you have learned to create in this chapter—charts, tables, graphs, and equations—are all objects. As objects, they have action settings and can be animated, just like any other object in a PowerPoint application. Something special happens when you try to animate a chart, however, because charts have special animation capabilities in PowerPoint. Follow these steps:

▷ Go to the slide that contains the chart you want to animate. In this example, open your *Practice* application, use the Slide Sorter to find the slide on which you created a chart earlier in this chapter, and double-click the slide to edit it.

▷ Right-click the chart, and when the menu pops out, choose Custom Animation.

▷ When the Custom Animation dialog appears, notice how the Chart Effects tab is active.

▷ In the Check to Animate Slide Objects list, check the box next to your chart. Even more of the options on the Chart Effects tab activate.

▷ Pull down the Introduce Chart Elements menu and have a look at your options for displaying the chart. As illustrated in Figure 38-8, you can introduce your data all at once, by series, by category, by element in series, and by element in category. For now, choose by Series.

▷ Use the Animation and Sound menus to set special effects according to your taste.

▷ Click the Preview button to preview the effect.

▷ Click the Order and Timing tab. If you want the data in the slide to appear in sequence automatically, set the start animation option to Automatically; otherwise, you click your mouse to sequence through the data.

▷ Click OK to close the Custom Animation dialog, then click the Slide Show button to rehearse the animation.

▷ To make changes in the animation, simply repeat these steps.

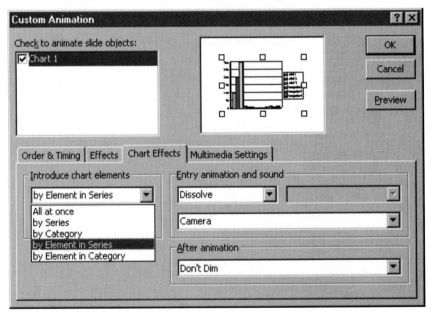

Figure 38-8   Pulling down the Introduce Chart Elements menu on the Chart Effects tab of the Custom Animation dialog.

exercises

1. Go to the slide in your *Practice* application that contains the chart you created in this chapter. Play with the animation effects. What is the most effective way, in your opinion, to present this data? How did you set the chart's animation settings? Did you decide to blast the chart onto the screen all at once, or did you choose to display the data in a sequence? If sequential, did you set the option to display the data automatically, or upon mouse clicks? Why?

2. Using the Windows Explorer, note the size in bytes of your *Practice* application. Then go to the last screen of your *Practice* application, use the Insert—Object dialog to link (with the link box checked) the *greeting.wav* file from the *Audio* folder of the *Multilit* CD, and save the *Practice* application. Using the Windows Explorer, note the revised file size of the *Practice* application. How much bigger did it get? Once again, go to the last screen of your *Practice* application. This time, use the Insert—Object dialog to embed the *greeting.wav* file. (*Note:* To embed the greeting, make sure the link box is unchecked.) Use the Windows Explorer to note the revised file size of the *Practice* application. How does the size compare? How much more did the file size increase when you embedded the *greeting.wav* file as compared to when you just linked it?

3. Use the Insert Object menu to create the following equation. Either put it on the last screen of your *Practice* application, or create a new screen for it.

$$x = \frac{-b \pm \sqrt{b^2 - 4ac}}{2a}$$

Part Eight
Distributing Multimedia Applications

You can do it.

—Bela Karolyi, 1996 Olympic U.S. women's gymnastic team coach, to athlete Kerry Strug

After helping you learn how to create multimedia applications, it is appropriate for this book to conclude with a tutorial on distributing them. Why? Because multimedia should not be a spectator sport. Everyone should be able to create and contribute, not just sit back and consume.

There are four ways to distribute a multimedia application created with PowerPoint. First, if you have Windows, you can use the Pack and Go Wizard to pack your application into a compressed format from which it can be installed onto other Windows computers. If your application is small, you can pack it onto diskettes. If your application is large, however, it may require too many diskettes for practical use; not to worry, because you can also use the Pack and Go Wizard to publish an application on higher capacity media such as zip disks or CD-Rs. You just need to make sure that the computer on which you are planning to install the application can handle the medium onto which you pack your application. Whether or not you plan to distribute your application, Pack and Go is a handy way to create a backup of your application onto another medium besides your hard disk drive, so you will not lose your work should an accident occur causing data loss on your hard disk drive. Chapter 39 teaches how to use the Pack and Go wizard.

Second, you can publish PowerPoint applications as Web pages on the World Wide Web. PowerPoint includes an incredibly capable Web publishing tool. Chapter 40 is a tutorial on World Wide Web publishing with PowerPoint.

Third, you can broadcast your presentation live over the Internet, using the Presentation Broadcast feature. Presentation Broadcast lets you invite people to attend the broadcast. If they cannot be there in person, you can archive the broadcast on the Web so people can view it later. Chapter 41 contains a tutorial on broadcasting an application with PowerPoint.

Finally, if you would like to take advantage of the collaborative power of the Internet, you can share your application during a live videoconference. Not only can you show your presentation as part of a videoconference, but you can also yield control to let another user navigate it. You can even permit another person to edit your presentation during the videoconference. Thus, you become a worldwide multimedia collaborator over the Internet. Chapter 42 features PowerPoint's collaborative capabilities that are based on the inclusion of Microsoft's NetMeeting technology into PowerPoint.

Publishing on Disks with the Pack and Go Wizard

After completing this chapter, you will be able to:

- **Understand the purpose of the Pack and Go Wizard**

- **Know how the wizard works and what it packs**

- **Distribute a multimedia application on diskettes**

- **Tell other uses how to unpack and install the application**

- **Pack a multimedia application for distribution on a CD-R, Zip, or other brand of read/write removable disk**

The Pack and Go Wizard makes it possible for Windows users to distribute PowerPoint presentations on disk to other Windows users. The wizard packs your PowerPoint *.ppt* file along with all of the sounds, graphics, and movies you inserted or linked into it. You can tell the wizard to write the packed application to any kind of media your computer can write to, such as diskettes, Jaz, or any other brand of read/write disks. You just need to make sure that the kind of disk you use can be read by the computer on which the application will be installed. You can even include the PowerPoint Viewer, which Microsoft permits you to distribute for free along with your presentation if you think your users do not already have PowerPoint.

Because multimedia applications tend to be large, you will need several blank diskettes if you choose to pack a presentation onto floppy disks. As this chapter will teach you, PowerPoint handles this well by prompting you to insert another disk each time the current disk fills up.

A large show might take up more diskettes than you care to distribute. Happily, the cost of CD-R (compact disc-recordable) drives has been declining steadily, along with the price of the CD-R discs, which cost less than a dollar each when purchased in quantities of 50 or more. For authors fortunate enough to have a CD-R drive, this chapter contains a special section showing how to publish PowerPoint applications on CDs as well as on diskettes.

Note for Macintosh users: When this book went to press, the Pack and Go Wizard was not available for the Macintosh. To check the status of PowerPoint publishing on the Macintosh, go to the PowerPoint Web site at http://www.microsoft.com/powerpoint and follow the links to downloads and support for the Macintosh version of PowerPoint.

Packing an Application Onto Diskettes

Show-Me Movie:

"Publishing on Diskettes with the Pack and Go Wizard"

To use the Pack and Go Wizard to publish an application onto diskettes, follow these steps:

▷ Get several blank, formatted diskettes ready. In this example, you will need about eight blank diskettes to publish the *History of Flight* application.

▷ It is important to keep the disks clearly labeled and numbered throughout the publication process. On the stick-on label of the first disk, write the name of your application, followed by Disk 1. For example, if you are publishing the *History of Flight* application you created in Chapters 26 through 31, write this on the label:

History of Flight
Disk 1

▷ Insert disk 1 into your computer's floppy disk drive.

▷ Use PowerPoint to open the application you want to publish. In this example, open the *Flight* application you created in your *Multilit* folder.

▷ To begin packing the application, pull down the File menu and choose Pack and Go.

▷ The first screen of the Pack and Go Wizard appears, as illustrated in Figure 39-1. Click the Next button to continue.

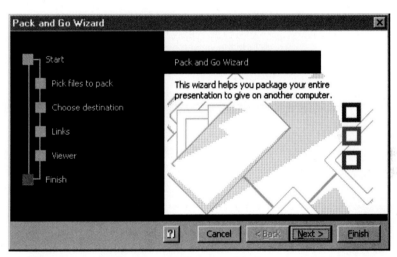

Figure 39-1   The first screen of the Pack and Go Wizard. Click the Next button to continue.

▷ The second screen asks what presentation you want to package. In this example, since you already have the *Flight* application open, check the box that says Active presentation, as illustrated in Figure 39-2. Then click the Next button to continue.

▷ On the third screen, the wizard asks what drive to which the presentation should be copied. In this example, since you are publishing to diskettes, click to select the A drive, as illustrated in Figure 39-3. Then click the Next button to continue.

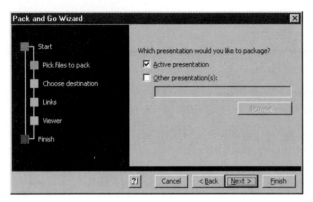

Figure 39-2   The second screen of the Pack and Go Wizard asks what presentation you want to pack.

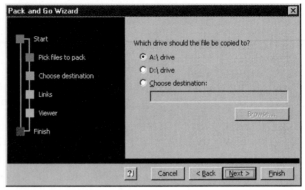

Figure 39-3   The third screen of the Pack and Go Wizard asks what drive you want to publish onto.

> On the fourth screen, the wizard asks whether you want to include linked files and fonts used in your presentation. In this example, since you want the linked files (i.e., the movies and ambient sounds) to be included, check the box next to the option to include linked files, as illustrated in Figure 39-4. If you used any exotic fonts not likely to be found on the targeted machine, you can check also the option to embed fonts, but be aware that the wizard does not permit you to publish fonts that have built-in copyright restrictions. Click the Next button to proceed.

> On the fifth screen, the wizard asks whether you want to publish the PowerPoint Viewer. As illustrated in Figure 39-5, you will probably want to click the option to include the viewer, especially if you suspect that one or more of the machines onto which you plan to install the application lacks PowerPoint.

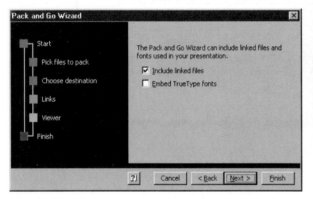

Figure 39-4   The fourth screen of the Pack and Go Wizard asks whether you want to include linked files and fonts.

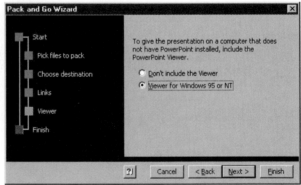

Figure 39-5   The fifth screen of the Pack and Go Wizard asks whether you want to include the PowerPoint Viewer.

> On screen six, the Pack and Go Wizard tells you what will happen when you click the Finish button to begin packing your presentation, as illustrated in Figure 39-6. If any of the settings are wrong, you can click the Back button to page back to previous screens of the wizard. In this example, if everything looks all right, click the Finish button.

> A status dialog will keep you informed as the Pack and Go Wizard packs your application.

> If the diskette fills up, which will definitely happen in this example in which you are publishing the *History of Flight* application, the wizard will prompt you to insert another blank diskette, as illustrated in Figure 39-7.

Figure 39-6 On screen six of the Pack and Go Wizard, if the settings look OK, click the Finish button to pack the presentation, or click Back to change the settings.

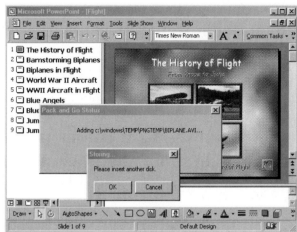

Figure 39-7 The Pack and Go Wizard displays a status dialog to keep you informed as your application gets packed. Here, the wizard is prompting you to insert another blank diskette.

> Label each disk before you put it into the drive. For example, if you are about to put in disk 2 of your *History of Flight* application, write this on the disk's stick-on label:

> **History of Flight**
> **Disk 2**

> If the Pack and Go Wizard reports any errors during the publication process, you should correct those errors, then repeat the process by pulling down the File menu and running the Pack and Go Wizard again.

> Do not distribute diskettes to your users if errors happened during the publication process.

Note: Beware of embedded objects when publishing an application onto disks, because the wizard may have trouble locating them. If you have embedded objects, the wizard may ask you to help find where they are. If so, help the wizard. Be aware that on playback, however, PowerPoint may also have trouble finding embedded objects. Therefore, it is best to link, as opposed to embed, objects if you are planning to publish via the Pack and Go Wizard.

Distributing Diskettes to End Users

Show-Me Movie:
 "Installing a Packed
 Presentation from Diskettes"

As always, before you distribute diskettes to your users, you should test the disks and make sure they work properly. Put disk 1 into your computer, and use Windows to run the *pngsetup* program on disk 1. Only after you verify that the application installs and runs properly should you consider distributing the diskettes. When you do distribute your application, you should include instructions on how to install it. Since the installation process is so simple, you can tell the average user something like this: "To install the *History of Flight* application, put disk 1 into your diskette drive and use Windows to run the *pngsetup* program on disk 1. The Installer will prompt you with additional instructions as needed. When prompted, enter *Flight* as the name of the destination folder."

If your users are more experienced, your instructions can be briefer. On the label of disk 1, you can write simply:

> **Run *pngsetup* to install.**
>
> **When prompted, enter *Flight* as the name of the destination folder.**

If your users are novices, however, you will need to supply more detailed instructions, explaining how to "run" the *pngsetup* program. Here is an example:

- **Insert disk 1 into your diskette drive.**

- **Use the Windows Explorer to locate the *pngsetup* program on the diskette.**

- **Double-click *pngsetup* to run it. The Pack and Go Setup dialog appears.**

- **When the Pack and Go Setup dialog asks you for the destination folder, enter c:\flight (assuming your hard drive letter is *C;* substitute a different letter if your hard drive is not *C*).**

As a courtesy, you should always recommend that the user specify a folder in which to unpack your application. Otherwise, the files will unpack to the root of the user's hard drive, resulting in clutter that could confuse or even irritate the user. The name of the destination folder cannot be longer than eight characters. If the destination folder does not already exist, the *pngsetup* program will create it. The *pngsetup* program will warn the user if any files on the distribution diskettes are going to replace any files on the user's computer, and if so, the user will have an opportunity to stop the installation or permit it to continue.

Publishing on Zip Disks and other High-Capacity Read/Write Disks

Because of the large file sizes of waveform audio, full-color graphics, and especially movies, multimedia applications tend to be large. If you publish a large application on diskettes, you will need many floppy disks! If you completed the tutorial earlier in this chapter, in which you packed the *History of Flight* application onto diskettes, for example, you discovered that it required eight (or more) diskettes, even though the application is relatively small. Many users have higher capacity read/write drives, such as the popular Zip drives. If you know that the computer onto which you are planning to distribute a PowerPoint application has a Zip drive, you can use it as your publishing medium. To do so, follow these steps:

- Insert a blank, formatted disk into your Zip drive.

- Use PowerPoint to open the application you want to publish. In this example, open the *Flight* application you created in your *Multilit* folder.

- To begin packing the application, pull down the File menu and choose Pack and Go.

- The first screen of the Pack and Go Wizard appears, as you saw in Figure 39-1. Click the Next button to continue.

- The second screen asks what presentation you want to package. In this example, since you already have the *Flight* application open, check the box that says Active presentation (see Figure 39-2). Then click the Next button to continue.

- On the third screen (see Figure 39-3), the wizard asks for the drive to which the presentation should be copied. Click to select the drive letter of your Zip drive. Then click the Next button to continue.

▷ On the fourth screen, the wizard asks whether you want to include linked files and fonts used in your presentation. In this example, since you want the linked files (i.e., the movies and ambient sounds) to be included, check the box next to the option to include linked files (see Figure 39-4). If you used any exotic fonts not likely to be found on the targeted machine, you can also check the option to embed fonts, but be aware that the wizard does not permit you to publish fonts that have built-in copyright restrictions. Click the Next button to proceed.

▷ On the fifth screen, the wizard asks whether you want to publish the PowerPoint Viewer. As was illustrated in Figure 39-5, you will probably want to click the option to include the viewer, especially if you suspect that one or more of the machines onto which you plan to install the application lacks PowerPoint.

▷ On screen six, the Pack and Go Wizard tells you what will happen when you click the Finish button to begin packing your presentation (see Figure 39-6). If any of the settings are wrong, you can click the Back button to page back to previous screens of the wizard and change the settings. In this example, if everything looks right, click the Finish button.

▷ A status dialog will keep you informed as the Pack and Go Wizard packs your application.

▷ If the Pack and Go Wizard reports any errors during the publication process, you should correct those errors, then repeat the process by pulling down the File menu and running the Pack and Go Wizard again.

Distributing Zip Disks to End Users

When you get your application published onto the Zip disk without any errors, you are ready to distribute the disk. Remember that the user will need to have a Zip drive in order to install your application from a Zip disk. Before you distribute the Zip disk, you should test it and make sure it works properly. Use Windows to run the *pngsetup* program on the Zip disk. Only after you verify that the application installs and runs properly from the Zip disk should you consider distributing the disk. When you do distribute your application, you should include instructions on how to install it. Since the installation process is so simple, you can tell the average user something like this:

> **To install the *History of Flight* application, put the disk into your Zip drive and use Windows to run the *pngsetup* program you'll find on it. The Installer will prompt you with additional instructions as needed.**

> **When prompted, enter *Flight* as the name of the destination folder.**

If your users are more experienced, your instructions can be briefer. On the label of the disk, you can write simply:

> **Run *pngsetup* to install.**

> **When prompted, enter *Flight* as the name of the destination folder.**

If your users are novices, however, you will need to supply more detailed instructions, explaining how to "run" the *pngsetup* program. Here is an example:

▪ **Insert the disk into your Zip drive.**

▪ **Use the Windows Explorer to locate the *pngsetup* program on the Zip disk.**

▪ **Double-click *pngsetup* to run it. The Pack and Go Setup dialog appears.**

▪ **When the Pack and Go Setup dialog asks you for the destination folder, enter c:\flight (assuming your hard drive letter is C; substitute a different letter if your hard drive is not C).**

Publishing on CD-R Drives

Happily, the cost of CD-R drives has declined steadily, along with the price of the CD-R discs, which cost less than a dollar each when purchased in quantities of 50 or more. If you have a CD-R drive, and if your users have CD-ROM or DVD drives, publishing on CD-R will be the least expensive method of distributing your application on disk. Since CD-ROM runs so fast, you can publish your application in an executable format that will run directly from the user's CD-ROM or DVD drive, thereby saving valuable disk space on the user's hard drive.

To publish a PowerPoint application on a CD-R in an executable format, follow these steps:

▶ Create a folder on your hard disk drive to hold temporarily the published application. In this example, since you will be publishing the *History of Flight* application, create a folder called *FlightPub*. Make sure there is enough disk space available to hold the published application. In this example, you will need about 15 megs.

▶ Use PowerPoint to open the application you want to publish. In this example, open the *Flight* application you created in your *Multilit* folder.

▶ To begin packing the application, pull down the File menu and choose Pack and Go.

▶ The first screen of the Pack and Go Wizard appears, as you saw in Figure 39-1. Click the Next button to continue.

▶ The second screen asks what presentation you want to package. In this example, since you already have the *Flight* application open, check the box that says Active presentation (see Figure 39-2). Then click the Next button to continue.

▶ On the third screen (see Figure 39-3), the Wizard asks for the drive to which the presentation should be copied. Click to select the option to choose destination, and browse to the folder you created in step 1 of these instructions. Then click the Next button to continue.

▶ On the fourth screen, the wizard asks whether you want to include linked files and fonts used in your presentation. In this example, since you want the linked files (i.e., the movies and ambient sounds) to be included, check the box next to the option to include linked files (see Figure 39-4). If you used any exotic fonts not likely to be found on the targeted machine, you can also check the option to embed fonts, but be aware that the wizard does not permit you to publish fonts that have built-in copyright restrictions. Click the Next button to proceed.

▶ On the fifth screen, the wizard asks whether you want to publish the PowerPoint Viewer. As was illustrated in Figure 39-5, you will probably want to click the option to include the viewer, especially if you suspect that one or more of the machines onto which you plan to install the application lacks PowerPoint.

▶ On screen six, the Pack and Go Wizard tells you what will happen when you click the Finish button to begin packing your presentation (see Figure 39-6). If any of the settings are wrong, you can click the Back button to page back to previous screens of the Wizard and change the settings. In this example, if everything looks OK, click the Finish button.

▶ A status dialog will keep you informed as the Pack and Go Wizard packs your application.

▶ If the Pack and Go Wizard reports any errors during the publication process, you should correct those errors, then repeat the process by pulling down the File menu and running the Pack and Go Wizard again.

▷ After the Pack and Go Wizard publishes your application with no errors, use the Windows Explorer to locate the *pngsetup* program in the folder to which you just finished packing it, and double-click the *pngsetup* program to run it.

▷ When the *pngsetup* program asks you where to install the application, type the letter of your hard drive, followed by the name of another temporary folder that is going to hold the files to be published onto the CD-R. In this example, name the folder *FlightCD*.

▷ Follow the on-screen instructions as the *pngsetup* program installs the appliation to your temporary folder, in this example, *FlightCD*. When the *pngsetup* program asks if you want to run the application, say Yes, and run through it to make sure it runs properly. Then close the application. Now you are ready to burn the files onto your CD-R.

▷ To create the CD-R, get your CD-R creation software running, such as Easy CD Creator, a very popular program that comes with many CD-R drives.

▷ Use your CD-R software to copy all of the files from the temporary folder you created in the previous steps (*FlightCD* in this example) to the root of the CD-R.

▷ After you are done creating the CD-Rs, you can delete the temporary folders (*FlightPub* and *FlightCD* in this example) if you want to free the disk space they consume on your hard disk drive.

Distributing CDs to End Users

Before you distribute a CD to your users, you should test the CD and make sure it works right. Use the Windows Explorer to find on the CD the published PowerPoint, which is *Flight.ppt* in this example. Only after you verify that the application runs properly should you consider distributing the CD. When you do distribute your application, you should include instructions on how to run the application. If your users are experienced, your instructions can be very brief. On the CD's label, you can write simply:

Use the Windows Explorer to run the *Flight.ppt* application on this CD.

If you do not have PowerPoint, use the *pptview.exe* program on this CD to run the *Flight.ppt* application.

If your users are novices, you will need to supply more detailed instructions, explaining how to run the application. Here is an example:

▪ **Insert the CD into your CD-ROM drive.**

▪ **Use the Windows Explorer to locate the *pptview* program on the CD.**

▪ **Double-click *pptview* to run it. The Run dialog appears.**

▪ **Make the *pptview* program run the *Flight.ppt* application on the CD.**

Setting Presentation Options

In Chapter 31, you learned how to set presentation options by pulling down the Slide Show menu and choosing Set Up Show. When you publish a PowerPoint application via the Pack and Go Wizard, the presentation options get published along with it. If your users are novices and your application has navigation buttons built in, you may want to disable PowerPoint's default navigation options. Otherwise, novices could be confused if they click outside a button and the slide advances. To disable PowerPoint's default navigation options, follow these steps:

▷ Pull down the Slide Show menu and choose Set Up Show; the Set Up Show dialog appears.

▷ Click the option to set up the application to be browsed at a kiosk.

▷ Click OK to close the dialog.

▷ Pull down the File menu, choose Pack and Go, and use the Pack and Go Wizard to publish the application.

The PowerPoint Viewer

Previously in this chapter, you learned how the Pack and Go Wizard asks whether you want to include the PowerPoint Viewer (see Figure 39-5). When you choose to include the PowerPoint Viewer, a program called *pptview32.exe* gets packed along with your application. The *pptview32.exe* program can run slide shows on Windows computers that do not have Microsoft PowerPoint installed. Microsoft permits you to distribute the PowerPoint Viewer freely with no additional license.

When this book went to press, some of the PowerPoint 2000 features, such as picture bullets and automatic numbering, were not supported by the Viewer. You can download the latest version of the Viewer and get updates and additional information from the PowerPoint Web site at http://www.microsoft.com/powerpoint.

e x e r c i s e s

These exercises are designed to help you develop your multimedia publishing skills. First you create a tiny application, then you publish it onto diskettes. Finally, you test the diskettes to make sure the application installs properly.

1. Use PowerPoint to create a new application called *Pubtest* in the *Multilit* directory on your hard disk drive. Use the Insert Picture tool to display the picture of the ocean on the *Multilit* CD in the file *backdrop\ocean.bmp*. Resize the ocean picture to make it fill the slide. Use the Insert Movies and Sounds—Sound from File tool to insert the following waveform audio file from the *Multilit* CD: *ambient\ocean.wav*. When PowerPoint asks if you want the audio to begin automatically, say Yes. Click the Slide Show icon to run the show. You should hear the ocean. Press Esc to stop the show, and save the *Pubtest* application in your *Multilit* folder.

2. Get a few blank, formatted diskettes ready. Pull down the File menu, choose Pack and Go, and use the Pack and Go Wizard to publish onto the diskettes the *multilit\pubtest* application you created in exercise 1. When the wizard asks if you want to include the PowerPoint Viewer, choose the option to include it. When the wizard prompts you to insert more diskettes, make sure you keep them clearly labeled as disk 1, disk 2, and so forth. This exercise will require about three diskettes.

3. Put the first disk you published in exercise 2 into the diskette drive and run its *pngsetup* program. Follow the installation instructions that appear on-screen. When the Pack and Go Setup dialog asks you for the destination folder, enter **c:\ocean** (assuming your hard drive letter is *C;* substitute a different letter if your hard drive is not *C*). When the Pack and Go Setup dialog asks if you want to run the presentation, say Yes. If you see and hear the ocean, you are well on your way to becoming a multimedia publisher. If not, review this chapter and try to figure out what went wrong.

40

Publishing a PowerPoint Presentation as a Web Page

After completing this chapter, you will be able to:

▓ Understand what happens when you choose the PowerPoint option to Save as Web Page

▓ Know how to set the Web Page publishing options so the browsers your users have will be able to view your presentation over the Internet

▓ Understand what kinds of links and objects get published to the Web, and which ones do not work over the Web

▓ FTP your published presentation to the Web

▓ Rehearse the presentation over the Web

● The most universal way to distribute a presentation is to publish it to the Web via PowerPoint's Save as Web Page tool. Once your presentation has been mounted on the Web, anyone in the world who has Internet access can run it with a Web browser. You need to be aware of some differences among the different Web browsers, however, because not all browsers can support all of the bells and whistles you can publish to the Web with PowerPoint.

This chapter teaches you how to publish PowerPoint presentations to the Web. You will learn how to save your application as a Web page, mount it on the Web, and provide worldwide access to it. You will be provided with an FTP tool that you can use to maintain and update your Web sites. You will also learn about the differences among Web browsers and how to cope with them.

Saving a Presentation as a Web Page

Show-Me Movie:
"Saving a Presentation as a Web Page"

When you choose the option to save a presentation as a Web page, PowerPoint goes through your presentation and creates a separate HTML file for each one of your slides. The filename of your first slide is the name of your presentation followed by the *.htm* filename extension. If you publish the *History of Flight* application as a Web page, for example, the first slide will be named *flight.htm.* The HTML files for the rest of your slides get placed into a folder that the Save as Web Page tool creates in the same place as the *flight.htm* file. This folder is also the place where any sounds and graphics used in your presentation get placed.

The best way to learn how to save a presentation as a Web page is to just do it. Follow these steps:

▷ Use PowerPoint to open the presentation you want to publish. In this example, open the History of Flight application you created in Chapters 26 to 31.

▷ Pull down the File menu and choose Save as Web Page; the Save as Web Page dialog appears as illustrated in Figure 40-1.

▷ Out on the Web, pages have titles. To set the title for this presentation, click the Change Title button.

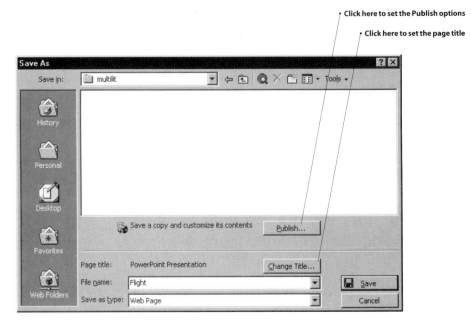

Click here to set the Publish options

Click here to set the page title

Figure 40-1   The Save as Web Page dialog.

▷ When the Set Page Title dialog appears, type the title you want. In this example, type **History of Flight**, as illustrated in Figure 40-2. Click OK to close the Set Page Title dialog.

▷ To set the Web page publishing options, click the Publish button. The Publish as Web Page dialog appears, as illustrated in Figure 40-3.

Figure 40-2   The Set Page Title dialog.

Figure 40-3   The Publish as Web Page dialog.

▷ In the Browser Support section, click the level of the browser for which you are publishing your application. Your presentation will work best if you click the high fidelity setting, but it may not be viewable by browsers other than the Microsoft Internet Explorer. If you want Netscape users to be able to view your presentation, for example, you will probably need to choose the lower setting. Choose the All Browsers option if you want to target all of the browsers. In this example, if you are using the Microsoft Internet Explorer, choose the high-fidelity setting. Otherwise, choose the lower setting.

▷ Click the Web Options button to make the Web Options dialog appear.

▷ As illustrated in Figure 40-4, the Web Options dialog lets you turn on or off the navigation controls; you will probably want them on.

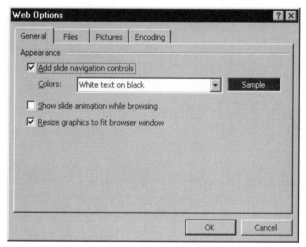

Figure 40-4   The Web Options dialog.

▷ If you want slide animations to appear, click to check the option to show slide animation while browsing. In this example, leave it unchecked.

▷ By default, the option to resize graphics to fit the browser window is checked; in this example, leave it checked.

▷ Click OK to close the Web Options dialog.

▷ If you want the finished page to appear in a browser after the presentation gets published, click the box near the bottom of the Publish as Web Page dialog where it says to Open published Web page in browser. In this example, since you will definitely want to preview your published page, click the box to check this option.

▷ Now you are ready to publish the page. Click the Publish button.

▷ Wait awhile as the page gets published.

▷ When the page is done publishing, the published Web page will open in a browser if you had chosen that option. If you did not choose that option, you can use your browser's File—Open menu to open the page manually.

▷ Figure 40-5 shows how the published page is displayed in a frame alongside the outline of your presentation. You can navigate by clicking buttons in the presentation or by clicking items in the outline.

▷ Please note that the movies and sounds will not play unless you chose the high-fidelity setting when you published the presentation.

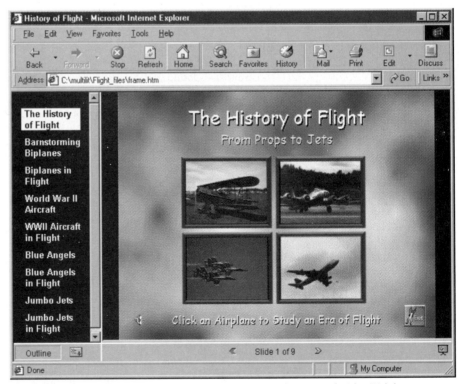

Figure 40-5   How the *History of Flight* application appears when viewed with a Web browser.

Mounting Published Files on the Web

After you have created the Web page and tested it locally by viewing it with a Web browser to make sure it published right, you are ready to transfer the files to the Web. You transfer the files with an FTP program. *FTP* stands for File Transfer Protocol, which is the standard way of transferring files over the Internet. FTP programs use the File Transfer Protocol to send and receive files over the Internet.

Installing the FTP Software

Show-Me Movie:
"Installing the FTP Software"

FTP programs are available in Windows and Macintosh versions that are free to users affiliated with educational or charitable institutions. For Windows users, the program to use is called WS_FTP. Macintosh owners use a program called Fetch. Both programs have a graphical user interface that makes it easy to upload and download files, inspect the contents of the folders at your Web site, delete and rename files, and create new folders.

Created by Ipswitch, Inc., *WS_FTP* stands for Windows Socket File Transfer Protocol. It is available in a professional edition called WS_FTP PRO and a freeware version called WS_FTP LE that may be used without fee by any U.S. government organization, by individuals for noncommercial home use, and by students, faculty, and staff of academic institutions.

Created by Dartmouth College, Fetch is licensed free to users affiliated with educational or charitable organizations. Other users can get an individual license for $25.

To download either WS_FTP for Windows or Fetch for the Macintosh, follow the steps in Table 40-1.

Table 40-1   How to Download and Install the FTP Software

WS_FTP LE for Windows	Fetch for Macintosh
▶ Click the link to download WS_FTP LE at the *Multilit* Web site.	▶ Fetch is distributed as a BinHex type self-extracting archive. In order to unpack this archive, you must first have StuffIt Expander installed on your Macintosh. If you do not have StuffIt Expander on your Mac, follow the *Multilit* Web site links to StuffIt Expander and install it.
▶ Follow the on-screen instructions that prompt you to fill out a form to download WS-FTP LE for Windows.	
▶ When your browser asks what folder you want to download the archive into, choose the folder you want to put it in. Normally you would use your *temp* folder.	▶ Click the link to download Fetch at the *Multilit* Web site.
▶ After the file gets downloaded, click your Start button, choose Run, and run the *ws_ftple.exe* program you will find in the folder where you downloaded the file.	▶ If StuffIt Expander has been installed on your computer, Fetch will automatically self-extract and put a Fetch Installer icon on your desktop.
▶ The WS_FTP LE install program will guide you through the installation; follow the on-screen instructions.	▶ Double-click the Installer icon to install Fetch.
▶ When you get to the screen that asks you what version of WS_FTP LE you want to install, the correct version for your system will be preselected. Do not change that unless you know for sure that you should choose something different.	▶ When the Installer asks whether you want to install Fetch as a fat binary or application only, you can choose application only to install a copy of Fetch with native code for your kind of Macintosh, or a "fat binary" that will run natively on any Macintosh.

How to Configure a New FTP Connection

Show-Me Movie:
"Configuring an FTP
Connection"

The first time you use your FTP software, you will need to configure a new connection for your Web site. The new connection configuration identifies the domain name of your Web server and your user ID on that server. To configure a new connection, follow the steps in Table 40-2.

Table 40-2   How to Configure a New FTP Connection

WS_FTP LE for Windows	Fetch for Macintosh
▶ Double-click the WS_FTP LE icon to get it running; you can also click your Start button, choose Programs, and in the WS_FTP group, select WS_FTP95 LE.	▶ Double-click the Fetch icon to get it running. If you cannot find the Fetch icon, choose File from the menu, then Find, and do a search for the file containing the word *Fetch*.
▶ The Session Profile dialog shown in Figure 40-6 appears. The first time you run WS_FTP, you need to create a new profile for your World Wide Web server. Otherwise, you just select the profile you created in a previous session.	▶ With Fetch running, pull down the Customize menu and choose New Shortcut; the Bookmark Editor dialog appears as shown in Figure 40-7.

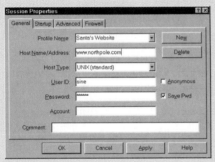

Figure 40-6   The WS_FTP Session Profile dialog.

Figure 40-7   The Fetch Bookmark Editor Dialog.

To create a new profile, follow these steps:

▶ In the Session Profile dialog, click New; this clears the fields in the Session Profile dialog.

▶ In the Profile Name field, type the name you want the new session profile to be called; for example, if your name is Santa Claus, you might call it Santa's Web site.

▶ In the Host Name field, type the domain name of your World Wide Web site, such as **www.northpole.com**

▶ Leave the Host Type set to Automatic detect, unless you have a reason to change it.

▶ In the User ID field, type the user ID by which you are known on your Web server; this will probably be the first part of your e-mail address, up to but not including the @ sign.

▶ If you are not concerned about the security of your password on your local PC, you can type your password into the Password field, but this is not recommended for security reasons; if you do not enter your Password here, your server will prompt you for it when you connect later on in this tutorial.

▶ Click Save to save the profile.

▶ In the Name field, type the name you want the new connection's shortcut to be called; for example, if your name is Santa Claus, you might call it Santa's Web site.

▶ In the Host field, type the domain name of your World Wide Web site, such as **www.northpole.com**

▶ In the User ID field, type the user ID by which you are known on your Web server; this will probably be the first part of your e-mail address, up to but not including the @ sign.

▶ Type your password into the Password field. If you are not using your own computer, you should erase the password field when you are done using Fetch, to prevent the user after you from accessing your Web site.

▶ Click OK to save the shortcut.

How to FTP Files to the Web

Show-Me Movie:

"How to FTP Files to the Web"

Figure 40-8 shows how the WS_FTP program has graphical controls that make it very easy for Windows users to FTP a file to your Web site. Figure 40-9 shows the Fetch controls that enable Macintosh users to do likewise.

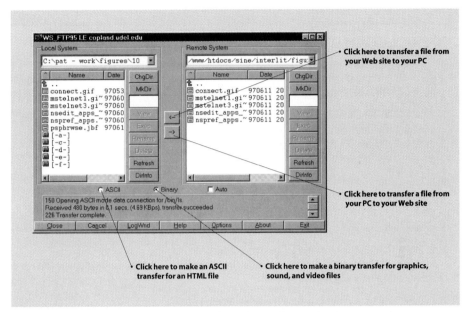

Figure 40-8 The WS_FTP program displays folder listings for your local system and the remote system.

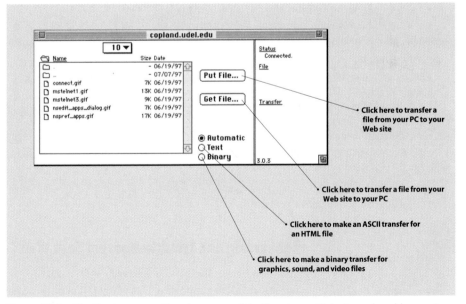

Figure 40-9 The Fetch program lists the names of the files at your Web site and enables you to upload and download files from the Internet.

Suppose you want to FTP the *History of Flight* application you published earlier in this chapter from your computer to your World Wide Web account. Follow the steps in Table 40-3.

Table 40-3   How to FTP Files to the Web

WS_FTP LE for Windows	Fetch for Macintosh
▶ If you are not connected to the network, establish your network connection now.	▶ If you are not connected to the network, establish your network connection now.
▶ 🖥️ If WS_FTP is not already running, double-click the WS_FTP icon; the Session Profile dialog appears.	▶ 🖥️ If Fetch is not already running, double-click the Fetch icon; the New Connection window appears.
▶ In the WS_FTP Session Profile dialog, pull down the Profile Name selection box and choose your Web site's profile; if your Web site is not listed in the selection box, follow the steps in Table 40-2 for creating an FTP Session Profile.	▶ Click cancel and then pull down File and choose Open Shortcut.
▶ To transfer files to the Web successfully, you must send them in the proper format, which is ASCII for text, and Binary for images, sounds, movies, and other kinds of documents. WS_FTP can do this automatically if you click the Auto button. Click the Auto button now.	▶ Click the Shortcuts menu, and choose the shortcut you saved when you configured your FTP connection in Table 40-2.
	▶ When you are connected to your Web site, the Fetch window will display a listing of the names of the files residing at your Web site.
▶ On the Local System side of the WS_FTP window, browse to the folder in which the file you want to transfer resides; in this example, browse to the *Multilit* folder on your hard drive.	▶ To transfer a file to the Web, drag-and-drop the file from your desktop into the Fetch window. Do that now with the *Flight.htm* file in your *Multilit* folder.
▶ On the Remote System side of the WS_FTP window, browse to the folder in which you want to transfer the files; in this example, that will be the main folder of your World Wide Web account.	▶ To transfer an entire folder to the Web, drag and drop the folder from your desktop into the Fetch window. Do that now with the *Flight_files* folder, which contains the rest of your published application.
▶ To transfer your application's startup file, click once on *flight.htm* on the Local System side of the WS_FTP window; then click the → button to transfer the file to the Web. After the transfer completes, you will see your *flight.htm* file listed on the Remote System side of the WS_FTP window in your World Wide Web folder.	
▶ To transfer the *Flight_files* folder, which contains the rest of your published application, click once on the folder's name on the Local System side of the WS_FTP window; then click the → button to transfer the folder to the Web. Be patient, or do something else, while the files transfer. After the transfer completes, you will see your *Flight_files* folder listed on the Remote System side of the WS_FTP window in your World Wide Web folder.	

Rehearsing and Troubleshooting Your Web Page

After you have transferred your application's startup page (*Flight.htm* in this example) and folder full of supporting files (*Flight_files* in this example), you should test them to make sure they work properly. Use your Web browser to go to the http address of the *Flight.htm* file you mounted on the Web. Follow all of the links and make sure everything published right. If you have trouble, you need to troubleshoot the problems.

One of the most common problems happens when the folder full of supporting files (*Flight_files* in this example) gets transferred to a different location in your Web space than the startup page (*Flight.htm* in this example). When you save your file as a Web page, all of the supporting files (e.g., icons, background textures, movies, sounds, and graphics) are saved in a supporting folder. If you move or copy your Web page to another location, you must also move the supporting folder to the same location in order that the links to your Web page remain intact.

If you have a problem you cannot resolve, PowerPoint's Web page troubleshooter may be able to help. Pull down the PowerPoint Help menu, go to the Help index, and key in Troubleshoot Web page options.

Things That Will Not Publish to the Web

If things on your Web page do not work quite the same way they do in your PowerPoint application, it is possible that your presentation contains something that does not publish to the Web. Check the limitations listed in Table 40-4 to see if your problem is due to a feature that is not supported in a Web presentation. More information about Web publishing limitations is documented in the Troubleshoot Web page section of the PowerPoint Help window.

Table 40-4   PowerPoint Features That Are Not Supported in a Web Presentation in a Browser

Animations	Action Settings	Other Limitations
Introduce text options *By Word* and *By Letter* do not work	The *Run Macro* option does not work	The ⌫Backspace key shows the last slide viewed, not the previous slide
The *After animation* option to make a shape appear dim does not work	The *Highlight click* and *Highlight when mouse over* check boxes do not work	The *Update automatically* check box does not work for dates and times
Sound only plays for a single slide (it does not continue playing when you jump to another slide)	*Object action* options do not work	The *Shadow* and *Embossed* font formatting effects do not work
Chart effects do not work	A hyperlink to a custom show does not play the show	
Linked and embedded objects do not play (but inserted movies and sounds do)	The play sound option does not play if the object is also formatted as a hyperlink (for example, a hyperlink to the next slide)	
The *Spiral, Stretch, Swivel,* and *Zoom* paragraph effects do not work	If a hyperlink on the slide master is covered by a placeholder (even an empty placeholder), the hyperlink does not work	
Rotated text is not animated separately from the attached shape; instead, the AutoShape and the text are animated together		
If you have automatic slide transitions, all mouse click animations on the slide behave as automatic animations		
Animated GIF pictures are static if they are grouped together		

Netscape Issues

Note: The information provided here was based on version 4.7 of Netscape Navigator. By the time you read this, a more recent version may be available. If so, you will need to reconsider these issues in light of the newer version.

By default, when you publish a Web presentation with PowerPoint 2000, the HTML file is optimized for Microsoft Internet Explorer 4.0 or later. If your Web presentation will be viewed by people who use any version of Netscape Navigator, you must click the option to include *All browsers listed above (creates larger files)* when you set the browser support level in the Publish as Web Page dialog (see Figure 40-3). If you run the presentation with Netscape Navigator, you will notice the following limitations:

- Animations and slide transitions are not supported.

- Animated GIF images might not be animated if the presentation is saved with a screen size setting of 640 × 480 or less. You set the screen size by clicking the Pictures tab of the Web Options dialog shown previously in Figure 40-4.

- The slide is not scaled to fit the browser window; instead, the slide stays at the screen size selected on the Pictures tab of the Web Options dialog, as illustrated in Figure 40-10.

- The presentation cannot be viewed full screen.

- You cannot open or close frames.

- The active slide title is not highlighted in the outline pane.

- The mouse does not highlight elements in the outline pane.

- Sounds and movies do not play.

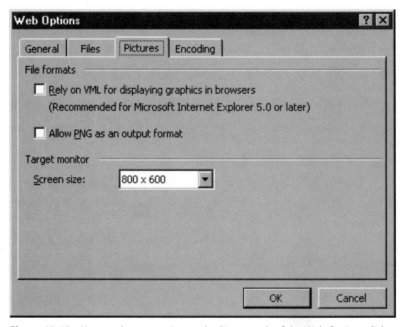

Figure 40-10   You set the screen size on the Pictures tab of the Web Options dialog.

How to Delete and Rename Files at a Web Site

If you do a lot of Web page publishing, you will encounter situations in which you want to delete or rename files at a Web site. Your FTP software lets you accomplish both of these tasks. To delete and rename files at a Web site, follow the steps in Table 40-5.

Table 40-5   How to Delete and Rename Files at a Web Site

WS_FTP LE for Windows	Fetch for Macintosh
▶ If WS_FTP is not already running, double-click the WS_FTP icon; the Session Profile dialog appears.	▶ If Fetch is not already running, double-click the Fetch icon; the New Connection window appears.
▶ In the WS_FTP Session Profile dialog, pull down the Profile Name selection box and choose your Web site's profile.	▶ Click Cancel and then pull down File and choose Open Shortcut.
▶ Click once on the name of the file you want to delete or rename on the Remote System side of the WS_FTP window in your World Wide Web folder.	▶ Click the Shortcuts menu, and choose the shortcut you saved when you configured your FTP connection in Table 40-2.
▶ To delete the file, click the Delete button. WS_FTP will ask if you really want to delete it. Click the Yes button if you really want to.	▶ Click once on the name of the file you want to delete or rename to select it.
▶ To rename the file, click the Rename button. WS_FTP will prompt you to type the new name for the file. Type the new filename, and click OK.	▶ To delete the file, pull down the Remote menu and choose Delete Directory or File.
	▶ Fetch will ask if you are sure you want to delete the file. If you are sure, click Delete.
	▶ To rename the file, pull down the Remote menu and choose Rename Directory or File. Fetch will prompt you to type the new name for the file. Type the new filename, and click OK.

Tip: When you publish a PowerPoint presentation to the Web, you can rename the *.htm* file to your Web server's default filename. If you do that, users can go to your presentation without having to type a filename. That is how the author made the URL of the *Necc Keynote* http://www.udel.edu/fth/necc instead of http://www.udel.edu/fth/necc/keynote.htm. If you rename the .htm file, do not rename the supporting files folder; it must retain the name PowerPoint gave it when you published the application.

Coping with Case-Sensitive File Servers

Remember that many World Wide Web servers are case sensitive. For example, the Unix operating system is case sensitive. On a Unix-based server, if a Web page is named *Flight.htm* and you try to access it as *flight.htm*, you will get a File Not Found error. Folder names are also case sensitive.

Make sure you are typing the case correctly when you advertise the URL address of your Web page. Suppose you invite someone via e-mail to visit your Web page, for example, and you need to type the Web address of your page into your e-mail message. To avoid making a typing mistake, first use your Web browser to go to the page. Then copy and paste the Web address from the Address field of your browser into your e-mail message.

How to Create New Folders on the Web

As the number of files at your Web site increases, you may choose to create folders to help keep your site organized. When the author published to the Web his NECC keynote presentation, for example, he first created a folder called *necc* to contain it; then he FTP'd the published application to the *necc* folder. To create a folder at your Web site, follow the steps in Table 40-6.

Table 40-6   How to Create a New Folder at Your Web Site

WS_FTP LE for Windows	Fetch for Macintosh
▶ If WS_FTP is not already running, double-click the WS_FTP icon; the Session Profile dialog appears.	▶ If Fetch is not already running, double-click the Fetch icon; the New Connection dialog appears.
▶ In the WS_FTP Session Profile dialog, pull down the Profile Name selection box and choose your Web site's profile.	▶ In the Fetch New Connection dialog, pull down the Shortcuts menu and choose your Web site's server. Then click OK to open the connection.
▶ On the Remote System side of the WS_FTP window, make sure your current directory is the one in which you want to create a new folder. If it is not, double-click on a directory name to select it, or double-click on the two dots at the top of the directory listing to move back a level of directory structure.	▶ In Fetch directory window, make sure your current directory is the one in which you want to create a new folder. If it is not, double-click on a directory name to select it, or double-click on the two dots at the top of the directory listing to move back a level of directory structure.
▶ Click the MkDir button to make the Input dialog appear.	▶ From the menu bar, choose Directories, then Create New Directory to make the dialog appear.
▶ Enter the name of the folder you want to create, and click OK.	▶ Enter the name of the folder you want to create, and click OK.
▶ Wait for a second or two, while the new folder is created. Then WS_FTP will refresh the directory listing, and the new folder will appear in it.	▶ Wait for a second or two, while the new folder is created. Then Fetch will refresh the directory listing, and the new folder will appear in it.
▶ If you want to enter the new folder, double-click its icon.	▶ If you want to enter the new folder, double-click its icon.

e x e r c i s e s

1. Following the tutorial steps in this chapter, use PowerPoint's Save as Web Page feature to save your *History of Flight* application as a Web page. When you get to the Publish as Web Page dialog (see Figure 40-3), set the browser support to the Netscape setting. After the Web page is saved, open it with your Web browser. Run through your presentation. Do the graphics appear? Do the sounds play? Do the movies play? Can you click and drag the border of the window frame to make the outline pane wider or thinner? If you resize the browser window, do your slides resize to fill the new window size?

2. Repeat exercise 1 but this time choose the high-fidelity setting. After the Web page is saved, open it with Microsoft Internet Explorer (if you do not have the Internet Explorer, open it with Netscape) and run through your presentation. Answer the same questions that appear at the end of exercise 1. Also, state which Web browser you used, Internet Explorer or Netscape.

3. If you have Netscape, use it to open the high fidelity version of the *History of Flight* application that you saved as a Web page in exercise 2. What differences do you observe in the way Internet Explorer and Netscape present the *History of Flight?* When this book went to press, Netscape users would get a message stating that "This presentation contains content that your browser may not be able to show properly. This presentation was optimized for more recent versions of Microsoft Internet Explorer. If you would like to proceed anyway, click here. . . ." What happens now, when you try viewing it with Netscape? Do you get the same message? What happens if you click to proceed anyway? How do you explain the differences you observe? Why doesn't the application display the same way in both browsers? What does the computer industry need to do about this dilemma?

41 Broadcasting PowerPoint Presentations on the Internet

After completing this chapter, you will be able to:

- **Understand what it means to broadcast a presentation**

- **Set up a broadcast for a private audience within an intranet, or for a worldwide audience over the Internet**

- **Schedule a broadcast and invite participants to attend it**

- **Broadcast the presentation with your voice narrating it live**

- **Include a live video window of yourself presenting the show**

- **Rehearse the broadcast before you do it live over the Internet**

- **Publish the broadcast to the Web so people can view it later if they cannot attend the live broadcast at the scheduled time**

● Presentation broadcasting enables you to schedule a day and time to present a PowerPoint show over a local area network (LAN) or worldwide over the Web. The people you invite to view the broadcast will see your presentation slides, hear your voice as you present the show, and, if you are using a video camera, they will see you as well. For people who cannot attend at the time you schedule the show, you can record the broadcast for future playback over the Web.

You should always rehearse the broadcast prior to presenting it. You can schedule such a rehearsal with yourself as the only participant and go through your presentation to make sure everything will broadcast properly.

Before you get started, however, you should be aware of some special needs. Presentation Broadcast is a Windows Media technology. When this book went to press, only Windows users could send and receive broadcasts. You must have the latest version of the Microsoft Internet Explorer, at least version 5.0 or later. As long as your audience has fewer than 16 people, you can use any named computer connected to a LAN-based Intranet or to the Internet to host the broadcast. If you have 16 or more people in the audience, however, you must have a special Microsoft product called NetShow Server to host the broadcast. NetShow Server will enhance any broadcast and is highly recommended if you choose to broadcast video to make yourself appear in a video window alongside your application. You do not need NetShow Server to complete the tutorial in this chapter.

Preparing a Broadcast

Scheduling a broadcast works a little differently, depending on whether you are using Microsoft Outlook, which is the e-mail part of Microsoft Office. If you are using Microsoft Outlook, you can schedule the broadcast as you would any other meeting. Outlook can be set to start PowerPoint automatically and prepare it for broadcast just before your scheduled broadcast time. If you are not using Outlook, the invitation mail will contain a hyperlink to the location of the broadcast. To attend the broadcast, the recipients follow the link to the broadcast.

Creating the Broadcast File Folder

Show-Me Movie:
"Creating the Broadcast File Folder"

If you or your system administrator has not already set your broadcast options, you need to use the Windows Explorer to create a shared file folder in which the broadcast files will reside. You only need to do this once, because you can use the same folder to contain all your broadcasts. PowerPoint will create a different subfolder within your broadcast folder for each broadcast you schedule. To create your broadcast file folder, follow these steps:

▷ File sharing needs to be enabled on your computer. To find out whether it is, click your computer's Start button and use Settings—ControlPanel—Network—File and Print Sharing to inspect the settings. If file sharing is not enabled, turn it on, then restart your computer to make the change take effect. Before you close the Network dialog, click the identification tab and note the name of your computer. You will need to know your computer's name later on when you set up the presentation broadcast and the instructions prompt you to enter the server name.

▷ Use the Windows Explorer to create a file folder. Name the folder *Broadcast*. If you want the live broadcast to be viewable over the Web, create the *Broadcast* folder in your computer's Web space. If you have the Microsoft Personal Web Server installed, for example, your Web space is *Inetpub\wwwroot* unless you named it otherwise when you installed it. Name the broadcast folder *Inetpub\wwwroot\Broadcast*. *Note:* If you want to install the Microsoft Personal Web Server, click your computer's Start button, click Help, search for the key word Personal Web Server, and follow the on-screen instructions.

▷ The folder you just created must be made shareable. Using Windows Explorer, right-click the folder and choose Sharing. When the Properties dialog appears, click the option to make the folder Shared As. Make the shared name *BROADCAST*, as illustrated in Figure 41-1. Do not close the Properties dialog yet.

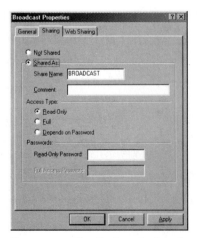

Figure 41-1 The Sharing tab of the Properties dialog.

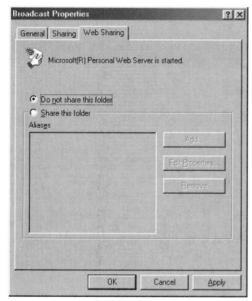

Figure 41-2   The Web Sharing tab of the Properties dialog.

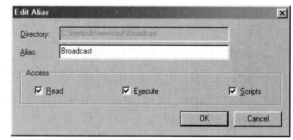

Figure 41-3   The Edit Alias dialog.

▷ If you created the folder in Web space, you need to make it executable. Click the Web Sharing tab on the Properties dialog. The Web Sharing tab appears as illustrated in Figure 41-2. Click the option to Share this folder; the Edit Alias dialog appears. In this example, enter the folder's alias as *Broadcast,* and check the box to make the files executable. All three boxes need to be checked—Read, Execute, and Scripts—as illustrated in Figure 41-3. Then click OK to close the Edit Alias dialog.

▷ Click OK to close the Properties dialog.

Setting Up and Scheduling the Broadcast

Show-Me Movie:
"Setting Up and Scheduling a Broadcast"

To set up and schedule the broadcast, follow these steps:

▷ Use PowerPoint to open the presentation you want to broadcast. In this example, open the *Keynote* presentation in the *Necc* folder of the *Multilit* CD. Because the CD is read-only, you need to put the presentation on your hard drive so you can save the broadcast settings you are about to make. To put the presentation on your hard drive, pull down the File menu, choose Save As, and save the *Keynote* presentation in the *Multilit* folder of your hard drive.

▷ Pull down the Slide Show menu, choose Online Broadcast, and click Set Up and Schedule. *Note:* If the Online Broadcast option is not visible, click the Slide Show menu's down-arrow to reveal more choices.

▷ The Broadcast Schedule dialog appears as illustrated in Figure 41-4. Click the option to Set up and schedule a new broadcast, and click OK.

▷ The Schedule a New Broadcast dialog appears. On the Description tab, fill in the information you want displayed on the lobby page of the broadcast. Figure 41-5 shows how you might fill this out for the NECC keynote presentation.

▷ To preview the lobby page in your browser, click the Preview Lobby Page button.

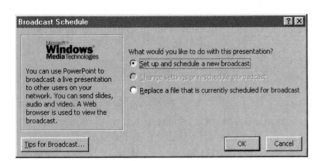

Figure 41-4   The Broadcast Schedule dialog.

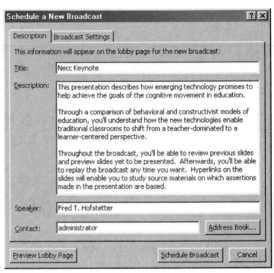

Figure 41-5   The Description tab of the Schedule a New Broadcast dialog.

Setting the Broadcast Options

If you or your system administrator has not already set your broadcast options, follow these steps:

▶ Click the Broadcast Settings tab; the Broadcast Settings appear as illustrated in Figure 41-6. Here you can set the options to send audio and/or video. The Send Audio box will be checked by default. Also check the Send Video box if you are using a camera.

▶ Click the Server Options button to set your server options. The Server Options dialog appears, as illustrated in Figure 41-7. Notice how the dialog has two steps.

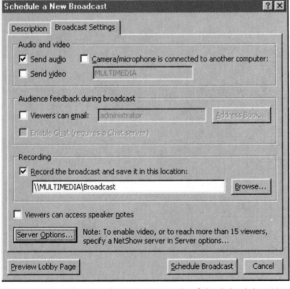

Figure 41-6   The Broadcast Settings tab of the Schedule a New Broadcast dialog.

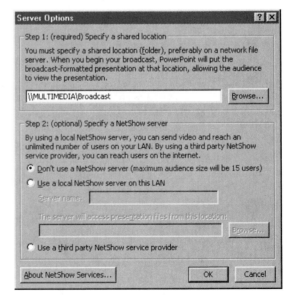

Figure 41-7   The Server Options dialog.

▷ In step 1 you must enter a shared folder location to which all participants have access. The format of the shared folder name must be *ServerName**FolderName* where *ServerName* is the name of your computer as identified on the Identification tab of your computer's network settings on Control Panel. In this example, assuming your computer's name is MULTIMEDIA, the shared folder name is *MULTIMEDIA**Broadcast*.

▷ In step 2, if you do not have a NetShow server, leave the option set to Don't Use a NetShow Server. If you have an audience of more than 15 people, you need to use a NetShow server on a LAN or a third-party NetShow service provider. If you are using a LAN server, contact your system administrator for the settings. If you use a NetShow service provider, follow its advice on how to set up and schedule a broadcast.

▷ After all of your server options are set, click OK.

▷ If you want the broadcast to be viewable afterwards for the benefit of people who cannot attend it live, click the option to record the broadcast, and in the *Record the broadcast and save it in this location* field, type the name of a shared folder to contain the recorded file. The format of the shared folder name must be *ServerName**FolderName*. In this example, assuming your computer's name is MULTIMEDIA, the shared folder name is *MULTIMEDIA**Broadcast*.

Scheduling the Broadcast

Now you are ready to schedule the broadcast. Follow these steps:

▷ Click the Schedule Broadcast button. Your e-mail program starts.

▷ If you have Microsoft Outlook, use it to schedule the broadcast. Figure 41-8 shows an example in which Santa Claus is being invited to attend a broadcast about emerging technology.

▷ If you do not have Outlook, enter the broadcast date and time in the message so your participants will know when your presentation will be broadcast. The URL of the broadcast will be included in the message automatically.

▷ If an Outlook window is open on your screen, pull down its File menu and choose Save to save the scheduling setup with your show. Then close the Outlook window.

Figure 41-8 Microsoft Outlook schedules the start time and end time of the broadcast.

Starting the Broadcast

Show-Me Movie:
    "Starting the Broadcast"

After you have set up and scheduled the broadcast, you can start it at any time. You should begin about 30 minutes prior to the scheduled time so you have enough time to check your microphone and make sure everything is ready. Especially if this is the first time you have done a broadcast, you should rehearse this process well in advance to make sure things are ready. Follow these steps:

▷ Open the presentation you want to broadcast. In this example, open the *Keynote* presentation from the *Multilit* folder on your hard drive.

▷ Pull down the Slide Show menu, choose Online Broadcast, and then click Begin Broadcast.

▷ The Broadcast Presentation dialog appears as illustrated in Figure 41-9.

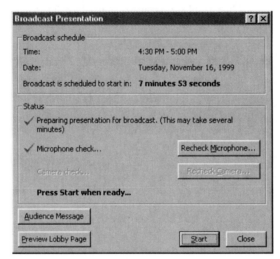

Figure 41-9   The Broadcast Presentation dialog steps you through a microphone check and a camera check if you are using a camera.

▷ If you want to send your audience any last-minute information, click Audience Message, type the message, and then click Update. Your audience will see the message on the broadcast's lobby page.

▷ To begin the broadcast, click the Start button. PowerPoint will ask if you really want to begin the broadcast now. Say yes.

▷ *Important:* When you start the broadcast, PowerPoint will attempt to create an instance of the NetShow encoder. If you get an error message indicating that the NetShow encoder cannot be found, you need to install the Windows Media Tools on your computer. Follow the link at the *Multilit* Web site to install the Windows Media Tools.

▷ As soon as your first presentation slide appears, you are broadcasting! Speak clearly into the microphone, and, if you are on camera, remember to smile. Make your presentation.

▷ When you are ready to end the broadcast, press Esc. You will get a dialog asking if you really want to end the broadcast. Say yes.

▷ If you set the option to record the broadcast for playback later, the broadcast file will get saved. Wait while this happens.

Viewing a Presentation Broadcast

To view a presentation broadcast, you must have Internet Explorer 5.0 or later. You should join a broadcast about 15 minutes early just in case the presenter has posted last-minute information on the lobby page. Follow these steps:

> If you are using Microsoft Outlook, you will receive an e-mail message reminding you to join the broadcast. When the reminder message appears, click the option to View this NetShow.

> If you are not using Outlook, you will have received an e-mail message containing the URL for the broadcast. Use Internet Explorer to open the URL for the broadcast.

> Your browser will display a lobby page that contains information about the broadcast and lets you know how much time is left before the broadcast begins. If the broadcast is late, the presenter can tell you by displaying a message on the lobby page. You can minimize the lobby page and continue working on some other task while you wait for the broadcast, which will begin automatically when the presenter starts broadcasting. Figure 41-10 shows a sample lobby page.

> When the presentation starts, it will appear in your browser as illustrated in Figure 41-11. You should be aware that there is a little latency in the broadcast. When the author broadcast a presentation to the Web using the Personal Web Server on a 266 megahertz (MHz) Pentium II laptop computer, for example, there was an 11-second lag time between what the author did and what the users heard and saw on-screen. This delay is normal and is due to the time it takes for the server to encode and broadcast the presentation. Remember that everything will work better if you purchase and install the Microsoft NetShow Server to host your presentation broadcasts.

> If you join a presentation late, you can click the option to View previous slides. This is a handy way to review what has already been presented. You can even use this option to look ahead at slides that have not been presented yet, as illustrated in Figure 41-12.

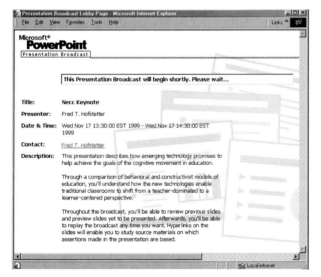

Figure 41-10   The lobby page for a presentation broadcast.

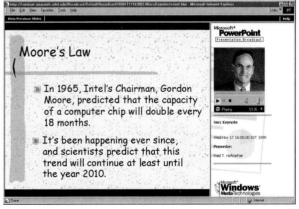

Figure 41-11   How the presentation appears while the presenter is broadcasting it.

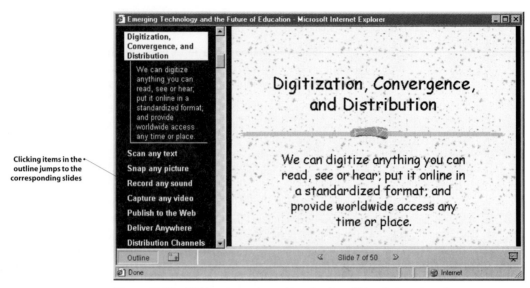

Clicking items in the outline jumps to the corresponding slides

Figure 41-12   Clicking the option to View Previous Slides during a broadcast brings up this window, which lets you view the presentation as a Web page and navigate it independently during the broadcast.

Replaying the Broadcast File

Show-Me Movie:

"Replaying and Reviewing the Broadcast"

If you chose the option to save the broadcast file when you set up your presentation broadcast (see Figure 41-6), it will have been saved in the designated file folder. After the broadcast has ended, users who visit the lobby page can press a Replay Broadcast button to review the broadcast, as illustrated in Figure 41-13. While replaying a broadcast, the user can click the option to View Previous Slides, which opens the presentation as a Web page and lets the user navigate via Next and Back buttons, or by clicking items in the presentation's outline, as illustrated previously in Figure 41-12.

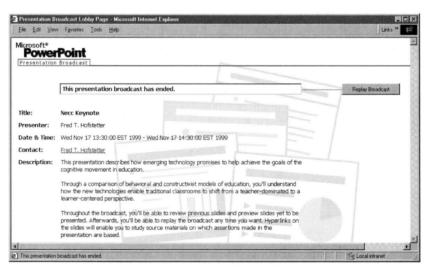

Figure 41-13   A Replay button appears on the lobby screen after the broadcast has ended.

Rescheduling or Deleting a Presentation Broadcast

If it becomes necessary to reschedule a presentation broadcast, you can do so. It is also possible to delete a scheduled broadcast, should you decide to cancel it altogether. To reschedule or delete a presentation broadcast, follow these steps:

▶ Open the presentation whose broadcast you want to reschedule.

▶ Pull down the Slide Show menu, choose Online Broadcast, and then click Set Up and Schedule.

▶ Click the option to Change settings or reschedule a broadcast, and then click OK.

▶ Select the broadcast you want to reschedule or delete.

▶ To reschedule the broadcast, click the Reschedule button and follow the on-screen instructions to create a revised e-mail message announcing the broadcast. Make sure you include the new time and date of the broadcast in the e-mail message.

▶ To delete the broadcast, click the Delete button and then use your e-mail program to send a message notifying your invitees that the broadcast has been canceled.

Changing the Lobby Page or Settings for a Scheduled Broadcast

At any time before or after a scheduled broadcast, you can change its lobby page or modify its settings. Whenever you need to change the setup, follow these steps:

▶ Open the presentation on which the lobby page or settings need to be changed.

▶ Pull down the Slide Show menu, choose Online Broadcast, and then click Set Up and Schedule.

▶ Click the option to Change settings or reschedule a broadcast, and then click OK.

▶ Select the broadcast you want to change, and then click Change settings.

▶ Make the changes, and then click the Update button.

Tips for Broadcasting

If your computer is connected to a network file server, you can boost performance by making the shared file folder in the Server Options dialog on the server instead of on your computer. If the shared folder is on your computer, users will be accessing files on your machine during the broadcast. This makes your computer do double duty, because it must both encode and serve the broadcast. More users will be able to view your broadcast if you place the shared file folder on a network file server when setting up a broadcast. If you have only one computer, however, you can still complete the tutorial in this chapter, because presentation broadcasting will work on a single machine.

If you want your broadcast to include live video, you should use a NetShow server. Broadcasting video without a NetShow server will tax your computer's resources and limit further the number of people who are able to view your presentation. If you do not have access to a NetShow server, however, you can still complete the tutorial in this chapter, because everything will work on a single machine.

If you want to host a chat as part of the presentation broadcast, you need to set up your computer to handle chat. For detailed instructions, follow the *Multilit* Web site link to Using Chat with Presentation Broadcasting. After the presenter's computer is configured for chat, the presenter can select the Enable Chat check box (see Figure 41-6) to allow chat, or clear the check box to prevent chat. If the presenter allows chat, the participants see an Online Chat button on the Event page. Clicking the button starts their chat client and takes them to the specified chat room.

To see more tips for broadcasting, pull down the PowerPoint Slide Show menu, choose Online Broadcast, and click Set Up and Schedule. When the Broadcast Schedule dialog appears, click the Tips for Broadcasting button.

e x e r c i s e s

1. Following the tutorial in this chapter, set up and schedule a presentation broadcast. If you happen to have more than one computer in the room with you, browse to the lobby page on one computer while you broadcast the presentation on the other. If you do not have two computers, see if you can open a browser window on your computer while it also broadcasts the presentation. What happens to the audio you broadcast via your microphone if you have the playback volume turned up in the room from which you are broadcasting? How many seconds lapse between echoes?

2. Invite a friend on another computer to view your presentation broadcast. What is the URL that your friend browsed to in order to view your presentation broadcast? How many tries did it take you to get the broadcast viewable by your friend? What were the major problems that you needed to overcome?

3. Set up and schedule a presentation broadcast with the audience feedback option turned on (see Figure 41-6). How well does the audience feedback option work? Do you think it would help to have someone on a nearby computer screen feedback messages for you? Or were you able to read the feedback messages in your e-mail window and still continue presenting effectively?

4. If you have a video camera installed on your computer, try including video in a presentation broadcast. If you have more than one computer at your site, can you broadcast acceptably across your LAN? What about over the Internet? Ask a friend at some remote connection to try accessing your broadcast. Does the video stream acceptably to your friend's computer? At what point do you feel you would need to install a NetShow Server to increase the performance of presentation broadcasting?

42 Collaborating Over the Internet in an Online Meeting

After completing this chapter, you will be able to:

▨ **Download and install the latest version of NetMeeting onto your computer**

▨ **Host an online meeting to share a PowerPoint show with participants you invite to the meeting**

▨ **Yield control of the presentation to the participants**

▨ **Regain control of the presentation**

▨ **Open a chat window and a whiteboard in which participants can collaborate**

▨ **Add and remove participants from an online meeting**

▨ **Participate in an online meeting to which you are invited**

▨ **Troubleshoot common problems that may arise in an online meeting**

● Perhaps the most powerful feature of the Internet is the way you can collaborate with other users. PowerPoint provides this capability with its built-in support for Microsoft's NetMeeting software. In this chapter, you join the worldwide network of NetMeeting users. You will learn how to join a meeting in progress or invite one or more users to join you in a meeting. You will be able to show them your presentation and discuss it with them in a chat window. If you want, you can yield control to the participants, who can then navigate and make changes to your presentation, while you watch. Figure 42-1 shows these features in action on the desktop of a meeting's host.

Before you can do these things, however, you need to make sure you have the latest version of NetMeeting installed on your computer. To find out what the latest version is, and to install it if you do not already have it, follow the *Multilit* Web site link to Microsoft's NetMeeting Web site.

Note: When this book went to press, NetMeeting was a Windows-only technology. Consequently, this chapter does not include instructions for the Macintosh.

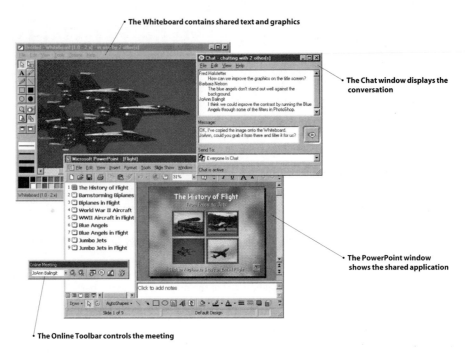

The Whiteboard contains shared text and graphics

The Chat window displays the conversation

The PowerPoint window shows the shared application

The Online Toolbar controls the meeting

Figure 42-1   An online meeting in progress.

Holding an Online Meeting

Show-Me Movie:
"Holding an Online Meeting"

Once you have the latest version of NetMeeting installed on your computer, you can use PowerPoint's built-in collaboration features. To host an online meeting, follow these steps:

▶   Open the presentation you want to share.

▶   You can either schedule a meeting or hold the meeting now.

▶   If you want to schedule a meeting that will be held later, you must have Microsoft Outlook installed. If you have Outlook, pull down the PowerPoint Tools menu, click Online Collaboration, and then click Schedule Meeting. When the Outlook window opens, use Outlook to schedule the meeting.

▶   If you want to hold the meeting now, pull down the Tools menu, click Online Collaboration, and then click Meet Now. The Find Someone dialog appears, as illustrated in Figure 42-2. Type or select the name of the first participant you want to invite to the meeting. Note that the participants you invite to an impromptu meeting must have NetMeeting running. It is easiest if they are all logged on to the same NetMeeting server you are on, otherwise, you will need to search for them in the Microsoft Internet Directory or type or select their directory server in the Select a Directory field in order to find them. If your participants are not logged on to the NetMeeting server, you may need to place a phone call to arrange the meeting.

▶   The first time you start an online meeting, you will be prompted to select a directory server. If you do not know what server to use, try the ils.chi-town.com server, which is one of the more popular NetMeeting servers available to the public. If the chi-town server is not available, follow the *Multilit* Web site links to publicly available NetMeeting servers.

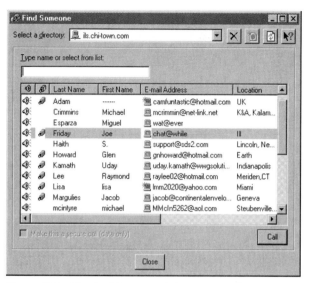

Figure 42-2 The Find Someone dialog appears when you
choose the option to hold a meeting now.

The Online Meeting Toolbar

During a meeting, the Online Meeting toolbar enables you to moderate the proceedings.
You can invite additional participants to join the meeting, remove participants, allow
others to edit and control the presentation, display the chat window, display the
whiteboard, and end the meeting when it is over. Table 42-1 lists and explains the
controls on the Online Meeting toolbar, which will appear on your screen as follows:

Table 42-1 Online Meeting Toolbar Controls

Control	Name	What It Does
JoAnn Balingit ▼	Participant list	Drops down a menu of participants currently in the meeting
	Call participant	Invites additional participants into the meeting
	Remove participant	Lets the host remove participants from the meeting
	Allow others to edit	Allows participants to edit and control the presentation during the meeting
	Display chat window	Allows participants to write messages in the meeting's chat room
	Display whiteboard	Allows participants to draw or type messages on the meeting's whiteboard
	End meeting	Allows an individual to leave the meeting, or lets the host end the meeting for the entire group

Only the host of the meeting gets to use the Online Meeting toolbar. If another participant wants more control of the Microsoft NetMeeting features during an online meeting, that participant must use the NetMeeting program directly by clicking Microsoft NetMeeting on the taskbar.

Adding Participants to a Meeting in Progress

Show-Me Movie:
"Adding Participants to a Meeting in Progress"

To invite another participant to join a meeting in progress, you place a NetMeeting call to the person. PowerPoint makes that easy to do by placing a control for that on the Online Meeting toolbar. Follow these steps:

▷   Click the Call Participant button on the NetMeeting toolbar.

▷   When the Find Someone dialog appears, as illustrated earlier in Figure 42-2, type or select the name of the participant you want to join the meeting, and then click the Call button.

▷   If the participant you call is available and decides to accept your invitation, the participant joins your meeting.

▷   If the participant you call is unavailable, you may need to place a phone call to deliver the invitation in person.

▷   To view a list of the participants who are currently in the meeting, click the Participant List button on the Online Meeting toolbar.

Answering a Call to Join a Meeting

Participants must have NetMeeting running on their computers in order to receive a call to join an online meeting. When you receive an online meeting call, the Incoming Call dialog will appear, as illustrated in Figure 42-3. Click Accept if you want to join the meeting, or click Ignore if you want to decline the invitation to join the meeting. The presentation that is being shared will appear on your screen. You will probably be curious to find out who else is in the meeting. To find out, switch to your NetMeeting window or click NetMeeting on your taskbar to inspect the participant list.

Figure 42-3   The Incoming Call dialog.

Removing a Participant from an Online Meeting

The host is the only person who can remove participants from an online meeting. If you want to remove someone, follow these steps:

▷   On the Online Meeting toolbar, pull down the Participant List and select the name of the person you want to remove.

▷   Click the Remove Participant button.

▷   The Online Meeting dialog appears as illustrated in Figure 42-4, asking whether you really want to remove the person from the meeting.

▷   If you click Yes, the person will be removed.

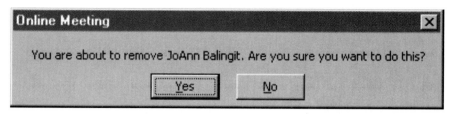

Figure 42-4   The Online Meeting dialog asks if you really want to remove the person from the meeting.

Ending or Leaving an Online Meeting

 Only the host of an online meeting can end it. If you are the host, you can end a meeting by clicking the End Meeting button on the Online Meeting toolbar. When you end a meeting, the other participants are automatically disconnected from each other.

If a participant wants to leave a meeting before it ends, the participant can do so by clicking Microsoft NetMeeting on the taskbar, then clicking Hang Up on the NetMeeting toolbar.

Collaborating in an Online Meeting

During an online meeting, there are many ways you can collaborate with the other participants. You can write text messages in the Chat window, work on the Whiteboard, and share the PowerPoint presentation in which the meeting began. The host can even click a button to permit other users to edit and control the presentation.

Yielding Control to Another Participant

 When an online meeting starts, the host is in control of the presentation. If you want to yield control to someone else, click the Allow Others to Edit button on the Online Meeting toolbar. Only one person can be in control at a time. To take control, the participant double-clicks anywhere in the presentation. A dialog box appears on the host's screen, asking if you want to let the participant take control, as illustrated in Figure 42-5. Click the Accept button if you do. The first time you try this, you will be amazed how the participant can take control of your presentation and have full access to your menus and toolbars.

When someone else is in control of the presentation, you will not have the use of your cursor. Instead, the initials of the person in control will appear next to the cursor. At any time, you can turn collaboration off by clicking the Allow Others to Edit button if you have control, or pressing [Esc] if you do not. This will return the cursor to you, and the

Figure 42-5   The Request Control dialog.

other participants then continue to watch you work. Remember that when collaboration is off, participants can still work simultaneously in the Chat window or on the Whiteboard.

Using the Whiteboard

Only the host of the meeting can open the Whiteboard from within PowerPoint. To do so, the host clicks the Whiteboard button on the Online Meeting toolbar. To close the Whiteboard, the host clicks the Whiteboard button again.

When the host opens the Whiteboard, it will appear on the participants' screens. If participants want to open the Whiteboard any other time, they must use the Microsoft NetMeeting program directly by clicking Microsoft NetMeeting on the taskbar.

Using the Chat Window

Only the host of the meeting can open the Chat window from within PowerPoint. To do so, the host clicks the Display Chat Window button on the Online Meeting toolbar. To close the Chat window, the host clicks the Chat button again.

When the host opens the Chat window, it will appear on the participants' screens. If participants want to open the Chat window any other time, they must use the Microsoft NetMeeting program directly by clicking Microsoft NetMeeting on the taskbar.

Sending a Message in Chat

Show-me Movie:
"Sending a Message in Chat"

When the Chat window is open, you can send a message by following these steps:

▷   Click once inside the message pane of the Chat window to position your cursor there.

▷   Type the message you want to send.

▷   Press ⌐Enter⌐ to send the message.

▷   If you want to send a private message to one of many participants, click that person's name in the Send To list before pressing ⌐Enter⌐, as illustrated in Figure 42-6.

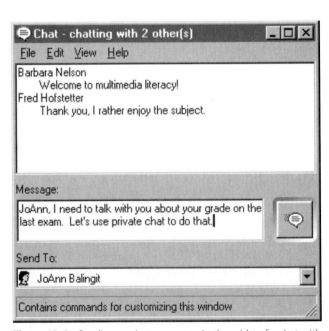

Figure 42-6   Sending a private message in the midst of a chat with other participants in a PowerPoint meeting.

Sending a File to All Participants

Show-me Movie:
"Sending a File to All
Participants"

During an online meeting, the host can send files to the participants. All of the participants in the meeting receive the files that are sent this way. If you are the host of a meeting and you want to send a file, such as a copy of the PowerPoint presentation you are sharing, follow these steps:

▷ Switch to your NetMeeting window, or click NetMeeting on the taskbar. The NetMeeting window appears.

▷ Pull down the NetMeeting Tools menu and choose File Transfer. The File Transfer window appears.

▷ Pull down the File Transfer window's File dialog, choose Add Files, and add the files you want to transfer. The files you choose appear in the window, as illustrated in Figure 42-7.

▷ You can send the file to everyone, or you can pull down the Send To menu at the right end of the toolbar to select a specific person to send the file to.

▷ To send the selected file(s), click the Send button.

▷ The participants who receive the file will see a dialog box that lets them refuse the file, close it, or open it. If they close or open the file, it will be stored in their *Program Files\NetMeeting\Received Files* folder.

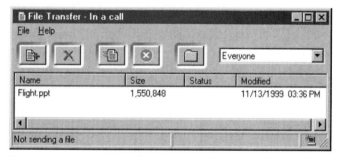

Figure 42-7 The File Transfer window.

Troubleshooting Online Meetings

The host of an online meeting should know about some common problems participants encounter in online meetings. By knowing about these problems in advance, you will know how to troubleshoot them should they occur.

1. If participants complain about a crosshatch pattern appearing on their screen, you probably have another window covering part or all of your presentation. Do not cover your PowerPoint presentation with other windows. This includes the Chat window and the Whiteboard. Any window that covers your shared PowerPoint presentation will result in a crosshatch pattern appearing in the covered part of the window on your participants' screens. The online meeting toolbar, on the other hand, is allowed to overlap your PowerPoint window. If you move the toolbar into the window, the participants will see it. Move the toolbar into the window if you want the participants to be able to observe how you moderate the meeting via the toolbar.

2. If participants complain about not being able to see all of the presentation, they probably have their screen resolution set lower than yours. Either make your

PowerPoint window smaller, or make your screen resolution match that of the participants. To change screen resolution, click the Windows Start button and choose Settings—Control Panel—Display.

3. Participants cannot print the PowerPoint presentation you are sharing with them unless you send it to them as a file, which they can then open on their computer and print.

Closing Comment

Because this is the last chapter of the book, it should probably conclude with some profound statement about the future of multimedia. This book is already full of statements attempting to be profound, however, so let's end instead with a quote from a famous old song: "We've only just begun." Now that you have started, enjoy the journey.

e x e r c i s e s

1. Check to see if you have NetMeeting installed on your computer. If you have trouble finding it, click the Start button, choose Find, and look for NetMeeting. Did you find NetMeeting on your computer? What version of NetMeeting is it? To find out, run NetMeeting, pull down the Help menu, and check the About box.

2. Go to the Microsoft NetMeeting site at www.microsoft.com/netmeeting. Find out what the most recent version of NetMeeting is for your computer. How does this compare with the version number you found in exercise 1? If your version of NetMeeting is out of date, follow the links at the Microsoft NetMeeting Web site to install the latest version.

3. Find a friend or a classmate who has NetMeeting installed. Following the steps given in this chapter for holding an online meeting, start an impromptu meeting, and invite your friend to join you. In order to make this work, before you start the meeting, you must ask your friend to get NetMeeting running and go to the same server you are planning to use. If you do not know what server to use, try the ils.chi-town.com server, which is one of the more popular NetMeeting servers available to the public. If the chi-town server is not available, follow the *Multilit* Web site links to publicly available NetMeeting servers. Try the following procedures with your friend, noting which ones work and which ones cause trouble at first:

Participant List	After the meeting starts, pull down the Participant List on the Online Meeting toolbar. Is your friend listed there as a participant?
Share the Show	Run through your show. Is your friend able to see it clearly? Note any problems your friend has viewing your presentation.
Chat	Click the Display Chat Window button to get a Chat window on screen. Use this window to communicate with your friend during this exercise. Ask your friend, for example, does your presentation appear OK?
Yield Control	After you run through your presentation, click the option to Allow Others to Edit, and see if your friend can take control of your presentation. Before you do this, however, be aware that if you yield control, your friend will be able to edit your presentation.
Remove a Participant	Send your friend a message in the Chat window saying you are going to try an experiment and remove your friend, then invite him or her back. When your friend acknowledges the message, click the Remove Participant button and remove your friend from the meeting.
Invite a Participant	Now click the Call Participant button and try to get your friend back into the meeting. How long does it take your friend to get back into the meeting?

Glossary

5.1 surround sound Dolby Digital surround sound; the nomenclature 5.1 describes the speaker configuration, which has five speakers (left-front, center-front, right-front, left-rear, and right-rear) plus one subwoofer for low bass sounds.

8-bit graphics A computer graphics mode capable of displaying up to 256 different colors simultaneously; 256 is 2 to the eighth power (2^8).

16-bit graphics A computer graphics mode capable of displaying up to 65,536 different colors simultaneously; 65,536 is 2 to the sixteenth power (2^{16}).

24-bit graphics A computer graphics mode capable of displaying up to 16,777,216 different colors simultaneously; 16,777,216 is 2 to the twenty-fourth power (2^{24}).

A/D converter Analog-to-digital converter. A device that uses quantization and sampling to transform a continuous analog waveform into a digital bit stream.

algorithm A sequence of processing steps that perform a particular operation, such as compressing a digital video to store it efficiently and decompressing it upon playback.

AltaVista A full-text key word search engine for the World Wide Web invented by the Digital Equipment Corporation. AltaVista is on the Web at http://www.altavista.com.

ambient sound A multimedia technique in which a waveform audio file keeps repeating to create the aural illusion that the user is in the place or situation where the sound was recorded.

animation In multimedia, animation is the use of a computer to create movement on the screen.

anonymous FTP A method by which computers on the Internet allow public access to certain files. These files can then be examined and downloaded by anybody. See *FTP*.

applet A little application that gets downloaded to your computer along with a Web page.

aspect ratio The relative width-to-height dimensions of a computer display's picture elements (pixels). The typical 800 × 600 screen has an aspect ratio of 4:3.

avatar An agent representing the user in a virtual reality system.

bandwidth The capacity of a device to process or transmit information. The more information it can handle per second, the greater its bandwidth.

baud rate See *bps*.

bitmap The picture formed by assigning different colors to the pixels on a computer screen; or the computer file that specifies how to color the pixels to create such a picture.

BMP The three-character filename extension for Microsoft Windows bitmaps. See *bitmap*.

bookmark A place in a World Wide Web document that you can jump to by name.

bounce To mix two or more audio tracks into one.

bps Bits per second. A measurement of the speed at which data is transmitted over a communications medium. Also known as *baud rate*.

cable modem A computer network connection device for providing high-speed Internet access over TV cables.

camcorder A combination of *camera* and *recorder*. A portable device that records video and sound onto videotape.

CAV Constant angular velocity. A type of videodisc that can hold 54,000 still frames per side, or 30 minutes of motion video. See also *CLV*.

CD Audio The use of a compact disc (CD) to play back recorded music. Compact discs can hold up to 75 minutes of audio. Multimedia computers can access the audio in increments as small as $1/75$ of a second.

CD Extra See *CD Plus*.

CD-I Compact disc–interactive. A multimedia delivery platform standard invented by Philips and Sony. The special players required for CD-I discs can also play CD Audio discs.

CD Plus   A multisession CD-ROM format in which a regular CD Audio session has been augmented by multimedia materials in another session. You can play back a CD Plus on a regular CD Audio player if you just want to hear the music, or you can install it on a multimedia PC and navigate through hypertext, buttons, pictures, and videos recorded in subsequent sessions. Also known as *Enhanced CD* and *CD Extra*.

CD-ROM   Compact disc—read-only memory. The use of a compact disc to store computer data. CD-ROMs can hold up to 680 MB.

CD-ROM XA   CD-ROM extended architecture. Increases to as much as 19 hours the amount of audio that can be stored on a compact disc by providing lower-quality recording and playback rates.

chroma key   Process whereby overlay cards display video on the screen and one of the colors becomes transparent. Any place the transparent color appears, you see the video input.

client   A computer seeking information on your behalf from a server on a network.

CLV   Constant linear velocity. A videodisc format that permits up to an hour of video to be recorded on each side of the disc. Most videodisc players cannot show still frames from CLV discs. See also *CAV*.

copyright   A law that secures for limited times to authors and inventors the exclusive right to their respective writings and discoveries. See *Fair Use*.

custom toolbox   An object-oriented set of multimedia development tools in the PODIUM multimedia application generator.

data rate   The speed of data transfer, normally expressed in bits or bytes per second. For example, the data rate of a single-speed CD-ROM is 150,000 bytes per second, or 150 KB; double-speed CD-ROMs are twice as fast at 300 KB per second.

dB   Decibel, a measurement of loudness. The higher the rating, the louder the sound. A whisper is 10dB; jet aircraft engines produce 130dB, which can permanently damage hearing.

DCT   Discrete cosine transform. A video compression algorithm that eliminates redundant data in blocks of pixels on the screen. It is used in JPEG (stills), MPEG (motion), and CCITT (fax) compression standards.

DejaNews   A search engine for Usenet newsgroups on the Internet. DejaNews is at http://www.deja.com/usenet.

digitizing   The process of converting analog audio and video signals into a digital format that can be stored, manipulated, and displayed by a computer. Digitizing is accomplished by A/D converters on scanners and audio/ video capture cards. See also *A/D converter*.

directory   An index to the files and subdirectories that are stored on a computer storage device.

dissolve   A transition effect between two sequential images on the screen. Dissolve patterns include splits, stripes, diagonals, and fades.

DLL   Dynamic link library. The expandable software technology that enables vendors to add features easily to the Microsoft Windows environment.

domain name   Allows numeric IP addresses (like *140.147.248.7*) to be expressed by names like *www.loc.gov*. See also *IP address*.

DSL   Digital subscriber line, a type of digital telephone connection that can send data at speeds up to 2 million bits per second.

DSP   Digital signal processor. A chip designed to process digitized sound and video quickly.

DVD   Digital versatile disc, an optical storage medium that uses CD-size discs (120mm diameter) to store 4.7 GB (gigabytes) per layer, which is seven times more than a CD can hold. Dual-layer DVDs can hold 8.5 GB on a single side, with 17 GB on a double-sided, dual-layer disc.

Enhanced CD   See *CD Plus*.

Ethernet   A high-speed network topology that provides access at speeds up to 10 MB per second, depending on how many users are connected to the network. Multiple users on an Ethernet can cause data collisions, which require data to be resent, causing the network to slow down. See also *token ring*.

fade   A gradual decrease in the brightness of an image or the loudness of a sound.

Fair Use   A section of the U.S. copyright law that allows the use of copyrighted works in reporting news, conducting research, and teaching. See the *Fair Use of Educational Multimedia* guidelines in the Demonstrations/Textbook Examples section of the *Multilit* CD.

FAQ   Frequently asked question. A list of frequently asked questions and their answers.

File Transfer Protocol   See *FTP*.

FireWire   High-speed serial technology for connecting peripherals to a computer; particularly popular on the Macintosh, where it is used to connect multimedia peripherals such as DV (digital video) camcorders and other high-speed devices like hard disk drives and printers.

flowchart   A logic diagram that illustrates the steps involved in an interactive decision-making process.

fps   Frames per second. A measure of the recording and playback rate of digital videos.

frame animation   Makes objects move by displaying a series of predrawn pictures, called frames, in which the objects appear in different locations on the screen.

frame rate   The speed at which frames are displayed on the monitor. Broadcast television in North America and Japan is displayed at 30 fps; in Europe it is displayed at 25 fps.

freenet   An organization that provides free Internet access to people in a certain area, usually through public libraries.

front-end   The creation or use of software to make it easy for people to perform computing tasks that would otherwise be too complicated or time-consuming for everyday use.

FTP   File Transfer Protocol. Allows users to send a file from one computer to another over the Internet.

full motion   Video played at the broadcast television frame rate. See also *frame rate*.

gateway   A computer whose role on a network is to reformat data sent from one computer into a form it can forward to another.

GB   See *gigabyte*.

GIF   Graphics Interchange Format. Invented by CompuServe for use on computer networks, GIF is the prevalent graphics format for images on the World Wide Web.

gigabyte   One billion bytes. A byte can hold a single character; a gigabyte can hold a billion characters. Abbreviated *GB*.

GigaPoP   One of the regional network aggregation points in the high-speed version of the Internet known by the name Internet2.

Gopher   A menu-based system for accessing Internet resources, including host computers, directories, and files.

Gopherspace   The connection of all existing Gopher servers.

graphics accelerator   A computer chip or circuit card that helps your PC process the specialized calculations required for 3-D imaging.

GUI   Graphical user interface. Allows direct manipulation of on-screen objects and events using icons, menus, toolbars, and dialog controls. Macintosh, Windows, and OS/2 Presentation Manager are examples of GUIs.

hard drive   A magnetic storage device on which computer programs and data are stored.

helper app   An application that helps a World Wide Web browser handle a file that the browser cannot deal with on its own.

home page   The Web page that serves as your main menu or home base on the Web. By linking things to your home page, you create a hierarchy that makes it easy to go to other Web pages and access resources on the Web. See *Web page*.

host   The main computer to which a user is connected when accessing the Internet.

hot spots   Places on the computer screen which, when selected, trigger the objects or events linked to them.

HTML   Hypertext markup language. The coding specification for creating Web pages. An HTML file contains the text you see on a Web page, plus special codes called markup that determine how the text gets displayed and how the user interacts with the Web page.

hyper   In multimedia, a prefix used to indicate that a link has given a new dimension to a word (hypertext), video (hypervideo), audio (hyperaudio), or part or all of a picture (hyperpicture).

IAB   Internet Architecture Board. The governing body that makes decisions about Internet standards.

IETF   Internet Engineering Task Force. A volunteer group that investigates and solves technical problems and makes recommendations to the Internet Architecture Board. See also *IAB*.

IMA   Interactive Multimedia Association. The IMA encourages the setting of industrywide standards for multimedia hardware and software.

Information Superhighway   A popular term coined by the White House to refer to the Internet with a metaphor the public could understand. See *Internet*.

input field   A blank space on a computer screen into which the user can type information.

internaut   A user who navigates the vast expanse of the Internet, much like an astronaut traverses outer space.

Internet   The worldwide network of networks that are connected to each other via the Internet Protocol (IP).

Internet address   Each computer on the Internet has a named address such as *www.loc.gov* (the Library of Congress Web site). See also *domain name*.

Interner Explorer   See *Microsoft Internet Explorer*.

IP address   A 32-bit numeric address of a computer on the Internet. An IP address consists of four numbers separated by periods. The numbers range from 0 to 255. The smallest address is 0.0.0.0 and the largest is 255.255.255.255. The number of IP addresses this scheme allows is 256^4, which is 4,294,967,296. See also *domain name*.

ISDN Integrated Services Digital Network. A high-bandwidth digital telecommunications network being installed gradually throughout the United States. This network handles voice, video, and data; it also supports videoconferencing.

ISO International Standards Organization.

IVD Interactive videodisc. A multimedia format in which a computer is connected to a videodisc player to provide interactive video capabilities.

Java An applet technology invented by Sun Microsystems. See *applet*.

JPEG Joint Photographic Experts Group. An ISO (International Standards Organization) body creating a new standard for digitizing still photographic images. The standard (which is also called JPEG) is cooperatively developed by more than 70 companies and institutions worldwide, including Sony, Philips, Matsushita, and Apple. The JPEG standard permits compression ratios ranging from 10:1 to 80:1—but the greater the compression, the lower the quality of the image.

K One thousand, a unit of computer measurement. For example, 150 K means 150,000. (Purists will tell you that the *K* used by computer scientists actually means slightly more than a thousand [1,024 to be precise], but for the measurements used in this book, a thousand is close enough and much easier to compute.)

KB See *kilobyte*.

kilobyte One thousand bytes. A byte can hold a single character; a kilobyte can hold a thousand characters. Abbreviated *KB*.

knowbot An information retrieval tool that you can train to go out on the Internet and find things for you.

layout The relationships among graphic design elements that appear on the screen, including text, pictures, icons, triggers, and buttons.

logic The use of conditional statements that act according to the values of variables. In multimedia, logic is used to make screens more sensitive to user needs and preferences. Logic is also used to increase the complexity, and hence the pizzazz, of multimedia special effects.

login To type your name and password to initiate a session with a host computer.

lossy Compression techniques in which decompressed images do not contain all the original information. JPEG and MPEG are lossy. The opposite is lossless compression. RLE (run-length encoding) is lossless but does not compress as much. See *RLE*.

markup Special codes inserted into a document, informing programs that read the document how to display or handle it. See *HTML*.

MB See *megabyte*.

meg See *megabyte*.

megabyte One million bytes. A byte can hold a single character; a megabyte can hold a million characters. Abbreviated *meg* or *MB*.

megahertz One million cycles per second. Processor speed is measured in megahertz. *Mega* means million, and *hertz* is one cycle per second. Abbreviated *MHz*.

megapixel One million pixels. See *pixel*.

metacognition Knowledge about your own thinking and learning.

metacognitive knowledge Knowledge about how tasks are performed and what makes some tasks more difficult than others.

MHz See *megahertz*.

Microsoft Internet Explorer Microsoft's World Wide Web browser.

MIDI Musical Instrument Digital Interface. The MIDI standard is a protocol by which electronic musical instruments communicate with computers and each other.

MIME Multipurpose Internet Mail Extensions. An Internet protocol that lets you attach a file to a mail message. When a user receives the message, the attached file gets decoded and stored on the user's PC.

modem A datacommunications device that connects a computer to a telephone line and lets the user transfer data at speeds ranging from 1,200 bits per second (bps) to 56 KB per second.

morph To transition one shape into another by displaying a series of frames that creates a smooth movement as the first shape transforms itself into the other shape.

Mosaic A World Wide Web browser created in 1993 by the University of Illinois supercomputer center. The graphical user interface in Mosaic made the Web very easy to use and led to the Web's becoming the most popular protocol on the Internet.

MPC Multimedia PC. An industrywide specification of the minimum hardware requirements needed for multimedia.

MPEG Motion Pictures Experts Group, an ISO (International Standards Organization) body creating a new standard for digital video. The standard (which is also called MPEG) was cooperatively developed by more than 70 companies and institutions worldwide, including Sony, Philips, Matsushita, and Apple. MPEG is emerging as the digital video standard for compact discs, cable TV, direct satellite broadcast, and high-definition television.

multiliterate   Understanding the principles of multimedia, its impact on the world, and how to use it for attaining business, professional, educational, and personal objectives.

multimedia   The use of a computer to combine and present text, graphics, audio, and video with links and tools that let the user navigate, interact, create, and communicate.

multisession   A type of CD-ROM drive that can play back CDs that have been recorded on more than once.

Netscape Navigator   One of the most popular World Wide Web browsers for the Internet.

NIC   Network Information Center. Every network on the Internet should have an NIC and a network administrator. Each NIC looks after the needs of the users connected to its network.

NOC   Network Operations Center. The organization responsible for the day-to-day operations of a network.

NTSC   National Television Standards Committee. The North American TV standard is named after the committee that created it.

overlay   To superimpose text and graphics on still or motion video images.

PAL   The European television standard that displays 25 frames per second. Used in all European countries except France; see also *SECAM*.

palette   A table of colors used to paint pixels on the screen.

PC Card   A plug-in credit card–sized PCMCIA peripheral for personal computers. See *PCMCIA*.

PCMCIA   Personal Computer Memory Card International Association. The name of a standards group that creates specifications for credit card–sized peripherals for personal computers. See *PC Card*.

Pentium   A microprocessor chip manufactured by Intel and its licensees. See *processor*.

pixel   Picture element—the tiny dots that make up the computer screen. Each pixel has a specific color and intensity level.

play list   A sequence of CD Audio clips, or MIDI or waveform audio files, that play back one after another.

point-to-point protocol   Establishes a TCP/IP connection to the Internet through a modem. Abbreviated *PPP*.

PPP   See *point-to-point protocol*.

processor   The brain in a computer where calculations and decisions get made.

protocol   A definition of how computers communicate with each other.

RAM   Random access memory. The main memory at the heart of a computer in which multimedia programs execute.

Red Book   The CD Audio protocol for recording audio onto compact discs. The minute-second-frame CD Audio addresses defined in the Red Book specification are known as Red Book addresses.

resolution   A measurement of the number of pixels on a display. The typical multimedia computer has a resolution of 800 × 600 pixels. See *pixel*.

RGB   Red, green, and blue. Each pixel displayed on the screen consists of a certain amount of red, green, and blue. For example, a black pixel has no red, green, or blue, whereas a white pixel has the maximum amount of each.

RLE   Run-length encoding. A lossless data compression technique that encodes the number of times a repeated data element recurs instead of recording each occurrence. For example, 12 red pixels in a row would be encoded as 12R instead of RRRRRRRRRRRR.

root directory   The primary directory on a hard disk from which all other directories branch. See also *directory*.

sampling   The process of measuring and recording the values of an analog signal at evenly spaced time intervals.

sampling rate   The number of times an analog signal is sampled each second. For example, CD Audio is recorded at a rate of 44,100 samples per second.

SCSI   Small Computer System Interface, a serial bus topology for daisychaining up to eight high-bandwidth devices, such as mass storage units, to a computer.

SECAM   Sequential Couleur Avec Memoire. The French national standard for color TV that is also used in Russia and eastern Europe. It operates at 25 frames per second.

self-extracting archive   A list of files that have been archived into a single executable file that decompresses itself automatically when the user runs the archive.

server   A computer on the Internet that provides information on demand to client computers. See also *client*.

shareware   Computer software distributed with no up-front cost. Users who try the software and wish to keep using it must pay a fee. Shareware is not free.

SMPTE   Society of Motion Picture and Television Engineers. Pronounced "sempty," SMPTE refers to a time code expressed in hours, minutes, seconds, and frames. SMPTE time code is written in the form HH:MM:SS:FF.

socket A portal on the Internet through which an application sends and receives information.

storyboard A time-based outline or script for a video or multimedia production.

subdirectory A directory inside another directory.

surf To browse an electronic medium for information. "Channel surfing" means to flip through the channels on a television set, looking for something that interests you. "Surfing the Internet" means to browse through the interconnected menus of information servers like Gopher and the World Wide Web.

surround sound See *5.1 surround sound.*

SVGA Super VGA. A screen resolution standard created by the Video Electronics Standards Association (VESA) that delivers a screen resolution of up to 800 × 600 with 256-color graphics.

tag A markup element in an HTML document. Tags are surrounded by brackets, such as the <P> tag that begins a new paragraph. See *HTML* and *markup.*

task analysis The process of hierarchically outlining an application's content.

TCP/IP Transmission Control Protocol/Internet Protocol. Computers connect to the Internet via TCP/IP.

telnet A protocol that allows users to log on to remote host computers on the Internet.

terminal The computer that connects to a host. The terminal can be a personal computer.

timeout A situation in a multimedia program in which the user must respond before a predetermined time limit expires and a default action occurs.

token ring A network topology that passes data in tokens that travel the network in a ring. Token ring networks run at 4 MB or 16 MB per second and are less prone to slow down as the number of users increases. See also *Ethernet.*

unzip To expand a zipped file back to its original uncompressed state. See *zip.*

upload To send a file to your host or to a remote host on the Internet. See also *host.*

URL Uniform resource locator. The address of a resource on the World Wide Web.

USB Universal Serial Bus, a popular way of connecting to your computer peripherals such as digital cameras, scanners, printers, fax machines, zip drives, and optical mice.

vector animation A vector is a line that has a beginning, a direction, and a length. Vector animation makes objects move by varying these three parameters for the line segments that define the object.

videodisc An optical disc on which video signals are recorded. Usually 12 inches in diameter, videodiscs are used for entertainment and to provide video in multimedia training applications. Videodiscs come in two formats: CAV and CLV. See also *CAV* and *CLV.*

WAIS Wide-area information servers. An Internet utility that provides full-text search capability.

waveform audio A method of creating sound by digitizing an analog audio waveform and storing the digital samples on a disk in a WAV file, from which the recording can be played back on demand. *WAV* stands for waveform.

wavetable A list of numbers that describe the desired waveshape of a sound.

WebCam Popular term for a videoconferencing camera designed for use on the World Wide Web.

WebMaster The person in charge of creating and maintaining a World Wide Web site.

Web page An HTML hypertext document on the World Wide Web. See *HTML.*

Webzine A magazine that is published on the Web instead of being printed on paper.

winsock The name of the dynamic link library (DLL) that enables the Windows operating system to open sockets on the Internet.

World Wide Web A networked hypertext system that allows documents to be shared over the Internet. Developed in Geneva at the European Particle Physics Center (CERN). Abbreviated *WWW.*

WWW See *World Wide Web.*

Yahoo A subject-oriented index of the World Wide Web. Located at http://www.yahoo.com.

zip To compress one or more computer files into a smaller file that contains the same information in a compressed format that occupies less space on a computer.

Bibliography

Alexander, Joanna, and Mark Long. "Cyber Sports." *VR World* (July/August 1995): 12.

Arnold, Kandy. "AT&T Braces for Blackout." *NewMedia* 3, no. 9 (September 1993): 33.

Bangert-Drowns, Robert L., James A. Kulik, and Chen-Lin C. Kulik. "Effectiveness of Computer-Based Education in Secondary Schools." *Journal of Computer-Based Instruction* 12, no. 3 (Summer 1985): 59–68.

Barron, Anne, Brendan Tompkins, and David Tai. "Design Guidelines for the World Wide Web." *Journal of Interactive Instruction Development* (Winter 1996): 13–16.

Beichner, Robert J. "The Video Encyclopedia of Physics Demonstrations." *Educational Technology Review* (Autumn/Winter 1993): 50–51.

Brill, Louis M. "Home VR: Electronic Playgrounds, Living Room Style." *Virtual Reality World* 2, no. 2 (March/April 1994): 18–32.

Brown, J. S., A. Collins, and P. Duguid. "Situated Cognition and the Culture of Learning." *Educational Researcher* 28 (1989): 32–42.

Bruning, Roger H., G. J. Schraw, and R. R. Ronning. *Cognitive Psychology and Instruction.* Englewood Cliffs, N.J.: Merrill/Prentice-Hall, 1995.

Buchanan, Leigh. "The Virtual Campaign." *CIO* (April 1, 1994): 66–70.

Cantwell, Steve. "Multimedia Transforms Union Pacific's Training Strategy." *Tech Trends* 38, no. 6 (November/December 1993): 21–22.

Cognition and Technology Group at Vanderbilt, The. "Anchored Instruction and Its Relationship to Situated Cognition." *Educational Researcher* 19 (1990): 2–10.

Computer Technology Research Corporation. *Multimedia Technology.* Charleston: Computer Technology Research Corp., 1992, 1993.

Connolly, Bruce. "Presentation Systems for the Electronic Classroom." *MultiMedia Schools* (May/June 1995): 29–37.

Cook, Nancy. "Mario Is Missing." *Technology & Learning* 14, no. 4 (January 1994): 7–13.

Coupland, Ken. "Declarations of Independents." *NewMedia* (October 1993): 48–54.

DeLoughry, Thomas J. "History, Post-Print." *The Chronicle of Higher Education* (January 12, 1994): A19–20.

Dennis, Verl E. "How Interactive Instruction Saves Time." *Journal of Instruction Delivery Systems* 8, no. 1 (Winter 1994): 25–28.

Doyle, Bob. "Crunch Time for Digital Video." *NewMedia* (March 1994): 47–50.

Duncan, Jody. "A Once and Future War." *Cinefex*, no. 47 (August 1991): 4–59.

———. "Morphing to the Music." *Cinefex*, no. 50 (May 1992): 18–19.

———. "The Beauty in the Beasts." *Cinefex*, no. 55 (August 1993): 44–95.

Eiser, Leslie. "Multimedia Science Programs: Moving Science Education Beyond the Textbook." *Technology & Learning* (March 1992): 16–30.

Escalada, L.T., R. Grabhorn, and D. Zollman. "Applications of Interactive Digital Video in a Physics Classroom. *Journal of Educational Multimedia and Hypermedia* 5, no. 1 (1996): 73–97.

Farber, David. "Cyberspace, the Constitution, and the Electronic Frontier Foundation." *Educators' Tech Exchange* (Summer 1993): 22–27.

Fetterman, David M. "Videoconferencing On-line: Enhancing Communication over the Internet. *Educational Researcher* (May 1996): 23–27.

Fitzsimmons, Edward A. Interview by Barbara Clinton in *Journal of Instruction Delivery Systems* 8, no. 1 (Winter 1994): 4–5.

Foremski, Tom. "Straight Outta Compton's: A Patent Play." *Morph's Outpost* 1, no. 5 (January 1994): 16–17.

Fox, John, Karen Loutsch, and Michelle O'Brien. "ISDN: Linking the Information Highway to the Classroom." *Tech Trends* 38, no. 5 (October 1993): 18–20.

Friedman, E. A., J. D. Baron, and C. J. Addison. "Universal Access to Science Study via Internet. *T.H.E. Journal* (June 1996): 83–86.

Frost & Sullivan. *Desktop Video Markets.* Mountain View, Calif.: Frost & Sullivan, 1993.

Gamble-Risley, Michelle. "Multimedia Makes the 1996 Olympic Team." *Government Technology* 5, no. 9 (September 1992): 1.

Gates, Bill. *The Road Ahead.* New York: Penguin, 1995.

Godwin, Mike. "Sex and the Single Sysadmin: The Risks of Carrying Graphic Sexual Materials." *Internet World* 5, no. 2 (March/April 1994): 56–62.

Goldstein, Jackie, and Mike Wittenstein. "Uses of Interactive Multimedia for Advertising, Marketing, and Sales." *Multimedia Review* 4, no. 2 (Summer 1993): 60–64.

Hilferty, Dan. "General Machinery: Show & Tell on the Plant Floor." *IBM Multimedia Solutions* 4, no. 1 (January/February 1994): 11–13.

Hitz, Martin, and Hannes Werthner. "Development and Analysis of a Wide Area Multimedia Information System." *Proceedings of the 1993 ACM/SIGAPP Symposium on Applied Computing* (February 1993): 238–46.

Hofstetter, Fred. "Multi Multimedia." *T.H.E. Journal* (February 1993): 6.

Hubbard, Janice. "Reflections of the Dead." *Cinefex,* no. 50 (May 1992): 82–83.

Hurtig, Brent. "CD Recorders Buyers Guide." *New Media* (June 3, 1996): 31–34.

Illman, Deborah. "Multimedia Tools Gain Favor for Chemistry Presentations." *Chemical and Engineering News* 72, no. 19 (May 9, 1994): 34–40.

Information Workstation Group. *Multimedia Opportunities.* Alexandria: Information Workstation Group, 1993. Call (703) 548-4320 to order this 600-page five-year forecast. $1,890 for the first copy; $200 for additional copies ordered at the same time.

Josephson, H., and T. Gorman. *Careers in Multimedia: Roles and Resource.* Pacific Grove, Calif.: Brooks/Cole Publishing Company, 1997.

Kaufman, Debra. "Effects in the Vertical Realm." *Cinefex,* no. 54 (May 1993): 30–53.

Kinnaman, Daniel E. "Compton's Re-ignites Patent Wars." *Technology & Learning* 14, no. 5 (February 1994): 14.

———. "Videodiscovery Files Complaint Against Optical Data." *Technology & Learning* 14, no. 3 (November/December 1993): 9.

Klinck, Nancy. "Back to School at Work: Training Strategies for the 90s." *Tech Trends* 38, no. 6 (November/December 1993): 32–34.

Krol, Ed, adapted by Bruce Klopfenstein. *The Whole Internet: User's Guide & Catalog,* Academic Edition. Sebastopol, Calif.: O'Reilly & Associates, Inc., 1996: 418.

Kulik, Chen-Lin C., and James A. Kulik. "Effectiveness of Computer-Based Education in Colleges." *AEDS Journal* (Winter/Spring 1986): 81–108.

———. "Effectiveness of Computer-Based Instruction: An Updated Analysis." *Computers in Human Behavior* 7 (1991): 75–94.

Kulik, Chen-Lin C., James A. Kulik, and Barbara J. Shwalb. "The Effectiveness of Computer-Based Adult Education: A Meta-Analysis." *Journal of Educational Computing Research* 2, no. 2 (1986): 235–52.

Kulik, James A. "Meta-Analytic Studies of Findings on Computer-Based Instruction" in Eva L. Baker and Harold F. O'Neil, Jr. (eds.) *Technology Assessment in Education and Training.* Hillsdale, N.J.: Lawrence Erlbaum, in press.

Kulik, James A., Chen-Lin C. Kulik, and Robert L. Bangert-Drowns. "Effectiveness of Computer-Based Education in Elementary Schools." *Computers in Human Behavior* I (1985): 59–74.

Lee, Yvonne, and Bob Francis. "PDA: Shooting Star or Falling Star?" *Infoworld* (May 2, 1994): 1.

Lerner, Eric J. "500 Channels: Wasteland or Wonderland?" *EDUCOM Review* 28, no. 6 (November/December 1993): 26–33.

Mack, Jennifer. "'Digital Divide' Gets Wide Outside U.S." *ZDNet News* [online]. [written 19 September 1999; cited 16 January 2000]. Available from http://www.zdnet.com/zdnn/stories/news/0,4586,2336552,00.html.

Matthew, Kathryn I. "The Impact of CD-ROM Storybooks on Children's Reading Comprehension and Reading Attitudes." *Journal of Educational Multimedia and Hypermedia* 5, no. 3/4 (1998): 379–94.

Merril, Jonathon R. "Surgery on the Cutting-Edge; Virtual Reality Applications in Medical Education." *Virtual Reality World* (November/December 1993): 34–38.

Moxley, Roy A. "Three Functional Advantages of Computer Word Processing for Children's Writing." *Educational Technology Review* (Autumn/Winter 1994): 30–36.

Nelson, Theodor H. "The Hypertext." *Proceedings of the World Documentation Federation,* 1965.

Neuwirth, Konrad. "Where in the World Is Carmen Sandiego?" *Educational Technology Review* (Autumn/Winter 1994): 46–48.

Newson, Gillian. "Virtual Valerie." *NewMedia* 2, no. 11 (November 1992): 42–43.

Olmstead, Jack. "Video Stores Starstruck by Multimedia." *NewMedia* 2, no. 11 (September 1993): 23.

Parham, Charles. "Interacting with the Past." *Technology & Learning* (February 1996): 8–11.

Pearson, LaTresa. "Multimedia Hits the Road." *Presentations* 7, no. 11 (November 1993): 29–39.

———. Releasing the Power of CD-ROM. *Presentations* 8, no. 2 (February 1994): 22–26.

Piaget, J. *The Mechanisms of Perception.* New York: Basic Books, 1969.

Rahlmann, Reed K. "Dave Grusin: The Gershwin Connection." *NewMedia* 4, no. 2 (February 1994): 56–57.

Rosenthal, Steve. "Mega Channels." *NewMedia* 3, no. 9 (September 1993): 36–46.

Rumelhart, D. E. "Schemata: The Building Blocks of Cognition" in J. T. Guthrie (ed.) *Comprehension and Teaching: Research Reviews.* Newark, Del.: International Reading Association, 1981: 3–26.

Skinner, B. F. *The Behavior of Organisms.* New York: Appleton-Century-Crofts, 1938.

———. *Science and Human Behavior.* New York: Macmillan, 1953.

Smith, Stanley G., and Loretta L. Jones. "Multimedia Technology: A Catalyst for Change in Chemical Education." *Pure & Applied Chemistry* 65, no. 2 (1993): 245–9.

Stefanac, Suzanne. "Sex & the New Media." *NewMedia* 3, no. 4 (April 1993): 38–45.

———. "Digital Carnage: Do Violent Interactive Games Promote Real-Life Violence?" *NewMedia* 4, no. 1 (January 1994): 72–77.

Stewart Publishing. *Interactive Healthcare Directories.* Alexandria: Stewart Publishing, Inc., 1995.

Turkle, Sherry. *Life on the Screen: Identity in the Age of the Internet.* New York: Simon and Schuster, 1995.

Tynan, Daniel. "Multimedia Goes on the Job JUST IN TIME" in John Hirschbuhl (ed.) *Computers in Education,* 6th ed. Guilford, Conn.: The Dushkin Publishing Group, Inc., 1993: 188–94.

Vivid Studios. *Careers in Multimedia.* Emeryville, Calif.: Ziff-Davis Press, 1995.

Vygotsky, L. *Mind in Society: The Development of Higher Psychological Processes.* Cambridge, Mass.: Harvard University Press, 1978.

Waltz, Mitzi. "Four-Wheeling with Two Megs." *NewMedia* 3, no. 11 (November 1993): 39.

Wasserman, Elizabeth. "Finding Money on the Web." *The Standard* [online]. [written 4 October 1999; cited 17 January 2000]. Available from http://www.thestandard.com/article/display/0,1151,6758,00.html.

Withrow, Frank. Guest editorial in *T.H.E. Journal* 21, no. 2 (September 1993): 10.

Image Credits

7-1	Courtesy of Graphic Education Corporation
7-2	The Dynamic Human: The 3d Visual Guide to Anatomy and Physiology by Unk. Copyright © 1996 Times Mirror Higher Education Group.
7-3	Courtesy of HT Medical Systems, Inc.
7-4	Courtesy of HT Medical Systems, Inc.
7-5	Courtesy of VTEL Corporation
7-6	Courtesy of Healtheon/WebMD
8-1	Courtesy of Grolier Interactive, Inc.
8-3	Courtesy of Microsoft Corporation
8-4ac	World Book graphics courtesy of World Book, Inc. World Book is a trademark of World Book, Inc. www.worldbook.com
8-5	Encarta logo reprinted with permission from Microsoft Corporation. Compton's Encyclopedia courtesy of The Learning Company. World Book graphics courtesy of World Book, Inc. World Book is a trademark of World Book, Inc. www.worldbook.com
9-1	Courtesy of Microsoft Corporation
9-2	Courtesy of Harvard Graphics
9-3	Adobe and Adobe Premiere are trademarks of Adobe Systems Incorporated
9-4	Courtesy of Kinetix
9-5	Courtesy of Macromedia, Inc.
9-6	Courtesy of Macromedia, Inc.
9-7	Photograph courtesy of TraCorp, Inc., Phoenix, Arizona
9-8	AOL@School screenshots copyright 2000 America Online, Inc. Used with permission.
10-4	Used with permission by Sony Computer Entertainment America. Playstation and the Playstation logos are registered trademarks of Sony Computer Entertainment, Inc.
10-5	Courtesy of Lightspan, Inc.
11-1	Reprinted by permission/International Business Machines Corporation
11-2	Reprinted by permission International Business Machines Corporation
11-3	Photo courtesy of Gateway, Inc.
11-4	DeskTop Theatre 5.1 DTT 2500 Digital from Cambridge Soundworks
11-5	Courtesy of ATI Technologies
11-7	Courtesy of IRIS, Inc.
12-1	Photo courtesy of Gateway, Inc.
12-2	Photo courtesy of Gateway, Inc.
13-1	Courtesy of Hauppauge Computer Works
13-2	Courtesy of Creative Labs
13-3	Jack Buxbaum
14-1	Courtesy of Len Bullard
14-13	Economics, 13E by C. McDonnell. Copyright © 1995 McGraw-Hill Companies. Reprinted by permission.
14-14	Economics, 13E by C. McDonnell and Stanley Brue. Copyright © 1996 McGraw-Hill Companies. Reprinted by permission.
15-1	Courtesy of Thomson Consumer Electronics
15-2	Jack Buxbaum
15-3	Jack Buxbaum
15-4	Courtesy of Teledesic
15-5	Courtesy of Teledesic
16-1	Courtesy of Gummess, Glen; Agnew, Janet; Hudson, Mike. Artwork: Glen Gummess/University of St. Francis
17a	Courtesy of NewMedia
17b	Courtesy of CNET
17c	Courtesy of Internet World
17d	Courtesy of T.H.E. Journal
17e	Courtesy of Technology & Learning
17f	WIRED logo reprinted with permission of Condé Nast Publications, Inc.
17g	Courtesy of Syllabus
17h	Courtesy of Cinefex. www.cinefex.com fax: 805-383-0803
17i	Courtesy of Computer Shopper
17j	Copyright 2000 Emerging Technology Consultants, Inc. Multimedia Compendium
17k	Courtesy of AECT
17l	Courtesy of SALT, Society for Applied Learning Techology
17m	INFOCOMM logo courtesy of International Communications Industries Association, Inc.
17n	Courtesy of COMDEX
17o	Courtesy of CeBIT
17p	Courtesy of the Association for Advancement of Computing in Education
17r	Courtesy of NECA
18-1	Courtesy of Grolier Interactive, Inc.
19-3	Courtesy of Microsoft Corporation
19-4	Courtesy of Microsoft Corporation
26-1	Photos by David K. Brunn. Copyright © 1994 Aris Multimedia Entertainment
26-3	Photos by David K. Brunn. Copyright © 1994 Aris Multimedia Entertainment
27-1	Photos by David K. Brunn. Copyright © 1994 Aris Multimedia Entertainment
27-4	Photos by David K. Brunn. Copyright © 1994 Aris Multimedia Entertainment
28-1	Photos by David K. Brunn. Copyright © 1994 Aris Multimedia Entertainment

Index